D0712274

RENEWALS 458-4574

DATE DUE

SEP 29			
GAYLORD			PRINTED IN U.S.A.

FOREIGN POLICY MOTIVATION

RICHARD W. COTTAM

Foreign Policy
Motivation

A General Theory
and a Case Study

Library of Congress Cataloging in Publication Data

Cottam, Richard W
  Foreign policy motivation.

  Bibliography: p. 357
  Includes index.
  1. International relations—Research.   2. Great Britain—Foreign
relations—Egypt.   3. Egypt—Foreign relations—Great Britain.   I. Title.
JX1291.C66   327'.07'2   76–6659
ISBN 0–8229–3323–3

Excerpts from Lord Cromer's *Modern Egypt* are reprinted by permission of Macmillan London and Basingstoke. Quotations from Wilfrid Blunt's *Secret History of the English Occupation of Egypt* are reprinted with the permission of the publisher, Howard Fertig, Inc.

Contents

Acknowledgments / vii

Part I. Foreign Policy Motivation

1. Introduction / 3
2. Status-Quo or Imperialist / 14
3. Motivation / 31
4. Perception / 54
5. Systems of Aims / 93
6. America in Vietnam / 133

Part II. The British in Egypt

7. The Case Illustration in Historical Perspective / 151
8. Fall 1876 / 157
9. Summer 1882 / 180
10. Summer 1887 / 211
11. Fall 1914 / 231
12. Winter 1921 / 258
13. Fall 1956 / 277

Part III. Conclusions

14. Eliminating the Perceptual Basis of Conflict / 313

Notes / 337
Bibliography / 357
Index / 365

Acknowledgments

The individuals who have been most helpful to me in the genesis and development of the ideas in this book are, for the most part, unaware of their contribution. They are my students, both undergraduate and graduate, who have listened to these ideas in the classroom. Their criticisms have helped me avoid many pitfalls and inadequacies. Several graduate students have made studies parallel to mine, and I have learned much from them. William Gilmore, Mahmoud Ismail, Ismail Makled, Marshall Hershberg, and Dorothy Donnelly are cited in the text. Not cited, but equally helpful, are William Markus, Benjamin Norris, Marsha Puro, Steven Schechter, Gerard Gallucci, and Sarah Crenshaw.

Colleagues who read the entire manuscript and gave me invaluable criticism are Carl Beck, Bert A. Rockman, Raymond Corrado, and Marshall Singer. I am particularly in the debt of Ole R. Holsti and Joseph Firestone, who work in the same conceptual area and gave me detailed critical comments.

PART I
Foreign Policy Motivation

1 / Introduction

The mid-1960s was a golden age of American academia. The ugliness of McCarthyism was a rapidly fading memory, and the academic community in general was enjoying almost unprecedented societal acceptance. Arnold Beichman wrote in 1965: "The college teacher today lives in a seller's market. If he is halfway good and productive, he can pick his employer and expect rapid promotion. And in a seller's market, the academician has the kind of power over his terms of employment that he lacked in previous generations."[1]

The social scientist shared this position with the traditionally more favored natural and physical scientists. This was the "end of ideology" era. A new and heady positivism had triumphed, and a fierce competition was engaged in to discover what Stanley Hoffmann referred to as the "magic key"[2]—a scientific method which would disclose the essence of man's sociopolitical behavior. General theory was preferred to middle-range theory, except in Cold War military strategy.

Leading figures in each discipline of the social sciences found ready acceptance in Washington. Indeed, formal or informal consulting with leading bureaucrats was as much a mark of achievement within a discipline as membership on boards of the relevant national foundations. Some theorists, especially those focusing on game theory and simulation, had the ultimate satisfaction of seeing their jargon incorporated into the bureaucratic lexicon. Universities established professional staffs in Washington whose function was to identify favored research themes and to advance the claims of faculty members for government contracts. Further blurring university-bureaucracy lines were the great institutes such as the Rand Corporation, which gained full academic acceptance and respectability even though they were designed primarily to serve bureaucratic research needs.

And then Lyndon Johnson decided to bomb North Vietnam!

Why should that essentially tactical decision have unleashed such an agonized response within the academic community? Stepped-up support for South Vietnam was almost certainly necessary if that American dependency was to survive, and the defense of South Vietnam was a Cold War goal of long standing. Previous decisions, which in the broader Cold War environment were more sharply escalatory, had not provoked a comparable response. American involvement in the overthrow of the regimes of Jacobo Arbenz in Guatemala in 1954 and Mohammed Mossadegh in Iran in 1953, and the abortive coup against Shukri al-Kuwatli in Syria in 1957 were at the time barely noted in the American academic world, although they were much discussed throughout the academic communities of Latin America and the Middle East respectively.[3] The crossing of the 38th parallel in Korea, the intervention in Lebanon, and the Bay of Pigs adventure were too open to be ignored, but they still produced only a fraction of the adverse response that followed the decision to bomb North Vietnam.

Furthermore, the bombing rhythm applied against North Vietnam was in tune with the sophisticated strategic bargaining theory incorporated in the McNamara doctrine, which was very much a product of academia. The doctrine of graduated compellence later articulated by Thomas Schelling is virtually a *post hoc* blueprint for the North Vietnam operation.[4] Certainly the more traditional air force generals were impatient with bombings which to them seemed hopelessly academic and which inexplicably delayed for months the interdiction of supplies at the Hanoi-Haiphong source.[5] What more could the new positivists ask? Here was the ultimate test of highly respected scientific theory.

But the agony in academia at the new bombing policy was real and broadly pervasive. It was expressed most dramatically in teach-ins, mass meetings of students, faculty, and townspeople which were held on campuses across the country ostensibly to debate but really to protest that policy. Opposition was far from universal within the academic community, however. Not surprisingly, those academics with the most extensive governmental connections tended at first to support the government position. Presidential assistant McGeorge Bundy, a former professor and dean at Harvard University, lashed out at his former colleagues with acid, contemptuous remarks. Even so respected a scholar and theorist as Anatol Rapoport was a rudely dismissed Bundy target.[6]

A group of scholars who appeared to regard themselves as the academic establishment of Southeast Asian studies issued a statement reminding the academic community that they were the experts and described the teach-ins as exercises in "name-calling, distortion, emotionalism and gross oversimplification."[7] This characterization was not really inaccurate, but it did miss the point. Biochemists, historians, and musicologists followed each other to podiums on dozens of campuses to give voice to the opinion that American involvement in the Vietnam war was not only a mistake, but profoundly immoral. That very few intellectuals could detail why they held this view or suggest an alternative policy only underlines the essential point. Opposition to the bombing was based on a sense of the situation, a sense that incorporated far more than Southeast Asia.

Professor Marc Pilisuk of Michigan asked the question and drew the conclusions that were in the minds of many academic participants in the teach-ins. He wrote:

What transformed us? For it seems obvious that we are not now wholly the same people we were before the teach-in. As social scientists, many of us had pursued a professional interest in the analysis of problems relating to the conditions of war in underdeveloped nations. Some were area specialists whose knowledge had not been called upon in forming Government plans. Some of the social scientists and philosophers among us believed that the dilemma was not in Vietnam but in the United States and that their knowledge was vital to an understanding of the crisis. But, for all of us, the most interesting aspect of our metamorphosis was the realization that our purely academic work was virtually irrelevant to American policy in Vietnam unless we chose to make it count.[8]

Here was reflected a sense of malaise and irrelevance and a determination to take a sharply activist and unscholarly turn to remedy the situation. But the diagnosis was typically a general feeling that the problem lay deep in fundamental and little-understood recesses of American political and social culture.

For the majority of those involved in the teach-ins, then, prescription was impossible simply because the problem was not comprehended. Methodological advances in the social sciences had been at a level of abstraction that was of little utility here. The more creative scholars generally avoided problem and case study foci. In the compilation of speeches and statements from the teach-ins included in *Teach-Ins: USA,* edited by Louis Menashe and Ronald Radosh, none really reflects a scholar's application of his favored method to the problem. Therefore the scholars can be regarded simply as laymen. That the members of a State Department team which toured various campuses at the time should have viewed the academics skeptically was understandable. One of them, Thomas F. Conlon, wrote: "What some of the academic critics lacked in factual knowledge and understanding, they made up for with emotional denunciations of 'immoral' policy actions, 'criminal' bombings, etcetera. The critics never defined what kind of moral standard they were using, and the team had the feeling that, for at least some of them, this was the most transparent kind of hypocrisy."[9]

Again, the description may be fair, but the hypocrisy charge indicates how little the phenomenon was comprehended by those supporting the administration. In all probability the teach-ins were in part a reflection of fundamental value change. The intensity with which national values were held had been in rapid decline for sections of American youth; and a sensitivity to the extent to which cultural parochialism and even racism had colored the American view of nonwhites at home and in the non-European world generally was growing. But the contention here is that a more important aspect of the explanation lies with the gradual alteration of the fundamental and yet rarely articulated assumptions that had formed the logical basis of Cold War behavior.

Professor Rapoport, with characteristic clarity, was one of the few to make these assumptions his focus. He pointed out that the keystone administrative assumption is that "communism—unless, perhaps, it is confined to the borders of the U.S.S.R. and her Eastern European satellites—is a menace to the security of the United States." If this and subsidiary assumptions are granted, Rapoport argued, "the Administration's case can be made to appear unassailable."[10]

That the simple truth of Professor Rapoport's statement was not more widely understood is in part explained by the undramatic way in which international images were altering. A decade earlier most of the academic participants in the teach-ins had agreed that communism was a "menace to the security of the United States." When the United States took its first steps in Vietnam in 1954, governmental officials, academics, and the interested public overwhelmingly regarded them as necessary to contain a Soviet Union which they saw as comparable in aggressiveness to Nazi Germany and more to be feared because of the wide appeal of its official ideology. By 1965 the picture for many of those participating in the teach-ins had changed drastically. In their eyes communism was no longer a great international monolith: China was weak and remarkably conservative in its foreign policy; and the Soviet Union not only was not sponsoring the war, but was openly using its influence to limit it. The United States was thus seen fighting North Vietnam, a fourth-class power that was receiving barely enough support to maintain the conflict. Whereas in 1954 American policy in Vietnam was accepted as a legitimate defense response to an international communist threat, in 1965 that policy was judged to be at best a manifestation of national vanity and hence profoundly immoral. What had changed drastically and fundamentally was the image of the "enemy." But only in rare instances was the fundamental assumptional change regarding the nature of the "enemy" spelled out.

The foreign policy debate that ensued was a classic example of two sides talking past each other. For those who persisted in holding the aggressive international communism image, the policy was defensible and as moral as defensive wars ever are. For those who no longer saw the international communist menace, the policy was immoral and possibly racist.

This pattern is in all probability typical of major foreign policy debates throughout history both within and between publics. Differing perceptions of the adversary's motivations are commonly the fundamental assumptional bases of differing policy preferences. What is startling about the appearance of this pattern once again in the 1965 teach-ins is that it involved many men who believed they had crossed new thresholds of understanding of man's international behavior. Instead they discovered, sometimes to their deep chagrin, that their methodological breakthroughs helped not at all in understanding how American policy had evolved or in prescribing a solution for the Vietnam problem.

But there was more than this to the intense involvement in the teach-ins. Once basic administration assumptions were at least implicitly questioned, the Cold War fusion of the academic world and the bureaucracy became shockingly and painfully evident to many of those in opposition. Not only did they see the conflict as having become a manifestation of national vanity, but they saw themselves as by now an integral part of the governmental process in support of that policy.

Self-judgments were harsh indeed. Rare was the participant who recalled that he and his colleagues had seen the early Vietnam involvement as we had seen most American Cold War interventions: as a legitimate exercise in national defense against aggressive international communism. Instead, his previous image of communism in Southeast Asia was forgotten, and the fact of his earlier support was recalled shamefacedly, if at all. The agony of Daniel Ellsberg which led to his release of the Pentagon Papers was symptomatic.

What this adds up to is a contention that Professor Pilisuk was exactly right. The purely academic work of even those social scientists closest to the problem had no relevance to and offered no insights for an understanding of the Vietnam conflict. But the academic world had to take credit for having provided the bargaining theory base that underlay the U.S. bombings of North Vietnam and indeed the operating tactical plan for the conduct of the war.

I have raised the example of the teach-ins for two reasons. First, it illustrates a point that is as true of interstate conflict as it is of domestic conflict over policy: Much of it rests on sharply differing but generally hidden assumptions concerning the motivations of adversaries. Every interstate conflict of significant intensity has both value and perceptual manifestations. In some cases the value conflict is so serious that resolution of the conflict without resorting to violence is hardly possible. Israelis and Palestinians value the same territory, and Hitler's ambitions called for German domination of Europe. Were the contestants in such disputes possessed of the most accurate assessments of each other's motivation, conflict would still persist. Even in such cases, however, the human tendency is to attribute motives to the adversary ugly enough that the conflict can be pursued without ambivalence. The resulting caricature is likely to lead to conflict exacerbation, since alternative strategies that call for something short of total defeat of so monstrous an opponent are simply not perceived.

In other cases the conflict may be primarily perceptual. Were each adversary in such conflicts to have perfect information regarding the motives of the others, the possibility of nonviolent resolution would be strong. I believe historians will record the Soviet-American Cold War as one that rested predominantly on motivational attribution rather than on conflicting objectives.

It follows, therefore, that basic to any major advance in conflict resolution is a description of the varying ways in which the conflict is perceived. The point is almost self-evident, yet progress in this direction has been and will surely continue to be slow. The motivations attributed to others are only rarely—and then only partially—explicated. Consequently, debate among adversaries typically will focus on competing policy proposals rather than on what may be the entirely contradictory assumptions on which the proposals rest. The task of the analyst is to infer motivational attributions largely from policy preferential statements. That is a major focus of this study.

The second reason for focusing on the teach-ins is to advance a basic prejudice:

that international relations theory must focus far more explicitly on the great problems man faces. The teach-in period produced two revelations about American social scientists. Their theory offered virtually no insights for understanding what was surely a great historical turn in the road. And they had become far more a part of the American bureaucratic process than they had ever suspected.

These remarks suggest opposing conclusions regarding the relevance of international relations theory in the area of conflict resolution. The charge of nonrelevance must be taken seriously in such areas as political environmental change. But the charge is emphatically not true of the type of theory that provides the underpinnings of the McNamara doctrine.[11] That theory was fully utilized by the customer bureaucracy and hence preeminently relevant. However, it was essentially tactical theory and would have been equally useful to the bureaucracy of any government with significant thermonuclear capability. It could accommodate just as easily to the tactical needs of a communist regime as to those of a Western democracy.

Such tactical theory offers the customer bureaucracy additional means for exercising its influence without regard for the ends it wishes to advance. Like the physicist working on the atomic bomb, the international relations theorist concerned with tactics and especially tactical bargaining added substantially to bureaucratic capability and gave not a thought to the problem of controlling bureaucratic use of his theory. It may comfort a Thomas Schelling to state that he opposed American bombing of North Vietnam,[12] but his own input is an integral part of the theoretical base for that bombing, and he cannot avoid the charge of responsibility for the "graduated compellence" nature of the overall policy.

The prescriptive utility of current international relations theory thus correlates with the level of concern. On the international system level it has yet to develop to the point of helping identify the major environmental trends, an understanding of which is essential for conflict avoidance. Similarly on the national system level, the need is for an understanding of values and of perceptual, attitudinal, and capability trends, since political strategy ultimately calls for trend alteration in these areas. Yet theory has little to offer here, and that is true even in the area of capability. The only level of theory at which prescriptive utility is obvious is the tactical level and even there only when dealing with an entirely hostile foe. Clearly the times call for a reexamination of the academic role in international relations—a reexamination with implications for democratic theory.

A basic challenge for democratic theory in advanced societies in all policy areas is the steady decline in the ability of elected officials, legislative bodies, and the public to comprehend and deal with the important problems of the day. There is far too much truth in Murray Edelman's *Symbolic Uses of Politics* for comfort.[13] The idea that publics and politicians will busy themselves in symbolic concerns essentially nonrelevant to policy is an easy projection from the observed decline in the layman's ability to understand increasingly complex public policy problems. That path leads toward an abdication of the reality of most policy-making to the relevant section of the bureaucracy. In foreign policy this trend is most advanced. The subject matter is esoteric and, except in crisis moments and crisis areas, public interest is low. Outside the concerned bureaucracy, only a few individuals will have the understanding to view in critical detail any aspect of foreign policy. Most of these few are to be found in the academic community.

What, then, is to be the role of nongovernmental experts? Should they, as they so frequently were during the Cold War, be offered contracts to make studies for the concerned bureaucracy? In all probability, many individuals will so involve themselves in times of clear national peril. But even in those times and certainly in noncrisis periods, in my opinion, the nongovernmental expert has a vital public role to play.

The history of the Cold War is a strong argument against leaving matters to a foreign policy bureaucracy, including one which in effect incorporates those academic experts whose theory is relevant to policy. In its essential features, the Cold War conflict comes close to coinciding with the Edelman model for both major adversaries. Two huge bureaucracies maneuvered in a competition more sluggish than deadly, though the dangers of unplanned catastrophe were omnipresent. But the history of that conflict makes clear as well the limits of the retreat from policy-making of those who preside over the bureaucracy. A John Foster Dulles will never see his role as that of an idle manipulator of symbols. On the contrary, his view will be that he makes policy and the bureaucracy executes it. Yet the fact is that for all his brilliance, except in narrow policy areas, Dulles was functionally incompetent. Time restraints are such that no single man can comprehend more than a fraction of what he needs to know of the political processes of other states which are of vital importance to American foreign policy.

What emerges is a foreign policy that resembles an iceberg. The vast majority of decisions are made subsurface in a routinized, noninnovative manner by a huge and highly differentiated bureaucracy. The visible decisions, those assumed to be most important, are made by political leaders or their appointees, often largely in disregard of the decisions made subsurface. Innovation does appear on this level, but in the Cold War era those innovations frequently exacerbated conflict. The decision to place Soviet missiles in Cuba was out of harmony with the dull, sluggish behavior of Soviet diplomacy generally but in close harmony with Nikita Khrushchev's personal flair. Similarly innovative performances in American diplomacy appear to have been suprabureaucratic. But such examples as Dulles in Suez, Nixon and Kissinger in Bangladesh, and the December 1972 bombings of Hanoi—innovations all—do not argue for me that disconnected executive actions should be the prime source of foreign policy innovation.

There is no point in lamenting the fact of bureaucratic domination of all foreign policy decisions except those at the tip of the iceberg. As in other decisional areas, this phenomenon reflects the complexity of the setting. Yet the history of the Cold War tells us as well that this iceberg policy arrangement is an extremely poor one for identifying the vital features of conflict and resolving it. Bringing innovation and overall direction to policy is the task of those at the apex of the decisional body. But the Cold War suggests that "innovations" and "direction" from on high have been disconnected from basic bureaucratic policy and have been associated with crisis. Presidential leadership typically will gain decisional control that is almost total in the area of the crisis of the day. The concerned bureaucratic sections and the policy thrust they have developed in the area can be, and to a large extent have been, ignored. But everywhere else, bureaucratic decisions are policy. As soon as presidential attention shifts, bureaucratic policy once again prevails in the previous area of focus even though it may in serious respects contradict presidential policy of only days before.

As Graham Allison makes clear in his *Essence of Decision*, the universe of the bureaucracy and the universe of the presidential decisional level differ in many vital respects.[14] The result is that the prevailing world view in each decisional area will differ, sometimes quite remarkably. "World view" is that construction of reality within which an individual perceives and chooses among policy alternatives. "Prevailing world view" is that construction of reality which is most congruent with the choice among policy alternatives that a decisional group makes. The most central aspect of world view is the motivation attributed to the various governmental actors. Therefore, what I am asserting is that presidential-level and bureaucratic-level policies will differ because implicitly, and only rarely explicitly, they are based on differing estimates of the situation, including especially the intent of governmental friends and adversaries.

The ability to perceive environmental change differs on the two levels, with both greater continuity and more gradual accommodation to be found at the bureaucratic level. The reason is that the role structure of a foreign policy bureaucracy is likely to mirror the needs of a foreign policy as those needs were perceived at a particular point in time. The point in time, the generic moment, is one in which major environmental change is perceived, the outlines of the altered environment are defined, and a general policy response agreed on. Such a point in time, for example, was the 1946–1948 period in the United States, when the perceived environment required a policy response for which the terms "Cold War" and "containment" were accepted as descriptive.

Once the structure is created, however, a bureaucratic vested interest naturally develops in perpetuating that structure and the world view on which it is based. Even extraordinarily competent bureaucrats, like other men, will tend to bring congruence to role and perceptions. Indeed, a central ingredient of bureaucratic inertia is the rigidification of perceptual assumptions. Thus, those whose vested interests would be adversely affected by a genuine Soviet-American détente quite naturally and sincerely persist in seeing a very dangerous foreign foe.

World views do change within bureaucracies, however. In chapter 5 I describe the process by which this occurs. The rhythm of change is typically one of long plateaus and occasional sharp rises—the rises reflecting a necessity to accommodate to change if role tasks are to be accomplished. But only rarely do the sharp rises lead to bureaucratic structural change. That is more likely to occur when an alteration in personnel at the presidential decisional level brings in individuals with very different world views. Townsend Hoopes has described one of the most dramatic instances of this variety.[15] A change at the Defense Department in 1967 from Robert McNamara to Clark Clifford produced (unexpectedly, given the histories of the two men) a leadership ready to accept a radically different view of the Vietnam situation.

Alteration in world view at the highest decisional level, therefore, may be sudden and radical. On the other hand, when individuals who are particularly rigid occupy key decisional positions, world view may be frozen. In any event, the role demands on those at the highest level will differ from those on the bureaucracy. Since role is a major determinant of how reality is perceived, this means that alteration in world view at the highest decisional level is not likely to parallel the kind of erosion pattern occurring in the bureaucracy. Consequently the gaps between the prevailing world views of the two decisional levels are likely to be greater the further the temporal distance from the generic moment at which foreign policy needs were spelled out—the one moment at which the two prevailing views will be approximately identical.

This argues that world view differences not only lie at the heart of interstate conflict and domestic debate on foreign policy but also are responsible for much of the difficulty in developing coherent policy intragovernmentally. It argues as well that a focus on motivational attribution is vitally important for prescriptive international relations theory. It is self-evident that a policy based on an accurate assessment of its target's motivations is more likely to achieve its objectives than one based on illusory or fantasied estimates. Yet the history of the last two generations argues that illusory estimates generally prevail. Hitler had to commit acts of violent aggression to convince his potential victims that Nazi Germany's motives would lead to an attempt to dominate the world. Conversely, years of passive diplomacy by the Soviet Union were required before other world leaders began to conclude that the Soviet Union's motives would lead to a policy preference for institutionalizing the status quo. Both of these motivational misassessments have led to unspeakable tragedy. A theory that addresses the problem of motivational misassessment or, more broadly, the problem of reducing the perceptual base of interstate conflict could truly be described as "peace theory."

What this amounts to is a suggestion that a vital public role the academic foreign policy specialist can play is that of challenging assumptions. To perform this function, the first requisite is to identify and map the world views and especially the motivational attributions that underlie the policy preference positions of those involved in policy-making. At the very least this should sensitize decision makers to the importance of looking at the assumptional underpinnings of each of several differing policy-preferential positions. Optimally it would persuade them to make explicit, to explore, to evaluate, and, one hopes, to revise their own assumptional positions.

A second requisite is for the analyst to infer the foreign policy motivations of target governments for comparison with the range of motivational attributions of decision makers. The point is not to substitute the academic motivational assessment for that of the practitioner. The point rather is to provide the practitioner with a comparative referent to help in his evaluation of his own motivational assumptions. Presumably the disinterested analyst operating from an explicated frame will infer somewhat different motivations than would the practitioner with career interests and an implicit but probably more elaborate frame.

With awareness of the need to explicate and explore operating assumptions could come a willingness to conduct systematized tests of competing assumptions. This calls for nothing more than a systematic application of diplomatic probing.

The focus of this study is on the perceptual base of interstate conflict. I believe that the state of theory is such that rapid progress can be made in understanding the motivation of governments in foreign affairs and in our ability to infer reasonably accurate world views. This optimism is based on the following assumptions:

1. In dealing with conflict at the interstate level, as in all areas in which conflict involves a multiplicity of variables, concerned individuals will simplify reality in order to confront the problem.

2. These simplifications are rooted in responses to perceived threat to or perceived opportunity for something highly valued, such as the nation.

3. These simplifications tend to fall into identifiable patterns which can be systematized.

4. This systematizing permits inference of motivation through a form of content analysis.

In chapter 2 I look at the unnecessarily narrow treatment of governmental motivation in the literature. Chapter 3 offers a taxonomy of motives and a device for looking at motivational systems. In chapter 4 I identify some world-view patterns that emerge in a variety of relationship types in response to perceived threat or opportunity. Chapter 5 brings together prevailing world views and motivational systems to construct a system of foreign policy aims. Much of the chapter is devoted to describing how and why alterations occur in systems of aims. Chapter 6 returns to a theme of this introduction—that differences in motivational attribution are the hidden basis of major foreign policy debate. This theme is illustrated with the debate in the United States concerning Vietnam policy in 1968.

Part II of this study is a case illustration of the approach. The case chosen is the British imperial episode in Egypt from 1876 to 1956. The scheme developed in part I is applied to six generic moments in the history of the British presence in Egypt. It is important to note that the scheme was not inductively derived from the case study. On the contrary, to avoid the pitfall of tautology I wrote part I before studying the British in Egypt. As expected, the case illustration revealed many inadequacies of the scheme and suggested several areas of development. Some of these are described in the conclusion, part III. The temptation was strong to revise part I on the basis of what was learned in the case illustration and then to apply the revised scheme to the case. I resisted that temptation and limited revisions of part I to clarifications.

2 / *Status-Quo or Imperialist*

Primitive Taxonomies

Motivation behind collective behavior is at least as difficult to infer as motivation behind individual behavior. Without question, both are extraordinarily complex and include such elaborate interrelationships that separate motives can be isolated and weighted only tentatively. Yet despite this complexity, scholars in international relations have tried to classify foreign policy motivation by dichotomizing the resultant policy, calling it status-quo or imperialist. However, most writers apparently find this twofold taxonomy inadequate to accommodate all variance. Hans Morgenthau adds a third category, "prestige";[1] Arnold Wolfers creates "self abnegation";[2] and William Gamson and André Modigliani have added "destructionist."[3] Apparently all can agree on status-quo and imperialist, but the obvious lack of parallelism in the third type for each of these writers speaks loudly of the noninclusiveness of the traditional dichotomy and any of the suggested trichotomies. And how is any particular foreign policy to be labeled? The answer is that the theorist with his own intuitive skills does the categorizing.

Nothing so well illustrates the limited contribution of international relations theory to the practice of diplomacy as does this primitive taxonomizing. A skilled diplomat will know and have a working analysis of dozens of major decision makers in his own area of concern. Probably unknown even to himself, he will have constructed a great many explanatory propositions regarding the motives of these men, including an implicit assessment of the pressures under which they operate. These propositions will have been tested in the real-life laboratory of diplomacy and will have been modified (refined) when expectations were not realized. What emerges is a "naive international relations," to paraphrase Fritz Heider, who spoke of a "naive psychology."[4] What it leads to is an implicit motivational theory that goes far beyond any simplistic dichotomy or trichotomy. A diplomat may see as a key to a particular foreign policy a deep factional struggle in which different ideological and vested-interest preferences are involved. To label that policy status-quo, imperialist, self-abnegation, prestige, or destructionist would be to replace refined analysis with crude.

The tendency to dichotomize or trichotomize complex phenomena has ancient

14

roots, but in international relations literature its dominance in the past four decades coincides with the disillusion associated with the appearance of fascism in Germany and Italy. Prior to the shock of Adolf Hitler, the view of the world that prevailed was that of nineteenth-century liberalism, and that view assumed motivational complexity. But there was little interest in dissecting that motivational complex into its component parts; the utilitarian view of a natural harmony of interest made this unnecessary. If peoples were allowed to give free expression to their national identity longings and if state and nation were made to coincide, a natural harmony of interest and—with the assist of a gentle legislator—peace would prevail. Woodrow Wilson's Fourteen Points gave programmatic expression to this national self-determination doctrine, and the League of Nations was a model of the kind of limited legislator the doctrine prescribed. But given this view of reality, the phenomenon of nazism in Germany should not have occurred. The Germans were in control of their own destiny, and the Weimar government was democratic. The advent of Hitler discredited the liberal utilitarian view, including the notion of complex but harmonizable motives.

Realism, Idealism, and Power Determinism

In his classic *Twenty Years' Crisis,* Edward Carr constructs the intellectual stage on which advocates of such schemes as Wilson's can be caricatured.[5] Every era has its incorrigible idealists who persist in seeing evil man as good. When they somehow gain power and seek to put their ideas into effect, Machiavellians who understand man's true nature appear and are more than willing and more than capable of exploiting this eternal naiveté. Hans Morgenthau, in *Scientific Man vs. Power Politics,* constructs the most bitter and most effective caricature of this genre.[6] His success in rigidifying what has become known as the realist-idealist dichotomy is remarkable. And as Inis Claude has observed, Morgenthau's preemption of the "realist" image gave him a psychological advantage.[7] Where could one find men with the temerity to embrace the idealist caricature?

The realists do not neglect motivation but make simplified assumptions about it. Thus, Morgenthau argues that individual motivations are for the international analyst essentially unknowable and hence a subject better avoided.[8] Nevertheless, his prescriptions are founded on motivational assumptions that are basic to his entire thought: that collective man, like individual man, is power-driven. A power determinism is almost but not quite fully constructed in *Politics Among Nations.* Morgenthau there develops and toys with what is possibly his most interesting concept, "nationalistic universalism."[9] With little effort he could have made that concept central to a philosophy of history whose basis would be a dominating will to power, ubiquitous in collective man, and which is concealed in appealing ideological garb.

It was left for William Riker to rush in where Morgenthau preferred ultimately not to tread. In *The Theory of Political Coalitions,* motivational monocausality is given its most extreme expression: "What the rational political man wants, I believe, is to win, a much more specific and specifiable motive than the desire for power. Furthermore, the desire to win differentiates some men from others. Unquestionably there are guilt-ridden and shame-conscious men who do not desire to win, who in fact desire to lose. These are the irrational ones of politics."[10] That the rational ones dominate is made clear later in the book. But also made clear is the logical reduction of political realism. Riker is hardly being the ideal Cold War theoretician when he makes the following remark:

In the journalism of the West the dominant interpretation of the events in the world society during the last fifteen years is that of an aggressive imperial power (i.e., the Soviet Union) constantly upsetting the status quo. In this theory, the main propulsion of change is the evil motive of the Communist leaders. In the interpretation offered here, on the other hand, a rational (rather than evil) motive is ascribed to the leaders of both sides. The changes in relative strength of coalitions is viewed as a normal political process. In both theories, the Soviet Union is interpreted as aggressive while the Western bloc is seen as a defender of the status quo. The difference between the theories is that, from the journalistic theory, one might infer that, were Communists to be replaced by liberals or democrats or aristocrats or kings, the aggression would cease. In the interpretation offered here, however, the aggression is a function of the total situation and would not be affected by a change of Eastern rulers except perhaps that kings might be less efficient aggressors than Communists.[11]

Given this motivational simplicity and immutability, Riker has no difficulty constructing a philosophy of history. Man naturally seeks the smallest possible winning coalition, but he unfortunately never knows precisely what that is. So he pays too large a price for his alliances and in so doing weakens himself into eventual defeat. Until theorists are able to calculate precisely the lowest possible price to be paid for a winning coalition, apparently the best that can be done is for those who understand this iron law to advise those who tend to be irrational as to what the law actually is. Is an alliance with South Vietnam too expensive? Is one with Israel? It is to be hoped that irrational men who might worry about the fate of the Vietnamese under communism or an American-supported dictatorship, or about the security of Israelis or the dignity of Arabs, will not be the prevailing American officials.

The realist school clearly points to a simple power determinism in which behavior flows inexorably from the relative power potential of various actors. Weak powers will naturally seek to appear morally self-righteous as an obvious but vain defensive device. Strong powers, capable of expanding their influence, are likely to wrap this national-interest objective in ideological garb such as fascism, Marxism, or even liberalism—the process of "nationalistic universalism." These ideologies are sincerely advanced, but they camouflage their instrumental nature. Thus *Politics Among Nations,* the most influential international relations textbook of the Cold War era, treats communism as an incidental factor. Communism is simply an instrument to advance Russian national, that is, power, interests.[12]

However, it is common for foreign policy practitioners and many academic writers to adapt realist premises in dealing with the communist menace. Typically they view the noncommunist world, regardless of its great power potential, as status-quo and hopelessly afflicted with the illusions of the idealist. Conversely, the communist world epitomizes the unsentimental power realist. Furthermore, Morgenthau's realism has a special appeal for practitioners. The diagnosis that collective man is power-driven is Hobbesian, but the remedy is not.[13] For Morgenthau, the remedy is more Platonic. What is needed is philosopher-king diplomats who understand the nature of man and the laws of collective man's behavior. Apparently something akin to the great diplomat Morgenthau seeks would be required to save the status-quo powers from their good selves.

Henry Kissinger's *Nuclear Weapons and Foreign Policy,* published in 1957, is one of the most acclaimed books of its generation.[14] Several reviewers took issue with his limited nuclear war prescription, preferring to consider as well the limited conventional war option. But of the reviews listed in the *Index of Book Reviews,* only one, that of Matthews Josephson in the *Nation*, referred critically to Kissinger's assumptions of Soviet and Chinese motivations.[15] Josephson, while not dwelling on the point, clearly did not share these assumptions. More typical was James E. King, Jr., writing in the *New Republic:* "There is a brilliant discussion of Communist doctrine and method in both the Russian and the Chinese incarnations with emphasis upon the military strategy of world revolution."[16]

In this "brilliant" discussion, Kissinger categorizes states into status-quo and revolutionary powers. The former accept "good faith" and "willingness to come to an agreement" as expected aspects of diplomacy. But, of course, the latter will simply take advantage of such naiveté.[17] Of the status-quo powers he writes, "All their instincts will cause them to seek to integrate the revolutionary power within the legitimate framework with which they are familiar and which to them seems 'natural.' " Then he adds, "Hitler could use the doctrines of his opponents in annexing Austria, because they wanted to believe that his aims were limited by the 'legitimate' claim of national self-determination. And the Soviet rulers have expanded their power into the center of Europe and along the fringes of Asia by coupling each act of expansion with protestations of peace, democracy, and freedom."[18] Conciliatory American statements will, therefore, appear to Soviet leaders either as "hypocrisy or stupidity, ignorance or propaganda."[19] "To us, negotiation tends to be an end in itself." To the communists, a conference is a means "to gain time or to define the political framework of the next test of strength or satisfy an 'objective' intuition. . . . To us, a treaty has a legal and not only a utilitarian significance, a moral and not only a practical force. In the Soviet view, a concession is merely a phase in a continuing struggle."[20]

Napoleonic France, Hitlerian Germany, the Soviet Union, and Communist

China are thus seen as following identical and apparently ineluctable patterns. These assumptions make it surprising that status-quo forms survive, in fact. Kissinger's account would seem to be a better basis for an epitaph than for a prescription. Nevertheless, it is the explicit assumptional base for his prescription. But what kind of scenario could emerge given such assumptions? One that obviously could not emerge is a scenario designed to move the United States and the Soviet Union in the direction of détente. After recounting the elaborate signals and diplomatic exchanges needed to keep Kissinger's limited nuclear war limited, Josephson explodes, "Why in Heaven's name cannot the same diplomatic effort be extended toward bringing about peaceful compromises?"[21] The answer is self-evident, given the assumptions. The elaborate signals are practical means for avoiding suicide. But peaceful compromise would only be a prelude to higher-level and less advantageous conflict for status-quo powers. It would appear that for Kissinger in 1957 negotiations going beyond the tactical would make sense only if the Soviet Union and Communist China ceased being "revolutionary." Disengagement in Europe, Southeast Asia, or the Middle East is the kind of policy that naturally appeals to the incorrigibly naive in the status-quo world. Such a policy could only play into the hands of the revolutionary powers.

Kissinger's prescription in *Nuclear Weapons and Foreign Policy* and his prescriptions as prime foreign policy formulator in the Nixon and Ford administrations may well be far closer than is implied by the description of his policy as one of "détente." Both prescriptions, moreover, appear to be in close harmony with the general prescription pattern implicit in Morgenthau's writings. Both see the great imperialist states pursuing ineluctable power objectives. Both see a defeating idealistic naiveté on the part of the people and leaders of status-quo powers. However, the inevitability of destruction can be circumvented by the great diplomat who somehow mysteriously appears. This diplomat will understand the ineluctability of imperialist objectives, but if he achieves decisional power—and sometimes he does—he will be able to contain imperialism by countering force with force. Seeing what they are up against, imperialist leaders, apparently always extraordinarily rational, will agree to an institutionalized *modus vivendi*. To be effective, that *modus vivendi* must be realistically constituted, with full awareness of the incorrigibility of imperial goals and a cold calculation of mutual capabilities.

Thus, the imperialist leaders of China and the Soviet Union, once they clearly understand that they have been contained by an American diplomacy which fully comprehends their aggressive intent, will agree to liquidate some of the expensive and dangerous Cold War side shows. A fierce bombing of North Vietnam and a blockade of Haiphong, like those done in 1972 just prior to a summit conference of Nixon and Kissinger with Brezhnev and Kosygin in Moscow and simultaneous with offering a major diplomatic concession, is illustrative of this thinking. The naive idealist would assume that such activity would both anger and bewilder Soviet leaders. But the great diplomat understands that "revolutionary" leaders do not indulge in sentiment. They will understand that these acts signal both America's willingness to disengage from this no longer important area and America's still firm strength of purpose. Similarly, in October 1973 the Kissinger approach to the Middle East crisis was to seek the liquidation of another Cold War side show. However, when the Soviets suggested that the United States and the Soviet Union jointly or the Soviet Union alone police the cease-fire agreement along the Suez front, this was interpreted as an exploration of American serious- ness of purpose. A major display of American will was then necessary. Kissinger's policy reflects just how serious he considered the perceived challenge: American forces were placed on limited nuclear alert.

Robert Levine, in *The Arms Debate,* looks at underlying assumptions of the most important authors who deal with the Cold War.[22] What emerges clearly from his study is the conclusion that Henry Kissinger had much company in his realist-based view of international communism. That view prevailed among practitioners as well. Townsend Hoopes illustrates this point in his *Limits of Intervention.* He first gives his own view that "the world was no longer neatly divided between Free World and Communist Bloc and while these new realities did not greatly diminish the dangers of an inherently precarious century, they did alter the shape and character of problems in ways that strongly suggested the need for new analysis and new responses." Hoopes then states: "It is of the greatest significance that those new perspectives did not materially alter the judgments of the men closest to President Johnson. The tenets of the Cold War were bred in the bone." He notes as particular examples Walt Rostow and Dean Rusk. Of the latter he says:

Not only in public, but in private conversation with colleagues and with President Johnson, Rusk expounded his thesis that Communist China was actively promoting and supporting aggression in Vietnam, that aggression in Vietnam was not different from Hitler aggression in Europe, that appeasement in Vietnam could have the same consequences as appeasement at Munich. In his always articulate, sometimes eloquent, formulations, Asia seemed to be Europe, China was either Stalinist Russia or Hitler Germany, and SEATO was either NATO or the Grand Alliance of World War II.[23]

If this was indeed Rusk's view, his judgment of the futility of negotiating with the Communists or of in any way letting up on the pressure follows most naturally. Equally apparent would be the futility of opponents' of American policy using arguments with Dean Rusk in which the contention of the conflict's immorality was central. To be meaningful, the debate had to focus on the question of Soviet and Chinese motivations. And this was only very rarely the case.

The path followed by Kissinger, Cold War theorists, and Cold War practition- ers has a starting point in political realism. They accept the status-quo–imperialist dichotomy. But they abandon the power determinism implicit in realism and proceed with the task of prescribing tactics for the defeat of the current imperialist evil. Motivation continues to be seen in the simplest of terms. Where this school is most impressive, however, in deterrence theory, it becomes virtually apolitical. Although the proclaimed objective of American containment policy in George Kennan's Mr. X article of 1947 was the alteration of communist Russia from imperialist to status-quo, the thrust of deterrence strategy was in the direction of military tactical bargaining.[24] But then Kennan was not finally a political realist. He saw containment policy leading to fundamental change in Soviet decision makers and the decision-making process and goals. In 1957, the year Kissinger's book was published, Kennan believed change so fundamental had occurred in the Soviet Union that a policy of disengagement should be explored. Soviet interest had drifted from political expansion to consumer production, and in the process Soviet foreign policy was becoming status-quo. To pursue containment energetically would be to risk frightening a new generation of Soviet leaders into returning, for defense reasons, to a policy resembling that of the early Cold War; in other words, it would be a self-fulfilling prophecy. Implicit here is a foreign policy motivational assumptional base far more complex than that of the realist.[25]

Deterrence strategy, however, rests on a simple motivational assumptional base virtually identical with Kissinger's. Even Thomas Schelling, who rebels against the zero-sum quality of Riker's work and asserts instead mixed motives, really theorizes in terms of an enemy who seeks to "win" and must be deterred from doing so. The range in values Schelling sees turns out to be confined largely to tactical values.[26]

In fact, however, the realist school seriously camouflages motivation. The power determinism which pervades it is allowed full logical development only by Riker. In his picture, all rational leaders seek a winning coalition. If they have one already, they try to maintain it at a minimal level and therefore are status-quo. If they are not part of a winning coalition, they make the effort to become one and therefore are imperialist. As the quote from Riker on page 16 illustrates, all other political values are irrelevant. If a collective ceases to be part of a winning coalition, its leaders, if they are rational, will (in Morgenthau's definition) take it from a status-quo to an imperialist policy. Were Morgenthau to be equally consistent and equally deductive, the answer to the puzzle of when a concession constitutes appeasement would be virtually self-evident. Demands from a government which is part of an effective winning coalition could be satisfied without any fear of appeasing. Conversely, if the government making the demand is not winning, to satisfy the demand would be to appease and thus to precipitate additional demands.

If Morgenthau and other realists did not follow this path it is probably because implicitly they see motivation as something more than the desire to win. In fact, what does it mean to "win"? As mentioned, Morgenthau had in addition to status-quo and imperialist policies a category which he termed "prestige." Its utility can be sensed by using it to explain French policy under Charles DeGaulle or U.S. policy in Vietnam once the conclusion was reached that America's opponents there were not the Soviet Union and China with a joint satellite in Hanoi. But Morgenthau resists any such easy association of the concept with nationalism and declining grandeur and leaves the cause of its appearance in the realm of mystery.

Revisionist Historians and Economic Determinism

Realism in the stark simplicity of power determinism dominates much of coalition theory and strategic theory. In a modified, less deterministic, but only slightly more complex form, it dominates as well the thinking of most American and Western practitioners. Not surprisingly, the most uncompromising opponents of both strategic doctrine and Western Cold War practice, the revisionist historians, operate from an entirely different motivational assumptional base. That base is hardly less simple or deterministic, but in place of a simple power determinism, the revisionists offer a simple economic determinism.

In doing so the revisionists are not being true to their primary progenitor, John A. Hobson. Writing in 1902, Hobson took a hard look at British imperialism. His influential book, *Imperialism,* does have archaic features. Who today, for instance, would entitle a chapter "Imperialism and the Lower Races"? And the pre-Keynesian theme of his economic theory may be of only historical interest to modern economists. But the motivational theory of imperialism he advanced remains in the forefront of international relations. Those who think of Hobson as an anti-imperialist publicist whose primary point was that imperialism in the capitalist era is motivated by the desire to "develop at the public force private markets for their surplus goods and their surplus capital,"[27] have missed the richness of his theory. Unlike revisionists such as Carl Oglesby, who wrote in 1967,[28] Hobson in 1902 understood the motivational complexity of imperialism. In the typology of motives of foreign policy advanced in chapter 3, every type specified can be seen in or inferred from Hobson's extraordinary book. Possibly because he was presenting an argument, his style camouflaged the complexity he implicitly noted. Still it is fair to say that Hobson placed inordinate stress on the economic determinants of British policy. Comparing his picture of imperialism in Africa with that which emerges in *Africa and the Victorians,*[29] the conclusion is strong that Hobson exaggerated the role of an out-of-balance capitalist system. But then the authors of the latter book had the benefit of diplomatic correspondence not available to Hobson and a half-century's distance to help produce analytic detachment.

Hobson's theories had great impact on both Marxist and non-Marxist writers. Among Marxists the point at issue was whether the capitalist system must turn to imperialism or whether an equilibrium can be achieved through altered monetary policies. Hobson had held the latter view, and the Marxist writer Rudolph

Hilferding shared his position. Rosa Luxemburg and Lenin argued that imperialism was inevitable because capitalists could not or would not alter what was an inexorable process. Both schools agreed with Hobson as to the preeminence of the economic factor in motivations of the great capitalist states.[30]

In the United States, Hobson's thinking was incorporated in the influential book, *Imperialism and World Politics*, by the non-Marxist Parker Thomas Moon.[31] A generation of Americans read this book in college courses and presumably found the Hobson thesis persuasive. The one explicit challenge to Hobson of real note came from the economist Joseph Schumpeter in his essay "The Sociology of Imperialism," which was first printed in 1919.[32] The Schumpeter thesis is brilliant and original, but it was meant to be a corrective. Just as Hobson may have been overimpressed with the economic motive, Schumpeter was determined to demonstrate the preeminence of societal factors. His contention that imperialism in the capitalist era is more likely the work of precapitalist aristocrats than of capitalists is unnecessarily disputatious. A far more compelling case could be made by looking at the role of both capitalists and landed aristocrats in many imperial episodes. But the "sociology of imperialism" was not central to Schumpeter's thinking. Had it been so, quite possibly a full-blown theory of imperialism would have appeared that went well beyond Hobson. As it is, the Schumpeter essay should be read alongside Hobson's study. Together they are highly suggestive.

As the replacement for Moon's basic text, a post–World War II book on imperialism included on a great many reading lists was E. M. Winslow's *Patterns of Imperialism*. The book is for the most part a high-quality critical review of the historical literature concerning imperialism. The author's own thinking, however, is made clear on his first page:

We shall use the terms "imperialism" and "militarism" repeatedly, and it may as well be said first as last that they are coeval terms representing the same general pattern of thought and behavior in the ordering of human relationships. It makes little difference whether one speaks of "militarism and war," or "imperialism and war." A nation that is militaristic is likely to want to give its militarism an aggressive outlet which can only mean an attitude of belligerency and an act of hostility toward some other nation. Imperialism is only a more concrete term for the same behavior; it suggests not only ability and willingness to use military power, but also the territory on and against which such power must be employed.[33]

Unfortunately, Winslow does not make the effort to develop analytically a case for "militarism" rather than the maldistribution problem of capitalism as the prime cause of imperialism. He simply asserts the determining nature of militarism.

In the Cold War era, each side has thought of the other as imperialistic, and the governments and peoples of the Third World have agreed with both of them. For all that, there has been remarkably little advance in the theory of imperialism. Yet this neglect is easily explained. In the communist bloc and in much of the Third

World, the Hobson-Lenin explanation is apparently fully accepted. As the New Left emerged in the United States and Western Europe, it too seemed to find a surface Marxist explanation satisfactory.

Carl Oglesby, in *Containment and Change,* spells out the operating assumptions of the radical left in the United States. Oglesby sees even Stalinist Russia as a state seeking to defend itself. In his view the Soviet Union following World War II had two concerns, "internal repair and development and territorial security."[34] But if Stalin was not an imperialist, his American counterparts emphatically *were* imperialists. Acting in support of American "supercorporations," the American government has inaugurated a new, less crude, but even more penetrating imperialism than that of the nineteenth century.[35]

With these assumptions, which are asserted more than developed, Oglesby obviously is in an excellent position to rewrite the history of the Cold War. Statistics indicating substantial economic relations between American corporations and Third World countries are allowed to stand as proof of imperial control. With such an assumptional base, it is little wonder that those who agree with Oglesby would see the primary task as internal revolution in the United States.

There is remarkably little serious interchange between advocates of a realist view and the revisionist historians. Robert W. Tucker has written a compelling critique of the revisionist image in his *Radical Left and American Foreign Policy,* but disappointingly he counters it with an asserted, power-focused realism.[36] Both Tucker's failure to develop a case for realism as compared with the revisionist position and the general disinclination of realist writers to look seriously at the revisionist argument may be explained in part by the difference in levels of analysis of the two schools. The realists, explicitly or implicitly, use the individual as analogue. Collective man appears to be interested in exercising optimal influence in interstate relations just as is individual man in interpersonal relations. The realists thus focus on gross foreign policy behavioral patterns and very little on a decisional process the driving force behind which, they assert, is power. The revisionists, Hobson, and Schumpeter look at the decision maker and the decisional process. Hobson saw decisional diversity, but within a process which reflects basically remediable ills of a capitalistic distribution system. Schumpeter saw decisional diversity as well, but the process he saw is given direction by the interests of societal elements whose influence and prerogatives are in rapid decline. Revisionists vary widely among themselves but tend to see a decisional homogeneity with a process given direction by cabalistic moneyed forces.

Bureaucratic Determinism

The power determinists deal with motivation sometimes explicitly but more often implicitly. The economic determinists are almost always explicit. A third group rarely if ever makes its motivational assumptions explicit, yet I believe it can be described as accepting a motivational determinism—in this case a bureaucratic determinism. Like the revisionists, writers in this group focus on the decisional process, but only as it relates to public officials. Richard Snyder sees clearly enough both the promise of a bureaucratic focus and the determinist pitfall in his collaborative *Foreign Policy Decision Making.*[37] The study makes a passing nod at the world environment with a flow chart uniting a few boxes which incorporate all the variables any analyst is likely ever to study. There is also the beginning of a suggestion of how conflict situations might be classified. But the body of the study consists of highly suggestive outlines of how the bureaucratic system and bureaucrats can be looked at. The accompanying case study is little concerned with relating the Korean decision to the international environment but much concerned with administrative process. Similarly, Graham Allison, much later, pictures almost in caricature form the admittedly primitive efforts of analysts to deal with determinants of policy external to the bureaucratic process. Then he too focuses on bureaucratic interaction.[38] No one, certainly not Snyder or Allison, asserts that "national interest" can be translated as the summary of the outcome of the bureaucratic process. But the impression is projected that the essence of decision lies in intra- and interbureaucratic habits, styles, values, and bargaining.

Personal Determinism

I suggested earlier that diplomats are less likely than the realist school or some revisionist historians to see motivational monocausality. They see too much of other governments' foreign policy decisional groups for that. Yet top-level diplomats do have their own brand of simplification. Living in a world of decision-making, they are susceptible to illusions regarding their own decisional roles. Anthony Eden's autobiographical diplomatic history, *Full Circle,* is an implicit estimate of Eden's own decisional role.[39] Reading it makes me wonder whether Eden had any need for a foreign office. Or, for an example of a lesser figure, the account of John Bartlow Martin of his tour as American ambassador in the Dominican Republic is an implicit assertion that Martin not only made American policy but also was the domestic kingmaker in the Dominican Republic.[40]

It would be absurd to conclude that Eden and Martin were unperceptive or egomaniacal. On the contrary, their accounts demonstrate that the perceptions of the decisional process of highly intelligent and sensitive participants will be extraordinarily personal. In the eyes of Eden, the policy pursued by Gamal Abdel Nasser, for example, was not the product of Nasser's internalizing the pressures placed on him in Egypt and the Arab world, but that of a puny Hitler who would respond to appeasement just as Hitler did.[41] Eden's was not an analysis of the Egyptian decisional process but a simple transference of one hostile relationship to another. Since Eden's own reputation resulted from his hard-line stand toward

Hitler, policy prescription for Egypt's minor imitation of Hitler was always obvious to him.

Anthony Eden did, of course, make many foreign policy decisions, but the analyst would be badly advised to take Eden's or any other diplomat's picture too literally. Theirs is a personal determinism which obscures just as surely as do power and economic determinisms. My contention is that Eden's perception of each situation was in harmony with the demands of the decisional unit prevailing at any time. As a sensitive politician he implicitly understood the range of interests he had to satisfy, and his view of the situation and his policy preference were brought into balance with the demands of interested elements. This process of perceptual balancing in fact is central to the foreign policy decisional process. Neither Eden nor any other decision maker is likely to recognize more than a fraction of the extent to which he has perceptually accommodated the needs of the situation.

The Limits of Determinism

The picture that emerges from this brief survey of attempts to look at foreign policy motivation is a series of efforts to simplify by discovering *the* primary determinant. The key offered may be the capitalist process (Hobson), a capitalist cabal (Oglesby), a military process (Winslow), a social class fighting decline (Schumpeter), a bureaucratic process (Allison), the individual diplomat (Eden), or a power process (Morgenthau). In the next chapter I suggest a typology of foreign policy motives that incorporates in some form each of the above determinants except the last, the power process. The typology incorporates as well other motives to which only Hobson refers. The object is to abstract from the decisional process, broadly conceived, a list of determinants of decisions made that approaches being inclusive. This is in tune with my general conclusion that efforts to look at foreign policy motivation, even including Hobson's, have badly distorted the motivational picture by failing to deal with foreign policy motivation in all its complexity.

Taken literally—and unfortunately my reading of Morgenthau and Riker suggests it is fair to take them literally—the realists are saying that collectives, governments or polities, have power drives. This is the most obvious of anthropomorphic fallacies. It is also the basis for the simplified view of international behavior that realism advances. But the realists are unfair to themselves. Were they to say that states behave in interstate relations *as if* they had power drives they could avoid the charges both of oversimplifying and of committing an anthropomorphic fallacy. They could instead focus explicitly on gross interstate behavior on a level far above the decisional process.

In fact, this is what realist writers, Morgenthau more than Riker, do much of the time. I mentioned earlier in referring to Tucker's book that Tucker and other realists fail to engage in full dialogue with the revisionist historians because they operate at different levels of analysis. Similarly, since the motivational typology I advance is abstracted from the foreign policy decisional process, I could not incorporate any assumptions of the realists, who are not fundamentally looking at the decisional process.

The test for the realists, if this amended version were accepted, would be the extent to which gross interstate behavior falls into the patterns they assert. Do states indeed behave in patterns that parallel the patterns of individuals seeking to optimize their influence? If so, future behavior could be predicted largely from a mapping of state capabilities. The prime goal for analytic refinement would thus be to sharpen and operationalize the check list of power factors the realists usually advance so that some kind of reliable capability equation could be inferred. A motivational analysis such as the one I am embarking on would be of academic interest only; and the perceptual basis of conflict would lie simply in failing to perceive accurately the capability of other actors.

The fact that I am making this study and consider it of more than academic interest testifies to my conclusion that in broad areas of interstate behavior the patterns the realists assert are not recognizable. There is an undeniably compelling quality to the realist argument, however. In my view this is because the moments in interstate behavior when those patterns are most recognizable are the moments of greatest crisis. When foreign policy decision makers perceive a great threat to or great opportunity for their policy, they very frequently act in parallel fashion to individuals seeking to optimize their influence positions. In noncrisis periods, however, they act in a fashion more parallel to that of individuals whose motivations are very complex.

In chapters 4 and 5 I will attempt to explain this difference between crisis and noncrisis behavior. The analyst who believes, as I do, that the realists are simultaneously compelling and in important respects wrong should explain both those judgments. Too much of modern diplomacy rests on realist assumptions to do otherwise.

Imperialism

Should a typological distinction be made between general foreign policy motivation and motivation for imperialism? In my view the answer to that question is no. The same types of determinants operate whether the degree of control exercised is minor or substantial. However, types of motivational complexes, that is, combinations of salient motives ranked according to intensity, will vary sharply with the degree of control exercised. Much of the focus of writers looking at foreign policy motivation in fact has been on those motives which lead to imperialism. It is important therefore to define clearly what is meant by the term *imperialism* in this study.

I believe imperialism is best defined within the context of an overall power definition. Power in international relations can be defined as the exercise of some control by the government and/or people of one state or community over the minds and actions of the people of another state or community. Any foreign policy involves the attempt to exercise some influence. Imperialism involves exercising a degree of control which goes well beyond that which is exercised in normal diplomatic, cultural, and economic relations. Where the line is drawn on a control scale which separates imperialism from normal diplomatic behavior, however, is a matter for individual judgment.

Is the United Fruit Company currently exercising control in Central America which is at the imperial level? Is United States cultural domination of Canada such as to constitute imperialism? Is Soviet political control of Syria at the imperial level? Citizens of the Central American republics, Canada, and Syria give different answers to these questions. So do Americans and probably Soviet citizens. The contention here is that it is far more important for the analyst to determine what percentage of a population and who within a population sees a particular relationship as imperialist than to try to determine the actual degree of control. Attitudes and policy preferences, and hence motivation, will vary enormously depending on whether or not imperialism is perceived; and the actual degree of control, even were that possible to establish, may not be too predictive of how the policy is perceived.

Figure I.1 is a device for charting the variance in perceptions of a particular foreign policy. The center of the circle is the theoretical point, never achieved in practice, where total control is exercised by one people over another. The outer circumference is the theoretical point of no control (or influence), reached only when there is no contact, direct or indirect. All the policies of one people designed to influence another people, individually or through organizations including governmental organizations, can be charted between these extremes. Governmental acts and policies and acts of individuals and nongovernmental organizations that are not perceived to infringe on the sovereignty of another people will be charted between the outer circumference and the broken line. This is the area of normal diplomatic relations. Acts and policies perceived to affect sovereignty will be charted within the circle defined by the broken line. The broken line therefore is the boundary between imperialist and nonimperialist activity. Acts and policies by one people which are perceived to involve such a degree of control over another people that the sovereignty of the latter has been transferred to the former will be charted inside the dotted line. The dotted line therefore is the boundary between acts and policies perceived to involve sufficient control to be classified as imperialist but not colonial and those involving control at the colonial level.

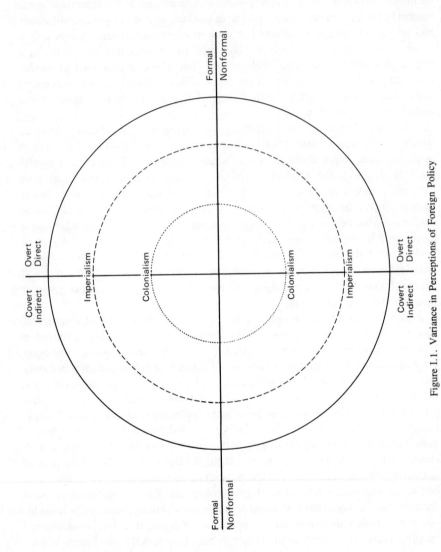

Figure I.1. Variance in Perceptions of Foreign Policy

The circular representation is divided into quadrants to allow charting of the perceived style of control exercised. Acts charted in the left half of the circle are those in which control is perceived to be exercised indirectly or covertly. Those charted in the right half are perceived to be characterized by direct or overt control. The upper half of the circle represents control perceived to be formally exercised, and the lower half represents control perceived to be nonformally exercised.

A policy is direct or overt and formal when the control exercised is officially admitted and the individuals exercising it are institutionally recognized. An example at the colonial level of control would be one in which colonial status is officially designated and colonial officers occupy formally designated roles.

A policy is direct or overt and nonformal when the control exercised is officially admitted, but those individuals exercising the control are not institutionally recognized. An example at the colonial level of control would be a temporary military occupation, where there is no pretense that the colonial power is not exercising control but where there are no formally designated colonial officers.

A policy is indirect or covert and formal when the control exercised is not officially admitted but is formally institutionalized. An example at the colonial level of control would be one in which most control is theoretically exercised by native officials but in which there is a formalized colonial relationship. Real control is perceived as emanating from a colonial staff usually identified as "advisory."

A policy is indirect or covert and nonformal when the control exercised is neither officially admitted nor formally institutionalized. An example at the colonial level of control would be one in which there is a native government and no colonial institutions but in which men who are in effect colonial officers are perceived to be exercising control from a "cover" position, usually an embassy.

Perceptions of motivation and response preferences will vary greatly depending on how a particular policy is classified. These variations fall into clear perceptual patterns that will be described in some detail in chapter 4.

Figure I.1 is useful for describing graphically major assumptional differences regarding particular foreign policies. For example, it would be possible to map assumptional variation regarding American and Soviet policy in Vietnam in the 1960s. From his statements on Vietnam, the perceptions of Barry Goldwater regarding these policies are easily inferred. He saw the relationship of the United States and South Vietnam as a direct, formal alliance with American control exercised at the normal diplomatic level. Conversely, he saw the Soviet–North Vietnamese relationship as being at the imperialism-colonialism level and as indirect and nonformal.[42] Carl Oglesby, an author of the revisionist school, is Goldwater's opposite. Oglesby saw the American–South Vietnamese relationship as indirect, nonformal colonial and the Soviet–North Vietnamese relationship as an alliance in which control was exercised at the normal diplomatic level.[43] This kind of mapping is a useful preliminary step, since it places in perspective the fundamental assumptional differences separating the two men.

A much more serious case is one in which two citizens of South Vietnam hold parallel views, one similar to Goldwater's, the other similar to Oglesby's. Each will consider the other a traitor. These patterns will be described in chapter 4.

The analytic utility of the device probably would be expanded were it possible to include in the mapping an estimate by "objective" analysts of the actual degree of control, how it was exercised, and by whom. Given the problems of access, to say nothing of theory, such a determination anywhere is unlikely. From the point of view of understanding responses to a policy, however, the inability of the analyst to describe actual control exercised is a minor problem. The degree and variety of control *perceived,* not that actually exercised, is what determines response.

Furthermore, the individual judgment today of what constitutes imperialism—where the line separating imperialism from normal diplomatic relations should be drawn—will certainly change tomorrow. Growing economic interdependence and the manifestations of the technological revolution in communications are likely to broaden the belt for normal diplomatic behavior. Developments such as the European Common Market and the seeming trend away from nationalism on the part of sections of European and American youth are reinforcing this trend.[44] As national sovereignty becomes less important either as an identity focus or for purposes of protecting economic interests, growing influence on the part of businessmen who live in other states will not be interpreted as approaching the imperialist level. A sudden resurgence of nationalism, however, could push the imperialism line out from the center. To repeat, what is important for describing behavior is to determine where various individuals and sections of the publics of different national communities draw the imperialism line and where they map the policies of any particular government and/or people.[45]

In spite of the fact that the line perceived as separating imperial behavior from normal diplomacy is a moving line and in spite of the fact that we are dealing in degrees of control, the distinction between perceived imperialism and perceived normal diplomacy is vital for a study of motivation. The overall view of reality associated with a perception of normal diplomacy is remarkably different from the view of reality associated with a perception of imperialism. These different views of reality are inevitably associated with different response alternatives which can be perceived. The response alternatives perceived in turn enter into the determination of motivation. Thus, even though the degrees of control exercised in two cases differ very little, the motivational response in a case where that control is perceived to be at the imperial level will be qualitatively different from the response where control is perceived to be at the level of normal diplomacy.

3 / Motivation

John Herz and Hans Morgenthau both warn of the perils of attempting to analyze motivation.[1] Other writers, by ignoring the matter, seem to agree. Yet Herz, Morgenthau, and the others as well operate from implicit and usually simplistic motivational assumptions. The naive optimism of idealist writers has been ridiculed and generally rejected today. Yet the idealists recognized motivational complexity and a vast diversity of individual and collective interests. Simplicity entered with the belief that with minor effort these competing interests could be brought into harmony. The idealist simplism has been replaced by two competing simplisms: the realist and the revisionist. The former, in the logical reductionist theory of William Riker, becomes a mechanical power determinism. The latter tends to be closer to C. Wright Mills's *Power Elite* than to Marx and thus is less an inexorable process dictated by the mode of economic production than a conspiracy of self-interested establishmentarians.[2]

In rejecting a focus on motivation, Herz and Morgenthau are really speaking of individual motivation. Their pessimism there is solidly based, for efforts by political scientists to deal with individual motivation have not been encouraging. Richard Snyder et al., for example, give "motivation" a psychological definition and seek to incorporate motivations of individuals into their decision-making scheme. The self-defeating elaborateness of the result underscores the pessimism of those who see no promise in this approach.[3]

Motivation in this study is defined as *a compound of factors that predispose a government and people to move in a decisional direction in foreign affairs.* For the most part the motivational factors pointed to are interests and forces presented in nonindividual terms. Although they could be translated into individual terms, this is not done because of an assumption that at this level of analysis individual differences can generally be disregarded. If it is concluded that a motivating force behind tribal imperialism is the desire for loot, analysts need not look into the range of individual intensities of interest in loot within the tribe.

However, certain leaders have had such important roles in foreign policy ventures that they must be looked at individually. The power drive of a Hitler and the ideological commitment of a Wilson, for example, must be considered. But I see no compelling reason for the student of foreign policy motivation to analyze

31

the personal history of Hitler's dislike of Jews or the extent to which Wilson would act out his love-hate relationship with his father.[4]

The point is not that psychoanalytic studies of exceptional leaders are unimportant, but that the dictates of parsimony do not allow the analyst to investigate the roots of any individual motivation. At most, individual motivation could be viewed as an analogue. As mentioned, Riker does this explicitly. His analogue is a corporate fiduciary agent, stripped of individuality, his only role being to optimize returns for his corporation. This accords with Riker's view of collective behavior as a zero-sum game.[5] Since my objective is to look at motivation in all its complexity, an individual used as analogue must exhibit individuality in all its complexity. The psychological literature dealing with individual motivation does this, but the parallel with my approach is only superficial. For example, David Birch and Joseph Veroff present a taxonomy of individual motives,[6] and this chapter includes a taxonomy of foreign policy motives. But the Birch and Veroff list did not guide the list of motives in this chapter. I do not believe individual motives and motives ascribed to a collective are sufficiently parallel to be used even homomorphically.

Abraham Maslow approaches motivation by developing a list of needs the satisfaction of which predisposes the individual toward various action patterns, depending on the level of need that must be satisfied.[7] Again there is a parallel in this chapter, but it is an even looser one: Ascribing needs to a collective carries far greater reification dangers than does ascribing motives. The parallel with Maslow's approach is simply that he attempts to explore the predispositional base for individual behavior and I attempt to explore the predispositional base for foreign policy behavior.

The predispositional base for foreign policy behavior, it seems to me, is reflected in the decisional process that results in a particular foreign policy decisional thrust. In investigating this decisional process, unfortunately, the international relations analyst is denied the evidence that is most critical. The official decisional process in foreign policy, far more than in other areas, is concealed. What the analyst sees is only a piece of policy outcome. Nor is the documentation available to the diplomatic historian much more helpful. It records formal communications and personal recollections, and this is important evidence; but it is evidence that reflects both conscious and unconscious distortion.

Nor is the approach of attempting to reconstruct a particular decision as promising as it might seem—even when the decision is fresh in the minds of individual decision makers. Most decisions, including most of those which in historical perspective appear to have inaugurated major new trends, are likely to have been incremental and additive. Few participants will be aware of anything beyond the increments in which they took part. Researching these decisions therefore calls for the prior construction of an analytic device (for example, a systems device) that permits the researcher to juxtapose different increments in order to create a propositional view of the interactive process—a process of which the participants were largely unaware. This interactive process will involve as well inputs from interest groups, both governmental and public, in various mixes. The analytic device should be constructed in such a way that the researcher seeking to understand directional movement of foreign policy will have a reasonably inclusive picture of direct and indirect influences on that policy. In chapter 5, I propose a system of foreign policy aims for this purpose.

But a core problem remains for dealing with the predispositional base: the construction of an analytically useful depiction of the decisional environment, including what Harold and Margaret Sprout call the psychological milieu.[8] Aggregate analysis is of some help in constructing the environment in which decisions are made. But the dangers in inferring from aggregate patternings are extraordinary and too rarely recognized. Since data aggregated tend to be economic, military, or vital statistics, inferring from such aggregations and ignoring "soft" evidence leads to predictably deterministic explanation.

My own choice is to move in the direction of perceptual analysis with "world view" construction as the primary device for depicting the decisional environment. In this approach, I identify a "prevailing world view"—that view of reality inferred as most congruent with actual foreign policy decisional direction. The prevailing world view is then compared with an inferred "modal world view" of a foreign policy interest group. Judgments as to the relative influence of groups in determining foreign policy direction are based in part on the proximity of a group's modal world view to the prevailing world view. If, for example, the American prevailing world view incorporates an extremely aggressive Soviet Union, then a public-interest group whose modal world view incorporates a status-quo USSR will be judged as not exercising much influence. Judgments as to which groups are and which are not influential in foreign policy then serve as a basis for judgments as to the motivation behind that policy. This analytic device is developed in chapter 4.

In this chapter, I present two preliminary steps before facing directly the problem of inferring the predispositional base of foreign policy. First I present a taxonomy of foreign policy motives. Then I suggest a device for looking at compounds of motives which will represent the predispositional base—a motivational system. The motivational types included here have been taken in part from the literature referred to in chapter 2 and in part were abstracted from a survey I made of the driving forces behind a large number of imperial episodes. The survey was the substantive base of an imperialism course I taught for several years. Since most of the authors referred to and the survey made dealt with policies that would be mapped within the inner imperial circle of figure I.1 (page 28), I originally conceived of the typology as motives for imperialism. Since then I have concluded that the list is also generally inclusive of motives behind foreign policy that is mapped in the outer "normal diplomatic activity" circle. It is the compound of motives, not the types of motives, that will vary, depending on whether the degree of control is perceived to be at the imperial or normal diplomatic activity level. However, to be true to their origin, I retain the imperial setting in describing them.

Motivational Types

ECONOMIC

Population

There is good reason to include among the types listed here some items that are of little importance in modern world imperialism. For example, the drive to gain control of other peoples for the purpose of relieving population pressure probably was a dominant factor in the conquest of new lands by Turkic tribes sweeping out of Central Asia.[9] There is much speculation that in the era of overpopulation and starvation which may be just over the horizon there will be a recurrence of imperialism designed to relieve desperate population problems.[10] If so, this will amount to a revival of an ancient motive. It would be difficult to demonstrate that a desire to provide an outlet for excess population has been important in initiating imperialist ventures in the modern era. Even when, as with Hitler and lebensraum, territory is demanded for a large population, actual policy suggests the demand was more rhetorical than reflective of a real need. However, instances in which a section of a population emigrates and then asks the country of origin to incorporate the territory they have settled are more common.[11] These will be dealt with in the category of "frontier dynamics."

Loot

Another motive that belongs largely to a tribal past, some of which is very recent, is the gaining of control over others for the purpose of acquiring loot. Even twentieth-century tribal behavior in the Middle East reflects this motive clearly.[12] It may well be that a careful look at the early stages of the imperialism of the great Persian Empire and others of that sort would lead to a conclusion that the desire for gaining loot was a major initial causal factor. The causal profile of later stages, of course, changes drastically.

Vested Interests: Trade

The great imperialist era that began in the late fifteenth century and persisted through the mercantile period was heavily motivated by a desire to import gold, spices, and exotic products from the non-European world. As the period progressed, an interest in exports developed as well. The history of this era suggests that as a causal factor of imperialism, a desire for trade is among those motives most capable of generating highly aggressive behavior.[13]

Vested Interests: Investments Abroad

This is the motivating factor that John Hobson particularly stressed. His contention that it was the most important determining force in the late-nineteenth-century imperialist surge was based on a prior conclusion that it reflected a fundamental imbalance in the capitalist economy: Given a very lopsided distribution of income, a surplus of capital had to be disposed of if the economy were to remain healthy. This could most easily be done through foreign investments. The British-in-Egypt study in part II looks at one of the prime instances for Hobson, and my analysis does not support his contention. That the desire to protect foreign investments was a motivating force, especially in the initial stages of the British involvement in Egypt, is unquestioned. But in my opinion, the evidence does not support the primacy placed on this factor by Hobson or by Lenin.

Vested Interests: Domestic Investments

Those critics of American Vietnam policy who argue that Vietnam is an instance of American, not Soviet or Chinese, imperialism would do well to base their argument on domestic rather than foreign investments. Too frequently they follow the Hobson line mechanically and place themselves in the untenable position of arguing that the very minor investments and investment opportunities in Vietnam were compelling for American policy.[14] Their argument could best be developed through the "military-industrial complex" theme.[15] The notion here really is that two gigantic and interlocking bureaucratic empires had very solid vested interests in that conflict's remaining unsettled, for in the event of its resolution both would suffer severe dislocation. That part of industry which receives huge defense contracts in particular is assumed to have been much in favor of protracted conflict.

It is not necessary to conjure up the image of evil men crassly engaged in planning that will prolong war and maintain their profits. The more sophisticated of those who accent this factor contend that individual actors are merely part of a process. It is the most elementary observation in the area of perception analysis that individuals tend to see their role-connected interests and other interests as congruent. Therefore, the defense industry executive hoping for lucrative contracts for his company will be predisposed to see a conflict situation that will necessitate heavy defense expenditures. It is far less certain that this executive would be sensitive to developments that might in the long run lead to an increase or decrease in defense contracts but have no short-run impact. Possibly the most tenuous of the assumptions of New Left writers is that the "establishment" in industry anticipates even distant developments with extraordinary prescience.[16] In fact this area deserves far greater analytic attention.

In the British-in-Egypt study this factor is of only minor importance. The military and foreign policy bureaucracies played major roles in that imperial episode, but the industrial bureaucracy did not. Therefore, this important contention of the revisionist school is not tested in my case study.

COMMUNAL

Grandeur

Terminal political community. Terms such as "face" and "prestige" are found with great frequency in speeches, commentaries, and discussions of imperialist ventures. They doubtless reflect the intuitive conclusion of those using them that they are a core determinant of imperialism. Man generally identifies intensely with one or several politically relevant communities, and he tends to treat slights and affronts to his communities much as he would insults to himself. Likewise, he will take great pride in the achievement of his community. Daniel Katz, among others, has in fact argued that frequently the individual can achieve vicarious glory from this indentity.[17]

Of the politically relevant communities with which the individual identifies intensely, the one likely to be involved directly in foreign policy is the largest or terminal community. In this era, that community is usually the nation organized as a state. The intense identification with and loyalty to the nation and the belief that the nation has a right to independent statehood is what we mean by the term *nationalism.* Where nationalism exists, concern for the prestige, dignity, and world respect for the nation-state can be a primary motivating force behind foreign policy. I would contend that where the state embraces several nations, as in the case of the Soviet Union or India, identification with the state is likely to be considerably less intense than where nation and state coincide. The contention is important and deserves examination because it suggests in contemporary world politics a means for differentiating among world powers regarding the predispositional force behind aggressive behavior. It suggests the hypothesis that concern with prestige, dignity, and face is likely to be less determining of imperialist behavior for the Soviet Union and India than, say, for the United States, France, or China.

The term *grandeur* is used here to refer to a concern for the dignity and prestige of a community with which a large group of individuals identify. Humiliation is certainly to be avoided, but whether influence aggrandizement is believed necessary for national prestige depends on other values prevailing in the community and on the opportunity for aggrandizement. A simple desire to avoid humiliation will lead to imperialism in some cases. If the interpretation of opponents of American involvement in Vietnam is correct, for example, this is a good example of an imperialist venture in which a major motivating force was the desire to avoid humiliation. In his address to the German nation in 1940 as German troops moved into France and the Lowlands, Hitler gave what must be the supreme example of influence aggrandizement for national prestige as a determinant of an imperialist venture. Whenever a perceptible gain or loss of influence is involved, in fact, national grandeur is likely to be affected. Consequently, this factor is among the most ubiquitous of determinants.

Other politically relevant communities. The terminal political community is not the only community with whose grandeur an individual may be concerned. In some cases the drive for grandeur of other communities will be a factor in imperialism. Two examples are church and political party. George Lichtheim argues, for example, that a concern with Protestantism was a major factor in British imperialism in Ireland.[18]

I have treated a concern for the prestige and dignity of the church as a motivation force for foreign policy separate from the desire to spread one's religion. The messianic motive is dealt with elsewhere because the imperialism in which influential churchmen wish to bring salvation to individual souls differs greatly in style and rhythm from that in which such churchmen wish to use the state to defend the dignity and advance the influence of the church. The Crusades would seem to qualify primarily in the latter category.[19] So would Islamic imperialism, in spite of the fact that vast numbers were converted.[20]

The Soviet Communist party can be viewed as a community with considerable relevance to a study of imperialism. Its leading members show every sign of wishing to play a major role in the affairs of international communism and to view any loss of influence to the Chinese Communist party with deep chagrin. Another very clear example is the Baath party of Syria and its bitter rival in Iraq.

Participant Excitement

John Hobson wrote that a spirit of adventure often lies behind imperialist ventures. No one can read Theodore Roosevelt's many speeches and statements on the subject of American influence expansion (he usually denied he was talking about imperialism) without understanding that this factor is important.[21] Modern observers of tribal raids have noted the intense excitement of the participants,[22] and Benito Mussolini's contention that the best of man emerges in warfare is a common enough theme. The vicarious excitement of the public is frequently observed as well. The British-in-Egypt study includes several instances in which the excitement of those not directly participating restricted the government's freedom of action. But those who seek to exploit excitement frequently discover (as did Joseph Chamberlain in the Boer War) that such excitement can be fleeting. In modern times it is not a factor on which to base a prolonged or high-cost imperial venture.

We would do well to subdivide this category further into active and passive —the excitement of the leaders of the Roman legions as compared with that of the citizens of Rome. With such a distinction, it is clear that in the era of mass politics the more important factor is that of passive participant excitement. The sense of adventure of a Theodore Roosevelt, a Joseph Chamberlain, or even a Lyndon Johnson should not be lightly dismissed or ignored. But as a determinant of fundamental political aims, the personal psychological needs of such leaders is of rapidly declining importance. In fact, in an age of fantastic and highly technical weapons, of a potential for calamitous suffering, and of conflict situations too complex for lay understanding, the factor of participant excitement generally is in rapid decline. Compare, for example, the wild send-offs for troops in World War I, the grim determination with which their counterparts were dispatched in World War II, and the extreme reluctance to fight in the Vietnam conflict.

Frontier Dynamics

When many individual members of a community perceive an opportunity to move into and settle underutilized territories occupied by another people, the basis is established for one of the more common determinants of imperialism. American Manifest Destiny is a classic example of imperialism thus motivated. As settlers move into the new territories, typically they run into serious conflict. The previous residents are threatened with extinction, forced migration, or adaptation to a new and unwanted style of life in a society in which they will face discrimination. Naturally enough they challenge their rivals, and the settlers call upon their original community for support. This is frequently granted, and when it is, the government of that community is likely to establish control at a level of colonial intensity over the previous inhabitants who remain. As the American Revolution testifies, this process can result in the settlers' indentifying with a new terminal community of their own creation. But the concern here is with the situation in which control by the parent government is broadened and intensified.

A major historical example is that of the Russian advance into the steppes of Central Asia.[23] The advance occurred in waves, each following the classical pattern: Settlers move into underutilized land; conflict with local inhabitants develops; the embattled settlers call for help from their home government; that help is granted and the original inhabitants are pacified; settlers move into the next area of underutilized land; etc. The best modern example is that of Israel after the war of 1967. Both Arabs and Jews understood very well that if the occupied area were settled by Jews, the demands placed on the Israeli government to make the occupation permanent would soon render any withdrawal politically impossible.

MESSIANIC

Religious Messianism

As stated earlier, I have made a distinction for analytical purposes between a desire to spread one's religion and a desire to defend it or to enhance the influence and prestige of the church. The desire to propagate the faith is especially strong, of course, among religious leaders and missionaries, but such men are often extraordinarily influential with secular authorities. Typically the missionary finds his task much easier if he is able to call upon coercive forces to aid in his efforts. This is in no way to denigrate the sincerity of the missionary. He is likely to believe that no greater good could be done than to bring the true faith to the infidel. Since he is likely to believe as well in the moral superiority of the culture of which he is a part, he is quite content to see old mores replaced with those more parallel to his own. The rhythm of imperial expansion when this factor is operative resembles that of frontier dynamics. In both cases government policy is a response to demands of citizens living outside state boundaries.

The best examples of imperialism with religious messianism as a motivating force are the Spanish in America and the British in Africa.[24] This, of course, is not to suggest that religious messianism is *the only* motivating force or even the most important. In no case will motives be that simple.

Cultural Messianism

Cultural messianism exists when the imperial power and its people seek to substitute a broad range of their own social mores for those of a people who are very much under their influence. Typically this will be referred to as the "civilizing" function. Thus, British cultural messianism has commonly been known since Rudyard Kipling as the "white man's burden."[25] The British-in-Egypt case study conforms to a picture of British cultural imperial intent in which the objective is to elevate the colonial subject, but with no thought that he could ever reach the British level. The French, on the other hand, with a very different culture and a very different self-image, seem to feel that it is possible to bestow that greatest of honors on a colonial—to be considered a Frenchman.[26]

Cultural messianism is a common motivating factor. For example, the importance Alexander the Great placed on cultural messianism is apparent from the centuries-long cultural influence of Greece on Parthia and Bactria.[27] It is probably true, however, that in the rhythm of imperialism, cultural messianism is rarely to be found as a first-order motivating force in the initial stages. However, it is not purely derivative and certainly not simply rhetorical. The agents of imperialism are frequently humanists who must feel their role is morally defensible. To bring the glories of civilization, therefore, to a people not even aware enough to know how miserable they are is a worthy task. Similarly, especially in the past hundred years, the intellectuals of the imperial powers need to believe in the civilizing role imperial policy plays. Indeed, this was just as true of American intellectuals in the post–World War II period until the mid-1960s as it was of British intellectuals during the period of empire.[28] Having convinced themselves of the worthiness of the task, they will often be found in the forefront of those advocating further extension of influence. Note in particular the exceptional role of antislavery societies in Great Britain in demanding that British influence be extended in order to bring Arabs and Africans latter-day British notions of the evil of slave-trading.[29] Americans since World War II have couched their cultural messianism in such terms as "modernizing" or "nation building."

Ideological Messianism

A fine line separates cultural from ideological messianism. Here culture is assumed to mean a very broad range of norms and values. Ideology refers to a more restricted set of values, clearly political, which offers at least programmatic direction and with which there will be a congruent picture of the political terrain. Thus defined, liberal democracy and Marxism-Leninism can both be described as ideologies even though the latter is far more sharply defined. The distinction serves the analytic purpose of placing the imperial ventures of a Woodrow Wilson and the imperialism of communist regimes in a different category from the late-nineteenth-century variety in which the "civilizing" function was manifest.

Given the importance of this motive factor in communist imperialism of the past generation, its historical importance may easily be exaggerated. The Wilson episode was unique in American experience. More typical is American policy in the 1950s, which was perceived to operate at the imperial level in many parts of the world. I would contend that American policy in the 1950s resembled far more the British cultural messianism of the late nineteenth century than Soviet ideological messianism of the twentieth century. Only rarely did the United States seek to impose its regime-level political values, its ideology, on other peoples.[30] These exceptions, during John Kennedy's presidency, were short-lived. For example, a momentary intervention for Juan Bosch and liberal democracy in the Dominican Republic did occur but was rapidly retracted in the face of the consequences of such folly. The United States has been charged with seeking to make over its political dependencies in its own image. But even the most cynical should have difficulty seeing a resemblance to the American system in the regimes of President Nguyen Van Thieu, President Chiang Kai-shek, President Park Chung Hee, King Hussein, the Shah of Iran, or the Greek colonels.

What this suggests is the proposition that Soviet post–World War II imperialism shows signs of a strong ideological messianic motivation but that American imperialism of the period reflects a much weaker and more selective cultural messianic motivation. This is not the place to develop the proposition, but it suggests the utility of placing ideological and cultural messianism in separate categories.

GOVERNMENTAL

Bureaucratic Vested Interests

Possibly one of the most important overall motivational factors and the one least noted by analysts is that which reflects the role interests of the imperial bureaucracy. A reason for its neglect may be that this factor is rarely a major determinant of the initial imperial venture. Once the imperial venture has been inaugurated, however, and especially if public attention begins to lapse, the role of the concerned bureaucracy in perpetuating and expanding the enhanced influence can become one of the most important of imperial determinants. This rhythm will be seen in the British-in-Egypt study in part II. It is important to note here, as in the economic vested interest sections, that I am not saying that the colonial bureaucracy engaged in crass and detailed planning with the object of preserving its position and enhancing personal career opportunities. Instead, the bureaucrats concerned inevitably see their roles as highly beneficial, and they see a situation in which the case is self-evidently strong for their continued presence and enhanced influence.

Military Vested Interests

It makes analytic sense to separate the military bureaucracy from the remainder of the relevant bureaucracy. This is true because of the peculiarly coercive role the military plays rather than because military bureaucrats are in some way fundamentally different. On the contrary, the military bureaucracy will behave in an exactly parallel fashion to the industrial and civilian governmental bureaucracies. They too will perceive a situation congruent with their interests. However, it is the fate of military bureaucrats to be responsible for the most important direct power instruments of foreign policy. Consequently, perceptual congruence in this case calls for an image of an enemy that necessitates the maintenance and improved effectiveness of those direct power instruments. In the present era, for example, one would expect the military bureaucracy to be the last to surrender Cold War images of the Soviet Union and China.

This category is not meant as a synonym for militarism. Military leaders remark with a frequency which itself generates suspicion that since they know the horrors of war best, they are the most anxious to avoid it. However, there is good reason to accept this sentiment at face value. Indeed, it is a commonplace to note that the military is most reluctant to risk prized hardware in combat. The proposition may well be defensible that imperialist ventures which flow largely from the urgings of military leaders will be more cautiously executed and more modest in goals than, for example, imperial ventures inaugurated by traders who see great economic opportunities or leaders such as Napoleon or Hitler who are consumed by a drive for personal power.

What is called "militarism" and is seen by Winslow as virtually synonymous with "imperialism" is, in this schematic effort, a conglomerate of several motives. Military vested interests, national grandeur, participant excitement, and a strong personal power drive of the national leader would be a typical mix of primary motives when "militarism" is described as causal.

Domestic Personal Power Drive

As the preceding suggests, the role of top national leaders is indeed important to consider in a study of imperialism. Those leaders may share with others of their countrymen an ideological messianism or a very strong perception of threat, and the resulting attitudes will be part of the determinants of imperialism. But national leaders will doubtless enjoy exercising influence and may have a strong desire to exercise more influence in world affairs than their position grants them. It is this aspect of the leader's personal motivation that is of primary concern here.

This factor is subdivided again for analytic utility into a personal power drive focused on the exercise of influence domestically and a personal power drive focused outside the domestic scene. The former is relevant to imperialism whenever a leader or leaders believe that the failure to expand external influence will lead to their losing influence domestically or that an expansion of external influence will enhance their domestic position. This motive is ascribed to leaders very frequently and certainly in some cases unjustifiably. It is a difficult factor to pin down. A politician who senses that a particular foreign policy venture would improve his political position is most unlikely to admit even to himself that his reason for adopting the policy is political expediency. Rather, he is likely to see, often suddenly, very strong national-interest arguments for adopting the policy. The British-in-Egypt study includes many such instances of sudden changes in perception of a situation by political leaders. Such sudden perceptual alterations, in fact, constitute the type of evidence on which inferences regarding the importance of a domestic personal power drive in a particular foreign policy venture are based.

External Personal Power Drive

There are examples of leaders for whom this factor is universally accepted as of prime influence: Napoleon, Hitler, Mussolini. Charles De Gaulle may qualify here as well. But with the exception of Theodore Roosevelt, how many American presidents so qualify? And does this category describe motivation behind the behavior of Georgi Malenkov, Khrushchev, Aleksei Kosygin, Leonid Brezhnev, or even Stalin? I believe a content analysis of particular leaders' statements would suggest an answer to this question. Should it reveal a projection of self into the collective such that the two become indistinguishable, the case would be a strong one. The point deserves further exploring because the history of imperialism argues that this factor, when present, can be responsible for extraordinarily aggressive imperial behavior.

DEFENSE

The most nearly ubiquitous of all causal factors behind imperialism is a defensive response to perceived threat. It must be understood that it matters very little whether the threat perceived is approximately equal to the threat that a detached analyst might identify. Reality for individual actors is that which is perceived. Therefore, whereas it may be extraordinarily difficult for a Barry Goldwater, given his view of the United States, to take seriously professed Soviet fears of American aggression, evidence that such fear is real for Soviet leaders is very strong. No less real, of course, is Barry Goldwater's own fear of aggression from international communism with its center in Moscow.[31]

As used here, this category refers only to perceived threats to the government and people of a state. It does not deal with political parties, religions, economic interests, or bureaucratic interests seen in isolation. Perceived threats to them should be considered in the previous categories. What is meant here is nevertheless broad-ranging. It includes perceived threats to external influence, to aspects of what is thought of as a "way of life," and to the very independence of the state itself. Reactions will vary in intensity depending on how strongly state independence is threatened. The perception of threat of many Israelis goes beyond independence to life itself, and the vigor of the Israeli response reflects this perception. On the other hand, the acquiescence of Great Britain in the loss of empire rather than pay the price of retention reveals a low level of interest in the defense of the empire. A similar point was implicit in General De Gaulle's distrust of the American commitment to the defense of Europe: He could not believe that the threat to American security was perceived with sufficient intensity to lead the United States to take major risks for the defense of Europe.

Motivational Systems

I have defined foreign policy motivation as that compound of factors which predisposes a government and people to move in a decisional direction in foreign affairs. The above list of motives is proposed as a reasonably inclusive taxonomy of factors which enter into the compound that forms the predispositional base of foreign policy.

But a motivational compound is far more than a sum of its parts. Rather, it resembles a chemical compound. With the techniques of quantitative and qualitative analysis now available, the chemist can describe the most complex compounds with an accuracy that the foreign policy analyst can only envy. The foreign policy analyst may understand that Soviet motivation is more complex than lunar soil and less stable than sodium peroxide, yet he lacks the qualitative and quantitative techniques comparable to those the chemist uses to analyze a compound as simple as water. To carry the analogy further, the foreign policy analyst is like a chemist who is allowed to determine the component parts of water by observation only. He can watch rain, snow, steam rising from the wet ground, an ocean storm, and ice forming on a pond. But he is not permitted to feel, boil, or freeze water. He must infer from the gross behavioral patterns he observes that water consists of two parts hydrogen and one part oxygen.

The utility of the taxonomy of motives outlined above can be seen in terms of this analogy as well. Its analogue is the periodic table of pure elements. The chemist, were he denied the use of his laboratory, would at least have a check list of elements, some of which combine to produce water. Drawing the conclusion that the elements involved were hydrogen and oxygen would still require creative genius, but the periodic table is at least a starting point. Before such a list of basic elements was advanced the ancient chemist concluded that water—along with air, fire, and earth—was a basic element. Entirely comparable is the conclusion of some foreign policy analysts that "power" is a basic motivational element. In my view, "power" is to a motivational element as fire is to a chemical element. And foreign policy analysts are to chemists as the alchemists of ancient Greece are to the scientists of the twenty-first century. Developing a list of motivational elements could help push us toward the Renaissance.

My intention is to construct a scheme for making both a qualitative and quantitative analysis of the ingredients that have gone into a particular foreign policy motivational compound. The substitute for the chemist's balance, centrifuge, and spectrograph will be a study of the decisional process, noting who was involved and what was said and done. This evidence should tell which of the above categories is relevant and should give some indication of the intensity of involvement. Who is involved in a decision tells a good deal about motivation. How interested is the general public in the issue? Which interest groups—economic, ethnic, ideological, bureaucratic, military—are most concerned? What decisional latitude is granted the foreign policy bureaucracy? The answers to these questions point to one or another of the motivational types suggested above and also suggest relative weightings of these types in the overall motivational picture. I believe, however, that a great deal more can be done to estimate composition and structure of motivation by comparing what is said and what is done. Verbal behavior by itself is not that revealing. If perception is defined as the mental picture on which action is based, perception and verbal behavior are not the same thing. My assumptions are that an individual will articulate even to himself only a small portion of the mental picture on which he bases his actions and, furthermore, that some of that verbalized behavior, even though sincere, is contradictory to the choice made.

For example, take an individual who was thoroughly socialized with the highly aggressive Cold War image of the Soviet Union but who has come over the years to expect conservative behavior from Soviet leaders. He may continue to describe the Soviet Union in Cold War terms, as he was trained to do, but at the same time advocate détente policies that would be absurd if he took literally his verbal descriptions. The distance separating the verbalized picture of Soviet motivations from the implicit picture of Soviet motivations that is in harmony with the individual's policy preferences is in this case substantial. Why not, then, simply ignore the verbalized picture and concentrate on inferring the individual's perceptions, since that is the picture on which action is based? My conclusion, unfortunate from the point of view of analytic neatness, is that both verbal descriptions and policy preferences must be considered in inferring perceptions. I believe there is always some distance between verbal description and policy preference. It is likely to be great, as in this example, when a stereotypical view of an actor became rigidified many years earlier in a generic diplomatic period, that is, one such as the early Cold War, in which general agreement was reached regarding the problem and major strategic lines for dealing with it. The stereotypical view continues to influence behavior, preventing the perception of some action alternatives and generally narrowing decisional latitude. Furthermore, it generates policy inconsistency. A decision maker who accepts the Cold War stereotype of the Soviet Union but who has engaged in détente policies is highly vulnerable to the arguments of those who describe these policies as appeasement. Responding to such arguments, the decision maker may well suddenly embrace policy suggestions more in tune with the stereotypical view.

Since the basic inferential device in this scheme is perceptual, it is important to note from the beginning that the analyst using such a scheme has broad judgmental latitude. These are the early days of perceptual analysis, and refinements in the direction of making this and related schemes operationalizable and thus ultimately replicable should not be ruled out.[32] For the time being, however, the motivational system device should be seen as a primitive first step in approaching the problem of explicating the predispositional base of a foreign policy.

Were I being true to the chemical compound analogue, the picture of American foreign policy motives implicitly accepted by a modal supporter of American foreign policy in the mid-1960s could be D_3Di_2NgCm, where D = defense, Di = domestic investments, Ng = national grandeur, and Cm = cultural messianism. Such a representation would have some definite advantages. Although the number of possible combinations is astronomical, only a few motivational elements would ever be depicted as being present in three parts, and the element or combination of elements granted three parts would suggest the flavor of the resultant foreign policy. Where defense alone is granted three parts, as above, the general thrust would be status-quo. My survey of imperial episodes suggests that the element in three parts most likely to be associated with aggressive imperialistic behavior are external power drive (Epd), especially in combination with national grandeur (Ng) and participant excitement (Pe). In an earlier era trade (T), when granted three parts, could lead to highly aggressive imperialism. Contrary to Winslow's view, I usually found military vested interests (Mvi), when present in three parts, in combination with defense (D) and associated with sluggish imperialism.

It is easy to envy the chemist, for his shorthand representation of a compound describes great complexity at a glance. But that representation demands too much of the analogue and could never be isomorphic for a motivational compound. The representation I do propose at least has the advantage of appearing more tentative. The major elements inferred by the analyst to be present in the motivational compound are placed in three intensity levels. The prevailing world view device, developed in chapter 4, and the system-of-aims device, developed in chapter 5, are the means for inferring the elements present in a motivational compound and their relative weightings. As I admitted earlier, however, the scheme at this stage requires the analyst to exercise far too much judgmental discretion, especially in ascribing weightings.

The device nonetheless has immediate utility for dealing with the perceptual base of conflict. It permits a systematizing of the motivational assumptions on which different policy preferences are based. Then, by juxtaposing competing assumptional positions, the analyst can point to the real basis of disagreement.

In the remainder of this chapter, I will illustrate the device and its utility for clarifying the perceptual basis of conflict by applying it to the foreign policy motivations of four states. For three of those states—the United States, the Soviet Union, and Israel—I propose two competing pictures of motivations. These pictures are the motivational systems that I suggest individuals representing opposing views would construct were they to use this scheme. In reality, foreign policy motivation is only rarely explicated. On the contrary, motivational assumptions either remain wholly hidden or are referred to in the simplest of terms—often symbolically.

The fourth state is Nazi Germany, and the motivational system proposed to describe Hitler's foreign policy is included for comparative purposes. The German motivational system is prototypical of the compound leading to extremely aggressive behavior. Do groups which call the United States, the Soviet Union, or Israel aggressive see motivational compounds comparable to that of Hitler's Germany?

American foreign policy motivation as seen by a supporter of American policy. My proposed assumptional base of a modal supporter of American policy is as follows:

A. (1st intensity)   Defense
B. (2nd intensity)   Economic vested interests: domestic investments
C. (3rd intensity)   National grandeur
                      Cultural messianism

This motivational system is essentially status-quo. It reflects the belief that American involvement in the affairs of others is primarily for the peace and security, in other words the defense, of the American people. However, my impression is that this modal American sees the well-being of the American people as a legitimate objective, which necessitates a concern with a healthy economy and a foreign policy which safeguards that economy. Therefore I place domestic investments at the second level of intensity. But this projection does not indicate that an expansion of American investments abroad is viewed as a primary driving force behind American foreign policy. I see a concern for the prestige and dignity of the nation; but I place national grandeur at the third level because I believe the modal American in the mid-1960s saw little threat to American prestige and dignity. The one motivational factor included in this inferred system that suggests expansion rather than maintenance of the level of world influence is "cultural messianism." Its inclusion reflects my belief that this modal American envisioned American policy as bringing a better life (that is, one closer to the American style) to our friends in Europe and the developing world. He therefore considered such programs as the Marshall Plan, Point Four, and the Alliance for Progress as in effect beneficently civilizing and certainly not as disguised imperialism.

American foreign policy motivation as seen by a New Left opponent. The motivational system proposed for a modal member of the New Left is as follows:

A. Economic vested interests: investments abroad and domestic
   Military vested interests
   Bureaucratic vested interests
B. National grandeur
   Cultural messianism
C. Defense

This motivational system is clearly imperialistic, although it lacks the kind of causal factors, such as external personal power drive or participant excitement, that would make for a highly aggressive imperialism. It incorporates the fundamental systemic nature of the New Left assumptions. The three factors placed in the first-intensity category are depicted by those holding this view as "the military-industrial complex." Defense is placed at the third-intensity level because the New Left questions the existence of a strongly held threat perception in which international communism centered in Moscow and, to a lesser degree, Peking, is the threatening object. Cold War rhetoric grounded in the assumption of such a threat appears to the New Left to be a cynical exercise.

Since the New Left generally describes American policy as designed to support traditional or reactionary regimes rather than as seeking to establish dynamic, bourgeois regimes, the inference has been made that ideological messianism is not regarded as a determining drive. But the imposition of modern bureaucratic values such as rationality and efficiency on such regimes is noted, and this falls into the cultural messianism category as used here. The second-level intensity rating may be too strong: Certainly the New Left writers do not articulate it strongly. But it relates very closely to the primary causal factors and is therefore inferred to be at the second level.

Nationalism, patriotism, and chauvinism are frequently cited and deplored by New Left writers. The fear of fascism, a characteristic feature of which is the use of national chauvinism to attract and maintain popular support, also pervades these writings. But national grandeur as a determinant of American imperialism is not stressed. Rather the factor appears to be subordinate to and derived from the needs of the industrial-bureaucratic-military establishment. It has therefore been placed in the second-level intensity category.

Soviet foreign policy motivation as seen by Senator Barry Goldwater. The motivational system I propose as congruent with Goldwater's views is as follows:

A. Ideological messianism
B. Bureaucratic vested interests
   Military vested interests
C. Defense

As comparison with the Nazi example given shortly will suggest, this inferred system, though imperialistic, does not support a highly aggressive imperialism. I have seen no suggestion from Goldwater that Stalin had a Napoleonic external power drive and certainly none that his successors did. The dull bureaucratic figures, Kosygin and Brezhnev, are not easily depicted as Hitlers. Nor is it easy to find in Soviet behavior the type of chauvinistic appeals made by the fascist leaders or any real public enthusiasm over imperial ventures. Still the perception of threat from the capitalist world that could explain much Soviet imperial behavior is downgraded sharply by those holding this view. Instead, they seem to see the driving force as the desire to bring to all the world the blessings of communism and to make Moscow the Third Rome of this new world. Soviet policy is seen to rest in the hands of military and civilian bureaucrats whose self-interest would of course be well served by the extension of communist world boundaries. Since Goldwater has the greatest difficulty believing the Soviet Union could seriously see the West as aggressive, were he actually to use this scheme he might well conclude that even the third-intensity ranking for defense is too high.

Soviet foreign policy motivation as seen by an American dove. My proposed motivational system as seen by, for example, former senator J. William Fulbright in the 1960s is as follows:

A. Defense
B. Bureaucratic vested interests
   Economic vested interests: domestic investments
C. Ideological messianism

This inferred motivational system resembles that of American foreign policy as viewed by a supporter of that policy and is essentially status-quo. Acts of imperialism have been carried out by both governments, but those who see policy as status-quo explain these acts as defensive in basic motivation. The remainder of the motivational system reflects the different political processes of the United States and the Soviet Union. I believe the presumption is the same, however: that

Soviet policy, too, is determined by the need to bring material satisfaction to its people. Thus, Soviet expansion into Eastern Europe at the close of World War II is seen as having been motivated by the desire to construct a cordon sanitaire and to aid in Soviet economic recovery. The desire to see communism spread cannot easily be denied since it is verbalized frequently by Soviet leaders. But this system places ideological messianism in the third category because men such as Erich Fromm, who believe the Soviet Union to be status-quo, see these statements as more rhetorical than indicative of a strong drive.[33] Here again, the parallel with American cultural messianism is close.

These contrasting motivational systems have been inferred to illustrate the construct and also to show how this device can be used for spelling out in more concrete terms the assumptional differences that commonly underlie major foreign policy debate. As the British-in-Egypt case study will demonstrate, the evidence for inferring motivations must be acquired painstakingly, and this has not been done for these illustrations. The point should be clear nonetheless, as has been argued throughout these early pages, that contending sides in foreign policy debates often have fundamentally different assumptions. Yet the debates almost always focus, not on the area of assumptional difference, but rather on competing policy recommendations. These policy recommendations may be perfectly defensible, given the assumptions on which each rests, but the participants in the debates will not often recognize where the real difference lies.

I stated in chapter 1 my belief that the international relations analyst can provide an exceptionally important service in domestic disputes over foreign policy alternatives simply by making clear the assumptional differences separating the contestants. If the 1957 Kissinger view was correct in seeing a Soviet Union driven by ideology to pursue single-minded and ineluctable imperialist goals, then a complicated *modus vivendi* in which American bargaining strength must always be optimal is an entirely defensible policy response. If the New Left view of defense and domestic economy as the motivating force is correct, the *modus vivendi* policy will perpetuate unnecessary conflict and could result in accidental war. Were the participants in the debate made aware of their real differences, the debate could focus on the central issue: Can the case that Soviet motivation is primarily one of ideological messianism be supported by careful and empirically based analysis?

An even more valuable service could be performed by detached analysts looking at conflict between nations and the motivational assumptions of each side. If the conflict is intense, these assumptional differences will be dramatic. Skilled mediators understand this point intuitively. An analytic scheme which helps to explicate assumptional differences could make even more clear to the contestants that, as real as some elements of the conflict may be, much of the conflict is based on a perceptually based misunderstanding. To illustrate, I will propose two

assumptional pictures of Israeli foreign policy. My purpose is to spell out con-
cretely the prevailing assumptional differences.

Israeli foreign policy motivation as seen by Israelis. I propose a motivational
system of Israeli policy that conforms to the Israeli prevailing view as follows:

A. Defense
   Cultural messianism
B. Economic vested interests: domestic investments
C. National grandeur

The similarity to the prevailing American view of American motivations is not
accidental. Both the United States and Israel have carried out acts of imperialism,
but I believe that neither the modal American nor the modal Israeli sees his
government as driven by a desire to increase its influence relative to that of other
governments and peoples. Rather, each sees his government as motivated by a
desire to defend itself against a strongly perceived threat.

However, the motivational system for Israel should reflect the unique relationship between Israel and Jews living in the Diaspora. This is schematically
indicated as cultural messianism—a desire to maintain for world Jewry a haven
where a unique Jewish culture can not only survive but develop and guide those
Jews of the Diaspora who are threatened with acculturation. Thus, Israel's policy
is placed further toward the imperialistic side than is the American. National
grandeur is seen as not requiring an expansion of influence, but since the very
survival of the nation-state is at stake, national grandeur is a determinant comple-
menting and interacting with defense. Israel is seen as compelled to be vigorous in
defending her economic well-being from Arab efforts to strangle her through such
tactics as boycott campaigns.

Israeli foreign policy motivation as seen by Syrians. The same evidence leads
many Syrians to a very different appraisal of motivation. The motivational system
that conforms to the Syrian prevailing view is the following:

A. National grandeur
   Participant excitement
   Economic vested interests: investments abroad and domestic
   Cultural messianism (toward Jews)
B. Military vested interests
   Defense
C. Cultural messianism (toward Arabs)

There are unique qualities to this representation which would support a vigorous
imperialism. The external investments refer not to Israeli but to world capitalist
investments. The close cooperation of Israeli and Western imperialism is always

noted in Syria. I believe, in fact, that this perception is one of the most deeply held in the Arab world. The support of Israel by the United States, for example, is seen as only in part a manifestation of pressure from American Jews. It is seen as motivated also by a desire to keep the Arab world a raw-material-producing area in which oil investments are well secured. In this view, Israel was created to help keep the Arab world under the imperial control of Western capitalists.

But Israeli nationalism is seen as increasingly independent of imperial control and almost limitlessly ambitious. That Israelis are immensely attracted to and excited by the prospect of a new Israel stretching from the Nile to the Euphrates is seen as self-evident. Western assumptions that Israel's prime motivation is defense are seen as examples of either extraordinary gullibility or guile. The parallel made in Arab propaganda between Israel and Nazi Germany is heavy with intentional irony, but it is too harmonious with the overall view to be considered simply shock propaganda. It would be a gross misunderstanding of the Arab position to discount the perception of threat herein involved.

Nevertheless, the second-level rather than third-level intensity rating of defense for Israel by Syrians does reflect some acceptance of the fact that many Israelis are, or are descendants of, people who have suffered horrible persecution, especially in the Christian world. That the Israelis fear genocide at the hands of Arabs is understood even though, of course, the Israeli fear is asserted to be groundless. However, the granting of a second-level intensity to the defense motivation of Israel is not sufficient to counter the dominant imperialist flavor. Instead, defense is seen in fact as a defense of world Jewry which in turn requires the establishment of a safe haven for their immigration if necessary. This in turn leads naturally to an energizing of the imperial drive. Interaction with what is typed as cultural messianism—that is, a special relationship with Jews in the Diaspora by which preservation of cultural uniqueness among the world Jewish community is enhanced—further adds to the imperial desire. Furthermore, the demands of imperialism have led to Israel's militarization, as Arabs see it, which results in the appearance of a military with a vested interest in protracted conflict.

A favorite Israeli propaganda statement that were there to be Arab acceptance of Israel the Israeli technical achievements could be shared with Arabs is seen as a further imperial manifestation. Arabs are to be offered aspects of Israeli culture in return for substantial Israeli influence gains.

Nazi Germany's foreign policy motivation. In the Syrian view just given, Israeli imperialism is seen to be the most aggressive of the examples described here. But the motivation system that could describe Nazi Germany's imperialism as seen by this writer is a model for an extreme in aggressiveness:

  A. External personal power drive
     National grandeur
     Participant excitement

B. Economic vested interests: investments abroad
   Military vested interests
   Cultural messianism
C. Domestic personal power drive
   Bureaucratic vested interests
   Defense

The basic foreign policy aims that could be derived from such a motivational system were perceived similarly by both the Nazis and their victims. The latter, of course, came to this conclusion reluctantly and only after evidence of aggressive intent was so overwhelming as to be undeniable. The placing of military vested interests in the second level of intensity does not conform, however, to the general perception of Hitler's victims. "Prussian militarism" was much too strong an image for that. But the reluctance of many of Hitler's general officers to carry out Hitler's audacious military policy is in tune with the generalized proposition that military vested interests lead to a far less aggressive kind of imperialism. Nazis, of course, would include defense against the Jewish capitalist powers as a first-intensity factor, whereas Hitler's victims would be unlikely to grant it any saliency. I conclude that there was a perception of threat on Hitler's part which warrants a third-level intensity rating for defense. Indeed, it is unlikely that a measurable threat perception is ever lacking in the perceptual basis of a motivational system for imperialism.

In the British-in-Egypt case study, British motivational systems for each of several periods will be inferred from a solid empirical base. The above systems are impressionistically derived to illustrate the potential utility of the scheme. If international relations specialists are to turn seriously to prescriptive theory, a focus on basic motivation is essential. Of equal importance are the tasks of constructing a scheme by which basic motives can be inferred and a scheme by which those motives which are perceived by various relevant actors can be inferred. The analyst seeking to prescribe a solution for the Arab-Israeli conflict, for example, must infer Israeli motivations and must also infer Israeli motivations as perceived by Syrians and by Israelis.

The importance of this point can be illustrated by the theory implicit in containment theory. The notion that the act of containment would result in systemic change in the imperialist state makes a good deal of sense as prescription for a motivational system such as that of the Nazis. That aggressive syndrome was dependent on nationalistic participant excitement, a phenomenon which can be sustained only if additions to national glory are frequent and relatively cheap. The internal control system itself depends on a perpetual state of outer-directed excitement. If such easy expansion is cut off, the imperial desire should quickly atrophy.

In that event the leadership would have to turn to other and inner-directed means of control—and in so doing lose freedom to engage in external adventure.

Applying this scheme to the Soviet Union, which has an entirely different motivational system, would make little sense. Yet if defense is granted a first-intensity ranking for Soviet motivation, the status-quo containment policy could have the unanticipated result of diminishing the Soviet threat perception and thus lessening the need for vigorous action to defend the Soviet people. Thus, inadvertently, the containment policy could have the desired effect of reducing the fear-induced Soviet imperial drive. A rollback policy, on the other hand, would surely intensify the perception of threat and thus the Soviet imperial response.

4 / Perception

Hans Morgenthau's discussion of the concept of appeasement[1] points to a simple truth: The most important requirement for foreign policy formulation is an accurate understanding of the motivations of other governments and peoples. To assume imperialist motivations where they do not exist is no less grievous an error than to assume status-quo motivations where in fact there is a strong imperialist motivational thrust. Either error is likely to heighten conflict. There is no margin of safety, as is commonly thought, in assuming the worst.

Yet this simple truth underlines even more sharply the modesty of the theoretical contribution of the field of international relations. The intelligent and politically sophisticated statesman or diplomat is likely to have a more complex estimate of other governments' motivations based on his own experience, knowledge, and judgment, than he could gain from the application of existing theory. His estimate, however, will certainly be simplistic and heavily influenced by his own perceptual blinders. The resulting distorted motivational assumptions will lead inevitably to faulty policy judgments.

The purpose of the previous chapter was to suggest a scheme for viewing motivations that would permit comprehension of the complexity and interactive quality of the motivational compound. A far more difficult theoretical task remains, however; and that is to devise a means, not simply intuitive, for inferring the operative motivational system. The analyst must identify the most important motivating elements and must ascribe to these elements relative intensity ratings. This is necessary even though none of the motivational types lends itself easily to quantitative analysis.

The evidence the analyst must rely on for understanding motivations is clear enough. He must discover who is involved in the foreign policy decisional process, what they say, and what they do. Weighting will be based in part on a determination of the importance of the roles played by those involved in the relevant foreign policy decisions. But weighting requires as well an evaluation of the decisional environment. Is there a prevailing sense of threat to the national community or opportunity for it which circumscribes narrowly the decisional freedom of those making decisions? Or is general interest low—a situation which allows the decision maker wide discretion but grants him little claim on national resource allocation?

Snyder et al., in *Foreign Policy Decision Making,* limited their concern with the question of "who is involved" to those with official competence, that is, those government officials whose roles led to some commitment of time to a particular decision.[2] Given the analytic purpose of these authors, this restrictive concern is defensible. But the analytic purpose here is to identify motivations and ultimately give them an intensity rating. To do this it is necessary to go beyond a determination of the role of those with official competence, which is difficult enough, and to include an estimate of the importance of the roles of the general public, various interest groups, and leading politicians, both government and opposition.

With this purpose in mind, the typology of motives suggested in chapter 3 can serve as a check list for a comprehensive identification of those who might be involved in foreign policy decisions relating to imperialism. But, more important, it suggests which aspects of behavior of those involved should be examined. The "domestic personal power drive" factor points to the leading political figures of a polity. If they are involved in the relevant decisions, the reasons will probably be varied. But the "domestic personal power drive" factor calls for a determination as to whether those leaders believe their maintaining or achieving power domestically would be enhanced by the support of a particular foreign policy venture. A judgment that this factor was indeed operative would be defensible if the leaders included an advocacy of such a program in speeches designed to attract public support. For historical figures, private statements might well be found explicitly to the effect that such a policy would or would not be politically helpful.

It would be far more difficult to draw a conclusion that the "external personal power drive" factor was operative. Here verbal behavior would be of little help, since a leader so motivated is unlikely to take public or even private note of his motivation—if indeed he is aware of it himself. A judgment that this motive applied would necessarily be based on a conclusion that the leader's actions far exceeded those necessary to attract domestic support and went well beyond those called for to satisfy any messianic mission important supporters might have had. Even so, the factor would not stand in isolation. A leader so motivated would in all likelihood have fused notions of personal and national grandeur with various messianic missions.

Least difficult to determine would be the bureaucratic elements involved in a decision. A judgment that bureaucratic vested interest is a factor, however, must be inferred. It is most unlikely that bureaucrats will take conscious note of the extent to which their own vested interests influence their policy proposals or make statements to that effect. Furthermore, a foreign policy decision of any importance will involve several bureaucratic sets with competing interests and conflicting interpretations of events reflecting these competing interests. The really difficult task is to assess the foreign policy thrust that results from bureaucratic interaction. Sections of the Central Intelligence Agency (CIA) and the Defense Department, for example, might favor supporting a military faction in a Third World state, but sections of the State and Commerce Departments might see such action as too risky and too costly. The analyst looking at the outcome can only infer the extent to which the role interests of these various bureaucratic sets influenced the decision.[3]

The general public role is best seen in the factors "participant excitement" and "grandeur." The presence or absence of the former is fairly easily determined. If the public is excited, their excitement will certainly be reflected in the communications media or in such direct action as demonstrations. If the society is open, politicians will certainly reflect the excitement in verbal behavior and are likely to do so even if the society is closed.[4]

Grandeur, when participant excitement is lacking, will be far less easily seen. Public opinion polls may suggest little nationalistic involvement of the public in a decisional area, but politicians will sense whether a particular policy under consideration would be likely to offend or excite the public sense of national grandeur. Furthermore, the decision makers will in all likelihood have internalized a devotion to national grandeur and yet be unaware of the extent to which that concern determines their behavior. Here again, the analyst will be compelled to infer from policy behavior whether the factor is significant.[5]

Bernard Cohen has described the activity of economic interest groups as being characterized by visibility and specificity of goals.[6] Carl Oglesby is typical of many writers of the left who operate from the assumption that economic interest groups are at the core of the military-industrial complex and therefore play a far more general role in foreign policy formulation than the Cohen thesis suggests and are far less visible.[7] This difference in viewpoint reflects the difficulty in discerning the role of economic interest groups in foreign policy formulation. Taking American oil interests in the Middle East as an example, there are moments in which the Cohen thesis is well demonstrated. In 1954, Onassis shipping interests made a determined effort to persuade the Saudi Arabian government that its self-interest would be served by giving Onassis interests a major share in the transport of Saudi Arabian oil. This would have broken the monopoly of Aramco, the giant American oil conglomerate. Aramco's response was highly visible, energetic, and successful; and American governmental response was clearly in tune with Aramco's desires.[8]

But to what extent did American oil companies play a role in the American-backed 1953 overthrow of Dr. Mossadegh in Iran, who had stubbornly insisted on Iranian control of its oil production? Specific evidence is lacking to support a conclusion that oil company influence here was of any significance. Yet the inference has been made with great confidence by Iranians and the left generally that the role of the oil interests was critical.[9] This latter conclusion is based on an assumption that vital economic interests are represented informally but decisively within the policy community of any capitalist state. The intensity weighting of this factor therefore obviously cannot depend on hard evidence. However, the circumstantial case is strong. CIA involvement in Mossadegh's overthrow is by now undisputed. Before nationalization, Iran's oil was controlled by the half-government–half-private Anglo Iranian Oil Company. Following Mossadegh's overthrow, the American-backed regime agreed to an oil consortium arrangement to manage Iran's oil production that was 40 percent American.

For most other public-interest groups, evidence of role should be more easily available and subject to less controversy. Possibly most easily identified and visible in their activities are religious interest groups. Where their role was significant, as in sixteenth- and seventeenth-century Spanish imperialism and nineteenth-century British imperialism, particularly in Africa, visibility was such as to offer very concrete evidence of activity. But religious messianism is not strikingly obvious in twentieth-century imperialism and is therefore largely of historical interest.

Similarly, cultural interest groups, so important in the imperialism of the pre–World War I period, have largely disappeared. The British antislavery societies, which placed great pressure on the British government to gain control of much of East Africa and suppress the local slave trade, have few modern counterparts. Cultural messianism remains an important motivating factor in the post–World War II era, but it is more difficult to identify. In place of easily recognized references to a civilizing mission are euphemisms such as "developing" and "modernizing." Furthermore, cultural messianism in this era is less likely to arise in response to pressures from an interest group outside the bureaucracy. It is far more likely today to be advocated by elements of the bureaucracy.[10]

Ideological messianism, advocated by public ideological interest groups, is again not an important factor in modern imperialism. Ideological pressure groups acutely concerned with national dignity and prestige, like the American Legion in this country, are common enough. But it is difficult to point to such groups which seek to spread a prevailing ideology to other peoples through imperialist activity. The Americans for Democratic Action is an ideological pressure group with a deep concern for foreign policy. It has found repulsive such regimes as those of Rafael Trujillo in the Dominican Republic, Francisco Franco in Spain, and the Greek colonels. Yet specific foreign policy recommendations concerning such regimes generally call for cutting off American support and never for a policy of replacement. Some men vital to foreign policy decisions will have deep ideological convictions and may seek to impose their ideological will on others. Wilson seems to have attempted this in Mexico. Leon Trotsky most obviously of Soviet leaders attempted the same. It appears that the ideological messianism factor is more easily inferred from the behavior of leading decisional figures than from the behavior of ideological interest groups.[11]

Another motivational type easily seen if present is that of frontier dynamics.

Here settlers constitute the public-interest group. Modern examples are not lacking. The French *colons* in Algeria, British settlers in Rhodesia, and Israeli settlers of Arab Territory occupied during the 1967 war play the same kind of role seen countless times in other parts of the world.[12]

One interest-group type which continues to play a vital role in determining American foreign policy is not clearly suggested by the motivational typology. That is the ethnic interest group. Such groups may identify both with their state of residence and with another state in which their ethnic group is a significant element of the population. In that case, they can be expected to see congruence in the defense and grandeur needs of both states and will advocate policies manifesting that congruence. Only in extreme cases will they feel compelled to choose between them. In this motivational scheme both identity communities will be dealt with under the captions "grandeur" and "defense." However, in chapter 5 a means for differentiating the two will be suggested.[13]

The purpose thus far in this chapter is to suggest a means for identifying, but not proposing intensity ratings for, the various motivational types operative in a particular imperialism. Were there a straight line from role interests to policy behavior, the task of identification would be much easier. In fact, not only is it extremely difficult to determine who is directly or indirectly involved in a decision, but it is impossible to argue that each participating individual or group is simply acting out role interests. When Secretary of Defense Charles Wilson made his famous remark, "What is good for General Motors is good for the country," he was simply being ingenuously explicit about something virtually everyone does, that is, bringing into congruence the needs as we see them of the various identity communities to which we grant loyalty.[14] Since most men owe allegiance to various communities and hold many values intensely, role values constitute only one set of the determinants of behavior.

The analytic device for proposing intensity ratings thus must deal with motivational compounds for individuals. These conclusions must in turn be reflected in the saliency profile of the motivational system which predisposes a government to pursue a particular foreign policy. Unlike the chemist who can isolate and ultimately measure with precision the elements of the compound he seeks to analyze, the international relations analyst must in large degree base his qualitative analysis on inference from behavior. Some circularity is thus unavoidable. Since qualitative analysis depends on fallible inferences, imprecision and tentativeness of results are inevitable. The modest threefold intensity categorizing scheme used here reflects this tentativeness. But even a three-level categorizing implies a precision beyond the capability of the scheme.

Intensity estimates will be based on the prevailing perception of the situation,[15] with "prevailing" defined as "most congruent with the policy being carried out." Having identified as far as possible who is involved in a decision, and having inferred the perceptions of the situation of those involved, the analyst is in a position to judge the relative congruence of the various perceptions with the decision ultimately made. If one group of individuals perceived the situation in such a way that the decision made is out of harmony with their view, the conclusion is that these individuals had little to do with the decision. However, if another group of individuals perceived the situation in such a way that the decision made was entirely harmonious with their view, the conclusion is not necessarily that these individuals were influential. Estimates of intensity also require information regarding the extent of individual involvement in the decision. Unfortunately for the researcher, that involvement may be indirect. In chapter 6 and in the case study the attentive public roles as described will appear to be far more influential than is generally believed. The point is simple. Psychological balance theory argues that an individual seeks to bring into balance his value-related goals and his view of a situation. If a political leader senses he will lose the support of a section of the public which includes many opinion formulators because of a particular foreign policy position he has taken, he will make some rapid and largely nonconscious alterations in his view of the situation. The amended view will accommodate as far as possible the various demands placed on him and yet will be one with which he personally can be comfortable. When this occurs, analysis should reflect it in a high intensity rating for the motive factor of domestic personal power drive. Yet, since the political leader will have so accommodated naturally and nonconsciously, even depth interviewing could not provide direct evidence. The primary "hard" evidence would be sharp alterations in verbal behavior. The rest must be inferred.

In chapter 5, two levels of situations will be examined. One will be the general international situation, and the prevailing perception of this situation can be described as the prevailing world view. The other will be the situation of immediate relevance to the specific policy area and will be described as the prevailing situational view. In the British-in-Egypt case study, for example, the latter will refer to the situation in Egypt and the British perceptions of it.

The primary evidential base for constructing these perceptions will be the verbal behavior of those judged to be involved, directly or indirectly, in the decisional area. Even the seeming platitudes of the diplomat will be of vital importance. But great caution must be exercised in the use of verbal behavior. No analyst would be so naive as to mistake a diplomat's public description of a situation for his perception of it. Yet, in the search for statistically reliable data, analysts do indulge in the kind of quantified content analysis of statements which amounts to equating verbal behavior and perception. Perceptions must be inferred just as motivation must be inferred, and an analytical base for inferring perceptions must be devised if we are to progress beyond the impressionistic level. Once inferential models are devised, quantitative techniques can and should be applied in content analysis for measuring perceptions. But applying these techniques prior to constructing inferential models will compel the analyst to rely on verbal behavior alone. The result will be serious distortion of meaning.

Inferential Base for World View

In the simple world of the realist school, inferring perceptions is almost ridiculously easy. The prevailing collective, in this era the nation-state, has an all-consuming role interest: to win or to optimize power. The human agents of that collective exercise its will and see the world in a way that is entirely congruent with that will. Morgenthau develops this point in his nationalistic universalism concept.[16] In chapter 2, I argued that the compelling quality of the realist argument rests on the fact that at moments of great interstate crisis, the human agents of nation-states describe reality in terms that are congruent with their states' interests. But at other moments this is not always the case. The noncrisis periods, therefore, call for an analytic scheme of great complexity.

To begin with, the determinants of an individual's world view are manifold. I would propose the following as an analytically useful categorizing of these determinants:

1. The historical experience of the national communities with which the individual identifies intensely
2. The defense and grandeur interests of the political communities with which the individual identifies
3. The other politically relevant values that the individual holds intensely
4. The individual's role interests
5. The individual's idiosyncratic socialization patterns

Items 2 through 5 categorize the values and attitudes that predispose an individual to view the world in a particularistic way. Item 1 suggests the external events that the individual, with his predispositional base, will have incorporated into a world view.

What is called for is a device for looking at the politically relevant aspects of an individual value system, categorizing them and describing their function in ordering world events into a world view. The above items could be a starting point for constructing such a device. I am suggesting quite a different value scheme than emerges from Milton Rokeach's efforts to discover value hierarchies.[17] An analytic distinction between intensity and salience seems to me vital here. Rather than value hierarchies, I see as most isomorphic to human behavior a construct which places values at different intensity levels but with a great many values occupying each intensity level. An individual may so value his nation that when the chips are down, as Rupert Emerson said, he would risk his life for that value.[18] We call him a nationalist. But that same individual, when the chips are down, may be willing to risk the ultimate sacrifice for that cluster of values over which is placed the umbrella term "liberal." Likewise, he may so value the achievement of a role of influence over others as to risk the ultimate sacrifice for its preservation. And he may value what he would describe as a "way of life," that is, social values he accepts and by which he defines personal comfort, intensely enough to risk everything in meeting a threat to those values.

All of these values are held at a first level of intensity and, as balance theory suggests, the world the individual perceives will be so ordered as to accommodate them all. But when this individual is compelled to choose among alternatives in any given situation, only a fraction of the values he holds will be affected or, in other words, will for that decision have any particular salience. So it is with nationalism. An individual may be a nationalist, that is, he may place a primary value in his national community, but only the rarest of decisions he makes will reflect that fact. The political scientist, who is interested only in the individual's political decisions, naturally has difficulty keeping in mind the fact that only a fraction of the decisions an average citizen makes have any political relevance at all, even though most individuals hold some politically relevant values at the primary intensity level.

It seems to me, therefore, that the simple notion of threat and/or opportunity has at this stage much to offer in political value analysis.[19] A particular politically relevant value becomes salient for an individual if he perceives either threat or opportunity associated with it. Does the individual perceive a serious threat to the survival of a nation-state community with which he intensely identifies? Does he see a magnificent opportunity to expand national influence and thereby enhance greatly the nation's world prestige? Does he see a threat to his way of life or the opportunity to give others its benefits? Does he see the possibility of a major career setback if international events take a certain course, or are those events likely to provide spectacular new career opportunities for him? My contention is that the individual's world view will be heavily determined by the answers to such questions. But the historical experience of the collective of which the individual is a part will have determined the boundaries of that world view. Furthermore, factors influential in the individual's socialization will have a significant and not easily discovered bearing on the world view. For example, the anti-Semitic attitudes with which Adolf Hitler was socialized strongly colored his world view and ultimately the policy choices he was to make.

West Germany and France have been allies for a generation, but the perceptual scars from previous generations in which enmity between the two people was intense remain clearly visible. Historically determined perceptions, therefore, will reflect eras of different relationships, and the resulting patterns will be mixed and often contradictory. Furthermore, the way Frenchmen perceive Germans and Germany is affected by the relationship each people has with all other peoples who are of significant concern. The result is a perceptual maze of such intricacy as to defy useful description. Nor is this atypical. The politically interested section of any population will have a world view of similar complexity.

This poses an enormous analytic problem. I see a foreign policy decision as involving a choice among alternatives made by individuals predisposed by their values to make certain choices but making them within the context of a world view. The concerned individuals could not, even in skillfully conducted depth interviews, articulate with any completeness either the predispositional value base or the world view which together resulted in their particular choices. What the analyst has, therefore, is limited evidence: some awareness of who was involved, a record of some of the verbal behavior of these individuals, and overt aspects of the decision itself. To get at world view and predispositional base, the analyst can only infer.

Perceptual Patterns

My reason for believing that a perceptual inferential scheme can be developed is that I think man behaves perceptually in patterned ways on the international as on the interpersonal level. If an individual perceives a threat to something valued intensely in interpersonal relations, he is likely to see a situation in a fashion tending toward paranoia. In its extreme form, the individual will perceive an evil force threatening him that is capable of the most elaborate conspiracies. Any lowering of his guard in the form of trust is likely to be exploited by that evil force. A friend who argues that the threatened individual is misjudging the situation runs the risk of being judged part of the conspiracy. Individual response to perceived threat is far from uniform. All will move toward seeing the situation in a paranoid pattern, but few will move so far that their reality view approximates the paranoid. The reality view of a few at the other end of the scale will be affected only slightly by the perceived threat.

Similarly, if an individual values his national community at the first-intensity level and perceives a terrible threat to that community, he will see the government and people threatening his community in a perceptual pattern that tends in the direction of the paranoid pattern in interpersonal relations. Here again, individual variance will be great, with some individuals perceiving the situation very close to the paranoid pattern while others see a situation that resembles the paranoid pattern very little.

The perceptual inferential scheme I am advancing takes as its starting point two perceptual patterns. One, called "hostile" or "enemy," is the paranoid extreme. The second, called "complex," is its opposite. My assumption is that, given a perceived threat from a state viewed as comparable in culture and capability to the threatened state, individuals will see the situation in a way that can be mapped somewhere between the enemy and complex poles. Given individual variation, the situation as perceived by some will approximate the enemy pole but never quite reach it, because the life experience and values of any individual will be such that he will not perceive reality in such clear patterns. The enemy and complex patterns therefore are to be regarded as ideal typical in the Weberian sense. As such they take the analytic role of comparative reference points.

In the perceptual inferential scheme I have developed, five basic patterns are to be treated as ideal typical. They appear in response to a perception of threat to or opportunity for something intensely valued which has relevance at the interstate level, most commonly the nation itself. In addition, these patterns correlate with two other aspects of the perceptual milieu—perceived capability distance and perceived cultural distance. As mentioned, the enemy pattern is correlated with an intensely perceived threat from a government or people viewed as similar in capability and culture.

A third extreme pattern to be treated as a perceptual ideal type is "allied." This pattern usually occurs in response to a perceived threat from another government. I assume that the people of a threatened state will see allies of their own state in identifiable patterns. The allied image is derivative: It varies directly with a hostile image of the perceived enemy. Like the enemy pattern, the allied pattern occurs near the ideal typical form if there is similarity in culture and capability between the threatened state and its ally. Less frequently, the allied image is approached when the people of another state see a need for the help of a third state while pursuing an opportunity in a second state.

A fourth extreme pattern is "imperial." This pattern occurs in response to a perceived opportunity to achieve something at the expense of another people. In its extreme or ideal typical form it is associated with a view of a government and people substantially inferior in capability and culture. In other words, there is a considerable capability and cultural distance.

A fifth extreme pattern is called "colonial." It is associated with perceived threat or opportunity from another polity viewed as substantially superior in capability and in culture. Here too there is a considerable capability and cultural distance. This fifth pattern has three variants which reflect three different control systems the colony or ex-colony has endured: direct, formal; indirect, formal; and indirect, nonformal.

The scheme is limited to five ideal typical patterns arbitrarily. Many other such patterns could be proposed. Several are suggested by the various combinations of the four situational correlates: threat, opportunity, culture, and capability. For example, there are patterns correlating with situations in which cultural and capability distances are narrow and yet opportunity is perceived, as with Hitler's Germany regarding France in 1940. Another pattern is identifiable when cultural distance is great but capability distance is narrow, as is becoming the case of Israel viewing the Arabs. One of the obvious directions for refining this perceptual inferential scheme is to multiply the number of ideal types, and I return to this point in chapter 14.

Figure I.2 incorporates graphically all five images.

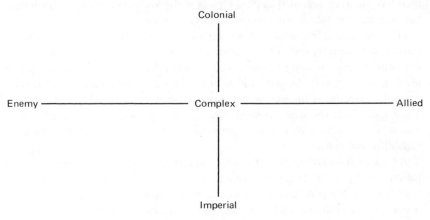

Figure I.2. Ideal Typical Patterns

The ideal typical patterns are systematized by breaking them down into several characteristic and standardized features which can serve as indicators. In each pattern the following features are described:

1. *Motivation.* Here the critical points to note are the relative simplicity or complexity with which motives are described and the relative readiness to evaluate as good or bad the resultant policy predisposition.

2. *Capability.* Since much of capability can be measured empirically (for example, industrial and resource base, size of population, extent of military preparedness), the variation will be seen in terms of intangible factors. These typically will be national morale, military training, quality of government, and most important of all, the will to act.

3. *Decisional style.* Variation here will be between a highly rational style in which elaborate orchestration is possible and an *ad hoc* incremental style.

4. *Locus of decision-making.* The range here will be between a monolithic, hierarchical decisional structure and a highly differentiated, diverse decisional structure which would be extremely difficult to coordinate.

5. *Domestic forces interaction.* Here the patterns to be looked for are associated with the harshness with which those who see the situation as different from the prevailing view are judged.

The enemy ideal typical image also includes a category for lesser allies of the enemy and for neutrals. These indicators are not associated with the other ideal types but are significant for identifying the enemy image.

ENEMY

Where extreme threat is perceived, the resulting image of the threatening government is likely to be very close to Henry Kissinger's image of the Soviet Union and China as developed in his *Nuclear Weapons and Foreign Policy*. It closely parallels a paranoid pattern. The image can be dissected into the following components:

Motivation. The enemy is by prevailing value standards adjudged to be simply motivated, evil, and highly aggressive.

Capability. Enemy capability is a derivative of the will, determination, and realism of the government and people of the threatened state. If their natural good will and faith persist, the enemy's capability is much enhanced, since the enemy will take full advantage of such weakness.[20] But when confronted with a single-minded will and determination to resist, the enemy will be exposed for what it is—a paper tiger.

Allies of the enemy. Lesser allies of the enemy are seen as part of a monolithic, hierarchical enemy decisional structure. All acts by the government of the lesser ally that are relevant to foreign policy are initiated by the government of the primary enemy. Lesser allies are satellites of the enemy.

Neutrals. Neutrals are viewed, much as are domestic elements which do not share the enemy view, with a great deal of suspicion. They are seen as easily duped or even as possible secret agents of the enemy.

Style and decisional locus. The enemy is monolithic in its decisional structure and highly rational in its decisional process. It knows exactly what it wants and will use negotiations as a cover for achieving these objectives. Any indication of willingness to compromise is simply a pose. The surface appearance is a charade designed to deceive wishful thinkers. The public of the enemy is disregarded in governmental decisions.

Domestic forces interaction. Those who perceive the enemy differently or are adjudged to be ideologically close or ethnically related to the enemy are to be viewed with the greatest suspicion. They are either traitors or the naive dupes of traitors.

COMPLEX

When there is little or no perception of external threat, the image of other governments and peoples will tend toward a detached, differentiated view in which reality is seen in all its complexity.

Motivation. Motivational complexity will be granted governments in this situation. There will be little tendency to ascribe a judgment of "good" or "bad" to the policy thrust associated with motivations. Defense is likely to be perceived as a significant aspect of motivation.

Capability. Capability judgments will be made on the basis of empirical estimates of industrial and resource base, armed forces, equipment, and training rather than on estimates of aggressive will and cunning from which power advantage derives.

Style and decisional locus. A highly diversified decisional process will be seen, with decisions made incrementally rather than coldly rationally in accordance with a detailed and preordained plan.

Domestic forces interaction. Those who perceive the target government and people differently, whether in an enemy or allied direction, will be described in complex motivational terms. Some will be judged as superpatriots who seek to create or to exploit mass fears for their own self-interest.

ALLIED

This ideal typical image is most nearly approximated when extreme threat is perceived. It is applicable only to states viewed as culturally on the same level. If the ally is perceived to be culturally inferior, the ideal typical referent will be the "imperial" image.

Motivations. Motivations will be seen as defensive, relatively simple, and generally benign. Imperial activity on the part of the ally will be considered to be for defensive and hence justifiable reasons. There will be a self-image projection of beneficent motivation to the ally.

Capability. A favorable estimate of capability will be made. This results from optimistic assessments of subjective factors among power potential indicators, especially national morale and quality of government. However, the ally is prone to grant good will to an enemy, and this counters the favorable judgment.

Style and decisional locus. The decisional process will be seen as diversified and incremental, but support for those leaders favoring the allied relationship will be perceived as substantial. There will, however, be a projection of the domestic diversity of the viewer state into that of the ally; and those elements in the allied population opposed to or less than enthusiastic about the alliance will be viewed as traitors or dupes of traitors.

Domestic forces interaction. Domestic elements who do not share this view, especially if they see the opposition to an ally's government more benignly, are seen as traitors or dupes of traitors.

What I am proposing is that these three ideal typical images serve as referents with which to compare the image an individual actually holds of a state. Since the image "actually" held must be inferred from both an individual's verbal description and his policy preferences, anything approaching exact scaling is, at this stage, out of the question. Crude, judgmentally based mapping should nevertheless be revealing.

To illustrate, I will take two individuals, Senator J. William Fulbright (F) and Senator Henry Jackson (J) at two times, 1962 and 1972 (figure I.3).

In 1962 Senator Fulbright supported strong action against Soviet missiles in Cuba, including an air strike. This was congruent with his favorable comments on

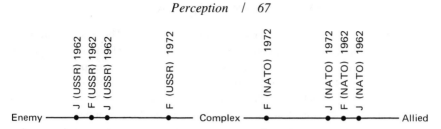

Figure I.3. Perceptual Images of Senators Fulbright and Jackson

Kissinger's *Nuclear Weapons and Foreign Policy* a few years earlier. On the scale in figure I.3, "F (USSR) 1962" refers to Fulbright's image of the Soviet Union in 1962. "F (NATO) 1962" refers to Fulbright's image of America's NATO allies at that time. My contention is that his USSR image approached that of the enemy ideal typical and his NATO image approached that of the allied ideal typical. This indicates very strong threat perception.

However, in the decade from October 1962 to October 1972, Fulbright's verbal behavior and policy recommendations changed remarkably. Presumably what had occurred was that Soviet foreign policy behavior did not conform to Fulbright's expectations. This led Fulbright gradually to alter his image of the Soviet Union to reflect a declining perception of threat. My contention is that by 1972 his image of the Soviet Union was considerably closer to the complex ideal typical image than to the enemy image. With the same evidence, verbal behavior, and policy recommendations, I conclude that his image of the NATO allies also moved sharply in the direction of the complex ideal typical image.

The judgment of Jackson's perceptual alteration over this ten-year period is that there was little movement. Presumably for Senator Jackson, Soviet foreign policy behavior conformed to expectations and the threat from the Soviet Union was perceived to have diminished only slightly. As the models suggest they should, Jackson in 1972 was inclined to see Fulbright as soft-headed and easily duped. Fulbright was inclined to see Jackson as exploiting Cold War fears for personal political advantage. Ten years earlier they had been in close agreement and evinced mutual respect for each other's positions.

Why these two senators, with similar role interests and sharing many political values, should respond so differently to the same evidence is, to say the least, puzzling. Later in this chapter I will make some tentative suggestions as to where to look for explanation.

IMPERIAL

These ideal typical image representations should have utility in most relationships where threat is perceived seriously and the concerned peoples do not perceive any of the others as significantly their cultural inferiors. They will have far less utility where perceived opportunity is more important than perceived threat and where some peoples view others as culturally inferior. There is, in addition, one relationship involving seriously perceived threat in which these ideal typical images have little utility. That is the situation in which the people perceiving threats are at a terrible power disadvantage which they cannot hope to rectify through diplomacy, that is, through coalition construction.

To deal with situations in which perception of opportunity is a more important determinant of policy than perception of threat and also with situations where one people perceives another as culturally inferior, I have developed the imperial ideal typical image. My contention is that those who make a decision to impose their will on another people will perceive their victims as somewhat culturally inferior. This was true of Hitler, Mussolini, and Napoleon in their great imperial ventures against fellow Europeans. It was true of the Japanese moving into China. But the perception of cultural inferiority is far easier to come by in this era if the people so judged are at an early stage of commercial development, industrialization, and technology. Opportunity to expand is much more easily perceived in such areas. British political leaders preparing to invade Egypt in 1882 would see an Egypt far closer to the ideal typical imperial image than would Nazi leaders preparing to invade Poland in 1939. In this study both the British view of Egypt in 1882 and the German view of Poland in 1939 are mapped between the complex and imperial poles. The German view of Poland is mapped closer to the complex than to the imperial pole, the British view of Egypt closer to the imperial pole. As mentioned above, however, a clear direction of refinement for the scheme is to develop another ideal typical pole for situations, such as that of Germany and Poland, where capability distance is great but cultural distance is narrow.

Perception of opportunity may relate to any of the motivational categories listed in the previous chapter. Most frequently, it will involve trade, grandeur, and personal power drive, both domestic and external. But it often involves defense. This occurs if a people perceives a serious threat from a great enemy and perceives the probability of that enemy's expanding its influence into a third country. When in response to this threat an opportunity is perceived to gain a controlling influence in the threatened third country, thus obviating the threat, that third country will be seen in a way that conforms to the imperial ideal typical image. Most frequently in our era, such third countries will be of the variety called "underdeveloped" (read "culturally inferior"). Third countries that are firmly within the enemy's orbit will be viewed in the prototypical satellite, hierarchical image described in the enemy ideal typical image whether or not they are seen as "underdeveloped." Thus North Vietnam was seen as a satellite, as was Poland. But South Vietnam was seen in the imperial image.

Motivation. A sharp differentiation will be made regarding motivation of native elites. Those willing to cooperate with the imperial power will be seen as "responsible" individuals with relatively benign motives. This view is well suggested by the British term WOG (Westernized Oriental Gentleman) in its early usage.[21]

WOGs were seen to be close in manner and motivation to the imperial officer but not quite there. Opponents to cooperation are perceived to range from the irresponsible self-seeking to agents of another power.

Capability. Capability is perceived as lower than the standard empirical indicators of power potential suggest. This is because of the "immaturity" of the people. They are not really capable of using advanced technology or of developing efficient administrative techniques, but with much tutelage they could manage reasonably well. However, the cooperating native elite is able to bargain with the imperial power with annoying effectiveness.

Style and decisional locus. The imperial power bureaucrats are seen to be pursuing efficiently and humanely a civilizing and modernizing task. The cooperative native elite are constructive and courageous men, though sadly lacking in the leadership or administrative abilities required for full independence. Those who oppose are at best agitators and extremists representing only themselves. At worst, opponents are agents of rivals of the imperial power. There is no real public opinion in the colony, no significant middle class, and certainly nothing that can be described as genuine nationalism. The people generally are best understood if considered as children.

√ *Domestic forces interaction.* There will be, especially in open societies, individuals who will perceive the people of the target society entirely differently. They will project their own values onto opposition leaders and view them as sincere, representing a genuine and growing demand for national dignity among the people, and increasingly capable of the sophisticated understanding necessary for independence. A. P. Thornton's *Imperial Idea and Its Enemies* develops this point at some length and over a long period of time.[22] Apparently this phenomenon is nearly ubiquitous. Individuals who empathize naturally and who hold liberal values are particularly likely to see a subject people as men and women much like themselves rather than as children.

Individuals holding such a view will be seen by the prevailing elite in the imperial power as soft-headed, naive do-gooders. If the imperial power is involved in an intense conflict with the target society opposition, the judgment will be much more harsh, though not quite at the level of treason.

To illustrate, I will take a situation in which the imperial power perceives both great threat and the opportunity to exercise substantial influence in a third country which is a target of the enemy. The case is that of Taiwan in 1962 and 1972. In this case I contend that the prevailing American view, that is, the one most congruent with policy, approximated figure I.4.

In the decade 1962–1972, the policy toward, and official verbal description of, China altered spectacularly. As this occurred, the image of both Japan and Taiwan changed in similar degree: All three moved toward the complex ideal typical image. Regarding Taiwan, American interest in maintaining some control over internal politics declined, and with that decline came an altered view. Chiang was

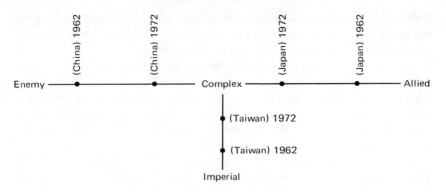

Figure I.4. American Prevailing View, East Asia

seen far less in the WOG image, and his opponents were no longer viewed as agitating dupes of the communist enemy. Detachment characterized the view toward each of the three peoples.

COLONIAL

We must still deal with the situation in which a people perceiving threat is at a substantial power disadvantage which cannot be rectified through diplomacy.

In perceptual terms a colony can be defined as existing when the view prevails among its people that the government and people of the imperial power are so deeply involved in the decision-making process of the colony as to deny it real sovereignty. The imperial relationship, therefore, need not be formalized. Indeed, the "hidden hand" concept is familiar in many parts of the world and is often currently referred to as neocolonialism. However, the world view of people living under a formalized imperial relationship in which the imperial bureaucracy rules directly will differ sharply from one in which a national elite is granted formal authority and rules in cooperation with a formally established imperial bureaucracy. It will differ even more sharply from the situation in which the colony is nominally independent but in which the imperial power's "hidden hand" is widely believed to hold final authority. Therefore three ideal subtypes will be offered.

Direct, Formal

Motivations. Motivations of the imperial power are commonly seen to be so close to those described by Hobson as modified by Lenin that this Hobson-Lenin picture can be thought of as the core motivational view held in all three colonial subtypes. The imperial power will be seen as interested in maintaining the colony as a source of raw materials and as a locus for investments and for selling manufactured products of the imperial economy.

Capability. Typically in this sort of imperial relationship, the imperial power's coercive force will be small. The ability to maintain order is considerably enhanced, however, by the assumption of technical superiority held by both the imperial-power elite and the colonial elite. Capability of the imperial power, therefore, is granted a much higher rating than troop numbers and military hardware would seem to justify.

Style and decisional locus. In style there is a perception of high technical competence on the part of the imperial-power bureaucracy. This leads to a view of the imperial decisional process as highly rational and clever. Incrementalism is not seen, and little ideological diversity within the imperial bureaucracy is perceived.

Domestic forces interaction. Because the imperial-power bureaucracy is assumed to be making important decisions itself and not to be working through a native elite, the onus for imperial control is placed on the imperial power directly. People who praise the imperial power's culture and ideology are suspect in the eyes of those in strong opposition. Members of the elite who appear to be profiting personally from the imperial relationship are also suspect. This includes particularly those who serve in a native bureaucracy in real if not formal subservience to the imperial bureaucracy. The citizens of the imperial power who empathize with an independence movement in the colony are judged highly favorably. Praise for and cooperation with this group is accepted as totally consonant with patriotism by those seeking independence.

Indirect, Formal

Motivations. As in the previous category, the Hobson-Lenin imperial explanation can be viewed as the core motivational perception. The imperial power's ideology is perceived as sincere, especially by the native elite with formal authority and by those who have studied in imperial-staffed institutions. However, the perception is that, regardless of the sincerity with which the ideology is accepted in the home country, it is not really for export. Quite typically, those cooperating with the imperial power seek to adapt both the ideology and the culture of the imperial power and hold a view of their fellow colonials which parallels exactly the prevailing imperial view.

Capability. Since in its control system the imperial power makes substantial use of the native elite and its traditional means of control, the imperial power's coercive forces will be smaller than in the previous category. Overestimation of imperial-power capability is far greater in this type. The imperial control strategy is believed to consist of manipulating opposing elements within the ruling native elite. This is the "hidden hand" perception which grants the imperial power a capability virtually on the level of omnipotence.[23]

Style and decisional locus. Here also the imperial bureaucratic advisors are perceived as being extraordinarily competent and technically advanced. However, close contact on a basis of formal equality leads to a picture of substantial diversity within the imperial bureaucracy, a diversity which can be exploited to the advantage of the more politically acute among cooperating native officials. Neither the populace generally nor the opposition sees this diversity. Incrementalism in decision-making is perceived to some extent within the cooperating elite, but otherwise the process is perceived as diabolical in its rationality. Conspiracies involving imperial manipulation of colonial affairs are commonly seen and described as brilliantly elaborate.

Domestic forces interaction. The cooperating elite is perceived by their domestic opponents to be maintained in power by and to gain immense personal benefit from the imperial relationship. Those seeking formal and real independence therefore see the cooperating elite as at best unpatriotic and flirting with treason. As mentioned earlier, the cooperating elite sees the opposition in the imperial ideal typical mode. The result is perceptual polarization in which the cooperating elite is very much on the defensive. In fact, elements of that elite, torn by the charge of betrayal, often see their intra-elite competitors as described by the revolutionary elite. As a consequence, the morale of the cooperating elite is usually low. Here, too, elements within the imperial-power population who sympathize with independence aspirations of the colony are very popular with the revolutionary elite, and cooperation with them will be acceptable behavior. In fact, their support is actively solicited.

Indirect, Nonformal

Motivation. In this subtype, motivation is perceived very much as in the indirect, formal case. There is likely to be greater cynicism about the ideology of the imperial power, including a strong perception of hypocrisy. In seeking to establish control over the political process, the imperial power is somewhat more likely to cooperate closely with a native elite that has modernizing values than is true where control is formalized. But the Hobson-Lenin motivational picture nonetheless prevails.

Capability. If the imperial power has a military force in the colony, that force will be there by virtue of an agreement with the formally independent government of the colony. The real strength of the imperial power is perceived to rest not with such a force but with the "hidden hand" manipulation potential. That potential exists because of the willingness of a section of the native elite to enter into a collaborative relationship with the imperial power in return for internal support.

Style and decisional locus. The imperial-power embassy staff and imperial agents under other cover are perceived to seek to exercise ultimate decisional control. Since this process is by definition sub rosa, the assumptions of monolithic quality, clear and persisting imperial goals, and a remarkably skillful and highly rational procedure are held outside the collaborating elite. Even within that elite, a similar perception is widespread. Since contacts between the imperial and native bureaucracies are likely to be less formalized and routinized, the awareness of imperial-power decisional diversity, even among the native bureaucracy, is slight.

Domestic forces interaction. Opponents will charge the collaborating elite and its domestic supporters with being of dubious patriotism. As in the formal, indirect situation, perceptual polarization is characteristic. But the collaborating elite is considerably less sure of itself than the "nationalist" elite. Even when the collaborating elite is moderizing and technocratic, as is frequently the case in post–World War II American relationships of this type, much of the politically attentive population will see that elite as flirting with treason. Members of the collaborating elite will see the "nationalists" in the imperial ideal typical pattern as irresponsible agitators and quite possibly agents of a competing imperial government. But in addition, members of the collaborating elite will typically see some of their colleagues much as the nationalist opposition sees them—as agents, witting or unwitting, of the imperial power.

Of the above three ideal subtypes, two are mainly of historical interest—the direct, formal and the indirect, formal. The third, the indirect, nonformal, approximated the post–World War II image held by vast numbers of people in Asia, Africa, and Latin America toward the important Western powers and in Eastern Europe toward the Soviet Union. It differs substantially from the ideal typical enemy image. In the enemy image, threat of a direct application of force against a polity is perceived. In the indirect, nonformal image, the threat is that an imperial power will, with impunity, be able to manipulate and gain effective control over the internal political process of the threatened state.

To illustrate, I will offer a propositional world view of Fidel Castro in 1960 and 1972 in figure I.5.

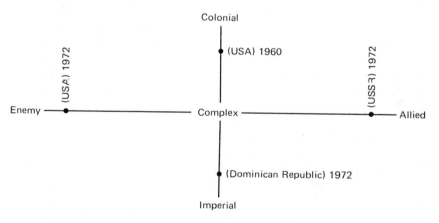

Figure I.5. Propositional World View of Fidel Castro

Spelled out, the proposition asserts that in 1960 Castro perceived a great threat from the United States. The United States was perceived as having the capability to gain control of the Cuban political process and to impose WOGs on the Cuban people; and there was little prospect of avoiding this fate through diplomacy. The Bay of Pigs episode was therefore highly confirming. But by 1972 there was real possibility of using diplomacy to deter the American threat, and most of the likely American collaborators had left the country. Intense threat was still perceived, but now the image of the United States was closer to the enemy ideal type than to the indirect, nonformal colonial ideal type. The allied protector, the Soviet Union, was perceived in parallel fashion close to the allied ideal typical image. By this time Castro, responding (in substantial part at least) to perceived threat, was sponsoring efforts to gain control of the domestic political process of a number of Latin American states.

In figure I.5, the Dominican Republic is shown for illustrative purposes. The propositional contention is that Castro's policy and his statements indicate a perception of opportunity for gaining substantial influence in the affairs of the Dominican Republic and that this is reflected in an image approximating the imperial ideal typical. Perception of threat has remained relatively constant, but the perceived situation has altered drastically. Were the intensity of that threat to decline, the relative importance of defense and ideological messianism as motivating factors would be tested. If defense is of primary importance and ideological messianism of tertiary importance, then a decline in threat perception should lead to an alteration of the image of the Dominican Republic toward the complex ideal typical image. Conversely, if the ideological messianism factor is of primary motivational importance, the image of the Dominican Republic might well approximate even more closely the imperial ideal typical image.

To sum up, mapping position is associated with four factors: the degree of threat perceived, the degree of opportunity perceived, perceived capability distance, and perceived cultural distance. Perception of threat associates with images which are mapped along the enemy-complex-allied line and also along the colonial-complex half-line. Images associated with perceived capability distance and perceived cultural distance are mapped along the colonial-complex-imperial line. Perceptions of opportunity-associated images are mapped along the complex-imperial half-line.

In one respect the representation used for mapping purposes is seriously misleading. It gives the impression that the enemy-allied line and the colonial-imperial line are scales on which the complex position is the center. In fact, movement occurs almost exclusively along the four half-lines, with the complex position polar. Nevertheless, in spite of this misleading quality, the utility of the representation is sufficient to argue for its retention. The reason is that actual perceptual positions are far better mapped in quadrants than along lines. For example, Taiwan was mapped in figure I.4 on the complex-imperial line. In fact, throughout the 1950s and 1960s Taiwan was regarded as an essential American ally, and the prevailing view of Taiwan incorporates elements of three ideal typical patterns

—imperial, allied, and complex. The location of the prevailing view should therefore be mapped at some point in the allied-complex-imperial quadrant.

The American prevailing view of the Soviet Union, on the other hand, should be mapped directly on the enemy-complex line. This is true because no significant capability or cultural distance is perceived, and no real opportunity is perceived to gain a substantial influence over the behavior of this great enemy. China, however, is seen as less powerful, technologically far behind, and, because of a deep fear of the Soviet Union, at a major bargaining and hence power disadvantage. The prevailing view of China should therefore be mapped in the enemy-complex-imperial quadrant, but considerably closer to the enemy than to the imperial ideal typical pole.

The Cuban case described in figure I.5 could therefore be far better mapped as in figure I.6.

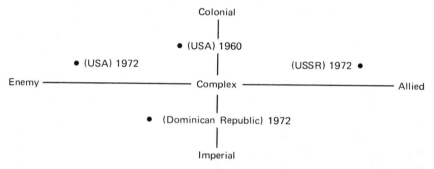

Figure I.6. Quadrant Mapping of Castro's World View

Perception of threat from the United States in 1960 is presented as great and the American power advantage overwhelming. Thus an image blend heavily weighted toward the colonial ideal typical but with some elements of the enemy ideal typical would be expected. In 1972 Cuba's power vis-à-vis the United States was much greater because of the bargaining strength it gained from its alliance with the Soviet Union. Now, the proposition is that the prevailing view of the United States should approximate more closely the enemy ideal typical but should contain elements of the colonial. In parallel fashion, the prevailing view of the powerful and technologically advanced Soviet Union should be a blend weighted toward the allied ideal typical but with some colonial ideal typical influence. The Dominican Republic, a friend of a great enemy but one in which an opportunity to intervene is perceived, should be seen in a blend of the imperial and enemy ideal typical images.

The scheme can be illustrated further by the proposed mapping of the American prevailing view of the Vietnam situation in 1960, 1965, and 1972 in figure I.7.

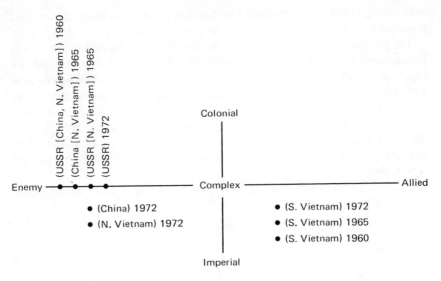

Figure I.7. American Prevailing View, Vietnam

The proposition expressed in figure I.7 is that in 1960 the Soviet Union was perceived closely enough to the ideal typical enemy image that its lesser allies, here both China and North Vietnam, were seen as satellites of the greatest communist power. South Vietnam, a weak, technically backward state in which the United States was actively combating communist inroads via internal intervention, was perceived in a manner closely approximating the ideal typical imperial image. By 1965, however, the perception of threat from the Soviet Union had declined to the point that in the prevailing view China was seen as an independent enemy. North Vietnam was seen ambiguously as the satellite of each of the large communist states. South Vietnam was seen with greater detachment, still primarily in the imperial image but with increasing allied and complex manifestations. Then by 1972 the perception of threat from the Soviet Union had dramatically declined. So had perceived threat from China. At the same time, China was seen as less rather than more powerful and as technologically retarded. Thus the image alteration reflected increasing complex and some imperial manifestations. North Vietnam now was perceived as an enemy in its own right so that a low capability rating and technological backwardness were clearly perceived, bringing the image of North Vietnam somewhat closer to the imperial ideal typical than that of China. This image would have been even closer to the imperial ideal typical were it not for the leverage gained from Soviet support. The image of South Vietnam reflected a perceived declining need for American intervention to thwart communist aggression. The major alteration was in the complex direction. Thieu thus was rapidly losing his WOG image and was seen more and more as the petty tyrant of a small state.

To illustrate the scheme further, this time with perceptual alteration which did not follow a pattern of declining perception of threat vis-à-vis the Soviet Union, Israel's prevailing view of the Soviet Union, Egypt, and the United States is given the propositional expression shown in figure I.8.

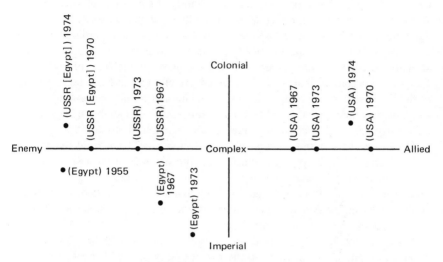

Figure I.8. Israeli Prevailing View

This proposition asserts that in 1955, the time of the Gaza Strip raid, Egypt was perceived mainly in enemy terms. The projection of President Nasser into Adolf Hitler was common enough in Israel. But the Gaza Strip raid reflected as well an imperial image of Egypt. David Ben Gurion felt that the Arabs would only halt their raids across Israel's borders if they were punished sharply for their infractions. That the Egyptian public would respond instead with a sense of outrage which would lead to exacerbation of the conflict was predicted by Israelis such as Moshe Sharrett, but the prevailing view was closer to a denial of an Egyptian public opinion. In this view Egypt's agitating leaders only understand force.

The poor Egyptian performance in the 1956 campaign and the Egyptian disaster in 1967 reduced the Israeli sense of threat and fortified the view of a weak, culturally inferior Egypt. Many Israelis perceived the opportunity to maintain control over the large territorial cushion occupied in 1967, and this was incorporated into the prevailing view. The proposed Israeli perception of threat from the Soviets is reflected in the mapping position of the Soviet Union in 1967 and the parallel allied position of the United States in 1967.

This view was sharply altered in 1970, when the Soviet Union began to bring SAM missiles and technicians into Egypt and to train Egyptians to man the missiles. Here it is proposed that Israeli threat perception intensified to the point that Egypt was perceived very much in satellite terms. The need for an ally to counter the Soviet Union led to a sharpened perception of the United States as ally.

Then when, in 1972, Egypt expelled much of the Soviet advisory force, Israeli threat perception, it is proposed, declined sharply. Egypt suddenly lost satellite status and was perceived instead as a technically incompetent, weak state whose agitating leaders need not be taken seriously. Israeli opinion regarding territorial concessions hardened, and the need for the United States as an ally was less strongly perceived. This perceptual picture argues for the lack of realism in Egyptian expectations that the United States, grateful for the Egyptian expulsion of the Soviets, would pressure Israel into making territorial concessions. It also suggests why the Israelis would feel reasonably secure on October 6, 1973, with only thirty thousand Israeli troops facing three hundred thousand Arabs.

The shock of the initial Arab advances in October 1973 was reflected perceptually in an overnight Egyptian return to satellite status vis-à-vis a Soviet Union sharply perceived in enemy-colonial terms. The view of the United States now reflects not only the desperate need for an ally but also the clear understanding of Israeli power disadvantage. Thus, aspects of the colonial image began to creep into the Israeli image of the United States.

These are, of course, untested propositions advanced only to illustrate the scheme. Empirical verification, to the extent that is possible, would call for a careful study of both verbal and policy behavior in each case. Such evidence is examined in the British-in-Egypt case study.

These ideal typical patterns, as the illustrations suggest, provide a device for mapping images held by individuals, images held by modal members of particular groups, and prevailing views at various moments. This device therefore offers the analyst a means for juxtaposing the prevailing world view and the world views of those whom the analyst regards as influential in foreign policy decision-making. "World view," it should be recalled, is the mental picture within which alternative policy choices are perceived. "Prevailing world view" is the construction of reality most congruent with the thrust of a government's foreign policy. All world views are inferred. In the case of world views of individuals and modal individuals, the inferring is based on verbal descriptions and on expressed policy preferences. Prevailing world view is inferred from policies adopted and, even more important, from policy direction.

This perceptual mapping is a vital first step in inferring foreign policy motivation. What is called for is an identification of the major participants, whether direct or indirect, in the making of decisions relevant to foreign policy. The perceptions of the participants, whether as individuals or as modal representatives of concerned groups, are then inferred and mapped. The prevailing view—the image judged to be most harmonious with the decision made—is then inferred and mapped. At this point the analyst can see a projection that suggests which decisional participants held images congruent with the decision and which held sharply divergent images. This projection is then of considerable utility in inferring motivation.

Yet it must be clear that the process of inferring cannot be mechanical. The image projection is suggestive only. If the image held by a modal individual of an interested group is located at great distance from that of the prevailing view, the conclusion could be drawn that the group played little part in the decision. If the group in question was a prime advocate of bringing to others the benefits of a prevailing ideology, the conclusion follows that ideological messianism was not a significant motivation. If the group in question was a collection of individuals seeking to gain official support for investing in a target state's economy, the conclusion follows that economic investment was not a significant motivation. But if the images held by the same modal individuals were close to the prevailing view, it would not necessarily follow that the influence of the group was great. Therefore, a judgment is still called for regarding relative influence of those participants whose images were close to the prevailing view. And this judgment must rest on evidence of activity and influence that is extremely difficult to come by.

There is a second major reason that makes impossible any simple, mechanical inferring of motives from the image map. There can be no one-to-one relating of role interests of individuals and groups to motivations. This is the essential mistake of the realist school. Riker's fiduciary agent analogue illustrates this. In its literal expression, realism tells us that power interests alone exist. To choose the most difficult example, to conclude that the president of an oil company with important interests in a policy outcome who participated actively in the decision was motivated exclusively by his investment interests would be incorrect. He might also be an intense American patriot who values highly America's prestige, dignity, and respect; he might be so opposed to restrictions on freedom of expression as to feel uncomfortable dealing with authoritarian regimes; he might have a natural empathetic ability which leads him to sense and value the national dignity concerns of the population of an oil-producing country. Psychological balance theory, which is consistently important in this study, argues that this oil company president would try, albeit unconsciously, to adopt an image that would bring into harmony the high value he places on his company's success and his other values. This argues that even where role vested interests are obvious and compelling, role values alone do not determine the image held by an individual. Rather, the image he holds will be one that relates best to a balancing of the various values an individual holds which have salience for the decision at hand.

Determinants of Individual Perception

The primary purpose of this chapter was to construct a perceptually based device for inferring foreign policy motivation. This has now been done. In chapter 5 this device will be integrated into an overall scheme which relates basic foreign policy motivation to aims. For the remainder of this chapter, I will pursue a purpose of less immediate concern but one which is ultimately essential if foreign policy motivation and the perceptual base of conflict are to be understood. My purpose in this section is to look at some major determinants of individual perceptions of the world in order to begin to explain some of the basis for individual variance. If this is not done, the temptation to assume a simple role determinism is likely to prevail.

To introduce this section, I have written a case history of a hypothetical Iranian. The purpose is to illustrate the major determinants of individual world-view perceptions in an interactive setting. The hypothetical Iranian will be called "Hossein."

In 1953 Hossein, the son of a middle-class family, was in the United States on a scholarship to study economics. As was true of most of his contemporaries of similar class and educational background, Hossein was a socialist, a democrat, and a nationalist. He believed that Iran's prime minister, Dr. Mohammed Mossadegh, was the greatest Iranian of the past several centuries and the only man who could restore to Iran a sense of national dignity and worth. But on August 19, 1953, Mossadegh was overthrown, and Hossein believed, as did virtually all of his educated contemporaries, that the main force behind his overthrow was the American CIA. Within two years a royal dictatorship had been established in Iran which Hossein saw in terms close to the indirect, nonformal colonial ideal type. The divergence reflected Iran's historical experience and Hossein's own personal good fortune in having received an American scholarship. Individual Americans had played an important role in the early Iranian national movement, and Hossein was aware of this. He also held the view that the British had had an indirect, nonformal relationship with Iran through much of the twentieth century. Soviet propaganda at that time was seeking to transfer this British image to the Americans, and some Iranians were accepting that transference. Hossein preferred to believe that the Americans had good intentions but that they had been misled by their evil British cousins into carrying out a stupid and immoral act. Acting under these assumptions, Hossein and many of his fellow students in the United States concentrated their efforts, as did their American-educated counterparts in Iran, on demonstrating to the United States the stupidity and immorality of its policy. But American persistence in a policy of total support for the shah led gradually to the weakening of the deception image and the strengthening of acceptance of the American role as the imperial power in an indirect, nonformal relationship with Iran. The shah and his government were thus seen to be on the edge of treason.

At that time, 1956, the prevailing view in Iran of the United States—the view held by the shah—approximated the allied ideal type. Hossein's view approximated the indirect, nonformal colonial ideal type with some enemy elements. But Iranian students not associated with America held an image of the United States even closer to the indirect, nonformal colonial. A projection is shown in figure I.9.

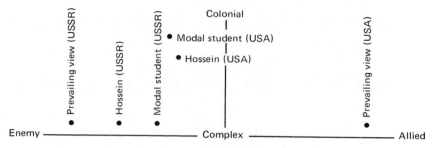

Figure I.9. Iranian Perceptions, 1956

When Hossein was in his last year in the United States before receiving a Ph.D., he was approached by a man whose values and attitudes were similar to Hossein's, who nevertheless was an employee of the Iranian government charged with the task of persuading bright young Iranians to return to Iran and enter an elite section of the bureaucracy, in the Plan Organization. After much soul-searching Hossein agreed to do so. As a strong nationalist, he very much wanted to return to Iran. But he needed an income, an outlet for his talents, and a sense of individual worth. He convinced himself he could enter the bureaucracy without becoming part of the ruling political elite, which he saw as little more than an appendage of American policy, and change the system from within.

Once in the bureaucracy, Hossein saw many things he did not like—such as inefficiency, nepotism, and corruption in high places. But he and others he respected did advance rapidly in the bureaucracy. Furthermore, his contacts with Americans indicated to him that, although they were supporting a corrupt ruling class, they were also sincerely interested in Iranian industrial modernization. This he had not expected, and his estimate of American motivation gradually changed from the rigid Hobson-Lenin image. Furthermore, as he rose to subministerial rank, he became increasingly convinced that the American decisional role was slight. He even wished it were greater and that the American ambassador would insist on the removal of men he knew to be corrupt. Gradually Hossein came to believe that the Iranian government now was responsible for its own mistakes and also for Iran's economic progress. He began to lose respect for those ideologues who continued to describe Iran in indirect, nonformal colonial perceptual terms. Indeed, he began to suspect their loyalty. Ultimately he became convinced that those who saw the shah as an American puppet were really Maoist agitators. When the shah offered him an appointment to the cabinet he accepted with alacrity. One of his first official acts was to make a trip to the United States during which he admonished American officials to behave more as the loyal allies of Iran he had always thought them to be. Hossein assured his American hosts that his fellow cabinet ministers were for the most part nonpartisan technocrats, as he was, and were motivated by a concern for Iranian progress.

The prevailing view of the United States in Iran had by this time shifted in the complex direction. This shift could be explained by a sharp reduction in perception of threat from the Soviet Union and hence a far less urgent need for an American alliance. In the projection shown in figure I.10, however, the Soviet image shifts even more sharply toward the complex ideal type than does the American image.

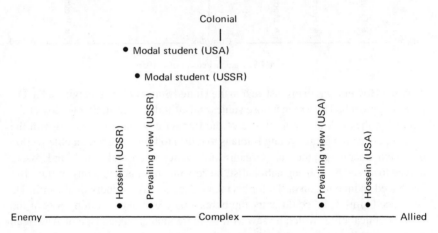

Figure I.10. Iranian Perceptions, 1975

Both verbal descriptions of the Soviet Union and policy decisions point to the radical shift in image. Most telling of the decisions was that resulting in Iran's purchase of Soviet army vehicles for the Iranian army. It is not exactly suggestive of deep fear of the Soviet Union to become dependent on Soviet spare parts replacements for military vehicles. I would propose without being able here to defend the proposition that the shah was motivated by two factors, domestic and external personal power drive, which explain the continued allied perception of the United States. The first motive, domestic personal power, was based on perceived threat from internal opposition. To deal with this the shah needed both equipment and technical aid. The second, external personal power, is based on perceived opportunity to expand Iran's and hence the shah's influence in the Persian Gulf region. For this he needed American arms and diplomatic support. Thus Iran's foreign policy motivation, reflecting a sharp decline in perception of external threat, shifted away from the primacy of defense.

Hossein's shift was even more dramatic. With the entrance of role values into his politically relevant value system and with the rapid growth in intensity of those values, Hossein's reality view was certain to change. His attachment to democratic and socialist values declined in intensity. He remained incapable of identifying with the shah and remembered the manner of the shah's accession to power. But, unlike Iranian students who a generation later remained generally hostile, Hossein perceived American policy as one of support for Iran's modernization, and modernization values had achieved great saliency for Hossein. He no longer saw the United States as approximating the indirect, nonformal colonial ideal type. Instead the United States moved even closer to the allied ideal type in Hossein's image than in the prevailing view.

The modal student had changed as well. He had previously hoped for Soviet balancing of the United States and, though fearing both, feared the Soviet Union less. Now he saw them as *de facto* allies, with the United States playing the dominant role. Both have moved to the indirect, nonformal, colonial-complex scale. The shah and Hossein were seen to be on the edge of treason.

The point of transference raised in the illustration deserves special attention. The proposition suggested is that when a government and people have emerged from historical relationship with one state and are entering into the same type of relationship with a third state, there will be a perceptual transference. That the Jewish nation, having emerged from an intensely hostile relationship with Germany and Hitler and having entered into an intensely hostile relationship with Egypt and Nasser, would identify Nasser with Hitler is only to be expected. Similarly, it has already been suggested that the containment theory articulated by George Kennan made great sense for retroactive application to Hitler's Germany but was faulty in its application to Stalin's Soviet Union. My contention was that expansion was required to maintain the participant excitement in Germany necessary for the survival of the regime. In the Soviet Union there is no real evidence of substantial public enthusiasm for external adventures. The transference phenomenon appears to be a natural one. In the illustration, the contention was made that the historic image of the British was indeed transferred to the Americans because the type of relationship was similar. Yet in most aspects, the two Anglo-Saxon nations, acting in different eras, favored different policies and were motivated differently.

Iran was chosen as an illustration because enormous disparities in reality views which occur in nonconsensual societies are typified there. Common historical experience is variously interpreted and hence does not lead to parallel world views. Given such disparity, the use of coercion to control those furthest from the prevailing view is highly probable if the deviants are politically important. The American experience in the late 1960s and early 1970s is not dissimilar. I contend that a major causal factor for this variation is to be found in differences both in historical experience and in value systems, especially in values grouped as follows: politically relevant community identity values, other politically relevant values, and role values. In addition, individual variation occurs, as the hypothetical Hossein illustrates, because of different personal experiences (for example, the cosmopolitan versus the provincial), different empathetic abilities, and different positions on a closed-open mind scale.

HISTORICAL EXPERIENCE

For individuals living in the same community, variation in historical experience is a factor of age. The point is by no means trivial. Americans who came into maturity after the last major Cold War episode, the Cuban missile crisis of October 1962, often have difficulty understanding the Cold War view of reality which their parents held. Historical accounts of an episode cannot project for the reader the rich perceptual milieu of the events described.

POLITICALLY RELEVANT COMMUNITY VALUES

Probably most important of the factors producing perceptual variation in this era of mass politics is that of the politically relevant communities with which individuals identify. Central here, of course, is the national community. Where the intensity of identification with the nation is at the first level and where the perception of threat to that community is strong, foreign policy is certain to be granted a high-priority claim on resources, and imperial policies designed to deal with the threat are probable.

The case is far less clear where there is a perception of opportunity for expanding the influence and hence prestige and glory of the nation. Benjamin Disraeli, Joseph Chamberlain, Theodore Roosevelt, and Otto von Bismarck profited from this drive; but Napoleon, Mussolini, and Hitler demonstrated its full potential. Most of these men also saw its limitations, however. Apparently the costs a people will pay, in values as well as material terms, for exploiting such opportunities are limited. In the post–World War II period, in which the costs of modern warfare are well understood, there is little real evidence of popular enthusiasm for policies of national aggrandizement.

But the national community is only one of the politically relevant communities with which an individual might identify. Predicting the influence of an individual's community loyalties in his reality construction is therefore most difficult. What is called for is the construction of an identity profile in which an individual's identity values are placed in intensity categories. The individual will naturally seek a reality view which will be comfortable, in which the interests of the communities valued are seen in harmony. At any particular time and concerning any particular decision, however, only rarely will all of these values be salient. That is, only rarely will the individual be confronted with a decision that involves either threat or opportunity concerning each of the communities with which he identifies.

A propositional illustration involving Arab perceptions of Israel will be developed to indicate how this factor can be handled analytically. The politically relevant communities with which Arabs might identify are fairly obvious. They include the following: clan, tribe, village or town, district, state, region (for example, Greater Syria, Maghreb), Arab nation (embracing all Arabic-speaking areas), religious sect. For purposes of constructing an identity profile, I propose a fourfold categorizing of intensities of loyalty. In the first-intensity category will be those communities for which an individual would be willing to risk life or career. The guideline for a second-intensity rating would be a willingness to make substantial material sacrifice for the concerned community. The third intensity would be reflected by a willingness to commit time and energy. A fourth intensity is indicated by a willingness to sacrifice peace of mind only.

The propaganda picture that emanated from Damascus in the months prior to the 1967 war was in essence as follows: The primary enemy is the United States in association with the old imperial powers, France and Britain. They seek to keep the Arab world in a raw-material-producing, exploited status—an outlet for capitalistic investment and products. In order to control the Arab world they have developed a brilliant formula: They work through two willing agents, traditional-minded Arabs, who are only too anxious to cooperate, and international Zionism. They have succeeded in gaining control of some Arab states ruled by their puppets, for example, Jordan, Saudi Arabia, Tunisia, and Morocco. They also have implanted a Zionist settler state in the Arab heartland. The only obstacles blocking imperial control are the will of the Arab people and the disinterested support given the Arabs by the Soviet Union. The Soviet leaders and people are strong and faithful friends.

Since Syrian policy response was congruent with this verbal picture, the projection of the Syrian prevailing view (PV) would be as shown in figure I.11. Divergence from this prevailing view in the Arab world is, of course, substantial. A sheik who rules in a small, oil-rich territory and sells his oil to the United States

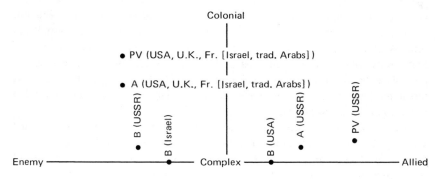

Figure I.11. Syrian Views Prior to the 1967 War

is likely to see a great threat to his income and position from Arab nationalist regimes and none at all from the United States or Israel. But at this point I am looking only at variation produced by political community identity values.

The perceived western imperial threat in 1967 was most closely associated with the Arab nation, the majority Sunni sect of Islam, and Palestine. Far less obviously threatened were other Arab states. Consequently a high-intensity loyalty to the Arab nation, to the would-be state of Palestine, and to Sunni Islam is likely to be associated with an acceptance of the prevailing Syrian view. A high-intensity loyalty to any of the other Arab states, a tribe, and Christian sects not represented in Palestine, especially the Lebanese Maronites and Egyptian Copts, is likely to be associated with divergence. The following are identity profiles of two hypothetical Maronite Christians, citizens of Lebanon:

A		B	
Arab nation	1	Arab nation	3
Greater Syria	1	Greater Syria	3
Lebanon	2	Lebanon	1
Maronite church	1	Maronite church	1
Mt. Lebanon		Mt. Lebanon	
(home district)	2	(home district)	1

Individual *A* will perceive a threat to two communities he values highly, the Arab nation and Greater Syria (which roughly incorporates Syria, Lebanon, Palestine, and Jordan). In dealing with this threat, however, he opposes policies that could lead to "unnecessary" threats to his home state (Lebanon), his district (Mt. Lebanon), and his church (Maronite). He therefore is likely to be somewhat more amenable to a settlement than were the Syrian leaders; and his image of the United States and Israel, while colonial and enemy, would be such that a settlement is distantly possible. His view is also given in figure I.11.

Individual *B* will diverge much more sharply. He values the Arab nation and Greater Syria but at an intensity level far below that for Lebanon, Mt. Lebanon, and the Maronite church. He is far less interested in other Arab leaders and sees little Western imperial control of Lebanon. Consequently he sees the United States somewhat more as an ally than as an enemy. Israel is seen as an enemy and possibly even as a creation of the Communists, but Israel is seen to be far less threatening than in the previous view. The Soviet Union is seen as an enemy, but not a highly threatening one.

In a relatively homogeneous nation-state, such as France, it can be assumed that virtually the entire population has a first-level intensity identification with the nation. Of other community identifications of Frenchmen, that of the member of the French Jewish community with the world Jewish community and Israel is likely to have a major impact on perceptions relevant to foreign policy in France.

French Jews who have a first-level intensity identification with both France and Israel are likely to have perceptions of reality congruent with this identity profile. If a strong threat to the Israeli community is perceived to emanate from the Arab states and the Soviet Union, such individuals, this scheme would predict, would be likely to see the Soviet Union in enemy terms and as threatening both the Israeli and the French communities. French Gentiles who do not identify with Israel and who perceive the Arabs more in accordance with the complex image are likely to be judged by French Jews in a manner parallel to that described in domestic forces interaction under the enemy ideal typical image. One difference, however, will reflect the unique history of the Jewish people: Instead of seeing such a view of the Arabs as suggesting treason, they would see it as reflecting anti-Semitism. This in turn could lead French Jews to an identity alteration, with identification with France declining in intensity.

OTHER POLITICALLY RELEVANT VALUES

The realist school tends strongly to see community identity values, in this era usually exclusively national values, as *the* determinant of foreign policy behavior. Morgenthau's nationalistic universalism notion goes furthest in that direction. He sees national ideologies as little more than a justification of national power interest expressed in universal symbolic terms.

This is, I believe, the fundamental error of the realist school. Yet the compelling quality of the realist argument is testified to by its widespread acceptance by practitioners of diplomacy and by probably most writers in the field of international politics. Indeed, many of the latter are unaware of the extent to which they accept the power determinism thesis.

The explanation for the persuasiveness of this argument is, it seems to me, fairly simple. A people which perceives great threat to their nation will indeed behave much as Morgenthau claims. This is the basic assumption underlying both the allied and enemy ideal typical images described earlier. Threatened people will see their allies as ideologically parallel, their enemies as ideologically polar. Furthermore, ideological projections change rapidly and imperceptibly when relationships change. It is fascinating, for example, to compare descriptions of Marshal Tito by American authors in periods when he was closely associated with Soviet leaders in a hostile relationship with the United States and descriptions by these and other American authors in periods when he was engaged in intense conflict with the Soviet Union and had a neutral relationship with the United States.[24] He appears to be two utterly different men in such periods, a simple satellite leader in the former and an almost liberal democratic leader in the latter.

Similarly, take the term "pro-West," a favorite journalistic short cut in describing ex-colonial world leaders in the Cold War period. In the Iranian example given above, the term "pro-West" was applied to those people who tended to favor an active alliance with the Western powers. Generally speaking, such men were members of the traditional elite who accepted the necessity of moderate change but who saw no relevance in liberal democratic institutions. Foremost of these men was Mohammed Riza Shah. But very rapidly the pro-West description evolved to mean men in our own ideological image. The shah became the "progressive," "liberal," and "popular" young monarch.[25] His opponents therefore were "anti-West" and obviously could not resemble us ideologically. Thus Mossadegh, whose devotion to liberal-democratic principles gave Iran a free election in 1952, was dismissed succinctly by *Time* as "red-lining."[26] His heir-apparent, Allahyar Saleh, American-educated and an irrepressible advocate of liberal democracy, was described as a naive dupe. When Mossadegh, in the days just prior to his overthrow by the CIA, turned in desperation to a staged plebiscite, the *New York Times* was quick to see (and correctly in this case) that the plebiscite was on the totalitarian model.[27] But when, ten years later, the shah won a referendum by 98+ percent of the vote, the *Times* congratulated him on his well-deserved popularity.[28] A few weeks later a spontaneous rebellion in Teheran embraced such a large section of the population that the regime almost fell.[29]

Such examples as these are legion, and they clearly support the conclusion that ideological descriptions are congruent with power interests. But consider the following example: In 1957 two coups occurred within a few weeks of each other in Jordan and in Colombia. In the latter the dictator Gustavo Rojas Pinilla was ousted, and in the former a royal dictatorship replaced the democratically elected government of Suleiman Nabulsi. In those pre-Castro days the United States had a complex relationship with Colombia, and in commenting on this coup the *New York Times,* manifesting an awareness of diversity within Colombia and the fragility of the democratic base, exulted over the triumph of liberal democracy there and wished it long life.[30] But in Jordan Nabulsi had had the temerity to seek to establish close relations with the Soviet Union in the middle of the Soviet-American Cold War. The *Times* in this case exulted over Nabulsi's ouster and the restoration of "responsible" government.[31]

The *Times* response in the Jordanian case follows the threat perception pattern. But the response in the Colombian case suggests that when a strong threat perception is absent, ideology is highly determining of the way in which reality is perceived. Indeed, this conclusion is incorporated in many definitions of ideology. Commonly, ideology is defined as a set of politically relevant values which together suggest a general program of action and which lead to a general picture of the sociopolitical terrain.[32]

Where there is no formalized and narrow ideological frame, variation in reality construction parallels the variation in value systems. But patterns are easily discoverable here too. I propose that in relationships close to the complex model, there will be a direct projection of one's own ideology and ideological conflicts into a foreign milieu. Parallelism will be perceived more on symbolic than on programmatic grounds. Thus, an individual who perceives himself to be significantly left of center in his own milieu will identify with individuals in another society who are similarly placed on that ideological spectrum.

An example that deserves full development is the former Belgian Congo in the days of Patrice Lumumba and Moise Tshombe. Tribal overtones, the fact that only a tiny veneer of the Congo public was in tune with the modern nation-state system, and the actual political values of the two leaders were not noted. In the United States the right saw Tshombe as one of them, and the far left equally identified with Lumumba. To the right, Lumumba was an instrument of international communism. To the left, Tshombe was an instrument of Western capitalist imperialism. For Egyptians, Lumumba was Nasser and Tshombe was the corrupt ex-King Farouk. For Indonesians, Lumumba was Sukarno; for Indians he was Jawaharlal Nehru or Mahatma Gandhi.

An excellent example for examining the role ideology plays in determining foreign policy perceptions is to be found in American perceptions of the government of Francisco Franco. William Gilmore has described the perceptions of the Franco government by four American groups—liberal Catholics, conservative Catholics, liberal non-Catholics, and conservative non-Catholics—in several historical periods, including some in which the relationship between the American and Franco governments was neutral, hostile, or allied. The results are revealing. In the early period before World War II, Catholics and conservative non-Catholics held a favorable image of the Franco government. Liberal non-Catholics held an unfavorable image. During World War II, when Franco was seen as the virtual ally of Hitler, all groups perceived his government according to the enemy ideal typical image. After World War II and in the very early stages of the Cold War, conservative Catholics again saw Franco as similar to themselves, conservative non-Catholics saw him as an ally, but all liberals persisted in seeing him in the enemy image. Then at the height of the Cold War, all perceptions altered in a favorable direction, although the liberal left, Catholic and non-Catholic, continued to perceive fascism.[33]

This suggests both the limits of ideology as a determinant of foreign policy perceptions and the patterns ideology generates when it is a determinant of perceptions. A threat to the nation, whether from right or left, produced a favorable or unfavorable image of Franco's Spain, depending on Franco's attitude toward America's enemies. When no threat was perceived to the nation but a threat was perceived to the Catholic church, as from the Spanish Loyalists in the Civil War, American Catholics responded by seeing Franco in allied terms. But when no threat to either national or church identity communities was perceived, Americans viewed Franco favorably if they responded favorably to conservative symbols. Programmatically, American conservatives had nothing in common with the Franco regime. Yet apparently his symbolic representation as a conservative led American conservatives to see themselves in him.

That domestic ideological conflict will be important in determining the speed with which a threat is perceived or a threat perception is dropped is also a defensible proposition. The American right came most reluctantly to the conclusion that Hitler was a threat to the American way of life, but it led the nation in seeing a threat from the Soviet Union. The left, conversely, saw the threat from Hitler but only reluctantly accepted the existence of a threat from the Soviet Union in the late 1940s. A comparison of American left and right projections onto Castro's Cuba and Trujillo's Dominican Republic is particularly revealing of the phenomenon.

The conclusion is clear. Perception of an intense threat to the terminal identity community will produce near-unanimity in seeing the threatening state in enemy terms. But when there is a no-threat situation, ideological symbol projection is a major determinant of the way in which other polities are perceived.

ROLE VALUES

Role as a determinant of perceptions is fairly obvious. Military leaders who understand that there will be severe allocation cuts if the international situation becomes placid, defense industry leaders, and political leaders who sense that their domestic support will be difficult to maintain in a secure, peaceful atmosphere are all likely to be impressed with arguments suggesting the aggressive intent of a national opponent. Bureaucrats concerned with urban development, industrialists wishing to export to a currently closed market, and opponents of a political leader with an image of dealing successfully with foreign opponents are likely to be more impressed with the counterargument. This should be true in the Soviet Union, Communist China, Egypt, and the United States. Nor is this meant to suggest cynicism or opportunism. On the contrary, the achievement of perceptual congruence with historical experience, political identity values, general ideology, and role interests is assumed here to be the most natural of processes. As will be seen in the British-in-Egypt case study, the role or vested-interest determinant of perceptions is central for at least that imperial policy.

IDIOSYNCRATIC

A most troublesome factor for this scheme is that of idiosyncratic socialization patterns. For example, an individual raised in a deeply religious family will doubtless differ considerably in his perceptions from an individual raised in a secular household. A John Foster Dulles[34] or an Ezra Taft Benson[35] processes all messages through perceptual filters formulated in early religious training. But the diversity of factors contributing to individual perceptual filters is much too great for any attempt at systematic treatment here. In this scheme, what must be determined about individuals whose decisional role is vital is an estimate of the intensity and duration of the personal power drive, the identity profile, and the politically relevant values held. Behavior of the individual should furnish a reasonable basis for reaching these statements, but there is no basis for estimating the remainder of their perceptual filter determinants.

In the British-in-Egypt case study, the idiosyncratic factor will be pointed to in many cases, and the remarks made are impressionistically based. But one observation was particularly striking. Men varied enormously in two ways: in the tendency to see another polity in enemy terms and in the rigidity with which perceptions are held. As mentioned, ideology is somewhat predictive of variations in the speed with which threat is both perceived and surrendered. But even when two individuals hold similar identity community values, political values, and role values, as in the earlier example of Fulbright and Jackson, variation is considerable. The following possibilities occurred to me as I made the British-in-Egypt case study:

1. An individual whose attachment to political values generally is shallow will easily surrender a world view when events are not clearly congruent with that view. Conversely, an individual of deep political conviction will explain away incongruities for a longer period of time.

2. The closed-open mind dichotomy is operative here. A closed-minded individual sees conspiracies naturally and tends to adopt an enemy perception quickly when early threats are perceived.

3. An empathetic ability leads to the opposite tendency. Whereas closed-mindedness is associated with seeing simple motivations, an empathetic ability is associated with seeing motivational complexity. The ability to empathize, a subject of substantial human variation, predisposes an individual toward detachment in world views.

4. More obviously, an individual with a cosmopolitan background is more likely to reject simple stereotypes and to be aware of the distorting effect of stereotyping.[36]

In the mid-1950s, the prevailing world view in the United States approximated that of the enemy ideal typical image regarding the Soviet Union. The Kissinger 1957 thesis of a highly rational monolith proceeding inexorably toward a preordained goal was an excellent articulation of that view. General public acceptance so approached unanimity that the small section which dissented was isolated and judged extremely harshly, as Joseph McCarthy's great influence demonstrated. General policy was in close conformity. A high priority was granted defense-related foreign policy objectives. No word of objection was raised in Congress or major periodicals to blatant interventions in the affairs of other states.

By 1970, some of the official rhetoric remained the same, especially that relating to Soviet motivation. But general policy suggested that little remained of the enemy image. Only far-right ideologues persisted in seeing the Soviet Union and international communism as monolithic. Polycentrism was widely assumed; the Chinese-Soviet split was fully perceived; incrementalism, bungling, and confusion in Soviet decision-making were assumed. Domestically a wide diversity of interpretations of Soviet behavior was tolerated. President Richard Nixon spoke with every expectation of approval when he described this as an era of negotiation.[37] The word *détente* could be used.

Old patterns did indeed prevail at times. The Soviet invasion of Czechoslovakia, rearming of the Arabs, and material support for Nigeria against Biafra were widely interpreted much as they would have been in the mid-1950s. Certainly there was nothing approaching a general willingness to follow the revisionist school in reinterpretation of Soviet-American Cold War behavior. Indeed, even that school was more intent on proving American imperial motivation than in carefully reassessing Soviet motivation.

The scheme introduced in this chapter would be useful in mapping this change, for it would make it fairly easy to demonstrate that a major new decisional element, that of a significant sector of the American public, had emerged and that the prevailing world view, the one most congruent with general policy, had shifted sharply in their direction. Using the perception frame for weighting, the conclusion would follow that American foreign policy motivation had shifted sharply away from defense and military vested interests.

But the scheme would not suggest the process by which this change had occurred. Nor would it reflect in any analytically useful way the alteration in intensities of foreign policy interest as reflected in the declining priority granted defense-related foreign policy objectives.

In the following chapter, the scheme will be developed further, using a system-of-aims device, to consider process. Then in chapter 6 the utility of the scheme will be tested briefly in an application to the dramatic alteration of U.S. policy in Vietnam.

5 / Systems of Aims

My normative purpose in this study is to deal with the perceptual base of conflict. I contend that peace theory as it develops should have a primary early focus on the perceptual rather than the value base of a conflict. The reason for that is the possibly too optimistic conclusion that if the perceptual aspects of a conflict can be eliminated or at least reduced, the probability of resolving value conflict would be enhanced. This should be particularly true of conflicts in which the perceptual base is more important than the value base. Since I believe the Soviet-American Cold War and probably the Sino-Soviet conflict are examples of conflicts based primarily on sharply opposed reality views, I believe this focus for peace theory could produce major benefits for the contemporary world. What is called for is a means of convincing foreign policy decision makers to consider at least the possibility of questioning their own implicit operating assumptions, especially those relating to estimates of other governments' motivations. Operating assumptions, once identified, can be translated into hypotheses, many of which could be tested by using the diplomatic probe.

My analytic purpose, in tune with this normative purpose, is to provide a means for identifying the perceptual base of conflict. To accomplish this I attempt to develop a scheme to systematize the foreign policy aims of a government in a manner that will reveal both the value and perceptual bases of those aims. The scheme should identify as well the directional thrust of foreign policy aims: Are they headed in an essentially status-quo or imperialist direction? And it should indicate the importance of foreign policy aims relative to domestic policy aims.

Inferring Foreign Policy Direction, Scope, Strategy, and Aims

Important aspects of this scheme have already been developed. In chapter 3, I suggested a taxonomy of motives and a systems device for looking at motives; and in chapter 4, I presented a perceptual inferential device to infer operating motives and to ascribe gross weightings to the identified motives in a motivational system. The perceptual inferential device is a map of the prevailing world view and the world views of important decisional elements. To illustrate how this device can be used to infer a foreign policy motivational system, I will continue with the example of the Iranian case described in the previous chapter, now not so hypothetical. The world views of the following are mapped in figure I.12:

1. A modal student (St), based on a careful reading of the Iranian underground press which speaks for the most politically active Iranian students abroad[1]

2. The shah (S), based on rich verbal evidence drawn from speeches and interviews

3. A modal military bureaucrat (Mil), based on private reports that the military is supportive of the shah's policy but not its initiator

4. A modal foreign policy bureaucrat (Fp), based on private reports that the Foreign Office, though necessarily supportive, not only has not initiated policy but has modally strong reservations about that policy

5. The Tehran newspaper *Kayhan* (K), one of two large dailies

6. The prevailing view (PV)

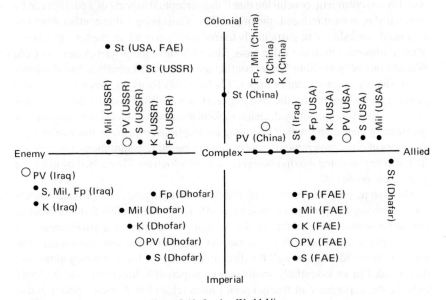

Figure I.12. Iranian World Views

The aspect of world view looked at for each includes the January 1975 images of the United States, the Soviet Union, China, Iraq, the Dhofar rebels (a Marxist revolutionary force operating in the Arabian peninsula state of Oman against which the shah has committed several thousand Iranian troops), and the Federation of Arab Emirates (FAE). The images are mapped as follows:

The perceptual inferential map and evidence suggesting which decisional groups are active in determining foreign policy together furnish the base from which the motivational system is inferred. The key is the mapping position of the prevailing view. As explained earlier, my operating assumption is that any individual or group mapped at a considerable distance from the prevailing view has had little to do with the decisions made. Therefore, those motivational elements which correspond to individuals and groups so mapped are not included in the motivational system. If individuals and groups are mapped close to the prevailing view, the associated motivational elements may or may not be included in the motivational system. The judgment to include them reflects a conclusion that the associated groups and individuals were significant elements in the decisional process and were actively concerned with the decisions in question.

For weighting purposes, however, a vital preliminary step is to note whether the perceptual inferential map suggests a policy responding more to perceived threat or to perceived opportunity. If the mapping of the prevailing view reflects perceptual response to fear with little evidence of any strong perceived opportunity, then defense is judged to occupy, by itself, the *A* category (first intensity) in a motivational system. If some substantial indication of opportunity perception can be inferred from the mapping, the judgment is far more difficult. In that event, groups and individuals mapped close to the prevailing view are the key. Associated motivational elements are the ones to be considered for inclusion in the motivational system.

In the Iranian illustration, the analyst can compare the perceptual inferential map with clear evidence about the Iranian decisional process. He will know that on the highest decisional level the shah's position is absolute. Thus, there is no point in mapping the prime minister, cabinet officers, or parliamentary and party officials. Given the complexity of decision-making, however, translation of the shah's wishes into policy will allow for bureaucratic interpretation. Therefore, reports as to modal bureaucratic response would reveal motivation, were they accurate. (Unfortunately, in this case accuracy is uncertain.) Similarly, although the press is controlled, interpretation of government directives necessitates some freedom. Thus, subtle differences in the positions of the dictator and his public can be inferred if a newspaper writing for the general public projects images that offer some directional differences from the shah's inferred images.

Looking at the map, the most obvious feature is the polar positioning of the shah's view and the prevailing view, on the one hand, and that of the modal student, on the other. It is a picture associated with a polarized and nonconsensual polity—a situation which makes the government vulnerable to internal manipulation by an enemy. This suggests the probability of a high weighting for the defense factor. However, a closer look at the map suggests a different judgment. The only actor placed in the enemy-colonial-complex quadrant, the position for a state perceived as having greater capability than Iran and hostile to it, is the Soviet Union. But the USSR is mapped much closer to the complex than to the enemy pole, suggesting a perception of only minor threat.

The "enemy" that could exploit the shah's internal difficulties is Iraq. But in the shah-prevailing view, Iraq is mapped in the imperial-enemy-complex quadrant, indicating an operating assumption that Iraq is considerably inferior in capability. The position of China along the complex-allied line but close to the complex pole suggests a potential alliance system which could counter the Soviet Union. But the position of the United States in the allied-colonial-complex quadrant, and much closer to the allied pole than the Soviet Union is to the enemy pole, is even more suggestive. It indicates that Iran sees an alliance with the United States as beneficial for nondefense purposes. Consequently, the defense factor is included in the inferred motivational system at the *B* level (second intensity).

Most revealing are the mapping of Iraq and the Dhofar rebels in the enemy-imperial-complex quadrant and the inclusion of the Federation of Arab Emirates in the allied-imperial-complex quadrant. This suggests a very strong perception of opportunity for influence expansion on the Arab side of the Persian Gulf and in the southern Arabian peninsula. Conservative Arab elites are viewed as WOG friends and revolutionary Arab elites as agitating enemies—a view entirely congruent with that expected when strong opportunity is perceived. The shah's extravagance in building a naval force in this area that is much more powerful than any probable hostile combination is in tune with this judgment.

But to what extent is the shah responding to other decisional elements in his policy of expanding Iranian influence? The map would suggest an answer of "very little." As I have mapped it, the position of the newspaper *Kayhan* suggests sluggishly faithful responses to the shah's adventures. My mapping of the foreign policy bureaucracy suggests clearly that bureaucratic vested interests are of little importance. However, the military is mapped closer to the prevailing view, and the military supports energetically the expensive training and equipment programs that can be defended in terms of the "Iran, protector of the Persian Gulf" image. I inferred as well a position for the military indicating a greater perception of threat from the Soviet Union than is apparent from the position of the prevailing view. Military vested interest is therefore included as the *C* level (third intensity) of the motivational system. Nothing I have seen indicates any particular foreign policy activity on the part of Iran's large and prosperous new middle class. Therefore, no private economic motivational factor is included in the system. Oil diplomacy is viewed as instrumental for achieving domestic economic investments at government instigation.

This leads to the conclusion that the motivational system must reflect the exceptional decisional position and ambitions of the shah. Given an irreconcilable opposition that is a matter of some concern, the shah has reason for internal control purposes to project himself as a heroic national figure. The image he projects very consciously evokes a comparison with his imperial Achaemenid predecessors—a new Darius. His constant personalizing of Iran leads me to infer that his is an example, the supreme example in the world at the time of writing, of external personal power drive as a foreign policy motivation.

The inferred Iranian foreign policy motivational system is thus as follows:

A. Domestic personal power
   External personal power
   National grandeur
B. Defense
   Economic: domestic investments
C. Military vested interests

To recapitulate, what I have done in this illustration is first to construct a perceptual map in which the prevailing world view and the world views of important decisional elements have been positioned. The evidence on which these judgments are based is drawn from two sources—the verbal behavior of individuals actively concerned with foreign policy decisions and the main lines of governmental foreign policy. The verbal behavior treated as evidence is of two varieties: that which describes other peoples and governments, noting in particular descriptions of motives, decisional loci and style, and capability; and that which expresses policy preferences. For purposes of mapping, groups of individuals who seek to affect policy are treated as modal individuals. The position of the prevailing view is the analyst's judgment as to what position on the map is most congruent with actual foreign policy lines.

The foreign policy motivational system is inferred from two sources—the map of the prevailing view and the world views of important decisional elements, and evidence of what decisional elements are most central in the foreign policy decisional process. Important decisional elements are identified, and the proximity of the world view of each decisional element to the prevailing world view is noted. Motivation types that are associated with the various decisional elements are given weightings in the motivational system that correspond to the relative proximity of the world views of the decisional elements to the prevailing world views.

This analytic process is described diagrammatically in figure I.13. The italicized items are areas in which there are some data. The others are inferred as the arrows indicate.

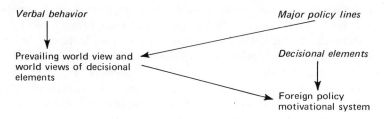

Figure I.13. Inferential Process

FOREIGN POLICY AIMS SYSTEM VALUES AND FOREIGN POLICY DIRECTIONAL THRUST

The foreign policy motivational system device that has been illustrated allows the analyst to list and give crude weightings to the factors which in his judgment give direction to a government's foreign policy. It offers a graphic representation of the foreign policy predispositional base. The next step in this scheme is to indicate how foreign policy direction can be inferred from the foreign policy motivational system. My approach, following Morton Kaplan,[2] is to use the device of "system values." In adopting this device, I am very much aware that the meaning of "system values" is anything but self-evident. I will try to make clear what I mean by the term.

"System" and "value" are both powerful analytic concepts. Their utility in producing order from which explanation seems to flow is so great, in fact, that the analyst must be particularly sensitive to the dangers of reification, of breathing life into an analytic device. Kaplan, a particularly well-disciplined analyst, nevertheless writes at one point about "that which the system values."[3] The "system" is, of course, his own creation and "values" nothing. But "value" is even more commonly reified by the analyst, and this reflects the fact that "value" is generally reified in usage by the layman. When an individual speaks of his values, he seems to have in mind something transcendental, like a soul, which is his essential being. I define value simply as a *choice pattern.* A value system therefore is a weighted listing of identified patterns of choice.

But what leads an individual to choose one from a set of possible alternatives in a particular choice situation? Part of the answer is his perception of the alternatives: Some possible alternatives are simply not perceived, largely because of past experience. But among the alternatives that are perceived, what leads to a particular choice? According to the definition used here, the system of "values" lists an individual's patterns of choice, some of which are relevant for this particular decision. The values do not lead an individual to make a particular choice, although they should be of some use in predicting the choice he will make. An individual is led to make a choice by a compound of needs that predisposes or "motivates" him in the choice direction.

In fact, lay usage of the term "value" is not far from the pattern of choice definition. Over the years, patterns of favoring particular outcomes and therefore alternatives which lead to these outcomes are consciously recognized. When asked to identify his "values," an individual will use terms which to him symbolize the patterned choices of which he has become aware. For example, he may be aware of a consistent pattern of choosing alternatives which advance him toward a career position of prestige and influence. He calls this "achievement" and says he places a high value on "achievement." Then if, when confronted with a particular choice among alternatives, some of which will advance his career and others damage it, he chooses a damaging alternative, he and we are likely to say he is behaving "irrationally." More likely, however, that particular choice was in accord with other patterns which the individual had not consciously recognized. In other words, the compound of needs salient at the moment of the decision, his momentary motivation, predisposed the individual to follow patterns of choice that surprised him. Needs of which the individual was unaware prevented a straight-line achievement choice.

Political scientists are primarily interested in that aspect of the individual's behavior which involves choosing among politically relevant alternatives. We therefore find it useful to discover choice patterns in such cases and to place labels on them such as "national," "liberal," and "role." When we begin to call these patterns "principles,"[4] for example, we start to reify and thereby to conceal the complexity of individual motivation. In this study, values are the choice patterns which reflect an individual's motivation.

To develop the concept of *foreign policy aims system values,* I use the individual and his values as an analogue. My definition therefore is parallel: *Foreign policy aims system values are those choice patterns of a government and people which reflect general foreign policy motivation.* Fortunately, however, the analytic difficulty of dealing with system values for a collective is minor compared with that of dealing with individual value systems. The number of choice patterns identifiable in individual behavior is unmanageably large. Probably the best way to deal with them is to look at narrowly limited choice areas, such as the political, and then begin to bunch patterns under umbrella terms such as "liberal," "modern," or "role."

At the level of generality of foreign policy aims system values, few choice areas are of interest. The analyst needs to identify only those in which the choices made give a general directional thrust to foreign policy. I propose three question areas as most basic: What priority is placed on the peaceful settlement of disputes? What level of relative influence in world affairs is satisfactory? What actor system in world affairs is called for? If a government consistently evinces a deep concern that conflict be settled without violence, seeks to do no more than maintain the relative influence it already exerts in world affairs, and makes no moves to undermine the prevailing actor system, the general directional thrust of its foreign policy can be described as *status-quo.* Different choice patterns in any of the three question areas may lead to the descriptive term *imperialist* for directional thrust. Precisely because these imperialist patterns vary enormously, analysts have, as suggested frequently before, coined other terms they see as more analytically descriptive, such as *destructionist.* Then, in addition, a government and people willing to accept a decline in relative world influence, historically a common and often painful choice, obviously have a foreign policy thrust which is neither status-quo nor imperialist.

To answer these three questions, the analyst must refer to major policy lines for evidence. In the Iranian example used to illustrate this scheme, the foreign policy motivational system clearly evinces a dissatisfaction with the level of influence.

But does Iran seek to alter the status of other state actors in the area in which it exercises substantial influence? My answer would be that policy evidence indicates at the very least a desire to become the hegemonic power of the Persian Gulf area, accompanied by a low interest in peaceful resolution of conflict. The seizure of three islands in the gulf, the military intervention in Oman, and the development of a military force far greater than that of all likely regional opponents add up to a judgment that Iran's foreign policy aims system values are imperialist in all three question areas.

Foreign policy directional thrust can range from acquiescence in declining influence, through determination to retain the current level of influence, to a resolve to increase relative influence. It can range from unwillingness to resort to force even in self-defense, through determination to defend oneself by force if necessary, to virtual disinterest in the question of peaceful resolution of disputes. It can range from acquiescence in evolutionary change in the actor system, through determination to freeze the prevailing actor system, to active support for a new model of the world actor system. Any combination of responses is theoretically possible. However, parallel responses are more likely; and depicting a governmental policy as status-quo, essentially status-quo, imperialist, or essentially imperialist continues to have crude analytic utility.

In this scheme I look at the answers inferred to the three questions that define the area of system values. Then, with reference to major policy lines, I construct a verbalized expression of system-level aims. The directional thrust is implicit.

For example, the supporter of American foreign policy who has a picture of American motivations as described in chapter 3 sees American policy as essentially status-quo. He sees a United States satisfied with the prevailing actor system, placing a high priority on the peaceful settlement of disputes, and satisfied with American world influence but determined not to see that level of influence erode. A reasonable translation of American foreign policy basic intent in this view would be: "to preserve the peace, well-being, and security of the American people." What "well-being," "security," and "preserve the peace" mean is fleshed out as foreign policy aims at a much lower level are specified. But this is a typical verbalization of a status-quo directional thrust.

The revisionist historian answers the question very differently. He sees an essentially imperialistic American government which (1) seeks actor alteration in the direction of an expanded role for capital increasingly organized on the multinational level; (2) places little value on the peaceful attainment of that objective; and (3) seeks expanded influence for the U.S. government as agent for international capitalist interests. A verbalized translation here could be: "to preserve the security of the American people and the capitalist system, and to support actively efforts to gain and secure investments and markets abroad for American industry and commerce and its international conglomerates." Were the revisionist to use this scheme, aims at a lower level would spell out applications of this system-level interest.

A translation of the Iranian picture that I developed is: "to preserve the security and well-being of the Iranian people and to restore to the Iranian people and their king some of the ancient glory that Iran knew." Implicit here is an imperialist directional thrust in all three system-value or question areas.

PARAMETRIC VALUES AND GENERAL STRATEGIC LINES

The motivational system and the foreign policy aims system values are designed to cull the essence of the foreign policy aspect of the political process, but they give no indication of how important the foreign policy manifestation of the political process is. In other words, they do not permit the analyst to estimate the priority foreign policy decision makers are granted in resource allocation. For example, the foreign policy motivational systems of two governments may be identical in terms of types of motives and the placing of motives in the three intensity categories. But the priority granted foreign policy decision makers may be high in one state and low in the other. In such a case, there will be little behavioral resemblance in the foreign policies of the two states. Indeed, a major difficulty in developing a weighting scheme for the foreign policy motivational system that is more isomorphic than three judgmentally ascribed intensity ratings is the fact that the distance between the three intensity categories varies, depending on the priority granted foreign policy decision makers.

My operating assumption is that a high or low priority granted foreign policy reflects the extent to which elements central to the decisional process perceive external threats or opportunities. The priority will be high if these elements perceive strongly a need for governmental action on their behalf in dealing with the perceived threat or opportunity. I propose that the greater the threat or opportunity perceived, the greater the distance between the three intensity categories in the motivational system. In practical terms, this simply says that if there is, for example, an intensely perceived threat to the nation, there will be a concentration on the needs of defense of the nation to the virtual exclusion of satisfying C-ranked motives, such as domestic investments, which could divert resources from the central task.

In systems terms, the priority granted foreign policy claims on national resources can be thought of as the parametric value of the system. The parametric value is a product of the intensity of external threat or opportunity perceived. It is relatively constant, but when it changes the effects will be felt throughout the system of aims. When it is high, the first-intensity motives will receive the all-consuming attention of national leaders. When it is low, there will be a relative lack of interest in foreign policy generally, but within that foreign policy greater relative importance will be granted to objectives that relate to second- and third-intensity motives.

The parametric value is inferred from the prevailing world view. If important decision-making elements perceive threat or opportunity intensely, this should be reflected in a position of the prevailing view far from the complex ideal typical image and close to the enemy, allied, or imperial ideal typical image, depending on the nature of particular relationships. Conversely, when little threat or opportunity is perceived, prevailing views in all bilateral relationships should approach the complex ideal typical image.

To illustrate, the prevailing view in the United States in the mid-Cold War period approximated the enemy image vis-à-vis the Soviet Union, the allied vis-à-vis the United Kingdom, and the imperial vis-à-vis Guatemala. By the 1970s, all three had shifted rapidly in the complex direction. My judgment is that this reflects a high-intensity threat perception in the early 1950s and a rapidly declining one in the early 1970s. Parametric value change is thus underway with a priority downgrading for decision makers concerned with foreign policy.

In the Iranian illustration, the location of the prevailing view of the Soviet Union, China, and Iraq on the perceptual inferential map suggests a moderately low perception of threat. But the position of the prevailing view of the Dhofar rebels and of the small Persian Gulf Arab states suggests a high perception of opportunity. Thus, the parametric value for Iran is judged to be at a high level, and the foreign policy–focused decision maker should have a strong hand in bargaining for scarce resources.

I use the term *parametric value* rather than the more descriptive "priority rating granted foreign policy decision makers" because I see this approach as prequantitative. My hope is that with refinements a point can be reached at which a numerical figure can usefully be ascribed to the parametric value and that this will allow for a more isomorphic weighting of factors in the motivational system. Refinement requires going beyond simply inferring parametric value from the mapping position of the prevailing view to looking as well at appropriations over time in the foreign policy area relative to the domestic policy area. The two foci are necessary because either taken alone can be seriously misleading. Important foreign policy decision makers who perceive threat intensely nevertheless are capable of such detachment that they see their enemy in complex terms. Their mapping positions therefore would be far less reflective of the intensity of threat they perceive than would be their appropriations request level. On the other hand, serious domestic disturbances having little to do with external affairs could lead to relative increases in appropriations in the domestic area that reflect perception of threat in that area but tell nothing of change in perceived threat from external sources.

FOREIGN POLICY GENERAL STRATEGY

I made the point above that foreign policy aims at the system level are rarely, if ever, debated. They reflect instead the overall foreign policy decisional process and the choice patterns this leads to in three gross question areas. They are inferred from the foreign policy motivational system, which suggests basic directional thrust, and from the empirical base of major policy lines. Foreign policy general strategy emerges to execute the foreign policy system aims. Again, debate and planning rarely focus on this decisional level. General strategy reflects the foreign policy decisional process but is only rarely mirrored in the verbal behavior of decision makers.

Since the foreign policy motivational system and foreign policy aims system values directly reflect the general decisional process, they constitute an important aspect of the inferential base for general strategy. In this scheme, I outline both general strategy and lower-level foreign policy aims in divisions that parallel the foreign policy motivational system. One division, or sometimes more than one, reflects the perceptions of threat or opportunity which underlie the motivational factors placed in the first-intensity category of the motivational system. Thus, in the Iranian illustration the perception of opportunity for enhancing the shah's world influence and Iran's national grandeur is reflected in one division. A second division reflects the perception of threat to the shah's position that is a consequence of political polarization in Iran.

Then there is always one final division which reflects the perceived threats or opportunities relating to the second- and third-intensity categories of the motivational system and other motivational factors which are of some significance but are ranked in intensity lower than the third level. When, as in the Iranian illustration, defense is given a second- or third-intensity rating, it is nevertheless given a division of its own which is placed next to the final division. All other second- and third-intensity categories are reflected within the final division.

Inferring from the foreign policy motivational system and foreign policy system values reveals the general *purpose* of strategy. The *scope* of that strategy is inferred in part from the foreign policy aims system parametric value. The parametric value ascribed indicates the priority position of those seeking resources to achieve foreign policy objectives and is therefore highly suggestive of the scope that can be given general strategy. In the Iranian illustration, the ascribed parametric value is high. Therefore, foreign and military policy decision makers can make heavy claims on Iran's mammoth oil income for their purposes.

But scope is dependent as well on another factor, that of capability self-image. How, in the prevailing view, does state capability compare with that of other state actors? The answer to this question can be inferred from the perceptual inferential map. It will be recalled that mapping position is associated with perceptions of threat, opportunity, capability distance, and cultural distance. If significant capability distance is perceived in a state's favor, the mapping position will be below the horizontal line in the direction of the imperial pole. If significant capability distance is perceived in favor of another state, the mapping position of that state will be above the horizontal line in the direction of the colonial pole. Inferring the perceived relative capability rating from the mapping position is complicated by the fact that perceptions of threat, opportunity, and cultural distance must be factored out. But that is not an impossibly difficult operational problem, especially if other ideal typical images are constructed which are associated with either cultural or capability distance but not both.

Obviously, if it is inferred from the perceptual inferential map that in the prevailing view a state's capability rating is three on a scale of five, the scope of strategy will be limited regardless of parametric value rating. In my judgment that is what a careful study of the Iranian prevailing view would reveal, although it would reveal as well an expectation of being in the second category with such states as Britain in the very near future. But as obvious as is the importance of capability self-image in inferring strategic scope, I did not understand this point until the British-in-Egypt case illustration was nearly completed. Thus, while in this illustration I follow the inferential scheme generally, I do not infer from capability self-image.[5]

With purpose and scope of strategy inferred, the next task is to consider the substance of strategy. Given limitations of scope and given general purpose, what direction should be assigned to strategy? The answer is inferred in part from the perceptual inferential map. The map should indicate the loci of greatest perceived threat and opportunity. In the Iranian illustration, the greatest opportunity is perceived in the Persian Gulf area. The greatest threat, one to the shah's internal power position, is just as clearly related to domestic political polarization which offers an enemy, the most likely being Iraq, the opportunity to play with Iran's internal political situation. Thus, some direction for strategy is suggested— exploiting opportunity in the Persian Gulf, reducing Iraq's opportunity to make mischief in Iran.

The final step in inferring general strategy is to refer to the major policy empirical data base. What policies conform to the directions that have already been inferred? With this final step the analyst is ready to verbalize the various strategies and to place a general strategic line at the head of each foreign policy division. In the Iranian illustration the heading of the first division, which relates to the first-intensity motivational factors of external personal power and national grandeur, would be "Enhance Iranian world influence, establish substantial influence in the region extending from the eastern Mediterranean to the Indian Ocean, and establish hegemonic influence in the Persian Gulf." For the second division, which relates to the first-intensity motivational factor of domestic personal power and reflects dangerous political polarization based in large part on the foreign origins of the shah's regime, the heading would be "Make clear the independence of Iranian foreign policy and reduce the potential for external exploitation of internal affairs." The third division, which relates to the second-intensity motivational factor of defense, would be headed by this statement: "In cooperation with the United States and China, contain the Soviet Union." The fourth and final division, reflecting the motivational factors given a third-intensity rating or lower, would have a generalized heading: "Satisfy the foreign policy–related demands of the Iranian people."

FOREIGN POLICY GENERAL AIMS

The task now is to order foreign policy aims by placing them in the appropriate divisions under general strategic line headings. As the illustration in this chapter of the American Cold War system of aims will make clear, there is no assumption that a particular policy fits neatly into one or another division. On the contrary, manifestations of a single policy may be found in each division. The utility of this ordering scheme, in fact, is in showing the multipurpose nature of particular policies.

The entire inferential scheme is depicted in figure I.14. It is important to keep in mind that the flow lines in figure I.14 are inferential, not causal. Change that is described within subsystems of the system of aims, in fact, may well lead to major alterations in every area of the system.

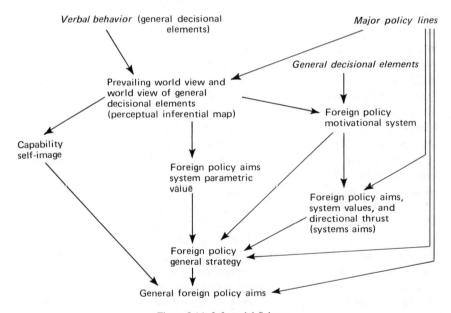

Figure I.14. Inferential Scheme

Change in System of Aims

When Lee Harvey Oswald shot John F. Kennedy, I believe he effected immediate and profound change in American foreign policy. Lyndon Johnson, in both verbal and policy preference behavior, evinced a world view which suggests to me a far more intense perception of threat than that of his predecessor. This was reflected in particular in Johnson's behavior in Third World areas of strategic concern. He saw South Vietnam, Latin America, and the Middle East in terms close to the imperial ideal typical image. This resulted in a sharp shift in the American prevailing world view and general strategy.

This illustrates important change which can hardly be predicted by any analytic scheme. Any sharp and sudden alteration in decisional element composition is likely to induce change, possibly even at the level of general strategy or system aims. These alterations may occur because of the sudden death of a prime decision maker or, more frequently, because of natural developments within that part of the political process which is not directly concerned with foreign policy. The most that can be done here with change so induced is to map its impact on the prevailing view and the motivation system.

This scheme attempts to deal more seriously with externally induced change. In line with my general approach, the focus of this attempt will be perceptual. An individual's view of reality incorporates his expectations of the response of others to his actions. If his expectations are not realized, he is compelled to adjust his view of the situation in such a way that he can explain his incorrect expectations and be comfortable with the explanation. Similarly, those making a decision in foreign policy will have expectations regarding the nature of the response to that policy. If expectations are consistently not realized and their nonrealization falls into a pattern, prevailing views will begin to shift. However, this process of change is likely to be subtle and nondramatic. If, for example, decision makers have expectations that are based on a perception of extreme hostility and aggressiveness but receive responses to their policy decisions that are consistently more in line with status-quo behavior, it is most unlikely that they will immediately conclude that the relationship has changed. On the contrary, past imagery is likely to persist in verbalizations. Consistent nonrealization of expectations of specific responses to specific policy decisions will lead first to almost imperceptible policy shifts until the two powers have a *de facto* changed relationship. Then at some point verbalization of the changed relationship may be brought up to date with the *de facto* change. At that point a government may erroneously appear to be inaugurating a fundamentally new general policy thrust.

Theorists concerned with the role of public opinion in foreign policy formulation have tended to refer to the boundary-setting role of the public.[6] The public is not seen as proposing and supporting specific policies or even as vetoing policies. Instead, the policy formulator is presumed to be able to sense how far his decisional freedom extends before he can be certain of running into public objections. The assumption just described suggests a somewhat different and far less conscious course of action. The balancing assumption suggests that the policy maker will be unlikely to consider policies which would evoke a strongly negative public response. If, as occurred with regard to Vietnam, the world view of an important element of the public begins to change and that of the policy maker remains static, a confrontation occurs—but a confrontation focused on alternative policies rather than on differing world views. If the opposed public is too strong to be persuaded or coerced into quiescence, the policy maker will respond, unknown to himself, by adjusting his world view. Then he can advocate with conviction policies a public can accept.

Across-the-board parallel perceptual alteration never occurs in response to a series of expectational failures. Role and value differentiations produce different predispositions to perceptual alteration. Take the illustration of a government and people for whom the prevailing perception coincides with the enemy image but the "enemy" responds to policies designed to deal with an incorrigibly aggressive foe in unexpectedly mild ways. Assume further that the "enemy" is perceived to be a leftist dictatorship. Although there is a prevailing view—the one most congruent with the policy lines operating in the situation—there will be wide variations in perceptions of motivation within the decisional unit. Those elements whose role interests would be adversely affected were the relationship to become less hostile (for example, men in the military bureaucracy or defense industry bureaucracy) would not be predisposed to perceive an altered situation. But those whose role interests would be favorably affected (for example, young men about to be drafted or consumer-oriented industrial bureaucrats) by the alteration in relationship would be predisposed to see change. The ideological projection theory developed in the previous chapter suggests that a rightist senator and a leftist magazine editor would have opposite predispositions as well.

Consequently, unexpected responses would lead to a serious disturbance within the decisional unit. A president, for example, may have listened to opposing views concerning an important policy decision. One side, predisposed to see no change, would explicate its expectations of the response to the policy. The other side, predisposed to see change, would explicate a very different set of expectations. Were the latter group's expectations consistently fulfilled, the president might begin to grant them somewhat greater credibility. A presidential appointment to fill a vacancy might well reflect this attitude and, with the new appointment, the decisional unit would acquire an altered modal view, one accepting change. This change could then be translated into changes in the weighting of motivations. Defense, for example, could begin to decline and with it the willingness to grant top priority to the foreign policy field in resource allocations. This alteration in the decisional unit would also be reflected in an altered prevailing world view and ultimately in altered major foreign policy lines. In chapter 6 the alteration of American policy in Vietnam in 1968 will be taken as an illustrative case along the lines of the above hypothetical outline.

When the analytic approach is perceptual, as it is here, a natural focus for viewing externally induced change is expectational realization or nonrealization.

In the pages that follow I will utilize this focus in looking at change as it occurs at four different levels within the overall system of aims. The first level is that of situational policy. A disturbance is felt, but an adjustment is made at such a low level that general policy, general strategic lines, and general system aims are unaffected.

The second level involves more serious change. Here some general policy lines are affected, and this leads to major adjustments in situational policies that are rooted in the affected general policy. But general strategy and general system aims are unaffected.

The third level of change considered is at the general strategy level. It results in some alteration of the perception of threat and/or opportunity which is reflected in the first-intensity level of the foreign policy motivational system. This is profound change which will be felt in all general and situational policy areas and will lead to alteration in general strategic lines. But the adjustment to this disturbance leaves the general system aims unaffected.

Then finally there is change at a level which is reflected in alteration of general system aims. Change at this level occurs when there is an alteration in one or more of the following areas: the priority placed on peaceful settlement of conflict, the degree of satisfaction with the level of influence in interstate affairs, and the degree of acceptance of the prevailing actor system. Change at this level is felt in terms of general strategy, all major policy lines, and all situational policy lines.

SITUATIONAL POLICY CHANGE

In August 1957 the U.S. government attempted unsuccessfully to overthrow the government of Syria. The case was of classic mid–Cold War vintage.[7] Perceiving an opportunity to deny to the Communists the Arab state of Syria, the United States decided to try to impose a cooperative military dictatorship on the country. Syrian political leaders, such as Michael Aflaq and Akram al-Hawrani, leaders of the socialist Baath party, were seen as agitators without following; collaborating rightist politicians were seen as men of responsibility. A coup was conceivable because, given the perceived lack of public opinion, it involved merely replacing one small elite, the "ins," with another small elite, the "outs." Expectations were that the coup would succeed, as had previous coups in Iran and the Sudan.

But the plan was uncovered, and the politicians who would have collaborated were imprisoned. American officials most directly involved were expelled, and the Syrian political right was thoroughly discredited, its leaders charged with treason. Change in the government following the coup included the appointment of a chief of staff who was believed to have been a member of the Communist party and of a premier who favored active collaboration with the Soviet Union. Confronted with these developments, U.S. diplomacy became active in Lebanon and Turkey. Turkish military maneuvers near the Syrian border soon after were assumed to be a consequence of this activity. In the uproar that followed, most of the Arab world expressed strong support for Syria, and the Soviet Union gained considerable prestige by threatening Turkey and offering support for Syria. The Syrian instigation of a union with Egypt to form the United Arab Republic was another direct consequence.

This is given as an example of a change in situational policy. A specific policy decision, to overthrow the Syrian government by a clandestinely supported coup d'état, was based on an imperial image of Syria. This image, in turn, was derived from an enemy image of the Soviet Union in accordance with which the Soviets were seen to be attempting to gain control for communism of the Arab Middle East. The operation was expected to succeed, installing a new government led by pro-Western and responsible men (WOGs), much like the leaders of Jordan and Iraq in 1957. The response, a Syrian crushing of the coup and an outraged public opinion throughout the Arab world, was not in accordance with expectations. But this failure did not much alter the views of participants in the American decisional unit. To them the failure simply indicated that the Soviet enemy had succeeded in winning this one and gaining control of Syria—which they had been in the process of doing anyway. Public support for the regime and public outrage over the attempted coup simply were not perceived. What happened was dramatic enough, however, and the prevailing image of Syria shifted from one close to the imperial ideal typical to one close to the satellite image, an aspect of the enemy ideal typical image. The union with Egypt, therefore, was seen as simply the union of two satellites.

There were changes in the decisional unit: The CIA contingent in Damascus was ousted. But no shift of telling importance occurred. Consequently the prevailing situational view reflected a perception of threat at about the same intensity level, even though the image type had altered. Specific policy now reflected the view of Syria as a Soviet satellite.

This example illustrates a serious disturbance which was met with an easy adjustment. Policy toward Syria specifically altered. But no major policy lines were changed, and the basic image of the Soviet Union remained unaltered.

The process is illustrated in figure I.15.

The specific decision (to overturn the Syrian government) had been congruent with the prevailing situational view. The response was not in accord with the expectations of decisional elements and altered their situational view to one in which Syria was perceived to be a satellite and no longer susceptible to the type of intervention just attempted. There is no evidence that the unexpected response strengthened some situational decision makers and weakened others. Personnel change occurred, but this did not upset the perceptual balance. Consequently, the new prevailing view was in harmony with unaltered major policy lines. Change had occurred but only concerning policy in a local situation. The impact on the overall system of foreign policy aims was no more than a ripple.

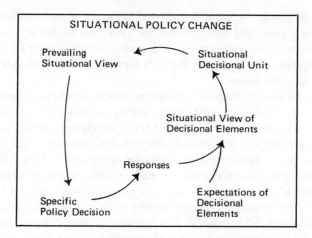

Figure I.15. Situational Policy Change Process

GENERAL POLICY CHANGE

"General policy change" refers to the adjustment to a rather severe disturbance which involves specific policy decisions and major policy lines, but not general strategy.

American intervention in Lebanon in July 1958, a few months after the Syrian fiasco, is a good example and a fascinating one for anyone interested in foreign policy perceptions.[8] This was another classic Cold War case. An absolute enemy, the Soviet Union, acting through its satellite, the United Arab Republic, was seen to be attempting to overthrow the Lebanese government. The president of Lebanon asked for American intervention. The U.S. government, perceiving the opportunity to preempt a Soviet subversive move, agreed. Lebanon was seen in terms closely resembling the imperial ideal type. Its responsible president, a classic WOG, was opposed by agitating and irresponsible dupes or agents of the Soviet Union. One leader of the "agitators" was Rashid Karami. Expectations were that the Lebanese would welcome American tutelage, that the agitators would flee, and that the Soviet Union would behave as paper tigers do when one stands up to them.

But nothing worked as expected. The commander in chief of the armed forces made clear his nonsupport for the president. The civil war continued, indicating real public support for the rebels. Leaders considered by Americans to be "responsible" argued that the president wanted American intervention to gain an illegal second term. And evidence of Soviet involvement was anything but hard. Confronted with this unexpected set of responses, American diplomats closeted themselves with Lebanese politicians and worked out a compromise. As a result, the commander in chief of the armed forces was made president in place of the man who invited intervention, and Rashid Karami became premier. This regime proved ultimately to be stable, and the American military withdrew.

Rashid Karami's transformation from agitating dupe of the Communists to responsible leader was not only wondrously swift, it was for Americans imperceptible. Neither public officials nor the press noted this seeming alteration.

This is typical of what is meant by general policy change. The determining image behind containment policy was that of a terrifying enemy. This episode was some small evidence that the image was overdrawn, but apparently this evidence went unnoticed. Instead there was a policy adjustment, one that made possible friendly relations with a "neutral" instead of a "pro-Western" government, without any verbalized recognition of the importance of the adjustment. General strategy remained undisturbed.

In this case there was a significant alteration in prevailing situational view. Unlike the case of Syria in 1957, the position of the prevailing view did not remain constant but moved toward the complex image. Rashid Karami moved in image from agitator to rather conservative Arab politician and one of a diverse group of Lebanese notables with a popular following. Furthermore, the image of the United Arab Republic in the prevailing view altered in the complex direction. A specific policy of aloof friendliness replaced the policy of hostility. Significant change in the situational decisional unit was made, with Robert Murphy, known for his cool detachment, coming in and the old Cold Warrior Loy Henderson losing influence. Yet the adjustment at the level of major policy lines was smooth. The shock waves were confined to the geographic area.

The process can be diagrammed as in figure I.16.

The civil war in Lebanon was a major world disturbance. It was perceived in the United States in close accord with a prevailing world view according to which the Soviet Union, acting through its Arab satellites, was seeking to subvert further the Arab Middle East. The opportunity to prevent this was perceived in Lebanon, and in the prevailing situational view Lebanon was seen close to the imperial ideal typical image. Policy was in tune with this view, but the response to that policy followed sharply unexpected lines. In this case some decisional elements apparently were less surprised than others. The situational view altered, and so did the composition of the situational decision unit. Robert Murphy's addition to that unit was very significant, and Loy Henderson's eclipse suggests that the shock effects were felt in major policy decisional units. As depicted in figure I.16, change was thus at the general policy level. However, the adjustment to the prevailing world view was apparently not serious. Although there was substantial evidence that the role of the Soviet Union had been grossly exaggerated, policy behavior does not suggest a policy shift which would lead to a mapping of the prevailing world view closer to the complex pole. However, the prevailing situational view did reflect

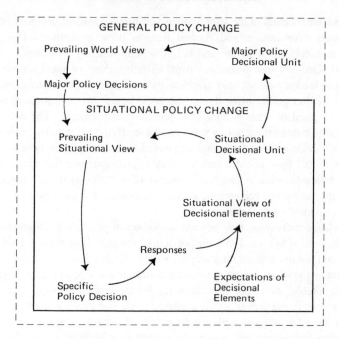

Figure I.16. General Policy Change Process

major change: Subsequent specific policy in the area was far more congruent with a situational view in which the images of Arab actors, friendly and unfriendly, were much closer to the complex pole.

By far the most important observation to make regarding this episode is that the major alteration in the American prevailing view of the area and in American policy went unnoticed both officially and in the media.[9]

GENERAL STRATEGY CHANGE

When a disturbance is severe enough that the intensity level of the determining perception of threat or opportunity is altered, the change is said to be at the general strategy level. This means that the relative priority granted the foreign policy side of the political process is altered. General strategy change will occur, but the foreign policy directional thrust will not shift.

Chapter 6 is designed to illustrate change at this level. In sum, the contention there is that early American escalation of the war in Vietnam in 1964 and 1965 was thoroughly in tune with a Cold War reality perception. South Vietnam and Thailand were seen in terms approximating the imperial ideal typical image. North Vietnam was seen as the satellite ally of a great power; to a lesser extent, so were Norodom Sihanouk's Cambodia and Sukarno's Indonesia. The Soviet Union and China were in the enemy mold. Escalation was designed to buoy up South

Vietnam's WOG regime and to show China and the Soviet Union for the paper tigers they were.

But from the earliest days, expectations were not realized. Ngo Dinh Diem was in many ways an ideal WOG, but the Kennedys saw him as unpopular. Placing that image against the ideal typical, the suggestion is that South Vietnam in John Kennedy's eyes was far from the ideal typical imperial image. President Kennedy saw a public opinion in South Vietnam and a differentiated leadership. Given that view, the replacement of Diem was reasonable. That American decision makers who perceived threat more intensely should see the removal of Diem as a tragic error is only to be expected. After Kennedy's death, the shift away from the complex pole appears to have been dramatic. But evidence that there was a public opinion in South Vietnam and that it was not attracted to the American-supported WOG leadership followed every American action.

If the South Vietnamese failed to respond according to expectations, so did North Vietnam. For a satellite population, the North Vietnamese fought very well—so well that the situational view of many Americans began to alter. Increasingly the Vietnamese conflict was perceived as a civil war rather than as aggression by a Soviet satellite acting out a surrogate role and invading a responsibly led developing country.

For those holding an extreme enemy view of China and the Soviet Union, the very mild response to American escalation was not unexpected. By this view, if you stand up to an imperialist foe it will prove to be a paper tiger. But for those whose views were further away from the enemy image, Chinese and Soviet behavior was far less aggressive than anticipated. Confronted with repeated escalations, the two communist powers appeared to move cautiously and sluggishly. Consequently, as time passed the very perception of threat from international communism began to fade for increasing numbers of Americans.

However, this attrition of the enemy image was uneven. An intense threat perception such as that which developed in the early post–World War II years leads inevitably to the creation of a huge industrial and bureaucratic complex to deal with it. The individuals who populate that complex will have a vested interest in its perpetuation. Only naturally, then, the defense, governmental, industrial, and academic bureaucracies held onto a view of the communist foe which made their own roles vital. Nevertheless, the intensity of the threat perceived generally did decline. As it did, the priority in allocation of resources to the defense bureaucracy declined, and so did the relative influence of that decisional element. The decline was accelerating, and the major policy decisional unit began to alter in composition.

Vietnam, then, is an example of a disturbance which resisted adjustment at the situational policy and general policy levels. It ultimately affected general strategy. But it did not produce a system aims change.

The combined picture is diagrammed in figure I.17.

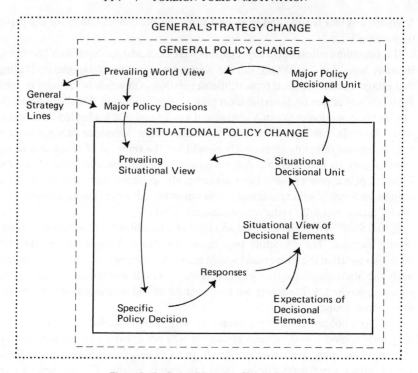

Figure I.17. General Strategy Change Process

The disturbance in this case was most seriously perceived: a real possibility that the government of South Vietnam might collapse and be replaced by a communist regime. Given the prevailing world view of the early Johnson administration, such an eventuality could only be seen as the successful conclusion of a Soviet-directed campaign of subversion and insurgency. Therefore, the United States adopted a policy of punishing the agent of Moscow's expansion, North Vietnam. This would be done according to a timetable of escalation until the Communists acquiesced in a Korea-type settlement in which the 17th parallel would become the Cold War boundary separating the two Vietnams.

The response to this strategy differed sharply from most expectations. Members of the decisional group most sanguine in their expectations of an increasing willingness of Moscow and Peking to acquiesce in North Vietnam's suing for a settlement were confronted with a hardening of North Vietnamese determination even though Moscow and Peking gave only minimal support. Members of the decisional unit who opposed or were skeptical of a decision made because of a fear of a strong Soviet Chinese response and a deepening of the Cold War were confronted with a remarkably mild response from both China and the Soviet Union. Only the rhetoric was harsh.

The result was a discrediting of both hard and moderate lines, especially among the major policy decisional elements in Washington. When Clark Clifford became secretary of defense, a major alteration in that decisional unit began.[10] This development accelerated a move of the prevailing view of the great communist states in the complex direction. This led to a general strategy change which was reflected in a lessening of the defense establishment's priority claim on resource allocation and in a shift away from containment and toward détente. With this shift, the major policy of opposing any internal drift toward communism in Third World countries began to change. In tune with this, South Vietnam was perceived less in the imperial image, and North Vietnam was rarely described as a satellite of the Soviet Union or China. With far less at stake, it became possible to shift specific policy dramatically in the direction of withdrawal.

SYSTEM AIMS CHANGE

American foreign policy of the last generation does not offer a good illustration of system aims change. There were signs of such a change, however. Both the Johnson and Nixon doctrines seemed to place a great responsibility on American shoulders for preserving world stability even in the face of a declining perception of threat from a great power. George Liska in his *Imperial America,* in fact, advocates an American equivalent of Pax Romana in this era.[11] Such a proposal was natural coming from members of the defense bureaucracy who believed, as Liska did, that external threat had all but vanished. But behavioral evidence is strong that the American political process would not support such an outlay of resources for this purpose. A decline in threat perception has weakened seriously any argument the defense establishment can make for continued high priority. The most that can be said, therefore, is that the tendency is manifest but unlikely to bear fruit.

However, there is an excellent example of perceived system aims change since World War II. George Kennan's containment thesis is simply a strategy for achieving Soviet system aims change and can be translated easily into a perceptual frame. Kennan saw a Soviet elite that had to be aggressive in order to attract the necessary popular support to stay in power. "Containment" was a strategy for denying the expectations of Soviet decision makers who planned to gain world domination. Kennan argued simply that a strong containment policy would defeat Soviet aggressive intent in a myriad of specific decisional areas. Expecting an easy expansion of influence, Soviet decision makers would be confronted with deep determination to resist. This in turn would confront the Soviet leadership with the necessity of satisfying its people with something other than cheap and exciting adventures. The alternative would be to satisfy some of their material demands, which would call for a lowering of priority for the foreign policy decision maker and ultimately for an alteration in overall decisional elements. Consumer industry bureaucrats with a vested interest in long-term peace would replace adventuristic ideologues. This in turn would change the motivational system and hence effect a system aims change. The foreign policy directional thrust would shift toward the status-quo. Many, possibly most, analysts would now disagree with the initial Kennan assumptions. Granting those assumptions, however, this is a good illustration of system aims change.

The entire change process indicating the boundaries in which situational policy, general policy, general strategy, and system aims change could be described can now be diagrammed as in figure I.18.

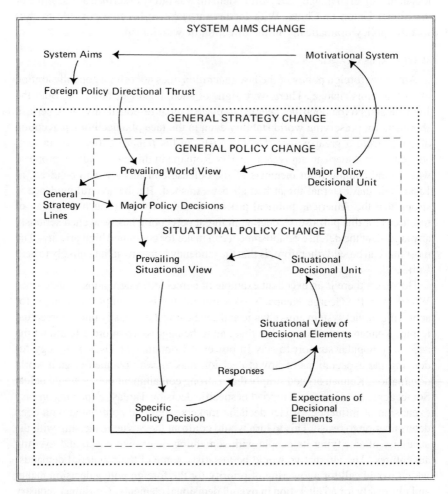

Figure I.18. System Aims Change Process

Mapping of General Foreign Policy Aims: American Cold War Policy

In chapter 3 I gave two opposing pictures of American foreign policy motivation in the mid–Cold War period to illustrate the foreign policy motivational system device. One was the picture a modal supporter of American policy would construct were he to use the scheme. The other picture was that of a revisionist historian using the scheme. My hope is that the scheme is sufficiently neutral that analysts with entirely different base assumptions will find it useful. It is simply an ordering device whose value lies in compelling its user to spell out assumptions and then to spell out the implications of those assumptions right down to the situational policy level. I see American motivations similarly to my modal supporter of American foreign policy, but I believe the revisionist historian's picture is just as fully integrated as that of the modal supporter. Were two such analysts to spell out their opposing views with this frame, the two constructions would amount to two fully developed and opposing descriptive propositions on which explanation and prediction could be based. The test would come in articulating competing expectations of outcomes from particular policies.

Since my object is to illustrate the procedure for mapping general foreign policy aims, the above remarks are intended primarily to alert the reader. The particular manner in which I map American Cold War policy aims is entirely in tune with my picture of an American foreign policy directional thrust that is essentially status-quo. The revisionist who sees an essentially imperialist directional thrust would map American aims in an entirely different manner.

I see an American prevailing view of the Soviet Union in the mid-1950s which is mapped on the horizontal enemy-complex line and close to the enemy pole. The parametric value of American foreign policy therefore is very high. Capability self-image is, as the Soviet position suggests, equivalent to that of the Soviet Union and superior to all others. The foreign policy motivational system I see is the following:

A. Defense
B. Economic investments: domestic
   Military vested interests
   Bureaucratic vested interests
C. National grandeur
   Cultural messianism

The foreign policy aims system values I see are choice patterns in each of the three areas that give a status-quo directional thrust to foreign policy aims. I verbalize system aims as "Preserve the peace, well-being, and security of the American people."

Inferring general strategic lines from this, however, is anything but mechanical.

We know that the primary purpose is defense and that the scope is very extensive, and we know the identity of the threatening state. But we must refer to the major policy evidence base in order to abstract a description of the general strategy lines.

In debate and general discussion, at least three general strategies have been proposed: containment, rollback, and Fortress America. But a strong verbal case was never made for any of the three.[12] Except in rare moments in history, meaningful debate in foreign policy does not focus on the general strategy level. Rather it focuses on major, substantive policy decisions. In 1970, for example, the so-called great debate focused on the advisability of an antiballistic missile program and on the wisdom of an invasion into Cambodia or of a definite timetable for withdrawal from Vietnam. Those calling themselves doves did not argue that containment, the name given to basic American strategy in the Cold War, was no longer valid. Nor did those who called themselves hawks argue its continued validity. Also, imagery referred to verbally is less than revealing. Both hawks and doves at times used pictures of the communist powers that coincided with an enemy image and at other times used pictures that were much closer to the complex image.

"Containment" itself was really an umbrella term that was reasonably descriptive of the sum of the general policy lines already operative when the term was coined. As mentioned previously, the image of the Soviet Union accepted by Kennan in his Mr. X article in *Foreign Affairs* enunciating containment was a simple transference from the image of Nazi Germany.[13] The alternative policy of "rollback" was never really spelled out even though its chief advocate in the 1952 election campaign became secretary of state with as close to a policy carte blanche as modern statesmen are given. Major policy lines remained remarkably the same. When, on the other hand (as will be described in some detail in the following chapter), Lyndon Johnson's policies in Southeast Asia began to look more and more suitable for the umbrella term "rollback" than for "containment," the debate focused heavily on specific acts of escalation. The conclusion therefore is that for purposes of mapping, little reliance can be placed on verbalization of general strategy.

Why did the American government choose containment rather than rollback or Fortress America? In the early post–World War II days, when the United States had a monopoly of nuclear weapons, rollback was surely a conceivable alternative strategy. Fortress America is self-evidently a defensible strategy: By making full use of the great oceans that separate the United States and the Soviet Union, the American government could have protected itself without the extraordinary sacrifice of its resources the Cold War was to claim. The answer may well be that a historically induced world view precluded seriously considering alternative strategies. Isolationism had become a pejorative symbol. Rollback smacked too much of the strategic thinking of the recently defeated fascist foe. This may well be an example of a case in which alternatives could not be easily perceived.

Nor was containment itself a well-formulated strategy. As stated above, it was really an umbrella term that defied exact definition but did seem to those using it to capture the spirit behind a conglomeration of more specific and definable policies. Some of those specific policies were blatantly imperialistic as the term is defined here. In the extreme, they included replacing one regime with another. Yet such individually undeniably imperialist acts were grouped under a rubric which was surely in tone status-quo. For defenders of containment—and only a tiny movement opposed it in the mid-Cold War years—this status-quo quality was reflective of status-quo general aims and a motivational syndrome in which defense was the vital factor.

Containment, therefore, was an excellent descriptive term for the policy of a government motivated chiefly by a desire to defend itself and perceiving an extraordinarily serious external threat to its security.

It follows that the impact of a general strategy change, one that involves, for example, a marked decline in the intensity of perception of threat but no alteration in the basically status-quo motivation system, will be felt in specific policies throughout the system. The argument that intervention on the level of regime alteration is in the national security interest will lose most of its persuasiveness for the center of the decisional unit. In fact, the willingness of their predecessors to execute such policies will be seen with astonishment and dismay. Arguments in favor of economic aid to minor allies, and increasingly of military aid as well, will also lose their force. A large American force in Europe begins to lose its defenders, and more ships move to the moth balls. Then a change in verbiage appears. "Containment" is effectively ignored and "era of negotiation," "détente," and "rapprochement" are heard. A generation which had never perceived intense threat begins to assert itself. Previous policy is utterly inexplicable for this group; and the older generation, unable to recall the perceptual climate of even a decade ago, is bewildered in its defense. However, islands of the previous perception remain, particularly concerning the Middle East, where even many of the new generation perceive serious threat. Discarded containment policies are thus infused with new life in this one policy island.

In sum, what I am arguing is that the external determination of foreign policy can be discovered in the form of perceived threats to or perceived opportunities for that which is highly valued by elements central to the political process. Reponse to these threats and opportunities will give direction to basic foreign policy thrust and will lead to a choice among strategic alternatives. Actual decision-making, however, rarely if ever occurs consciously at the level of general strategic lines. Consequently, policy and verbal evidence dealing with a lower level of concern must be aggregated and collated in order to discover and describe the strategic choice that was made. The analyst is helped, however, by the tendency of participants in the decisional process to see and describe the pattern of strategic response, usually in metaphoric terms. "Containment" is a case in point.

In looking at policy and verbal evidence for constructing my outline of American Cold War foreign policy aims, one problem quickly became obvious. One threat deriving from the menace of world communism was almost as important as the parent threat. This was a threat to the survival of the American system from the nuclear weapons that were central to the strategy of containing the communist enemies. I therefore subdivided the strategic line division referring to the perceived threat from communist enemies into two sections. The first, under the umbrella term "containment," is designed to order major and specific policies primarily concerned with stopping communist aggression in whatever form. The second, given the umbrella term "avoid thermonuclear war," is designed to give order to policies concerned with preventing both accidental war and resort to warfare on the thermonuclear level.

General strategy is therefore translated into the following three levels:

A. Contain international communism directed from Moscow

B. Avoid thermonuclear war

C. Satisfy the economic and other internationally relevant demands of the American people

The first of these, containment, gave essential definition to the era. But avoiding thermonuclear war is unique to the nuclear age. It was recognized not only that nuclear war would destroy civilization but that it could occur accidentally. Thus, although nuclear deterrence was the core of military containment policy, policies were inaugurated simultaneously to give the major participants as much control as possible over accidental events which could spark an unwanted nuclear exchange.

The derivative nature of the "avoid thermonuclear war" division is indicated by looking at the impact a decline in perception of threat from the communist states would have on policies in that division. There would likely be serious interest in nuclear weapons control agreements, but there should also be a decrease in attention given areas in which local conflicts threaten to precipitate major power conflict. Their potential for producing accidental war would decline, and insofar as this potential was responsible for great-power interest, that interest should decline as well.

The third area mentioned, satisfying foreign policy–related demands of the domestic political process, is a constant reflecting second, third, and lower motivational intensity levels. Variation occurs within it, of course, as the domestic political process alters. Generally speaking, however, its relative importance in giving definition to policy thrust varies inversely with perception of threat intensity.

In order to explain further the utility of focusing on general aims and general policy thrust and to explain what is meant by "major specified policy lines" and "specific policy," I have detailed a system of aims which, in my view, describes the American foreign policy aims system at the height of the Cold War.

In this example, system aims are given in the heading, roman numeral I; general strategy is spelled out under A, B, and C; general policy lines are related to the general strategy and listed by number; specific policy lines are given within each general policy line, with lower-case letters. Situational policy lines are not mapped.

I. Preserve the peace, well-being, and security of the American people
  A. Contain international communism directed from Moscow
   1. Deter militarily the primary enemies and their satellites
      a. Communicate the impression that a nuclear attack would be intolerably expensive
      b. Communicate the impression that expansion utilizing conventional warfare, guerrilla warfare, encouraged insurgency, or subversion would be too expensive
      c. Establish and develop military alliances on the communist periphery
      d. Give unilateral guarantees of support to noncommunist regimes of strategically important states.
   2. Encourage the liberalization trends of communist states
      a. Reinforce the positions of those leaders, frequently consumer-oriented, who perceive coexistence to be possible
      b. Increase trade selectively as liberalization trends become manifest
   3. Encourage tendencies toward autonomy in satellite states
      a. Grant economic aid selectively and, where autonomy is well established, military aid
      b. Encourage trade patterns reducing satellite dependence on the USSR
   4. Work for the economic stability and the economic, military, and political integration of developed noncommunist states
      a. Advance credit and monetary support where necessary
      b. Provide diplomatic support for integrationist moves
      c. Encourage the evolution of military pacts into the institutional base for broader alliances
   5. Work for noncommunist stability in developing states
      a. Grant economic and technical assistance necessary to produce short- and long-run stability
      b. Support economic aid through regional and international agencies
      c. Encourage investment, domestic and foreign
      d. Grant military assistance to enable an embattled noncommunist regime to withstand a communist challenge
      e. Through symbol manipulation, present a case for development outside the communist frame
      f. Through overt and covert diplomacy, develop stable regimes capable of withstanding the communist challenge

B. Avoid thermonuclear war
  1. Deter any nuclear power from launching a nuclear attack
     a. Develop weapons systems necessary to make any attack intolerably expensive
     b. Develop credibility for the use of these weapons
  2. Proscribe certain military behavior
     a. Set the stage for phased arms control
     b. Outlaw certain procedures such as above-ground nuclear testing
  3. Stabilize accidental war areas
     a. Stabilize states divided as a result of the Cold War: Germany, Korea, Vietnam, China
     b. Stabilize conflict situations in which the great powers are not directly involved but have serious interests
  4. Support and encourage international organizations
     a. Work to preserve the peacemaking prerogatives of the United Nations
     b. Support a vigorous role for the secretary general
     c. Encourage international cooperation generally through the United Nations, the specialized agencies, and regional organizations
  5. Work for the development of international law
     a. Observe accepted international law
     b. Support the International Court of Justice in current practices
C. Satisfy the economic and other internationally relevant demands of the American people
  1. Maintain a foreign policy and civilian defense bureaucracy capable of executing American foreign policy efficiently and well
  2. Maintain an armed force capability sufficient to meet the security needs of the American people
  3. Provide for the health of the American economy in its foreign policy–related aspects
     a. Encourage, support, and protect American investments abroad
     b. Protect defense-related industry
     c. Protect against the impact of economic crises abroad
     d. Encourage American foreign trade; negotiate tariff reductions on products of competitive industries; seek to protect American domestic production from foreign competition
     e. Take measures to prevent an adverse balance of payments
  4. Give diplomatic support and assistance to people for whom there is special concern
     a. Support the independence and well-being of Israel
     b. Help improve conditions for the people of Eastern Europe
     c. Support the drive for independence and equality of the African peoples

5. Encourage democracy, support independence, and advance the welfare of other peoples
   a. Establish especially friendly relations with democratic states, aloof but correct relations with authoritarian regimes
   b. Engage in aid projects and encourage the use of the United Nations simply for humanitarian purposes
6. Ensure that the prestige and dignity of the United States are at all times protected
7. Advance the cause of world peace and avoid risking the loss of American lives in foreign conflict

Included in the first division are the major policy lines and related specific policies which in sum add up to containment. The second division contains those policies which add up to "avoid thermonuclear war." And in the third division are at least a few of the major policy lines and their specific manifestations which are encompassed by the umbrella term "satisfy the economic and other internationally relevant demands of the American people."

It should be recalled that this scheme is meant to be simply an ordering device. It explains nothing. The hope is, though, that the description, so ordered, will suggest explanatory propositions, especially when two or more successive time periods are compared.

To illustrate this point, we will take a brief look at American policy toward the Arab-Israeli dispute at two moments in history: mid-1957, when the Cold War system of aims as detailed above is presumed to have been prevailing, and mid-1970, when a general strategy change is presumed to have been occurring. In both cases, my assumptions as to the prevailing system of aims are undefended. In the British-in-Egypt case study, the entire scheme will be illustrated and there will be no undefended assumptions. The purpose here is simply to explain this aspect of the scheme by means of a familiar illustration. As mentioned, those analysts who are convinced that American policy was basically imperialist in motivation would, of course, have an entirely different system of aims in mind.

In mid-1957, the Dulles-Eisenhower policy had crystallized. The pre–Suez crisis ambiguity regarding American relations with the revolutionary Arab states, more or less following the lead of President Nasser, had been replaced by a policy of isolation and if possible overthrow of the revolutionary regimes. A successful and American-backed royal coup had a few months earlier toppled the pro-Nasser Nabulsi regime in Jordan. Saudi Arabia had broken its ties with Egypt, and an American-backed plot (which was to fail) against the Kuwatli regime in Syria was crystallizing. Relations with Great Britain, France, and Israel had all improved greatly since the Suez war of 1956 and since American pressure had been placed on Israel to withdraw to her prewar boundaries.

Looking at the system of aims in the containment division, it is quickly apparent that the major policy line which applies is A.5, "Work for noncommunist stability in developing states." Specific policies listed in this category had been carried out in the Arab world, which was considered a prime target for Soviet subversion. Economic and technical aid had been given; American investments were encouraged; military assistance had been granted and far more offered if the government would associate itself more closely with the American-backed Baghdad Pact; psychological warfare was vigorously pursued; and intervention in domestic affairs had been common since 1949, as detailed by Miles Copeland in *The Game of Nations*. These interventions by mid-1957 came to follow a pattern that was in tune with the imperial ideal typical image. In the early days of the Cold War, before images crystallized, a willingness to look with favor on nationalist regimes was apparent. Early American support for Egypt's junta suggested a conclusion that a popular modernizing regime which was noncommunist but not anticommunist might nevertheless be preferable to a verbally anticommunist regime which was unwilling to modernize rapidly and was bitterly disliked by important segments of the population. By mid-1957, this question had finally been resolved in favor of traditional elites that were willing to collaborate. Efforts were made to move these regimes toward reform. Clearly the economic and technical assistance programs were designed to help collaborating regimes move more rapidly in a modernizing direction, since modernization was seen as necessary for stability. Policy by mid-1957 was thus to isolate and/or overturn modernizing elites and to support traditional elites but push them toward gradualistic modernizing programs.

Another item in the containment division applies to the Arab-Israeli case. That is A.1, "Deter militarily the primary enemies and their satellites." The situational response here relates to the subsidiary aim, A.1.c, "Establish and develop military alliances on the communist periphery." Efforts to persuade Arab states to enter into American-associated military alliances were intense but successful only with the then leading traditional government of the area, that of Iraq.

Where does American support for Israel fit into the containment scheme? None of the major policy lines obviously applies to Israel. In fact, a study of the policy lines aggregated in the containment division of the foreign policy aims outline suggests a conclusion that the American *de facto* alliance with Israel not only did not reinforce the containment policy but actually subverted it. The belief of many Arabs that Israel was a part of overall Western imperial policy toward the Arab world, a policy which included an implicit alliance with both Israel and traditional Arabs, was likely to lead to instability among Arab states and a willingness to ally with enemies of the West. By mid-1957 the perception of an unholy alliance of the United States, Israel, and traditional Arab leaders was widespread and worked against the legitimacy of traditional regimes that the United States supported.

This point, in turn, suggests some explanation of the seeming pro-Arab position of the American defense and foreign policy bureaucracy connected with the

Middle East. In pursuing role objectives these bureaucrats naturally perceived the existence of Israel as complicating their task of advancing American security interests. A classic case of this can be seen in Secretary of Defense James Forrestal's diary.[14]

Under the second general policy thrust, that of avoiding thermonuclear war, the Arab-Israeli conflict is of deep concern. Under B.3, "Stabilize accidental war areas," the need to prevent local conflicts that are independent of great-power conflict but interact with it is a major specific policy line. But again, the range in choice for devising the best policy for stabilizing the Arab-Israeli conflict is wide. Assuming that a commitment to Israel's survival as an independent Jewish state is unquestioned, how can Arab acquiescence in the existence of that state be gained? Since the point is clear that revolutionary Arab regimes are far more implacable in their hostility to Israel than are traditional Arab regimes, the relevance of the direction of this specific policy decision to that concerned with promoting stabilizing noncommunist regimes in the Arab world is obvious. A popular, noncommunist Arab regime might be more fundamentally stable, but it would certainly be less acquiescent in the existence of Israel. Thus, the case for an American policy focus on traditional Arab elites is much strengthened. The mid-1957 policy therefore conforms nicely to both of these objectives, if the assumption is made that traditional elite-based regimes can be made stable.

With this focus, the case against a unilateral American guarantee for Israel's independence emerges as a strong one. Such a guarantee would multiply American involvement in a dispute over which the United States can exercise little control. The danger in such a guarantee is that the dictates of the local conflict could so control behavior in the area as to produce an inadvertent great-power confrontation. In fact, the basis of this general policy thrust is to gain greater control over forces that could inadvertently trigger nuclear conflict.

In the third division, where the concern is to satisfy "the economic and other internationally relevant demands of the American people," a number of major policy lines and related specific policies could be seen to apply. However, under closer scrutiny, only two are of vital importance: 3.a, "Encourage, support, and protect American investments abroad," and 4, "Give diplomatic support and assistance to people for whom there is special concern." This conclusion implies that only two major American pressure groups are involved, economic and ethnic. The economic objective is to gain and protect American investments, particularly in oil. The ethnic objective is to satisfy the demands of American Zionists for support of the independence and well-being of Israel. Eliminated as inconsequential are ideological pressure groups such as Americans for Democratic Action, which generally favor support for Israel but are ineffective in pressing for such support, and the Arab-American ethnic group.[15] The latter, though at least a million strong, is remarkable for its lack of interest or activity on behalf of the Arab world in the conflict with Israel.

The two vital pressure groups could easily be rivals, but much of the attractiveness of the 1957 crystallizing of policy focus on conservative Arab regimes was that both pressure groups were pleased. Israel had little to fear from traditional Arabs as long as words do not hurt, for traditional elite opposition to Israel remained on the rhetorical level. At the same time, these Arab regimes were quite willing to provide a comfortable climate for American investments, especially oil. Popular regimes, on the other hand, were more serious in their proclamations against Israel and far less willing to accommodate to the interests of American investors. Nationalization, in fact, was an omnipresent threat.

What this adds up to, therefore, is a contention that the mid-1957 focus on support for conservative regimes reflected a neat balancing of all the major policies relevant to the Middle East. Of course, policy formulators did not recognize this congruence. But a basic claim in this study is that perceptual accommodation to diverse demands is a subtle process and one of which those accommodating are hardly aware. The major point to be resolved was whether traditional elite-based Arab regimes could be made stable; and although there were proponents on both sides of this question, the debate was not resolved on the basis of the case either side presented. Rather, as American involvement in the area became more intense and appeared increasingly to concern a core area of the Cold War confrontation, policy in tune with the enemy and imperial images crystallized. Neutral-minded regimes were soon seen as favorable to the monolithic enemy, and anticommunist Arab regimes and Israel were seen in the favorable stance granted close allies in an intense conflict. Therefore, the policy of isolating and overturning Nasser and his allies came to appear central to American security interests.

This description provides a base within which the abortive CIA-backed coup against the Kuwatli regime in Syria, outlined above, must be seen. In this context, it is understandable that the Eisenhower administration responded so vigorously to this failure that the Soviets threatened explicitly to counter American intervention. This description also provides a base for viewing American military intervention in Lebanon's civil war—surely one of the most bizarre acts of American diplomacy in a generation.

I contend that by 1970 general strategy change was well under way in American foreign policy aims. The presumed cause of this change was a marked decline in perception of threat from the Soviet Union which in turn reflected a long series of Soviet responses not at all in tune with expectations based on an enemy image. But this perceptual alteration was reflected in policy far more than in official verbalizations of Soviet motivation. Thus, a verbal construct of a highly aggressive Soviet foreign policy can be juxtaposed against a policy which would appear to be designed to deal with a conservative and only sluggishly aggressive antagonist. This pattern appears to be common enough to suggest a general proposition: In perceptual alteration, verbal alteration will lag behind policy alteration. The length of the time lag depends on historical experience and value congruence support for the previously prevailing perception. In this case, the historical experience was long and intense, and the negative perception of the Soviet Union and international communism was highly congruent with prevailing American values.[16]

In the following chapter this overall scheme will be applied to American policy in Vietnam at the time of Johnson's March 31, 1968, decision to reduce sharply the area of bombing in North Vietnam. The contention will be that communist failure to respond as expected did ultimately lead to a major alteration in prevailing world perception and therefore to a general strategy change reflected in the entire system of foreign policy aims. By 1970, general policy aims alteration had occurred extensively but unevenly. The area of least change appears on the surface to have been American policy in the Middle East. The specific objective of this section, therefore, is to describe the system of general policy aims as it applies to the Middle East and to advance some tentative explanatory propositions for the lack of change. The general objective is to illustrate the utility of the scheme when comparing two systems of foreign policy aims of the same polity which existed at two different moments.

Using the outline of American foreign policy aims for the mid–Cold War as a check list, it is easy to point to change in American policy in the Middle East. This is particularly true of items in the containment division. Take first A.1, "Deter militarily the primary enemies and their satellites" and A.1.c, "Establish and develop military alliances on the communist periphery," which was presumed earlier to describe American policy in the Middle East in 1957. The evidence is overwhelming of growing American disinterest in this objective. The United States acquiesced in the departure of the Baghdad government from the Baghdad Pact. The truncated pact, the Central Treaty Organization (CENTO), was allowed to evolve into more of a regional economic development alliance. Improving Soviet relations with CENTO members evoked no surface evidence of American concern, and there was no real effort to expand CENTO's membership.

Moving to A.5, "Work for noncommunist stability in developing states," the six specific policy lines under that major policy line can be used to compare policy in 1970 with that of the mid–Cold War. In each case—economic and technical assistance, multilateral aid, encouragement of American investment, military assistance, psychological warfare activity, and overt and covert domestic policy intervention—there has been a sharp decline. Arabs, frequently the target of CIA intervention, are most unlikely to admit the point, but the decline in number of both official and nonofficial Americans in the Arab states strongly suggested a decline in American capability to intervene.

The case for the contention of general strategy change is far less self-evident in the next division. But here, too, a strong case can be constructed for the contention that American interest in stabilizing the Arab-Israeli conflict as a potential trigger of nuclear confrontation had declined. The active use of the hot line in the June war and the subsequent Glassboro Conference reflected both a determination that the conflict not become a Soviet-American conflict and a perception (not verbalization!) that the Soviets shared that determination. American policy after the June war was, under President Johnson, desultory. It followed Israel's diplomatic lead and responded sluggishly to President de Gaulle's efforts to give life to a Big Four endeavor. Under President Nixon there was for a time more independence; and the so-called Rogers Plan, though highly generalized, did concern itself with Israeli security needs and an Arab need to regain some national self-respect. Furthermore, Soviet acquiescence in the Rogers plan was out of tune with verbalizations within the Nixon administration of Soviet aggressive intent in the area. Still, only when the local conflict, mainly on its own momentum, moved in 1970 and much more seriously in 1973 toward a crisis which could result in an unwanted East-West confrontation was diplomatic activity really energetic.

This picture, much too briefly developed, is congruent with the contention that change in the "Avoid thermonuclear war" division is manifest in the form of a more energetic concern with attacking the potential of technical failure resulting in accidental war and with arms control than with stabilizing accidental war areas. As trust begins to develop, fear of overreaction in the accidental war areas declines, as does the bargaining position of local combatants with the great powers.

However in the third division—C. "Satisfy the economic and other internationally relevant demands of the American people"—two major changes occurred between 1957 and 1970. First, the perception of threat to Israel on the part of those Americans who identify to any significant extent with that country had multiplied in intensity. Second, the possibility that conservative Arab regimes (in whose countries American oil interests by and large are located) would continue to furnish a comfortable environment for those interests was being steadily reduced. Anger at American support for Israel persuaded more and more Arabs that Americans should not have the luxury of huge profits from Arab oil while ignoring the political demands of the Arab people. Thus, pressure was increased on American oil interests to use whatever influence they had to alter American policy.

A perception of threat for American Zionists thus not only persisted but intensified. As the close ally of those basically responsible for the threat, the Soviet Union was commonly perceived in its Middle East policy in classic Cold War terms. It was fairly common for Zionists to compartmentalize the Soviet image, although increasingly they adopted the hostile image for Soviet behavior in all parts of the world. An untested hypothesis here would be that the ability to compartmentalize varies inversely with intensity of identification with Israel and with conservative political attitudes.

American policy under the Nixon administration, which was heralded before the inauguration as likely to be more "evenhanded" in the Arab-Israeli dispute, was at first viewed by Zionists with suspicion. The above description of an inexorable movement toward withdrawal and decreasing interest in the area, if valid, would naturally be classified as appeasement by those who perceive aggressive imperialism. Proponents of "evenhandedness" within the bureaucracy and among economic interests that would be adversely affected by a more vigorous pro-Israeli policy were naturally seen as hostile, even anti-Semitic. Jews holding such a position were likely to be thought of as traitors.

The response of the economic interest groups, including oil, to the dilemma they faced from angry Arabs on the one side and angry American Zionists on the other, must remain in the area of conjecture. The great advantage of the Zionist ethnic pressure group lies in its perceived ability to influence the outcome of elections in several important states. Senators and congressmen dutifully signed whatever pro-Israeli petition they were offered. Given the quiescence of the Arab-American ethnic pressure group, the only potentially countervailing force within the general public was in the Black community. Among militant Blacks, there was indeed a strong preference for the Arabs. But the behavior of Black politicians, such as ex-Mayor Carl Stokes of Cleveland, suggests that this view was not at all widely held within the Black community.[17] It is unlikely that affected economic groups, particularly oil, could have mustered comparable public support for their interests.

Therefore, the oil lobby needed to pursue its aims through quiet contacts with friendly political leaders and with key members of the bureaucracy. Since data on these contacts are unlikely ever to be available in a form that permits careful assessment, the impact of these contacts must be inferred. Obviously the inference of those whose perception of Soviet and Arab behavior approaches the pure enemy image will be strikingly different from the inference of those whose perceptions are closer to the complex image. There has been since October 1973 much evidence that the oil lobby is indeed seeking to alter American policy.[18] The detached analyst must therefore refer to both verbal behavior and policies adopted by the Nixon and Ford administrations to infer the relative influence of the economic interests in the situational decisional unit.

If the above schematically based description is valid, there is a striking irony in the efforts of proponents of more vigorous support of Israel to convince the American administrations of their situational view. As proposed above, there is a significant time lag between policy behavioral alteration that reflects real perceptual change and verbal behavioral alteration. The verbal behavior of the Nixon administration was not sharply different from that of the Israeli leaders and their American supporters. In other words, the administration might well have responded favorably to the symbol manipulation of pro-Israeli lobbyists. And if the latter ever succeed in reestablishing a perception of threat from the Soviet Union which approaches in intensity that of the 1950s, then the Cold War system of aims could be expected once again to describe American policy.

But the general strategy change occurring in the early 1970s was a consequence of a declining perception of threat, so that defense bureaucrats and the defense industry could no longer claim a resource allocation at the previous level. This in turn was reflected in a relative increase in Zionist influence on an American foreign policy which, up to October 1973, was of declining interest to the American people. Policy manifestations of this change included declining pressures on the Israeli government to settle the dispute.

Were this trend reversed and a general strategy change to occur in the opposite direction, that is, one in which the foreign and defense decision makers would be able to claim a higher priority in resource allocation, the bureaucratic foes of support for Israel would be given a greater voice. This would be especially true given the greatly enhanced bargaining position of economic pressure groups, mainly oil, as a result of the energy crisis. This would renew strong interest in creating stable, noncommunist regimes in the Arab world, since that area is of the utmost strategic significance. Once again Israel would appear as a force for instability to those whose role interests are directed toward the goal of Arab stability, that is, the concerned defense and foreign policy bureaucracies. Because Arab hostility to Israel has increased dramatically since 1967, it is unlikely that the formula of achieving all major system aims by supporting conservative Arab regimes is possible any longer. Consequently, in its revitalized efforts to contain the perceived Soviet threat, the bureaucracy would probably respond by turning away from support of Israel. The impact of such a shift on those who identify intensely with both the United States and Israel would certainly be destructive and probably anomie-creating.

If, on the other hand, efforts to bring peace to the area are successful, the impact on the system of aims should reinforce the direction of change. The Rogers cease-fire proposal, though certainly not by design, was a test of perceptions of the Soviet threat. Those favoring it perceived a Soviet Union interested in the status-quo objectives of stability in the area. Those opposing it generally perceived an aggressive, imperialist Soviet Union which would utilize the negotiation to its advantage. Acceptance of the peace plan by the Soviet Union coincided with the expectations of the former group; but violation of the cease-fire coincided with the expectations of the latter group. Soviet behavior in the Jordanian crisis once again confirmed the expectations of those who see a Soviet interest in stability.[19]

The Arab-Israeli war of October 1973 severely strained the credibility of the view that the Soviet Union was pursuing a status-quo policy in the Middle East. This was most clearly demonstrated when President Nixon placed American armed forces on nuclear alert on October 25, 1973. But Soviet support and encouragement of subsequent peace efforts helped restore some of the lost credibility. Since the Middle East is the situational area in which the enemy image most prevails, a conclusion that Soviet policy favors peace and stability in the Middle East could bring a rapid acceleration in the general strategy alteration of the system of aims away from that which prevailed in the mid-1950s.

As described above, the impact of the Arab-Israeli conflict on the American foreign policy system of aims is almost diametrically opposed to the impact of the Indochina conflict, as will be described in the following chapter. That is, the Indochina conflict tended to reduce the perception of threat in the prevailing view, whereas the Arab-Israeli conflict tended to work against such an alteration.

The entire scheme will be developed in a far less impressionistic manner in part II of this book, using the British in Egypt as a case study. Since the last major episode in that drama occurred in 1956, fairly extensive historical evidence can be examined. British involvement in Egypt was lengthy, and therefore strikingly different phases of imperialism can be compared and explanatory propositions advanced.

But I would like to stress here as I did in the introduction that my primary interest is to construct a frame for viewing contemporary international conflict. To what extent is the conflict a result of real value conflict, and to what extent is it a result of perceptually based misunderstanding? For example, both Arabs and Israelis value Jerusalem and its holy places with inordinate intensity. But the overall view of Arab motivations held by Israelis and the overall view of Israel as an integral part of capitalist imperialism held by Arabs prevent a focus on very real value conflict. An intention of this scheme is to explore motivations to determine the extent to which a conflict is more value-based or perception-based.

In both the Arab-Israeli and the Vietnam cases considered here, the conclusion is that a perception of threat flowing from assumptions regarding Soviet foreign policy motivation is a root factor. Had I looked at the same two cases using a Soviet foreign policy aims system, it is entirely conceivable that I would have concluded that the root factor in explaining Soviet behavior in each is perception of threat flowing from assumptions regarding American foreign policy aims. This conclusion is strongly argued by William Gamson and André Modigliani.[20]

If this proved to be the case, the prescriptive implications would be obvious—a case of nothing to fear but fear. Prescription simply calls for the elimination of the basis of perceptual misunderstanding. Can this be anything more than a pious wish? Certainly it cannot if the problem is understated. The perceptual base of an intense conflict can be reinforcing. Furthermore, anyone appearing to disagree with the prevailing view runs the risk of being cast outside the arena of even marginal effectiveness. Added to this is the uncertainty of the findings of such a scheme. There is a basic pessimism throughout this discussion concerning what is called hard data. The most important aspects of the scheme are inferred by juxtaposing verbal and policy behavior. The resulting inexactitude makes every conclusion little more than systematized conjecture.

The one concept in this scheme that offers real prescriptive promise is that of expectations and their realization or nonrealization. I have described at some length the process by which expectational nonrealization can affect a prevailing situational view and a prevailing world view. I have also suggested that explanatory propositions based on the ordering of a government's foreign policy aims can be tested by stating expectations in the form of hypotheses. Given a real, specific decision, what outcome is expected? The scholar who wishes to explore the validity of his own conjecturing can thus make his expectations into hypotheses and the response to policies on which these expectations are based into his "proof." In the unlikely event that his expectations are exactly realized, he will not have proved his case, but he will have supported it. More likely, his hypotheses will have proved faulty to some degree and the assumptions behind them will have to be reexplored.

As the one dynamic aspect of this scheme, expectations can therefore be used to refine analysis. But expectations can also be used far more systematically in active diplomacy. The diplomatic probe used throughout man's history is in fact a use of expectations by policy makers much as has been suggested above for scholars.[21] But expectations can be a focus of strategy as well, with the object of correcting the misunderstandings of other governments and peoples. If, for example, we conclude that the Soviet Union does not perceive the seriousness of American interest in a resolution of Arab-Israeli conflict, a strategy designed to alter perceptions would be called for.[22] Soviet policy and Soviet official statements should suggest the Soviet situational view and Soviet expectations of American policy behavior. Policies that do not conform to these expectations but would be appropriate for an America interested in settling the dispute could thus produce an unsettling effect on the Soviet situational view and eventual alteration in a desired perceptual direction.

Likewise, for scholars interested in suggesting alternative policies that might result in peaceful conflict resolution, the expectation focus is promising. The following chapter, which looks at American policy toward Vietnam in early 1968, develops further the argument for the utility of this focus.

6 / *America in Vietnam*

On March 31, 1968, President Lyndon Johnson made one of history's most dramatic speeches. He announced on that day his determination to test the willingness of the communist world to begin to negotiate peace in Vietnam. He drastically reduced the area of North Vietnam that would be bombed and called for formal discussions among the combatants. To underline the seriousness of his intent, he announced that he would not run for reelection. President Johnson had proclaimed on many occasions his deep interest in building a broad consensus among the American people, but the tragic irony of his administration was that as it neared an end an atmosphere of bitter division prevailed. That Lyndon Johnson hoped and believed his speech would help end this division is hardly to be doubted. That he expected a favorable response from the Communists is subject to every doubt.

In the weeks prior to his speech, President Johnson's foreign policy critics, led by Eugene McCarthy, had come to believe that a cessation of bombing of North Vietnam might well lead to peace talks. United Nations Secretary General U Thant was of that opinion.[1] But within the Johnson administration there had been a most vigorous rejection of that conclusion. U Thant's expectations therefore amounted to a sharply challenged hypothesis. For those followers of Eugene McCarthy and Robert Kennedy who saw the Vietnam conflict as a civil war with massive American intervention, the likelihood of negotiations was great. For administration supporters who saw American involvement as deterring international communist aggression, the likelihood of negotiations for anything other than American surrender was negligible. Townsend Hoopes, who served in the Johnson administration, has written that Johnson fully expected his overture to be rejected.[2] With that rejection, he could legitimately reason, would come a realization that McCarthy, Kennedy, and their followers had seriously misjudged the foe, and their movement could be expected to dissipate.

The Johnson proposal therefore amounts to one of the most spectacular tests of a foreign policy hypothesis in diplomatic history. Had an unequivocal rejection followed, those who argued that the Vietnam conflict was in essence a civil war and not a test of the West's ability and willingness to contain a major challenge issued by international communism would have had difficulty defending their reality view. Their one out lay in Johnson's unwillingness to halt the bombing altogether. But even with only a limited bombing halt, Hanoi's response was close to the expectations of those who perceived a civil conflict.

After Hanoi's acceptance, the date March 31, 1968, looked as if it would go down in history books as one of those magic dates which signify the end of one era and the beginning of another. Two years later, however, President Richard Nixon announced a limited intervention in Cambodia, and two years after that a resumption of bombing. For many Americans the date of Johnson's speech had lost its significance and had become no more than a minor, temporary retreat from a burgeoning American imperialism. The contention here is that the original estimate was correct and that the Johnson decision had allowed what had been an important but still counterpoint theme to become the main theme. Furthermore, I contend that the perceptual alteration which followed had reinforced and given great impetus to a general strategy change in the American foreign policy aims system. This contention will be developed in the pages that follow.

In the foreign policy aims system outlined on pages 121–23, American policy in South Vietnam following the Geneva Agreements is defined in two categories. A.5, "Work for noncommunist stability in developing states," clearly applies. Also applicable is B.3.a, "Stabilize states divided as a result of the Cold War." Within months after the division of Vietnam, it became apparent that the noncommunist South Vietnam regime would, with American support, refuse to take steps that could lead to Vietnamese reunification under a communist regime. This behavior was fully in tune with that of the other divided states, Germany, Korea, and China. World polarization then was far too bitter to allow for a resolution in any of these cases which would appear to be a victory for either side. Unwilling to risk defeat and yet fearful of a local conflict which could escalate into thermonuclear war, the great powers at either pole sought to maintain sufficient control of the situation to prevent local responses from threatening the delicate balance. Indeed, Korea stood as mute evidence of the great dangers of losing control. Only a decline in the intensity of overall conflict gave promise of a more permanent solution. American behavior, therefore, was in full conformity with the Cold War system of aims.

Also in harmony with Cold War behavior was the interpretation of the Soviet announcement at the Twenty-Second Party Congress that "wars of national liberation" would be supported.[3] Whatever the Soviet leaders intended to say, it is clear how their statement was translated after passing through American Cold War perceptual filters. It read in effect "expand Soviet influence through contrived indigenous insurrection." This fits well with expectations based on an image of rationality, monolithic quality, and aggressive intent. Therefore, when insurrection in South Vietnam began to become serious, Americans were not at all likely to look to local conditions for the real explanation. Instead, the assumption that Moscow and/or Peking was furnishing direction and planning even on the tactical level was not likely to be questioned. At that point the response that flows from the Cold War aims system would clearly be A.1.b, "Communicate the impression that expansion utilizing . . . encouraged insurgency . . . would be too expensive." The critical point was reached under the Kennedy administration, and the response was as would be expected—an increase in material support and a much expanded military technical aid program.

Five years earlier, this response would probably have gone unnoticed by the American public, but by the early 1960s many unexpected events had occurred. Polycentrism in the communist world and, even more dramatically, the Sino-Soviet dispute belied a monolithic decisional image for the entire bloc. Soviet policy had been so inconsistent and so unsuccessful that its rationality was hard to defend.[4] Furthermore, although rhetoric still described ineluctable aggressiveness of intent, Soviet behavior and Chinese behavior as well seemed no more than sluggishly aggressive. Highly vulnerable areas, such as Iran, Afghanistan, and the Indian peninsula, remained outside the communist world even though the American ability to protect them was subject to grave questioning. Furthermore, the spectacular Soviet avoidance of confrontation in Cuba in 1962 and the almost instantaneous reduction of tensions in Berlin following the Cuba crisis were hardly in tune with the aggressive image. Of the enemy image, only the expectations based on the paper tiger component were being realized.

Although there was no direct challenge to the enemy image, perception of threat was beginning to decline in intensity. As it did so for increasing numbers of Americans the Soviet image began to move along the line from the enemy toward the complex position. As always, verbalizations lagged, but the prevailing world view showed signs of beginning to change. Obviously many of those included in the general decisional unit, for vested-interest or ideological reasons, did not alter their perceptions.[5] Others, especially those with a Hobson-Lenin view of imperialism, moved so far as to perceive the focus of imperialism as lying in Washington rather than in Moscow.[6] Manifestations of perceptual alteration could be seen in renewed tolerance of descriptions by scholars of a highly diverse Soviet governmental elite and of an incrementalist decisional process. Even more significant was the stance of President Kennedy, who though clearly still a cold warrior, frequently showed accommodationist inclinations. There had been a major change from the Dulles days.

Within the Vietnamese situational area, however, there was little reflection of this altered prevailing world view. Prior to 1964, the situational decisional unit included virtually no public elements. There was little economic interest group concern or ethnic interest group involvement, and ideological interest groups had not focused on this area. The decisional unit, therefore, was almost exclusively bureaucratic. That is not to say that it was monolithic. Only a few months after Kennedy's decision to send advisers to Vietnam, bureaucratic disagreement was so open as to overflow into the American press.[7] But the prevailing situational view, the one most congruent with specific policy, reflected the perceptions of those bureaucrats with a Cold War perceptual syndrome so rigid as to approach the enemy ideal typical image outlined above.

What this argues is that in the early 1960s an incongruence existed between the prevailing world view and the prevailing Vietnamese situational view. The incongruence was parallel to but less extreme than the existing between the prevailing world view and the Middle East situational view in 1970 as described in the previous chapter. The difference was that perception of threat, which was the major determinant of the prevailing world view, was much more intense in 1960 than in 1970. As in the Middle East case, this perceptual incongruence was strikingly persistent and for the same two reasons. First, verbalizations continued to follow the Cold War form and thus helped blur the incongruence. Second, the discussion here also focused on specifics of policy and almost never on the basic assumptions on which that policy was based. Prior to 1964, even future opponents of America's role in Vietnam, such as Hans Morgenthau and William Fulbright, accepted the prevailing situational view and policies based on it. Nevertheless, as the situation became increasingly grave, visibility increased and with it serious public concern. The situational decisional unit lost its exclusively bureaucratic character, and inevitably the prevailing situational view was to be challenged. That challenge, however, was slow in coming and was never made directly.

By the summer of 1964 the Vietnamese situation had deteriorated to such an extent that a major decision regarding the level of American involvement was unavoidable. Understandably, the Johnson administration, which had carefully nurtured an image of strength plus moderation in dealing with the communist foe, would not if it could possibly avoid doing so in the months prior to a presidential election make a decision which could shatter that image. Yet it is clear in retrospect that, unbeknownst to the public, one of the gravest decisions in American history had been made. Furthermore, the Tonkin Gulf episode, which occurred prior to the election, clearly forecast the dimensions of that decision.[8] As Senator Fulbright's sponsorship of the Tonkin Gulf Resolution in the Senate indicates, however, many future opponents of that decision were unable to perceive what was so "clearly" forecast.

The dilemma can be simply stated. The international estimate on which the Johnson administration based its decision was that the South Vietnamese were facing defeat that could only be avoided by very substantial American involvement. Given the prevailing situational view, a decision to intervene massively was inevitable. Otherwise the essence of deterrence policy—credibility for the expressed American determination to prevent the expansion of international communism, in this case through encouraged insurgency—would be lost. The form that intervention would take, however, was by no means predetermined.

In the introduction to this study I made the point that one section of American academia during the Cold War era was preeminently "relevant," if that word is to have any meaning. These were the bargaining theorists at both universities and great semipublic research institutes such as the Rand Corporation. President Kennedy and even more so his secretary of defense, Robert McNamara, were predisposed to turn to technology and advanced theory in their conduct of American defense policies. There emerged from this predisposition a symbiotic relationship with a highly talented group of men who did their theorizing in defense strategy.[9] Possibly most interesting of these men was Herman Kahn, whose tendency to think about the unthinkable had already horrified more romantically inclined scholars.[10] The deterrence strategy that evolved from this association came to be called the McNamara doctrine.[11] It amounted to a sophisticated bargaining scheme designed to meet contingencies on a wide variety of conflict levels. But behind it stood a motivational assumptional base that was virtually the enemy ideal typical image. It was to deter the enemy, not change him. The possibility that a particular policy might reinforce the power position of "enemy" leaders who believed in accommodation was not seriously faced, because the assumption of a decisional monolith was too firmly held. In his *Strategy of Conflict,* Thomas Schelling asserted the existence of mixed motives, but he only rarely remembered that point as it related to broad political values when he wrote his substantive work on policy, *Arms and Influence.* Mixed motives were given expression on the tactical level only.

Because of the great influence of these intellectual military bureaucrats out of uniform, the decision of 1964 was not to be a traditional military one. A more conventional approach would have called for American armed forces in South Vietnam to confront the communist forces directly. Then if the situation became increasingly grave, interdicting enemy supplies at the most critical point, the port of Haiphong, through aerial bombardment and marine blockade would be a reasonable policy. The decision instead was to supplement direct American participation in South Vietnam with a sophisticated bargaining strategy which fits well Schelling's *post facto* term, "graduated compellence."[12] The "enemy" was informed through numerous (and unfortunately, since most policy makers did not play the game, contradictory) signals that he could have peace and a Korea-style settlement if he would come to the negotiating table. If he did not, he would be punished. The punishment in this case would take the form of saturation bombings of supply lines in the southern part of North Vietnam. However, signals told him that a failure to comply would be followed by expansion of the zone in which he would be punished. Once the entire country was being bombed, presumably the punishment would cross a threshold into a different and even more expensive form.

Such a strategy had serious theoretical weaknesses. First, it assumed far more decisional control than exists within any bureaucracy. State Department officers concerned with American policy toward Asian neutrals and traditional military leaders could hardly be expected to harmonize their verbal behavior in such a way that signaling would be clear. The basic premise that such disciplined orchestration of the foreign policy community was possible was obviously too sanguine.

However, the core of the problem was not here, but in the perceptual base of the strategy. If the enemy image is accepted, the strategy makes a good deal of sense. A monolithic, highly rational foe will make a simple cost analysis and conclude that this particular tactic is excessively expensive and must be abandoned. He therefore will order his North Vietnamese puppet to acquiesce in the terms offered, and the focus of conflict will move elsewhere. In retrospect, what is truly breathtaking is the dimensions of the risk involved. To follow such a course of brinkmanship, those making the decision could not have entertained real doubts as to the validity of their perceptual premises.

If the same strategy is viewed through the eyes of those who had surrendered much of the enemy image, the basis of the intense and bitter policy debate becomes clear. For them Soviet and Chinese leadership was diverse, policy process was more incremental, and fear and suspicion were factors determining communist policy response. Furthermore, the communist world was equally diversified, and the term "satellite" applied to North Vietnam was a misnomer. The Vietnamese conflict was perceived as in essence a civil conflict complicated by great-power interference.

With this perceptual filter, graduated compellence raises serious, even terrifying questions. Would not the unintentional results of such bombing be to strengthen suspicions, reinforce the most hostile communist leaders, and grant to the North Vietnamese government the benefit of nationalist outrage at the foreign-inflicted destruction? If so, the bombings would produce exactly the opposite results of those intended. Ironically, indeed, they could become a self-fulfilling prophecy producing the very hostile and aggressive foe that had been perceived. In that case, the implicit cost analysis assumption would apply, but since the "enemy" would see itself under siege with its very survival in question, the level of enemy cost tolerance would be so great that punishment would have to be inflicted on the great-power heartlands. This risks civilization itself.

Happily, expectations based on this latter perception were no more to be realized than were those based on the former.

As soon as the full dimensions of Johnson's 1964 decision became apparent, manifestations of the incongruence of a rapidly altering world view and an unchanging prevailing situational view appeared. Even under John Foster Dulles, policies had evolved that were more in tune with a sluggishly aggressive and diversified view of communism than with the highly aggressive monolith. These are noted in the foreign policy aims scheme in A.2 and A.3, "Encourage the liberalization trends of communist states" and "Encourage tendencies toward autonomy in satellite states." This suggests that as early as the late 1950s a general strategy change was beginning to occur. "Containment" was a little less descriptive of the sum of specific policies relating to the Soviet Union. "Coexistence," a

Soviet term, was used more often, and a few people were ready to agree with George Kennan that "disengagement" would be an even more appropriate umbrella strategy. Furthermore, in many parts of the world, both Lyndon Johnson and Dean Rusk acted on this altered image. Strangely, in fact, Dean Rusk appeared to view the Middle East in this sense. Encouraging the liberalization trends of communist states implies a recognition of diversity within the decisional structure and advocates strengthening the position of Soviet and Chinese leaders whose focus is more on internal consumption than on external adventure. Such leaders should by role interest be predisposed to see a United States that can be lived with, a United States that is not intransigently hostile and aggressive. But a graduated compellence strategy has an entirely different assumptional base: Convince an aggressive, monolithic, and rational leadership that the costs of incursions in South Vietnam are oppressively high and the prospects of victory low, and such leadership will agree to cut its losses. Given the assumption, the case is neat and convincing. But a graduated compellence strategy applied against a government, some of whose leaders perceive the United States to be highly aggressive and others of whom perceive the United States to be inclined toward the status quo, is likely to reinforce the position of the hard-liners, for it would be their expectations that would be realized.

My contention, therefore, is that the prevailing situational view in Vietnam in 1964, very much out of tune with a rapidly evolving prevailing world view, created a foreign policy aims system disturbance of universal importance. Its impact, like that of the Middle East situation, was to reverse the developing trend away from general perception of threat and hence from the enemy image of the communist states. But there could be no return to the status quo ante. For example, in the days of the Cold War aims system, America's European allies had perceived the communist threat similarly to prevailing American perception. By the 1960s, however, this was no longer true of the French government and less true of the British and West Germans. General DeGaulle in particular made clear his fundamental disagreement with American hostile perceptions. Demands for dissociation from the United States were severe enough in Europe that none of the allied governments gave any serious support to the United States in Vietnam. Furthermore, such basic general policy lines as A.1.c, "Establish and develop military alliances on the communist periphery," and A.4, "Work for the economic stability and the economic, military, and political integration of developed noncommunist states," were placed in serious jeopardy. "Go it alone" slogans, appearing among those in the United States for whom the communist threat was most real, reflected this extraordinary change.[13] As prevailing world view began to inch back toward the enemy pole, general policy lines everywhere were affected. Weakening of the alliance with Western European states was only one example of this adjustment.

With regard to policy toward the so-called developing world, there was a move back in the direction of the Dulles period when "stability" came to mean conservative regimes that deal with social and economic reform in a measured and controlled manner. Among more revolutionary states, suspicion of American motives was significantly heightened.

Furthermore, this trend reversal could not occur smoothly so long as basic perceptions among Americans of Soviet, Chinese, and North Vietnamese motivations varied so sharply. As American policy in Vietnam was suddenly catapulted into a position as the primary foreign policy issue, major sections of the American attentive public became deeply involved for the first time. In terms of this scheme, they now became part of the situational decision unit. But the public role in the formulation of American policy in Vietnam was sharply different from the case of the Middle East, where two interest groups with great influence in the decisional process had deep and specific interests in policy. There were no American interest groups concerned with Vietnam parallel to the Zionists and the oil interests.

Revisionist writers tend to see as self-evident a conclusion that a conflict which produced government contracts for most of America's great corporations would be supported by if not created by those corporations. My view is different. I see no evidence of early interest, to say nothing of support, for Johnson's Vietnam policy on the part of corporate executives. Once government contracts became numerous, however, those with a vested interest in that policy supported it. This was even more apparent among academics with such contracts than among corporation executives. But evidence of a common view in the business community is no more forthcoming than evidence of a common view in the academic community.

The reader will recall that the final division of foreign policy aims in the system-of-aims scheme is reserved for those aims which flow from secondary, tertiary, or even less intense concerns in the motivational system. These are placed under the rubric here of "Satisfy the economic and other internationally relevant demands of the American people." As the Vietnam crisis deepened, most of the aims listed in this division began to apply.

Item C.1 refers to foreign policy and defense bureaucratic interests; C.2 refers to military bureaucratic interests; and C.3 refers to economic vested interests. The Vietnam crisis led to an expansion in all three areas and hence generated industrial and bureaucratic interest. As the earlier discussion of the corporate community indicates, this vested-interest involvement was derived from the conflict rather than generative of it. Once the conflict expanded and led to the creation of new jobs and contracts, however, vested-interest support followed for its perpetuation, and even its expansion. This was not, of course, a conscious advocacy. Rather, individuals in this category were predisposed by their roles to see the situation in such a way that their material interests would be satisfied.[14]

Item C.4 refers to ethnic interest support and is not relevant here.

Item C.5 is relevant. It is "Encourage democracy, support independence, and advance the welfare of other peoples." There is general agreement among foreign policy analysts that, in the era of mass politics, publics determine the boundaries of policy and the general decisional latitude of those who make policy. This scheme reflects that conclusion as well. But a disinterested public role in specific decision-making is not often described. Interested publics, such as those with professional, economic, or ethnic interests, are seen and their role described.

In the Vietnam case, a disinterested public role was manifest, and ideological differences were important. Presumably, virtually all Americans would agree with the symbolically phrased objective, "Encourage democracy, support independence, and advance the welfare of other peoples." But would this objective be best satisfied by support for the various South Vietnam regimes or by support for the National Liberation Front? The ideological projection theory outlined earlier would suggest that the answer depends on the individual's position in the American political spectrum. Taking two prototypical individuals, a liberal left American and a conservative right American, very different interpretations should be expected. The conservative would be expected to construct a benign picture of the Saigon government but a hostile picture of the NLF. The liberal would be more likely to see the NLF as it claims to be —that is, as a broad-based nationalist alliance which favors socialism, democracy, and neutralism—while the Saigon regime would be judged very harshly.

Similarly, the differential in perception of North Vietnam was predictably great. Those whose world view was one of declining threat—and the liberal would be presumed to be more predisposed in this direction—would have a perception of the Vietnamese Communists that would accept diversity and assume decisional incrementalism. Thus, such an individual would be far more willing to consider favorably the view that the North Vietnamese and Viet Cong were indigenous nationalist Communists fighting a civil war. On the other hand, an individual whose world view continued to parallel that most common in America in the Stalin-Zhdanov period of Soviet foreign policy—and the conservative would be predisposed to such a view—would reject that picture and instead assume North Vietnam and the Viet Cong to be agents of international communism testing the American will to resist. These two individuals could be expected to have equally contradictory views of the importance to the United States of the Saigon regime. The liberal would see a South Vietnam of no critical security importance to the United States and would therefore accept the complex image, rather than an allied or imperial image. The conservative, viewing the Saigon regime as important to American security, would perceptually accommodate the Saigon leaders to a Western democratic model. The liberal would be certain to have a far more critical view.

Debate between two such prototypical individuals would likely be as bitter and inconclusive as was the actual debate. The individual who perceived little threat would be inclined to see American policy as morally untenable. His opponent would see opposition to American policy as suggestive of treason. The participants in the debate might agree on the desirability of a democratic regime in Vietnam, but their own ideological lenses would focus on fundamentally different interpretations of what constitutes a democratic regime.

C.6, "Ensure that the prestige and dignity of the United States are at all times protected," also applies and seriously complicates the above picture. Even by 1964 and increasingly in the following four years, many Americans perceived that the United States, history's most powerful nation, was being humiliated in Vietnam. In spite of overwhelming manpower and equipment superiority, the United States and its ally were not winning the war. For individuals who identified intensely with the American nation, liberals as well as conservatives, a different but still serious perception of threat was developing, this time more to national dignity than to the preservation of independence and way of life. The perceptual accommodation of this factor opposed the trend toward a declining threat perception. It added to the inclination of those whose perception of threat remained intense to judge those who criticized American policy as flirting with treason. Since identity attachments do not correlate in a one-to-one fashion with "conservative" or "liberal" ideological postures, responses varied sharply among both conservatives and liberals. It appears on the surface to be likely that liberals would be less upset by perceived national humiliation than conservatives; certainly the peace movement elite was heavily liberal and left.[15] But this may be a function of ideological projection rather than an indication that the left is less nationalistic. Before and during World War II it was a conservative elite which appeared less sensitive to national affronts. In any case, the present offense to national dignity added to the bitterness of public opinion polarization on this issue.

A third aspect of public response is indicated by C.7, "Advance the cause of world peace and avoid risking the loss of American lives in foreign conflict." This objective, too, tended to exacerbate rather than reduce public opinion differences. Those perceiving a declining world threat and hence seeing the Vietnam war as a civil conflict of little consequence to American security saw U.S. policy leading to increased communist belligerency and hence adding to international conflict. For those people, the loss of American life was senseless at best. Young men holding this view were frequently willing to accept jail terms or exile rather than participate in a policy which to them threatened world peace. For those persisting in a world view of intense threat to national survival and suffering with the view of a threat to American dignity, the cause of peace was seen to demand a policy of strong, unyielding resistance to this episode in international communist aggression. Furthermore, opposition to such policy was viewed as directly threatening the lives of American men, since it added to the enemy's sense of opportunity for victory.[16]

Politicians, of course, have a vested interest in being elected to office. Since they presumably have a well-developed sensitivity to public attitudes, they should be expected to accommodate their own situational perceptions to the demands of conducting a winning campaign. But given the ambiguities of the picture, there should be little surprise in the fact that no clear trends appeared among politicians regarding the Vietnam conflict in the early months of severe crisis. The public response factor was much too confused, a conclusion reflected in inconsistencies in opinion polls.[17]

It was in this setting that the new American graduated compellence policy began to take shape. Expectational differences were sharp, and few policies in modern history offer a better test of hypotheses implicit both in the administration's policies and in the opposition's critique.

Administration expectations were not realized. These were that the highly rational foe would understand that a continuation of his policy of staged insurgency would cost far more than he was prepared to pay and that he therefore would be willing to accept the 17th parallel as the permanent border between the two Vietnams. Likewise unrealized were the expectations of one section of the opponents of administration policy that more belligerent leadership would triumph in Moscow, Peking, and Hanoi. The bombing of North Vietnam indeed reinforced a nationalistic will to resist, as opponents expected. But neither the Soviet nor the Chinese leadership balance moved as substantially in the direction of those favoring confrontation as expected.[18] Even when the zone of bombing targets was extended to include the Hanoi-Haiphong area, neither the hopeful expectations of the administration nor the fearful expectations of some opponents were realized.

In a study of the Pittsburgh area peace movement elite in 1967, Arnold Miller found two sharply different perceptual and attitudinal patterns.[19] One slightly more numerous group tended to view the Vietnam conflict as just described. They saw a Soviet Union which was increasingly conservative and nonaggressive and a United States which was behaving in accordance with the passé Cold War image of a highly aggressive Soviet Union and China. The other group, however, perceived the United States as by far the more imperialist power in its motivations. Their picture of motivations tended to coincide with the Hobson-Lenin syndrome described in chapter 2. This group, therefore, had expectations of continued American aggression, Vietnamese nationalist resistance, and a sluggish Soviet and Chinese response. It was the expectations of this group that were most nearly realized in each particular.

With each American escalation, expectations were tested anew, and each time the same pattern emerged: a passive response from China and the Soviet Union, a fierce determination to resist from the North Vietnamese and the Viet Cong. The enemy image began to atrophy. This is strongly suggested by the administration's efforts to persuade the Soviet Union to pressure North Vietnam into going to the negotiating table. That would not be reasonable were the North Vietnamese simply a satellite power. Chinese rhetorical belligerence and policy passivity led inexorably toward a perception of weakness. References to the primary enemy as "Hanoi" rather than "international communism" or "Moscow" crept into administration statements and then became the most common enemy reference.[20]

Countering somewhat the impact of consistent expectational nonrealization was the perception that the domestic peace movement itself was a major factor in keeping the enemy from the negotiating table. Schelling makes the point that an essential bargaining device is what he calls commitment, or burning your bridges behind you.[21] In the graduated compellence tactic in North Vietnam, commitment depended on the enemy's belief that the U.S. investment of prestige in the tactic was too great to allow retreat. Any American leader who failed to follow through would surely be punished by an electorate furious at national humiliation. But given the existence of a strong peace movement, the entire basis of credibility was destroyed. Thus, failures in expectations could be blamed on the doves.

Another serious determining factor for administration officials was their extraordinary ego investment in the tactic applied against North Vietnam. The public charge against them was not simply that they were in error but rather that they were guilty of immoral, even criminal, behavior. Understandably, administration officials resisted a perceptual accommodation which would appear to give substance to such a charge. Consequently, the normal time-lag factor was seriously strengthened. Personnel changes, such as the replacement of Robert McNamara with Clark Clifford, therefore became vital to the administration's eventual partial accommodation. Clifford did not have any serious ego involvement in the prevailing situational view and found it rather easy to accommodate to the long series of expectational failures.

Nevertheless, the generally unexpected communist response to American escalation weakened seriously the prevailing world view of serious threat. A conservative Soviet Union, a weak China, and a North Vietnam suffering murderous punishment did not add up to an intensely threatening combination. The result was that both the image of South Vietnam and the image of the communist states moved toward the complex image for many Americans. As it became increasingly possible to look at the South Vietnamese regime in all its diversity, the argument that defense of such a regime was an ideological duty steadily lost force. That regime, once the allied-imperial perceptual filter was removed, was not seen to accord with the ideological model of men as liberal, democratic, and incorruptible as WOGs can be. Indeed, they were quite the opposite.

But administration leaders with an ego investment in the correctness of their situational assessment were not to be abandoned by the public en masse. On the contrary, the very diminution of the perception of threat from a great enemy resulted in an aggravated perception of American humiliation. This was a threat of a somewhat different variety, but a threat nonetheless to huge sections of the American public. How was it possible that the greatest power known to history could not defeat a power which, had it not been for this conflict, would have been relegated to a footnote in history?

What this suggests is that not only was the alteration in threat perception leading to a general strategy change, but there was a real possibility of general system change. In the American motivational system, defense was being downgraded, but bureaucratic vested interests, domestic personal power, and national grandeur were being sharply upgraded. Furthermore, the repeated demonstrations of communist weakness offered a great opportunity. The United States had failed to take the kind of military measures that would produce a North Vietnamese defeat because of expectations of Soviet and Chinese retaliation. Repeated testing had failed to produce any serious response from either great communist state, so why not take the necessary military steps now to defeat the Vietnamese Communists? Many bureaucrats and important sections of the public advocated such a policy. The end result could be a Pax Americana in which America, working through surrogate powers, could eliminate conflict, disorder, and instability.

One book, referred to earlier, appeared at this time which accepted a complex image of the communist states and advocated a policy that would meet anyone's definition of imperialism. This was George Liska's *Imperial America*. Indeed, in the Pax Americana Liska prescribed, the Soviet Union would be allowed to play the hegemonic role in its area of influence, Europe. For Liska, America would be the New Rome beneficently granting the world an era of peace and stability.

Liska's book is noteworthy particularly because both the abortive Johnson doctrine and the Nixon doctrine showed unmistakable tendencies of moving in such a direction.[22] But although the motivational drive behind such policies may have been present, particularly bureaucratic vested interests, the cost in terms of resource allocation would have required intense commitment. And that intense commitment was denied because of the very ambiguity of the situation. Great public excitement would be necessary, and such participant excitement was unlikely in a situation in which "victory" was so ill defined. Thus, even though nationalist symbols did evoke a response, that response was not strong enough even to affect seriously voting behavior.[23]

At the moment of Johnson's historic speech, then, the American foreign policy system of aims was in an advanced state of disequilibrium. From one significant attentive public group with considerable representation in Congress, there was pressure in the direction of détente and hence an end to containment. From another section of the attentive public, from important members of the bureaucracy, and from the president himself, there was pressure in the direction of an enhanced American role as gratuitous peace supervisor. But these were simply tendencies. Much of the attentive public favoring détente in Southeast Asia saw a highly aggressive and threatening Soviet foe in the Middle East. And those willing to drift toward a Pax Americana, unlike Liska, persisted in seeing an aggressive international communist movement.

Whatever the ambiguities, however, the point remains that the expectational test implicit in Johnson's policy change was as sharp as modern diplomacy produces. Two sets of expectations resting on two very different views of reality had been articulated. One position echoed the prediction of U Thant that an offer such as Johnson made would be accepted by North Vietnam. Those advocating this position saw a largely independent North Vietnam, engaged in a civil war, motivated more by nationalism than by communism and willing to accept a compromise with America. The other view was that the North Vietnamese, still acting under at least the active encouragement of the Soviet Union and/or China, would only agree to compromise if compelled to do so. When the expectations of the first group were realized, there was an almost overnight general perceptual alteration. Implicitly and nonconsciously the world view of the first group became the American prevailing world view and the image held of North Vietnam moved dramatically in the complex direction. Richard Nixon, whose image of the Soviet Union had been as close to the ideal typical enemy image as that of any American politician, was within months giving a presidential nomination acceptance speech in which he described this as the era of negotiations. Cold War rhetoric virtually disappeared in a presidential election campaign year. For the first time in a generation, politicians were offering competing images of peacemakers rather than Cold Warriors.

This, I would contend, is an uncommonly dramatic example of a common process by which a public manifests its influence on foreign policy. Johnson's speech came at a moment when two positions on the Vietnam conflict were being spelled out sharply. One position called for increasing commitment, the other for a negotiated American withdrawal. Such men as Senators Fulbright and McGovern spelled out assumptional differences clearly.[24] President Johnson and his administration were not allowed the luxury of failing to perceive that responses to their policies did not conform to expectations. On the contrary, each such expectational failure was pointed to with brutal eloquence. Then, when the president began to see that a large section of the most activist American youth were turning for leadership to elements within the Democratic party which he most disliked and that this coincided with the strong charismatic pull of Senator Robert Kennedy among other sections of the public, his vested interests for the first time pushed him in the direction of perceptual accommodation with his opponents on Vietnam policy. He needed to defuse the political charge behind the Kennedy candidacy. His offer of negotiations that did not specify a Korea-type solution was an ideal instrument. If it were rejected, and Johnson probably believed it would be, much of the credibility of the peace movement would be destroyed. If it were accepted, Johnson could claim the peace innovator role for himself and his chosen successor, Hubert Humphrey. When the offer was accepted, Johnson moved comfortably to the perceptual position of those who had expected acceptance. There was no dramatic admission that he had changed his mind. Nor was there even an overtly manifest awareness that a dramatic perceptual alteration had occurred. Mr. Humphrey's acceptance speech in Chicago that year is a beautiful example of assumptional dichotomy.[25] The first part, defending the Johnson policy, implies a strong threat perception. The second part, calling for rapid progress toward resolving the conflict, implies very little perception of threat.

This suggests a means for looking at what is meant by the "boundary-setting role of public opinion in foreign policy." Johnson, a proud and confident man, had entered the presidency with a view of reality consistent with that of the latter-day Cold War. Division in the communist world was seen, and some degree of incrementalism and decisional differentiation was implicitly accepted; but communist aggressive intent remained strong, and their policy thrust remained essentially imperialistic. Johnson's Vietnam policy was consistent with that view. However, policy based on his view did not produce the expected results, and many Americans moved away from the aggressive communist image almost to the point of seeing a status-quo Soviet foreign policy directional thrust. Johnson and his bureaucracy developed deep ego and vested-interest investments in the 1964 world view and tried to hold to that view until 1968. Then Johnson was faced with exceptional value conflict. To resolve it in a way that balanced his need to salvage a favorable historical image, to deny the presidency to Robert Kennedy, and to be true to nation and ideology, he accepted a fundamentally altered perception of the situation. There is every reason to believe he was not aware of that alteration. In the British-in-Egypt case study that follows, there will be several instances of this sudden and unnoticed yet dramatic kind of perceptual alteration. The Lebanon intervention as described earlier is a similar example. It suggests that the public role in policy determination is much greater than has been assumed but is impossible to measure with any precision.

The picture that has been drawn is one of drift along the enemy-complex image path in the complex direction. This is true for both the administration and its leading critics, with the critics always substantially closer to the complex position. Then, in 1968, a startlingly rapid movement occurred of administration supporters toward the complex position. Vice-President Humphrey, Senator Edmund Muskie, and Senator Walter Mondale were typical representatives of this move. Almost overnight they saw the world very much as Kennedy, McCarthy, McGovern, and Fulbright had seen it. Yet two important groups of Americans did not share in this perceptual transformation. They represented groups mapped at opposite ends of the enemy-complex spectrum. One of these, referred to above as the revisionists, had never been really surprised by events in Vietnam. Seeing an imperialist America and a typically weak and unresponsive status-quo Soviet Union, they expected American initiatives and Soviet passive responses. Given the consistent accuracy of their expectations, why had others not joined them in their world view? The answer, I believe, lies in the inability of most opponents of the Vietnam war to see the American government in the near ideal typical enemy terms of the revisionists. Many American initiatives were hard to explain with this view. Why, given an economically aggressive America and a passively submissive Soviet Union, should Johnson ever have made his offer? The Nixon-Kissinger policy from 1969 through 1971 could be described as one that revisionists could reasonably anticipate. But they should have great difficulty in explaining the May 1972 surrender of the insistence on a Korea-type solution—a concession that led to the withdrawal agreement.

The second group has an even more impressive anticipation record. This group included men such as Senators Goldwater and Jackson and columnist William Buckley, who persisted in seeing the communist foe in terms close to the ideal typical enemy. In its ideal typical form, enemy capability is seen as derivative from one's own domestic softness, good will, and lack of understanding. It follows that firmness of purpose will be rewarded with enemy responses that follow the paper tiger pattern. Individuals holding such a view can see a highly aggressive Soviet Union which, in the 1948 Berlin blockade, would have shrunk before the challenge of an armored train sent to crack the blockade.[26] Or they could see an American threat to invade Cuba producing a meek Soviet withdrawal of missiles.[27] Similarly tough American policy in Vietnam would be rewarded with Soviet passivity. This was the pattern they saw in Soviet behavior, and they therefore could not see a strong argument for the kind of retreat in which Johnson and Nixon engaged. Certainly the communist willingness to negotiate was not unexpected. Kissinger, in more orthodox days, had explained that a revolutionary regime will negotiate because it has the advantage of seeing negotiation as a way station on the road to an end, never as an end in itself.[28] Thus, the Communists were more than willing to go through the motions of pretending to agree to a settlement in Vietnam. They saw it as a means for getting rid of the United States and only as a temporary delay in their objective of swallowing the entire region.

Why should this group not have been rewarded for the accuracy of its predictions? Why wasn't the perceptual drift in their direction? The answer may be found in the broader world setting, where the Communists seemed to be passing up far too many opportunities to sustain a highly aggressive image. But the longevity of the Goldwater-Jackson position should surprise no one, given the perceptual reinforcement provided by the American experience in Vietnam.

PART II
The British in Egypt

7 / The Case Illustration in Historical Perspective

In 1880 William Ewart Gladstone became prime minister of England. The election effort he waged for his party's victory, the Midlothian campaign, carried a strong flavor of anti-imperialist indignation.[1] In particular, he warned against the growing involvement in Egypt which, he argued, could lead to the occupation of Egypt and the creation of a British African empire. Then, in the summer of 1882, Gladstone's government ordered the invasion and occupation of Egypt, an occupation that would last more than seventy years and would indeed stimulate further British expansion into Africa. Even more, the occupation of Egypt catalyzed the late-nineteenth-century wave of European expansion in Africa and Asia.

This imperialist episode, from its almost imperceptible beginnings in 1876 to its devastating climax in 1956, is the case study that will illustrate the theory developed in the first part of this book. But the word "episode," covering, as it does, eighty years, is carefully chosen. This is a study not of Egypt, but of the motivation for British imperialism in Egypt. Because the episode is recent, because Great Britain epitomizes European culture, and because Egypt is in American and European eyes "underdeveloped," this imperialism may seem to late twentieth-century Western man more a civilizing epic than an imperialist episode. But Egypt is an ancient land and has shown a particular susceptibility and ability to accommodate to imperialism Hyksos, Persian, Greek, Roman, Arab, Mameluke, and European. The imperialists have been remarkably the same. Typically they came, set up their own communities with their own language and culture, looked with contempt on the Egyptians, and regarded their own presence as benign and civilizing. They did vary, of course. The Hyksos seemed to lose their identity; the Persians were culturally least demanding; the Arabs were culturally most hospitable. For cultural arrogance, the Greeks and the Europeans must compete for top honors. Both regarded Egypt as "underdeveloped," to use today's culturally value-ridden expression, but neither really believed that the Egyptians—though they would advance far—could ever become "developed." It is easy to lose perspective in days of seeming apocalyptic crises, but the very breadth of Egypt's history carries an insistence for perspective.[2]

Egyptians were influenced fundamentally and enduringly by each wave of imperialism. The Arabs, who gave their language and their religion to Egypt, had an influence so profound that today Egyptians think of themselves to some degree as Arabs. There is no identity confusion regarding the Greeks or the English: The Fatimids, the rulers of Egypt in the early Moslem era, may not have been quite sure they were Egyptian, but Cleopatra was clearly more Greek than Egyptian and the aristocratic Evelyn Baring, first earl of Cromer, the great man of the British presence, had no question about his identity—he was the civilizing agent and very much an Englishman. Yet the Greek and European cultural impacts on Egypt have been second only to that of the Arabs. Since the European imperial impact has not yet reached its final chapter, only preliminary assessments can be made, but perspective demands that it be seen for what it is—one more in a long succession of imperial encounters for the Egyptian people.

Since this is not a study of Egypt, no effort will be made to look at the impact on Egyptian identity of such a history as they have endured. The descriptive term "docile" appears with great frequency in the generalizations of those who describe Egyptian character.[3] That Egyptians should appear docile to their overlords is not surprising; nor should be the anger and contempt of these same overlords when Egyptians betray this judgment. In the last and current imperial episode, a number of the Egyptian leaders who occupy the pages that follow have gained this anger and contempt. The most noteworthy of them have been Ahmed Arabi, against whose agitating presence the original invasion was made, Mustafa Kamel, Saad Zaghlul, and Gamal Abdel Nasser. In the bloodless analysis that follows, British opinions of these men will be looked at as evidence of motivations, but these leaders should be seen as well as the men to whom Egyptians turned as they felt the impact of European culture. Arabi, Kamel, Zaghlul, and Nasser thus reflect both the cultural impact and the identity demands of a people undergoing profound change.

The tendency of those who are part of European culture to patronize these men is shared by statesmen and social scientists, by agents of imperialism, and by critics of imperialism. The latter in particular, possibly because of their guilt feelings, indulge in a romantic analysis which may be even more patronizing and ultimately infuriating to those patronized than the analysis of men secure in their judgment of cultural superiority. Imperialists such as Cromer and Alfred Milner may ultimately have respected the Egyptians as much as that marvelously transparent, self-appointed, and aristocratic English patron of Arabi Pasha, Wilfrid Scawen Blunt.[4] The difference lies in empathetic ability. The agony of Blunt in describing Arabi's behavior in battle—which in a British cultural context can be described only as cowardice—testifies to his seeing a savage, not quite noble and not yet British, but a man nonetheless.[5]

The distinction between the "civilizing" goal of nineteenth-century imperialism and the "nation-building" or "development" goal of the twentieth century is not readily apparent. "Development" as a partial ideology is really a latter-day American phenomenon. The British, whether one speaks of the imperialist Cromer or the anti-imperialist Blunt, never seemed to have doubted the superiority of British culture or the value of Britain as a model toward which the "lower races" would be well advised to strive. Indeed, even though his outrage at Ottoman treatment of Bulgarian rebels was real enough, Gladstone's Midlothian anti-imperialist argument was pragmatic more than ethical. Not only does imperialism not pay, but its dynamics lead to ever increasing, resource-draining responsibilities. The Tory Blunt stood virtually alone in focusing his opposition to imperialism on the belief that it was demeaning to the dignity of a people he loved more than respected.

American development ideology, however, simply makes explicit that which the British allowed to remain implicit. The hidden assumptions and concealed ends were closely parallel. "Development" and "change" are very different terms. "Change" can be value-neutral, but "development" cannot. Change toward a particular and probably good end is "development," and in today's usage the end is clearly good. For the British when their imperialism began in Egypt in 1876, and for the Americans in the Cold War, the end was progress toward selected aspects of the imperial society as a model. For the British in nineteenth-century Europe, development included change toward the model in the following areas: infrastructure, including communications, transportation, and irrigation; administrative rationality, especially in departments concerned with financial order; commercial and industrial expansion; increases in agricultural yield per acre; legal norms to resemble more closely the European secular system; and elimination of practices such as slavery and the corvée, draft labor, that offended British ethics. The rate of change advocated varied sharply, with highest priority granted administrative rationality and infrastructure change and lowest priority placed on legal and ethical change. In two other areas of vital importance in the model, expansion and reform of education and growth in liberal democratic institutions, the rate of growth, especially in the latter area, was so slow as to be imperceptible. In a third, that of development of an identity with an Egyptian nation as worthy of world respect and as entitled to dignity as was the British nation, there was some rhetorical support but functional resistance.

In making the above statement, I do not intend to condemn British behavior. Rather, my purpose is to describe that behavior. In the chapters that follow, a central proposition will be that British imperial expansion into Egypt in the nineteenth and early twentieth centuries was motivated primarily by a desire to defend British commercial, financial, and imperial world interests. For this, stability in Egypt—and a stability achieved at minimal cost to the British public—was the objective most likely to satisfy basic aims. But the Englishmen responsible for British policy in Egypt believed profoundly in the goodness of

British culture, including the prevailing political values. Therefore, they had to accommodate perceptually British policy in Egypt and the British political ethic. In that accommodation, the program just described is totally natural. Those aspects of the British model which could be incorporated in Egypt and which would help in achieving stability were naturally stressed as central to Egyptian development. Others, such as education, liberal democratic institutions, and nationalism, would make control more difficult and expensive and, naturally, were either given low priority or deferred. Typical perceptual accommodation was that Egyptians were not yet sufficiently "mature" to be able to incorporate these institutions and norms into their culture. This in no way suggests that the British lacked sincerity in expressing hope and belief that someday the Egyptians would be able to incorporate liberal democratic institutions or to become an independent nation-state. On the contrary, as will be proposed shortly, part of lower-priority British motivation was to accomplish precisely that.

The assumption here is that American Cold War imperial policy was parallel both in objectives and in style to this outline of British policy. American policy, too, called for stability, especially in the littoral areas of the communist world. The difference lies in the more explicitly programmatic and ideological exposition of American policy. American statements of purpose may ultimately be more of a national embarrassment than the less apparent but remarkably parallel statements of Englishmen in the nineteenth century. In Iran and Jordan, for example, U.S. policy was a vital ingredient in the overthrow of two popular leaders, one of whom, Mohammed Mossadegh in Iran, was the symbol of a restored Iranian sense of national dignity and the other, Suleiman Nabulsi of Jordan, was recognized as a leading proponent of restored dignity for the Arab nation. Both successor regimes were royal dictatorships in which liberal democracy was tabled indefinitely as premature and in which the kings owed their consolidation of power to imperial support. Both were described by Americans as prototypical regimes engaged in "nation-building" and as examples of "political development." Their prede- cessors were described as prototypical models of regimes embarked on a course of action leading to "political decay." Iranian and Jordanian victims of American policy see great hypocrisy in proclaiming as "nation-building" a policy initiated by ousting national heroes and supporting the consolidation of a regime selected by the imperial power.[6]

The purpose of part II of this book is to illustrate the scheme developed in part I. The case study, the British in Egypt, was chosen because of its importance in modern imperial history, because of its duration and the variety of its forms, and because of the abundance—indeed, overabundance—of information regarding it. But there are serious disadvantages in its choice. Although British motives were very different from one period to another, they were never of the variety which led to the highly aggressive behavior seen in Napoleonic, Hitlerian, or Japanese imperial behavior. Nor do they resemble very much the motivational syndrome behind a sluggishly aggressive Soviet imperialism. They do, as the previous pages suggest, however, resemble fairly closely American post–World War II imperialism. The scheme is designed for universal applicability, but the case study illustrates only one sort of application.

In addition, as the first part of this chapter suggests, the case study rips out of context an episode in Egypt's very long history and even in this episode looks only briefly and superficially at the impact of imperialism on Egypt. The temporal and contextual perceptual distortion that results is serious, and the preceding pages can do no more than alert the reader to that distortion. There is little to be learned in the pages that follow of the great men of modern Egyptian history or of the profound social, economic, political, and cultural impact of British imperialism on Egypt.

The approach in part II will be to follow the scheme as outlined in chapter 5. Much of that scheme consists of looking at sets of variables placed in system constructs. Thus, the scheme only lends itself to describing momentary situations. No attempt was made to bring a dynamic quality to those constructs as, for example, Morton Kaplan seeks to do with transformation values.[7] Instead, the strategy for looking at the imperial process was what Stanley Hoffmann called comparative statics.[8] The plan of the case study is to look at six different momentary situations in the eighty-year period extending from 1876 to 1956. Description of the imperial process and explanatory propositions will be based on a comparison of the constructs for each period. However, one aspect of the scheme does lend itself to a somewhat structured look at change. That is a comparison of the expectations of decision makers regarding the consequences of policies they inaugurated during the critical days of the period studied with the actual results of those policies. This leads to identifying alterations in perceptions resulting from the nonrealization of expectations—alterations which result in a changed decisional environment.

The periods that will be examined are the following:

1. 1876: the nonspectacular beginnings of a British imperial presence in Egypt

2. 1882: the year of the landing of British troops, the capture and imprisonment of Ahmed Arabi, and the "temporary" occupation of Egypt

3. 1887: a year in which British institutional control of Egypt was firm and in which a major effort was made to adjust the British imperial presence to formal Ottoman imperial control and French imperial jealousies

4. 1914: the declaration of a British protectorate and the cutting of formal Ottoman imperial ties to Egypt

5. 1921: the decision to grant or impose a constitution on Egypt and to grant formal, though not functional, independence

6. 1956: the return of the British to Egypt in the Suez crisis and the temporary occupation of part of the Suez Canal in cooperation with the French, in collusion with the Israelis, and in opposition to the United States and the Soviet Union

Detailed application of the scheme focuses on these momentary situations. However, each chapter includes a historical narrative briefly describing relevant events that occurred prior to each of the periods studied in depth. This is essential if the situational environment of the decisional moment is to be understood. In each case the historical narrative is developed within the framework of the overall scheme. The focus is on perceptions and motivation.

8 / Fall 1876

Historical Narrative

Although British troops landed in Egypt in 1882 and departed in 1956, the boundaries of British influence in Egyptian affairs at a level which can fairly be called "imperialist" were 1876 and 1956. Before 1882 and since 1956, British interest in Egypt has been intense, but there is little reason to expect any future British intervention with the dramatic force and intensity of the 1956 Suez invasion. The British humiliation in 1956 had the effect in both the United Kingdom and the Middle East of destroying the illusion of any British claim to great-power status. The illusion had unquestionably been stronger in Egypt than in the United Kingdom. In a very real sense, British influence in Egypt had always rested on an illusion of power—an illusion that was a result not of design, but rather of the interaction of British intervention, always peculiarly extralegal, with an Egyptian expectation of imperial control based on millennia of historical experience.

It is impossible to select a moment at which all will agree British influence in Egypt crossed the boundary of imperialism. There can be no agreement as to what that boundary is and, in any case, no real possibility of reconstructing the Egyptian decisional process in such a way as to measure British involvement. Yet unless an extraordinarily narrow definition of imperial boundaries is employed, Britain was exercising imperial-level control in Egypt well before the troops arrived in 1882. I have chosen 1876 because by that year a number of Englishmen were serving in the high bureaucracy of Egypt and because three major investigations of Egyptian finance were made, two exclusively British and one Anglo-French, which had a decisive influence on Egyptian financial policy. But the choice remains arbitrary. It should, however, serve as a good starting point for constructing an imperialist map, even though the degree of control was far greater later on.

An intense British interest in the internal affairs of Egypt dates from the Napoleonic invasion of Egypt at the turn of the nineteenth century. That event inaugurated a clash of French and British imperial interests that was to endure well past World War II. During much of the nineteenth century, the British were responding to French expansionist tendencies in North Africa generally. The

157

British were convinced that any substantial French influence in the Mediterranean and Middle East would threaten the security of the empire, and Egypt, a vital link in the imperial life line, was a natural focus of this conflict.

Conflict over Egypt raised other complications as well. Formally Egypt was a province of the Ottoman Empire, and the Turks were by the nineteenth century fighting to prevent the dissolution of their empire. Since neither France nor Britain could take possession of Egypt without incurring the extreme displeasure of the other, and since the Ottoman Empire was no threat to either, an ideal compromise would seem to have been for each to support the Ottoman position. It was long-standing British policy, associated with the name of Henry John Temple, third viscount Palmerston, to buoy up the Ottoman Empire in order to cushion Anglo-French rivalry and provide a buffer against any Russian drive to the south.

Unfortunately, however, Ottoman control over its Egyptian province was both casual and weak. On rare occasions, when the Egyptian government was exceptionally recalcitrant, Ottoman troops were sent to correct the situation. More commonly, Ottoman control was maintained by playing on intense intraelite rivalries. The potential for this type of control was great. Following Napoleon's defeat, Mohammed Ali, an Albanian officer in the Ottoman military force in Egypt, gradually achieved primacy among Egypt's ruling elite.[1] Eventually he established a dynasty which lasted until King Farouk was sent into exile in 1952. However, this was no simple dictatorship. Mohammed Ali managed to kill most of the leading members of a Turkish-speaking, landowning elite known as the Mamelukes, who had exercised major influence in Egypt long before the Napoleonic invasion. By the mid-nineteenth century, the ruling elite consisted of a numerous royal family, a still large Turkish-speaking landowning element, the leaders of a sizable European and Levant trading community in Alexandria, Moslem religious leaders centered at the great Al Azhar University, Arabic-speaking landowners, leaders of the large Coptic Christian community of Egypt, and leading officers of the army, most of whom were Turkish-speaking. No community of interest was likely in such diversity, and the formula for control was to manipulate the personal rivalries and ambitions of leading personalities representing the various groups.

A history that describes the Egyptian political process of this era in all its complexity has yet to be written. At the time, European observers tended to see little beyond the royal family and the top Turkish-speaking elite, and today little effort is made in historical analyses to go beyond these two elite levels. But the Ottoman representatives in mid-nineteenth-century Cairo had a clear understanding of the entire complex and how it could be manipulated to serve goals that went little beyond the acceptance of formal Ottoman suzerainty and the receipt of revenues. The British and French interests were both more specific and more intense. The rivalry of the two powers was therefore expressed in competing efforts to gain influence with those primarily and immediately responsible for decisions, the royal family and the Turkish-speaking landowning elite. There is little evidence to suggest that either the British or the French were sufficiently concerned with expanding their influence to explore the potential of dealing with the other elites.

Two decisional areas were of primary concern to the British and the French: money-lending and trade routes. In the mid-nineteenth century, large banking concerns and a multitude of petty satellites sought to interest oriental leaders such as the Egyptian khedives in large loans for ventures that were often ill considered or frivolous but were sometimes of great benefit to the people.[2] The Egyptian Khedive Ismail and his predecessor Said proved susceptible to this siren call. Ismail, in particular, saw in the competition to gain his support for these ventures an almost magical opportunity to improve the economy of his realm, to add to the splendor of Egypt's cities, and to acquire for himself a living standard of unparalleled luxury. Thus, he sponsored irrigation improvements, railroad construction, public building and city beautification projects, and visits of European entertainers to Cairo. Individual Englishmen and Frenchmen and representatives of the great financial houses of England and France were involved in this competition, but the governmental role of the two rival states was minor, although British and French consuls frequently assisted their countrymen. The critical year in this competition was 1876, when bankers and financiers came to understand that the interest charges on a public debt of the magnitude of £76 million and on a private debt of £15 million were greater than the government could pay.[3] When this point was reached, both the British and French governments realized that Egyptian government financial policy decisions must be a matter for British and French concern.

The other decisional area of deep interest to both governments reflected Egypt's place in world trade routes. Separating the northern tip of the Red Sea and the southeastern shores of the Mediterranean is a brief stretch of Egyptian desert. The argument for cutting a canal from the Mediterranean to the Straits of Suez had been made for centuries. Indeed, a canal had been dug during the seventh century B.C. and redug by the Ptolemies and again by the Arabs, but then had been allowed to silt over. However, the British government saw serious disadvantages in constructing a canal which they realized would quickly become a primary security concern to the empire and a source of jealous attraction to many governments. Therefore, they preferred to see developed a rapid overland transport system linking Alexandria to the Red Sea. The French government was understandably less reluctant to see a canal built. Ferdinand de Lesseps, a Frenchman and the chief instigator of the canal construction, found his government's attitude to change from neutrality in the first days of negotiation to full diplomatic support. Constructing the canal became essentially a French project, and French citizens gained controlling interests in the Suez Canal Company. The diplomatic and political maneuvering associated with this transaction mirrors the interaction of the full scale of influences on Egyptian decision-making: European finance, the

French and British governments, the Ottoman government, and the entire range of competing elite influence in Egypt.[4]

As foreseen by British statesmen, from the moment of its opening the Suez Canal altered British policy in the eastern Mediterranean. Egypt could not become the dependency of France or any other European state without endangering the almost instantaneously massive British trade interest in the Suez Canal. Thus, when Benjamin Disraeli learned that the khedive in his financial difficulties wished to sell his 15 percent share in the company, he purchased the interest on behalf of the British government without consulting Parliament and with such speed that he had to borrow the money from the house of Rothschild to make the purchase. However, parliamentary response was mild and, as will be seen below, reflected a widespread view that the purchase would enhance British influence in Cairo. The debate demonstrated as well a broad acceptance of the view that the crisis in Egyptian finance threatened a marked increase in European influence in Cairo.

Prevailing World View

The first half of the 1870s witnessed a series of events that altered substantially the world view of Englishmen. Most important of these was the Franco-Prussian war of 1870. Napoleon III was compelled to abdicate, and French influence in world affairs sharply declined. Germany emerged as a great power, and Prince Otto von Bismarck became one of the most influential leaders in the world. Then in 1875 rebellion broke out in the Christian lands of the remaining parts of the Ottoman Empire in Europe. Bismarck made clear his willingness to see Constantinople in Russian hands, and Englishmen were compelled to consider that possibility.[5] Of far less importance, but of great significance to the English view of themselves in the world, was the continuous difficulty the British had in maintaining their control in Ireland.

Englishmen in 1876 perceived neither the great threat nor the great opportunity which could lead them to see a world of enemies, allies, and peoples yearning for British imperial tutelage. The account of A. J. P. Taylor, *The Struggle for Mastery in Europe, 1848–1918*, on which I rely heavily for inferring world view, makes clear that the prevailing view toward all the major states of Europe in 1876 approximated the complex image. The British were suspicious of the motives of all European states, but almost without discrimination. The British foreign secretary, Edward Stanley, fifteenth earl of Derby, remarked in an 1876 letter that "one can trust none of these Governments."[6] There was no serious drift toward seeing one state as closer to allied and another as closer to enemy, and this is exactly the pattern to be expected if perception of neither threat nor opportunity was exceptional. Prevailing French perceptions of Germany understandably approximated the ideal typical enemy image. On at least one occasion in 1875 the French were able to alarm the British and Russians with strong suspicion of German motives, and the two foreign secretaries protested to the Germans.[7] British suspicions of aggressive and evil Russian motivations regarding India and the Middle East were a constant throughout this period.[8] French motives in Egypt and the Mediterranean generally were suspect, as will be detailed.[9] But in sum, perception of neither great threat to Britain nor great opportunity for an expansion of British influence in Europe appears to have prevailed.

Nor does a reading of this period in British history reveal any strong perception of threat or opportunity relating to Europe on the part of any interest group of policy importance in Britain. There was one significant exception, however, and it is of particular importance to this study. By 1876 the revolt of the southern Slavs, most of them Christian, against the Ottoman Empire, had led to a demand for national self-determination. Furthermore, stories of Turkish brutality against Christian Bulgars were widespread and increasingly accepted in England. The extent of public outrage at these acts was mirrored in the great popularity of Gladstone's tract attacking the Turks for their atrocities.[10] Clearly there was a very serious, indeed horrifying, threat to fellow Christians who were proclaiming their right to national self-determination; and national self-determination was an integral part of British liberal ideology. A threat to both religion and ideology was perceived, and public pressure was strong enough that even the lethargic Lord Derby was moved to call a conference at Constantinople in November 1876 to pressure the Turks into making reforms.[11] Disraeli was singularly unmoved by these stories of Turkish atrocities and by the southern Slav insistence on national self-determination. For him the argument for preserving the Ottoman Empire as a buffer state was apparently so compelling that he found difficulty in even accepting the stories of atrocities. However, he could not ignore the popular appeal of Gladstone's campaign or the willingness within his own cabinet—Robert Gascoyne-Cecil, third marquis of Salisbury, being the most important example —to consider abandoning the traditional approach to the Ottoman Empire.

Another interactive factor that enters this equation was the continued terrorism in Ireland. Here too the demand was clear for national self-determination, but with Britain cast in the role of oppressor. Englishmen were being killed, the honor of the empire was being attacked, all in the name of national self-determination. It was not easy to reconcile sympathy for the aspirations of the southern Slavs with annoyance at the parallel aspirations of the Irish.

What was called for was perceptual and policy accommodation to these diverse interests. Both the Irish and Slav revolts constituted problems for the security of the empire, and the Irish revolt was damaging national dignity. The ideological symbol of national self-determination was manipulated by both and, in the case of the Slavs, a threat to the Christian identity group was involved as well. Because of the Slavic situation, the importance of Constantinople for the security of the empire was downgraded both verbally and in policy. But the impact of the Irish rebellion and the perceived threat to the imperial life line mitigated the impact on the public of southern Slav appeals. As a result, anger and outrage did not become so great that British policy was led to cooperate in Bismarck's plan for the partition of the Ottoman Empire in which Britain would receive preeminence in the Ottoman province of Egypt.[12]

Experience in another area, this time India, apparently had perceptual consequences for any expansion of British influence in Africa. The authors of *Africa and the Victorians* summarize a point that appears repeatedly in diplomatic correspondence and in parliamentary debate:

> The experience of governing Hindus and Moslems strongly prejudiced the later Victorians against acquiring more Oriental possessions. . . . The Indian Mutiny and the social upheavals which followed hard on the heels of European penetration throughout the Near and Far East left a lasting disenchantment in London and Calcutta about the possibilities of westernizing the Oriental.
>
> The Victorians had learned that westernization was a dangerous and explosive business. Perhaps non-Europeans after all were not potential English gentlemen who had been unluckily retarded, but were inherently different and apart.[13]

Such a perceptual alteration was favored by a coincidence of economic and government vested-interest perceptions that further imperial expansion would be, if anything, a liability. As Ronald Robinson and John Gallagher conclude, "For one thing, the merchant and manufacturer could easily overcome all competition, given an open market; for another, the Treasury normally had little money to spare for more colonial activities.[14]

The one clearly discernible interest group with a minor decisional impact tending toward imperial expansion was, ironically, the antislavery movement. Any evaluation of the dynamics of British expansion into Africa must incorporate the decisional role of this element, but assigning a particular weight to the associated motivational factor is most difficult. For example, in February 1877 the British consul in Cairo suggested to the Khedive Ismail that an eccentric and bitterly antislavery Englishman, Charles Gordon, be appointed "Governor General of all the Sudan and Equatorial Provinces." Not surprisingly, given the rapidly expanding British presence, private and semiofficial, and given Ismail's concern with maintaining a British-French balance in Egypt, Ismail made the appointment. The British consul, Henry Hussey Vivian, was ecstatic:

> I can only say that the Khedive had made this choice spontaneously, without any pressures on my part. I simply warned His Highness that he would find no sympathy in England with the extension of his territory in Central Africa, so long as slave-hunting and slave-trading practices were carried on in the provinces he was annexing. His answer to my remonstrance is the selection of the Englishman who had denounced the practices, for the government, with almost independent authority, of the provinces where the slave trade has its source; and

I cannot but submit that this concession of the Khedive, which is all the more valuable because it is spontaneous, is deserving of the highest praise.[15]

The number of dispatches from Cairo to London in this period that dealt with the slave trade was very large. As in the case above, British officials appear to have so internalized the antislavery case that they could misconstrue a clear case of crass pressure as ideological persuasion. Throughout these dispatches concerning the slave trade there runs an official enthusiasm that seems to reflect the motivational factor of cultural messianism. As *Africa and the Victorians* shows, the force of the drive to eliminate the cultural institution of slavery in Africa was never great enough to be more than a force of lower-level intensity in producing a decision for expansion. When operating alone, this factor could not expand influence, but in conjunction with economic pressures or imperial rivalry, it became a significant part of the equation. It allowed British officers to believe that theirs was a civilizing presence. In the scheme here, it is granted a third-level intensity rating.

Figure II.1 maps the prevailing world view (PV) in England in 1876. Disraeli's divergent view of the Ottoman Empire is mapped (D),[16] as is the antislavery view of Africa (A). Other group modal or individual views are not mapped because of their general convergence with the prevailing view.

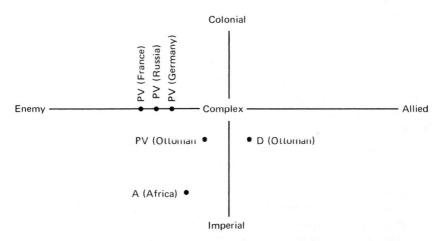

Figure II.1. British World Views, 1876

Motivational System—General

Clearly 1876 was a period in which British interest in expanding influence was very low. The only serious pressures on the government from public opinion and interest groups appear to have been religious (a concern with fellow Christians), ideological (an interest in national self-determination for the Slavs), and cultural (a desire to persuade Africans to adopt British cultural attitudes toward slavery). The judgment made is that these interests were fairly minor and that British political leaders and the British foreign policy bureaucracy had substantial freedom in the foreign policy decisional area. In fact, the clearest limitation was on Disraeli, who, without these pressures, would probably have maintained a high priority for the goal of buoying up the Ottoman Empire.

The representation of general British foreign policy motivation in 1876 is as follows:

A. Defense
B. National grandeur
   Trade: exports and imports
C. Ideological messianism
   Religious messianism
   Cultural messianism

This reflects the inference that British official activity was primarily concerned with defending Great Britain and the British Empire against the appearance of any hostile combination in Europe, such as the League of Three Emperors, and with protection of the empire against Russian or French inroads. National grandeur has been placed on the second level because a concern for the dignity of the nation was clearly omnipresent. Trade has been included because of the somewhat mildly perceived threat to the trade channel of the Suez Canal, but there is no serious indication of either a major perception of threat to the dignity of the nation or an interest in seizing the opportunity to expand influence for the sake of grandeur or for trade. The parametric value, the priority granted foreign policy, is therefore judged to be low.

General System of Aims

British foreign policy aims reflect the prevailing system values, which are all status-quo. Thus, a high priority is placed on peaceful settlement of disputes; an acceptance of the prevailing international actor system, which consists of a combination of nation-state, nation-state-empire, and empire; and satisfaction with the prevailing world configuration of power.

In the outline that follows, the system of aims is charted in three divisions, each headed by a general strategy line response to perceived threat and/or opportunities: (1) a perception of threat from the development of a hostile combination of powers in Europe. Since no polarized allied-enemy perceptual images appear, this perception of threat is judged to be of low intensity; (2) a perception of threat of moderate intensity from Russian expansion southward toward India and the imperial life line, and a less intense perception of threat of French control of Suez Canal shipping; and (3) perceptions of threat or opportunity by British governmental, economic, and ideological interests of such low intensity as to be only a minor determinant of the aims system.

I. Preserve the peace, well-being, and security of the British people and safeguard the British Empire
  A. Prevent the development of a hostile combination of states on continental Europe
    1. Maintain France as a major power in Europe
    2. Counter any tendency of the League of Three Emperors to develop into an effective alliance
    3. Work to prevent the weakening of Ottoman control in the Balkans from leading to major warfare or a serious alteration of the European balance of power
  B. Defend the empire and the imperial life line from Russian and French threats
    1. Defend the Ottoman Empire and the imperial life line from Russian and French threats
    2. Prevent Russian expansion southward toward India from engulfing Afghanistan
    3. Counter any French move to gain further control over Egypt and the imperial life line through the Suez Canal
  C. Satisfy the foreign policy–related demands of the British people
    1. Maintain a colonial and foreign service bureaucracy capable of administering British foreign policy and the British Empire efficiently and well
    2. Maintain armed forces capable of providing for the defense and security of Great Britain, the empire, and the imperial life line
    3. Defend and advance the interests of British industry, commerce, and finance on the high seas, in the empire, at home, and abroad
    4. Defend the dignity and enhance the prestige of the British nation
    5. Encourage and support moves abroad toward national self-determination and democratic rule
    6. Defend Christian people against oppression by Moslem or other infidel rulers and support Christian missions abroad
    7. Help spread civilized values to the people of the Orient and Africa; in particular, work to stamp out the slave trade
    8. Advance the cause of peace

This outline is a verbalization of the foreign policy aims system congruent with a low parametric value rating and a foreign policy which has a low-priority claim on resource allocation. The system of aims developed in the first part of this book is the model for this representation. When the outline and the representation of general motivation on p. 164 are juxtaposed, the inference becomes clear as to which policy lines are most important in British efforts to influence world developments. Low-intensity though they may be, the defense objectives in divisions A and B of the outline are inferred as most important. In division C the aims of protecting and encouraging trade and of protecting the dignity and enhancing the prestige of the nation are seen as being on the next level of importance. On the third level of importance are those policies in division C which relate to the defense of Christianity and to the encouragement of freedom and of those cultural norms the British people thought of as "civilized."

The primary analytic utility of the system of aims is to provide a descriptive base for viewing the interaction of conflicting tendencies in aims determination. In the British system of aims in 1876, the most threatening disturbance was the sharp weakening of Ottoman control evidenced by the southern Slav revolt. Affected aims were A.3, which reflected a determination not to allow this disturbance to strengthen any European state or bloc of states to the point of threatening British security; B.1 and C.3, which reflected British interest in preserving the Ottoman Empire as a buffer against a southern drive by Russia toward the imperial life line; B.3 and C.3, which reflected British interest in maintaining a casual Ottoman control in Egypt as a deterrent to further French inroads there; C.5 and C.6, which reflected a British sympathy for the aspirations of the southern Slavs for self-determination and the end of colonial dominance by an oppressive and terroristic Moslem regime; and C.7, which reflected an extreme reluctance to become involved in warfare over these issues. A British response which incorporated an acceptance of Bismarck's proposal to partition the Ottoman Empire would satisfy some of these objectives: It would be reasonably satisfactory from the point of view of maintaining a European balance of power, and it would satisfy British sympathies for the southern Slavs. But in all likelihood it would increase perception of threat to the life line of the empire from both Russia and France to the point that a general strategy change could occur. In that event, major transformation of virtually every British foreign policy aim could be expected. This point was well comprehended by Disraeli, who was in any event unburdened by any real sympathy for the southern Slavs. Even Gladstone, whose concern for Ottoman genocide against the Bulgars came close to being an obsession, did not allow it to lead to advocacy of the Bismarck position.

Prevailing Situational View

The British view of the Egyptian situation must be seen in the broader context of the prevailing British world view. There is little evidence that a perception of opportunity to expand British territorial control or British investments prevailed generally. Nor did British investors in Egypt exert significant pressure for governmental assistance in expanding their investments, although they clearly perceived threat to these investments strongly. Apparently the British creditors in Egypt were unable to draw attention to their case at home, for the prevailing world view indicates little concern for the worries of local investors in the general foreign policy decisional process. The aspects of the prevailing world view that did affect seriously the situational view in Egypt were the perception of threat to the life line of the empire at the Suez Canal, incorporated in the decay of quality of government in Constantinople, the perception of Ottoman Moslem leaders as enemies of Christendom, and the self-determination of peoples.

The parliamentary debate of February 21, 1876, prior to an endorsement of the purchase of the Suez Canal Company shares by Disraeli, reflects the range in attitudes toward British defense needs in the area. Gladstone, speaking for the Opposition, referred to the purchase made some weeks earlier:

The general belief at that time, promoted by nearly the whole of the metropolitan Press—I think by the whole of the metropolitan daily Press—was that a great blow had been struck for the assertion of British power, that, in the critical circumstances of the Turkish Empire, notice had been given in the world that, so far as Egypt was concerned, we intended to have the first and largest share in determining what would be its destiny.[17]

Sir Stafford Northcote, chancellor of the exchequer, denied there was any interest in "surrounding our policy in Egypt with a great halo of glory." He asserted:

Our object, I repeat, was simply to see clearly what we were about, and to give the assistance we could to our friend the Khedive. . . . Well, when you see a friendly country squandering its resources, when you see it engaged in financial courses which you know to be bad and which must lead to embarrassment. When you see that this embarrassment may and probably will affect not only that country, but European Powers—and I would here remind the House that Egypt lies on the highway of Europe to the East—when you recollect what advantage might be taken of the embarrassment of that country by some European Power, and how the peace of Europe might thereby be jeopardized, it is surely good policy to come forward and prevent that country from getting into difficulties.[18]

During this debate, the government side made no reference to the interests of the creditors even though several members of the House were among their ranks. The opposition made negative references typified by those of Sir George Campbell, who, in approving the purchase, said, "Let us take our chance, but not allow ourselves to become a cause of oppression, and a source of stockjobbing and intrigue."[19]

Diplomatic correspondence evinced a mild defense concern. The immediate threat of foreign intervention in the Egyptian financial crisis came from France, but official behavior suggests a perception of the French in Egypt far closer to the complex ideal typical image than to the enemy. The two governments were in close communications throughout the year. At one point Derby instructed Richard Pemell, first earl of Lyons, in Paris that Her Majesty's government "could not view with indifference any attempt to gain administrative control over Egypt by another power."[20] But for the most part diplomatic dispatches contained such phrases as that transmitted by Lyons to the Duc Decazes in which he was to say that Her Majesty's government "join with him in deprecating any idea of international rivalry."[21]

Policy was in tune with this overall mild perception of threat. In response to an urgent request from the Khedive Ismail that the British and French governments each nominate a national bank commissioner who would presumably have a role in debt management, the French responded favorably but the British agreed only to study the matter. When a financial mission headed by Stephen Cave was sent to investigate and report, even this was too much for the opposition. In Parliament there were sarcastic taunts and the suggestion that the Cave mission was gratuitous interference in Egyptian affairs.[22] Sending the Cave mission was thus indicative of the moderate seriousness with which the government viewed the Egyptian case. This was reflected as well by their sending Sir Rivers Wilson, a prominent financial expert in Treasury, to investigate and to advise the khedive. Both Cave and Wilson found the finances to be in a highly critical state, and both made recommendations for debt consolidation, conversion, and payment. Subsequent efforts of the khedive to persuade the British to nominate a commissioner of the debt were rejected, because the British officials involved sensed serious difficulties. The khedive would not accept a scheme giving the British and French commissions real control. Without that, the British saw themselves increasingly drawn into responsibility, uneasily shared with the French, but with no real authority.[23]

By August 1876, Liberals in the House expressed a deeper concern. Opposition spokesmen charged the government with a desire to take control of Egypt for the glory of the empire. There was still no suggestion on their part that the government had responded to protect the creditors, of whom Sir George Campbell was quoted as saying:

He pitied those poor people very much; but if we were to adopt this mode of assisting them a great many other people might similarly get into difficulties. He believed the first loss was the test and that it was not wise to prop up the credit of any foreign State that might be in a rotting or tottering condition.[24]

From the London side of the situational decisional process, the case seems overwhelming that there was a moderate perception of threat to the Suez Canal link in the imperial life line and a somewhat less compelling perception of opportunity for enhancing imperial prestige in the acquisition of the Suez Canal shares. But moving to the Cairo end of the decisional process, a considerably different view of the situation becomes evident. That view reflected the interaction of British officials and British residents in Egypt, many of whom were deeply fearful of financial ruin.

The foreign population in Egypt was concentrated in Alexandria. Of forty-seven thousand foreigners in that city, forty-five hundred were Englishmen, but a great many others, especially Greeks, carried British passports. The foreign community was a world unto itself. It reflected all the rivalries of Europe and the Near East, but it did have something of a social and political structure. Five hundred members of the community were granted the social status of "notable" by virtue of their wealth and personal influence. Of these, forty-five were English. The political structure was more reflective of interaction with governmental representatives. This is seen in the composition of a list of twenty-four assessors who were in effect the political spokesmen for the community. Of these, five were British; four each were French, Italian, and Greek; three each were Austrian and German; and one was Russian.[25] In the struggle for the ear of the khedive, the consuls played a major role in support of their respective fellow nationals. Career success demanded that they do well by their compatriots, and it is unreasonable to assume that they did not share many of the perceptions of the community. In addition, by 1876, individual Englishmen held high positions in the Egyptian Departments of Law, Finance, Commerce, the Post Office, the Army, and the Navy.[26] Interaction of these officials with the consul was a constant, and in effect there existed an unofficial British bureaucratic interest group in Cairo.

Reports of the *London Times* correspondent in Cairo in this period are presumed to reflect prevailing views of this community. Certainly the correspondent so represented himself, and if that is accurate, a fair record is available of that community's perceptions. Perceptions of British motives in the purchase of the Suez Canal shares paralleled those already seen in London, although the intensity of interest was much greater:

The transaction, carried on as it was by the English Government though Parliament was not sitting, is considered here of great political importance and as almost amounting to a declaration on the part of England that she will permit no foreign intervention save her own in any affairs of Egypt which may have a political bearing. A second view of the matter is current. . . . England, it is said, has stretched out her hand to save Egypt from following the wreck of Turkey.[27]

In other respects a sharp differential appears. The mild parliamentary and governmental view of the French had no parallel among the British in Egypt, who saw France in enemy terms. Furthermore, French actions in Egypt lent themselves to this interpretation. In fact, a conflict overwhelmingly perceptual in base was developing.

In France, the British lack of interest in the khedive's suggestion of a joint

Franco-British commission in Egypt and the dispatch of the Cave mission were viewed with alarm. The *Times* correspondent in Paris reported on French opinion there: "England . . . was said to have consented to save Egyptian finance, to direct the administration, and to bring her strength, influence and credit to its regeneration and independence. It was to prepare for this role, to study the possibility of this exclusive protectorate and to solve this problem that Mr. Cave was sent to Egypt."[28]

To avoid being frozen out by the British, the French sent a mission of their own, the Outrey mission. In the eyes of the British community in Egypt, however, the Outrey mission was the advance guard of a gigantic plot. The mission even intervened in small matters such as the competition for control of a railroad franchise. According to the *Times* correspondent, the British assumed, (naively, as is the wont of the status-quo power) that the matter would be settled according to regular procedures. "There has been no thought of intrigue, consular or diplomatic influence, and it has been taken for granted that the highest bidder would win the prize." But Outrey chose to misrepresent the British position entirely. "In the name of France, the protecting Power of the Levant, he has represented to the Khedive that the English are looking for annexation and must not be allowed to obtain such a hold on the country as this operation would give them." As would be expected, given this perception of threat, images of other European states began to polarize. The *Times* continued in the same story:

The Russo-French rapprochement seems more than a possibility or a rumour, and there is no doubt that agents of both Powers, accredited and unaccredited, are unusually active here at the present moment. Fortunately for England, she has at present the most cordial support from Germany in all she does in Egypt, and we English here believe that the two Teutonic Powers together can direct the world.[29]

The momentum of this perceptual drift could not be maintained. British passivity was too clear for the French to deny, and the French lost interest in the proposal for a debt commission. The focus of the British community in Egypt returned to the threat to investments from Egyptian finance, not French intervention. Writing six months after the above dispatch, the *Times* correspondent reported: "So great is the anxiety here that the financial equilibrium should be somehow or other restored, that any feeling of international jealousy which may have existed as regards this Commission has died away—at any rate, in English circles."[30]

Now the perceptual response was to see an Egypt closely resembling the ideal typical imperial image. This is the response expected when an interest group sees an opportunity to achieve an objective with government support at the expense of a community viewed as inferior in culture and capability. The image of a people needing tutelage emerges in Cave's report. He wrote that Egypt "suffers from the ignorance, dishonesty, waste, and extravagances of the East, such as has brought her Suzerain to the verge of ruin and at the same time from the vast expenses caused by hasty and inconsiderate endeavors to adopt the civilization of the West." Referring to one model British bureaucrat assigned to Egypt, E. H. Acton of the Commerce Ministry, the Cave report says, "If men of such character and position were appointed to higher offices in the Civil Service, they would, as we believe, bring about most excellent results."[31]

Even more in tune was the description of the resignation and probable murder of the one Arabic-speaking member of the khedive's cabinet, Minister of Finance Ismail Saddiq. The story appears only in fragments. In the fall of 1876 a final mission went to Egypt, this time not an official mission but one that represented all foreign bondholders. It was headed by a leading liberal politician, MP, and bondholder, George Joachim Goschen, and a leading French banker, M. Joubert. From the beginning, it was clear that they would recommend, among other things, enhanced British-French control of finances. Saddiq, who was regarded as the second most powerful man in Egypt,[32] was the chief opponent of increased European influence. Viscount Goschen refused to meet with Saddiq, who shortly thereafter was dismissed.

The *Times* correspondent was mystified by Saddiq's power role: "Equally wonderful was his rise, as he is the son of an Egyptian peasant who speaks no language but Arabic and had no education but that which would fit him for ordinary clerk's work."[33] But in none of the known accounts did a European author ponder why an exclusively Arabic-speaking minister should wield such influence when the khedive was personally not comfortable in Arabic and hence was most unlikely to have granted him this influence because of a close, intimate relationship. The most logical answer would seem to be that Saddiq represented an important, Arabic-speaking, landowning elite. Having been made forcibly aware of British hostility to Saddiq, the khedive may have felt forced to choose between the British and the Arabic-speaking landowners. Saddiq's dismissal and mysterious drowning in the Nile may well have been the khedive's solution to what he saw as a serious conflict of interest between the British and the Arabic-speaking elite.

If so, the British evinced no awareness of his dilemma: To people who were oblivious to the importance of the Arabic-speaking elite, this proposition obviously could not have occurred. Rather, they described Saddiq as an agitator. "Early last week . . . reports came in from the Provinces that mischievous agitation was being promoted among the village fellahs and the mullahs of the larger towns, in which . . . the Viceroy was accused of betraying the interests of the country to foreigners." Saddiq had had the audacity to send a letter of resignation to the khedive "charging him with all the misdeeds alleged by the provincial agitators and almost in terms indicting him for this virtual treason to Islam and to Egypt."[34] While some members of the native elite were described in ideal typical terms as agitators, those willing to cooperate were described as "responsible" men, or WOGs (Westernized Oriental Gentlemen). The khedive was so described: "The Khedive has fully realized how necessary it is to real progress to utilize European experience in the establishment, for instance, of an honest administration of justice and a good system of education."[35] The report confirms that the entire European population of Egypt was overjoyed at the disappearance of Saddiq from influence.[36] But their joy was short-lived. Within a few months the khedive was behaving"irresponsibly" and was himself seen by the same people as an agitator.

The perceptual mapping of the situational view (figure II.2) reflects three positions. There is the liberal opposition in London (L), which sees little threat in the area. There is the prevailing view (PV), that inferred for the modal view in the conservative government, which reflects slightly more threat perception. There is the view of economic and bureaucratic interests in Egypt (I), which perceive substantial threat from France and substantial opportunity in Egypt.

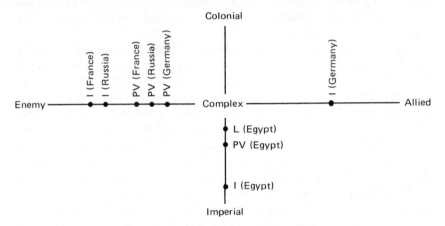

Figure II.2. British Situational Views, 1876

Situational Motivational System

Evidence suggesting who was most prominent in the decision to move tentatively and cautiously into a deeper involvement in Egyptian decision-making is inferential. Parliamentary opposition to so careful an approach was somewhat more obvious than support. Press response ranged from that of the *Economist*, which reflected the Liberal opposition position, to that of the *Times*, the *Spectator*, and the *Saturday Review*, which were somewhat skeptical government supporters.[37] Certainly there is no reflection in the press of a broad public interest.

The role of the bondholders was both direct and indirect. Whereas there is little in diplomatic correspondence, newspaper reports, and parliamentary debates from which bondholder influence on the British government could be inferred, diplomatic correspondence with the French is filled with clear evidence of bondholder influence with the French government. For example, Lord Lyons described a conversation with French Foreign Minister Decazes as follows:

A deputation from French capitalists . . . had come to him and represented to him that if he would appoint the French Commissioners at once they would renew the bonds; . . . These gentlemen had been very persistent and had come to him more than once and had indeed on one occasion waited for him till he came home at midnight, and stayed with him till 3 o'clock in the morning.[38]

Bondholder influence on French policy, in turn, added to the British perception of threat of increasing French involvement in Egyptian affairs.

Direct influence appears mainly at the Cairo end of the decisional process. The tentative nature of London's position is seen in the treatment of the important Goschen-Joubert mission. The bondholders asked for and received a British government statement to the Egyptian government suggesting interest in the mission. Derby wrote to Charles Cookson in Cairo, "I have to add that you may inform His Highness that Mr. Goschen was a member of the late Cabinet, and is a person of high position and reputation in this country."[39] When the consul, Mr. Vivian, was presenting Goschen at court he was asked by the Egyptians whether the mission should be regarded as diplomatic. Vivian replied that it should not and that he was to give it only unofficial aid.[40] However, in reporting on his mission Goschen said, "They had had very great assistance from Mr. Vivian, the English Consul, and from Baron de Michel, the French Consul-General throughout the whole of the negotiations."[41] The most important achievement of the Goschen-Joubert mission was the khedive's agreement to appoint a Briton and a Frenchman as controllers-general with substantial authority over the debt repayment. The British government persisted in refusing to nominate a candidate, but the khedive found this policy stance of symbolic importance only.

Although a direct bondholder role was obvious only in interactions with British officials in Egypt, in a subtle way, the British community in Egypt began influencing London. The prevailing situational view of the British commercial interests in Egypt was apparently easily communicated. Cave, Sir Rivers Wilson, and Viscount Goschen all appear to have adopted it and to have drifted toward favoring a policy of competition with France for establishing imperial control in Egypt. The prevailing situational view and therefore situational policy were still much closer to the perceptions of British officials in London, but strong pressure was developing in London for a more activist policy.

Figure II.2 describes the decisional picture. The images of France and Egypt held by British bureaucrats and agents of bondholders in Egypt are judged to be much closer to the enemy and imperial ideal typical images respectively than are the prevailing views. A basic assumption of the scheme is that the distance from the prevailing view of the situational view of a modal member of a decisional element is a major indicator of the relative importance of that element in the decision that is made. This, in turn, is translated into motivational terms. In this case, actual policy reflected little fear of France and little interest in placing increasing numbers of Englishmen in Egyptian decisional positions. I judge it therefore to be most in tune with the position of those in London who did some worrying about defense interests. Defense is given first-level intensity in the situational motivational system. My conclusion, based on both the lobbying activities of investors as described and on the substantial distance between a modal investor's view and the prevailing view of the Egyptian situation, is that the factor of economic investments abroad is at best of second-level motivational importance. The British bureaucratic set in Egypt is mapped similarly, but their personal activities, of which there is record, were not particularly vigorous in the decisional area. Bureaucratic vested interests are therefore placed at the third level.

Were Liberal opposition members of Parliament doing the judging, national grandeur would be the primary factor and defense tertiary. Statements by the government, in fact, reflected concern with prestige; certainly scenarios suggesting intense threat perception were lacking. However, none of the statements by the government suggest a strong compulsion to add to the grandeur of the nation. The defense–national grandeur–cultural messianism combination, respectively primary, secondary, and tertiary in importance, is judged to represent most accurately both verbal and policy behavior of the government.

The inferred motivational system is as follows:

A. Defense
B. Economic investments abroad: security
   National grandeur
C. Cultural messianism
   Bureaucratic vested interests

Specific Policy, Expectations, and Response

The policy adopted in the fall of 1876 was clear. The British government would not nominate Englishmen to serve as an elite bureaucracy for Egypt or as the controllers of debt repayment policy. It would, however, acquiesce in the appointment of individual Englishmen, and the British consul in Cairo and other diplomatic officials would be in close contact with these men. Thus, an illusion of noninterference would be maintained, but in effect there would be an involvement in the Egyptian decisional process at a level that in this study meets the definition of imperialism.[42]

Prevailing expectations were also clear. The Khedive Ismail would behave as a good WOG. Highly competent British and other European officials would bring the rules of Western civilization to bear on Egyptian financial and governmental policy. The British government need not involve itself directly. Ottoman suzerainty with its casual control would remain, and British-French relations, both cooperative and competing, would be conducted within the context of this formal suzerainty. With the removal of Saddiq, agitation among the fellahin and religious leaders would cease. Most important, the likelihood of a French move into a chaotic Egypt would be much reduced.

British Liberal opposition expectations were less specific but as clearly stated:[43] The government's policy would result in an ever deeper involvement in Egypt, and this would lead to increased international rivalry in the Mediterranean and Africa and to an expansion of the British Empire.

In fact, virtually none of the governmental expectations were realized, while all the Liberal expectations ultimately were. Logic would suggest that expectational nonrealization and realization in this pattern would lead to an acceptance of a world and situational view closer to that of the Liberals. In fact, it was to be a Liberal government headed by Gladstone that would occupy Egypt and would, in doing so, surrender its own situational view. A task of the following section will be to suggest a set of propositions to explain that phenomenon.

Here it is necessary to describe briefly expectational nonrealization, because that nonrealization must be viewed as a disturbance in the system of aims as developed in the outline on page 165.

Saddiq was replaced as minister of finance by an Armenian, Nubar Pasha, who was possibly the Egyptian official closest to the ideal typical WOG image. But the Khedive Ismail was proud and assertive, unwilling to accept a subordinate position to a European decisional superstructure. He consequently began to maneuver with the very elite group of which Saddiq had been the informal representative. Nubar Pasha in the meantime sought to use his leverage with the European powers to compel Ismail to agree to the limitation of his own power. Nubar wanted the appointment of an Englishman as minister of finance and a Frenchman to another ministerial post relating to finance. In Vivian's opinion, Nubar "would infinitely prefer to see Egypt govern herself, but he recognizes that this is impossible and that the native element is neither sufficiently apt for administration nor independent enough to attempt to cope with the despotic authority of the Chief of State."[44] The khedive agreed, appointed Nubar Pasha prime minister, and pleased Vivian immensely. "The result is all the more satisfying in that it has been brought about without any semblance of pressure on the part of foreign Governments."[45] But then, in the eyes of both the British and the French, Ismail began to be perverse. The danger of inadvertent involvement the British had perceived in 1876 was by 1878 very real. Step by step they had accepted increasing responsibility for the behavior of British and WOG officials in Egypt, yet the basis of their authority and the ability to enforce it were weak. Reports began reaching them that Ismail was busily undermining the position of Nubar, whom he had so recently appointed "without pressure." The two governments thus instructed their consuls to present a démarche to Ismail. Vivian was to say:

Both the British and French Governments earnestly desire to see the establishment of a stable Government and a sound Administration in Egypt, and they rely upon steady support being given on the part of His Highness the Khedive to the endeavors of Nubar Pasha and his Cabinet to reestablish the financial credit of the country.[46]

By then agitation was apparent to Vivian, and his picture of Egyptian public opinion approached closely the imperial ideal typical image: "If this fermentation was natural it would not be an unhealthy symptom, but I have good reason to suspect that it has been secretly fomented by agents, probably employed by the Khedive."[47]

British impotence became humiliatingly obvious when in February 1879 a military riot occurred in which twenty-five hundred officers who had been placed on half-pay surrounded and jostled Nubar and Sir Rivers Wilson. Ismail came rushing to the scene and quickly restored order. Later evidence strongly suggests that Ismail had connived with the officers;[48] the British drew that conclusion without much evidence. They also well understood the fact that the officers had a financial grievance. But the nearly ideal typical imperial view of Egypt that the British in Egypt held prevented their seeing the early stirrings of a major political development there: a coalition of liberal, religious, and nationalist elements. The liberals consisted mainly of wealthy Turkish-speaking notables of whom Sherif Pasha was most prominent. The religious element consisted of reform-minded Moslem leaders, many of whom had been influenced by Jamal-ud-Din al-Afghani and whose best-known leader was Mohammed Abdou. The nationalists were a nascent Arabic-speaking Egyptian movement soon to crystallize around the leadership of an Arabic-speaking colonel, Ahmed Arabi.[49] Such a coalition had no place in a view of an immature Egypt badly in need of long-term tutelage.

Ismail won a temporary victory. He was able to force Nubar out and to reestablish clear predominance over European officials. In desperation Vivian called for the dispatch of French and British warships to Alexandria.[50] The British action reflected a judgment that their only real problem was Ismail's irresponsibility. None of the diplomatic dispatches and none of the descriptions of the period by contemporary Englishmen even consider the possibility that Ismail's behavior reflected demands placed on him by politically important elements in Egypt. Vivian did worry when Ismail bowed to army demands for back pay, but his concern was with the officers only.[51] He made no mention of their connection with Egyptian nationalism.

Of course, Ismail was a politician trying desperately to retain his position. Having rid himself of Saddiq and accepted in his place Nubar, who performed as a representative of the European bondholding and official elite, Ismail found himself without the means to keep Nubar and the people he represented from eroding court influence and robbing him of his personal fortune. He therefore sought to reestablish the pre-1876 elite balance as the vehicle for his own return to preeminence. He could reasonably hope that the British and French would prefer this to a revolutionary alternative. But far from vying with the liberal-religious-nationalist elite for the khedive's favor in the traditional fashion and thereby granting the khedive a strong bargaining position, the Europeans did not even perceive their competitors. Instead they saw the khedive as the focus of their problem of restoring lost influence. They therefore confronted him with strong demands for Nubar's reinstatement and a restoration of European financial influence. Since he was in serious need of European support to balance off the newly activated domestic elite alliance, Ismail had little choice but to make major concessions.[52] There is nothing in the diplomatic correspondence to indicate British awareness of the price Ismail paid by angering the domestic elite alliance with these concessions. The British persisted in seeing his resistance to their demands as perversity based on personal vanity—and surely personal vanity was a factor. They were unable to see him as a politician seeking to satisfy a diverse clientele. Indeed, they did not perceive the diversity. In the imperial image, public opinion is not perceived.

In the weeks that followed in the spring of 1879, the British persisted in seeing their problem in the simple terms of one man: Ismail, the one-time WOG now turned agitator. Diplomatic correspondence makes clear that the British did receive reports of liberal, religious, and nationalist ferment, but they interpreted all such evidence as manifestations of Ismail's agitating presence. An example of this phenomenon was the report of the British consul, Sir Frank Lascelles, on a meeting with two entirely friendly Egyptians, one a future first minister and a prototypical WOG. Lascelles wrote:

Riaz Pasha had been denounced in the mosques as a friend of the Europeans, and had been declared to have forfeited all claims to be regarded as a Moslem.

A meeting was to be held at the house of the Sheikh El Bakri, and it was believed that it was intended to rouse a religious feeling against the European Ministers and the Christians generally.

Lascelles then quoted a trusted British observer of the Egyptian political scene to the effect that such meetings were coordinated with Ismail's efforts to pressure the Europeans.[53]

Shortly thereafter Ismail made his move toward the Liberals. A new cabinet was formed, headed by Sherif Pasha. The cabinet would exclude Europeans and would be responsible to a Chamber of Notables.[54] This was an Egyptian Magna Carta. That Ismail, whose preference for despotic rule was clearly perceived, would accept this Magna Carta was in no way seen by the British as indicative of the price Ismail had to pay for domestic support. On the contrary, the two powers were outraged. Salisbury instructed Vivian as follows:

The breach of these engagements, and the precipitate and causeless dismissal of the Ministers whose services the Khedive had solicited the Governments of England and France to place at his disposal, are not only at variance with the spirit of Reform of the 28th August, but constitute a grave and apparently intentional discourtesy to a friendly power.

But if he continues to ignore the obligations imposed upon him. . . . it will remain for the two Cabinets to reserve to themselves an entire liberty of appreciation and action in defending their interests in Egypt, and in seeking the arrangements best calculated to secure the good government and prosperity of the country.[55]

Ismail's efforts to convince Vivian that he was not a free agent in his activities were flatly rejected. Vivian wrote that he saw no evidence that Ismail had surrendered any power to the native elites. The entire episode was treated as an elaborate charade.[56] Consequently, in June 1879, the two governments prevailed on Ismail's formal suzerain, the Sultan of the Ottoman Empire, to dismiss Ismail and replace him with his pliable son, Tewfik. But within months the agitation was again too visible to dismiss, and the suspicion began to grow that more drastic action would be called for.

Robert Lowe, the MP for the University of London in the House of Commons in 1876, made two speeches ridiculing the government's behavior in Egypt. He did so by describing the events surrounding the Cave mission as they would look if a nonimperial view of Egypt were held. He said the khedive had asked for two clerks, but the government responded by sending an unsolicited mission to Egypt, apparently not "to find out how much of a salary the two clerks should have," but to make public an outrageously critical report of Egyptian finance. And all this was done at Egyptian expense. "It was bad enough to go without leave to examine into the state of Egyptian finances and to publish them to the whole world without quartering ourselves on the Khedive."[57]

The contrast of this detached picture with the essentially imperial picture held by the government was shocking. By 1879 perceptual alteration in the imperial direction had proceeded so far that arguments in favor of military occupation of Egypt began to be heard. The case is instructive. Confronted with expectational nonrealization based on an image that approached the ideal typical imperial, the perceptual response was to move even closer to the ideal typical imperial. Lowe's perception might well have accommodated the evidence in its full diversity more easily, but all the verbal evidence suggests an underlying perception of threat to vested bureaucratic interests, to vested economic interests, and to the dignity of the British Empire. Overall perceptual accommodation to the demands arising from these interests and to the flow of events apparently could best be achieved by seeing Egypt in terms of an imperial image.

This episode deserves a comparison with the Vietnam study in chapter 6. Three very different situational views were advanced concerning the Egypt seen in 1876. Events betrayed the expectations of those who held the prevailing view. My assumption has been that in such cases a perceptual migration would occur toward the view most congruent with expectations. In this case, however, both the Liberal opposition and the investor-bureaucratic elements could claim that failure would not have occurred had their preferred policy been followed. Unlike the Vietnam case, where the extreme hardliners could as well claim expectational exoneration, perception migrated toward the more hard-line position. This occurred because of a rapidly increasing perception of threat to British interests, prestige, and security. The operating assumption in this study is that such a development leads to migration away from the complex pole and toward enemy and allied poles. In this case, in spite of striking expectational failures, the classic pattern resulting from increasing fear did unfold. In the case of Vietnam, the declining perception of threat led to a U.S. perceptual migration toward the complex pole.

The feedback from these expectational failures into the world view seems to have produced no significant disturbance in the Egyptian case. There were differences between the British and French, but the chief disturbance was of local Egyptian origin and was so perceived. The prevailing world view remained essentially unaltered, so that the disturbance should be classified as being at the level of situational policy.

However, this classification probably understates the importance of the case to general British policy. The situational view of Egypt that prevailed in London differed sharply from that which prevailed among Englishmen in Egypt. The view of the latter was typical of the view held by officials in any era who are deeply involved in the internal affairs of a people perceived as culturally inferior. (The same pattern was clearly apparent during the Cold War.) Publics and elites in the decisional process of the "inferior" society are not differentiated; decisions concerning the governments of such societies are made instead on the basis of a simplistic WOG-agitator distinction.

This simplistic image soon becomes implicit in official policy. Policy directives from the capital must be constructed in general terms, and translations of these general policy directives in the field are likely to push the prevailing situational view in the direction of the situational view held by officials in the field. This was certainly true of the British in Egypt after 1876. Furthermore, as noted earlier, English officials traveling to Egypt quickly adopted the situational view prevailing there and took it back to London with them. As the distance separating the two views eroded, the neatness of the simplistic field view became increasingly apparent in London.

9 / Summer 1882

Historical Narrative

National self-determination was an ideological cornerstone for nineteenth-century English Liberals of the radical persuasion. The national awakening of Greece had captured their imagination, and all were moved, none more than Gladstone, by the plight of Christian nationalities in the Balkans. Irish nationalism, held in check by the force of British arms, was therefore a source of embarrassment and anguish. By 1882 most informed Englishmen had recognized and many had welcomed the first clear manifestations of Egyptian nationalism. But that nationalism was inevitably highly disruptive of the foreign policy goal of Britain in Egypt: an acquiescent, friendly, and stable government.

Egyptian nationalism in 1882 had a profile that now is familiar in non-Western societies caught up in the early stages of profound change. Whereas in France and England nationalism appeared in men's consciousness as the property of large and politically significant sections of the population, nationalism in non-Western communities usually makes its appearance as the property of a tiny though often politically influential section of the population. So it was in Egypt. By definition, nationalism can exist only when the nation becomes a primary identity focus for a significant portion of the population. In Egypt, the fellahin, the vast majority of the population, had an identity focus confined within the boundaries of the visible horizon. For this great peasant majority, "nation" was and could only be a meaningless abstraction. Nationalism could be comprehended only by those educated few whose lives had been much affected by the nationalist West. These people, in turn, fell into four groups, three of which either could not embrace or were threatened by Egyptian nationalism. The first was the sizable community of Europeans and Levantines living primarily in Alexandria who in no way identified with Egypt. The second was the Turkish-speaking element, representatives of which constituted the ruling Moslem elite. Egyptian nationalism was inevitably threatening to this group as well, since they were classified as foreign by the Arabic-speaking Egyptians. The third were the native Christian Copts. For them nationalism would seem to be, at first glance, more an asset than a liability, since they were in their own minds thoroughly Egyptian. But identity is always a complex of factors, and the association of Islam with Egyptian nationalism was natural since the overwhelming majority of the people were Moslem. As the new national identity penetrated Egyptian society, few Moslems distinguished the secular Egyptian element from the spiritual Islamic element.[1] Thus, for the Copt, too, the identity alteration was implicitly threatening. Only the fourth group, the Arabic-speaking Moslem Egyptians, was highly receptive to Egyptian nationalism.

This differentiation has to be made if the role of Egyptian nationalism in the British occupation of Egypt is to be understood. As described in the previous chapter, the French and to a lesser extent the British insisted on considerable influence in Egyptian decision-making. Yet neither wished to establish direct control, in part because of an acute awareness of their own conflicting interests. Largely oblivious to the decision-making role that had been played by Arabic-speaking Egyptians, both Copt and Moslem, the Europeans effected an alliance with Ismail and the Turkish-speaking ruling elite. They accepted with relief the ouster and probable murder of Finance Minister Ismail Saddiq, who had represented the view of the Arabic-speaking small landowners. His replacement by Nubar Pasha, almost a classic WOG, was not recognized as a symbolic replacement of the representation of one power group, the Arabic-speaking Egyptians, by the representative of another power group, the European governments. Nor was the price Ismail paid for executing this maneuver comprehended.

Governmental control in "traditional societies" is remarkably casual. The overwhelming majority of the population accept habitually and without question a normative system which virtually eliminates them from the decision-making process. Thus active control, whether through satisfaction of material and power demands, an appeal to accepted symbols, or acts of coercion, is required for only that small minority which to some degree participate politically. But the change produced by the Western impact is quickly manifest in a breakdown of habitual norms and the rapid growth of the percentage of the population which is to some degree politically participant. As this occurs, the casual control system of the traditional ruling elite will certainly be ineffective, and some adaptation will be required if that ruling elite is to survive. Nationalism becomes a major catalytic force in breaking down the habitual normative system. Ascriptively based identity distinctions begin to crumble as the notion of common membership in a community grows. In Egypt, thus, Arabic-speaking representation in decision-making was being eliminated at the very moment that nationalism was beginning to spread rapidly. With this growth in political awareness came an increase in the percentage of the Arabic-speaking population which had to be controlled by active means.

As described in the previous chapter, Ismail's efforts to reestablish a role for the Arabic-speaking element were simply not perceived by Europeans. Since the latter were oblivious to Ismail's control problem, they saw his maneuver as a pure reflection of avarice and unreliability. He was replaced by his WOG son, Tewfik, and briefly a control system even more casual than its predecessor was established. In the British situational view, Ismail was the source of most difficulties; once he was removed, control could be relaxed. They saw no problem for Egyptian politicians in meeting the British demand that close to half of Egyptian government revenues be earmarked for debt repayment. They therefore concerned themselves exclusively with establishing European-style fiscal institutions and left the control of the population to the most docile, acquiescent, and least respected section of the Turkish-speaking elite. Support for such a regime was, of course, confined to the European and Levantine populations.

The primary coercive instrument in this control system, the army, included many Arabic-speaking officers, particularly in the lower ranks. Conceivably, the support of these officers could have been purchased by satisfying their material and power demands, for example, with salary increases and promotions into the higher ranks. But the British recommended an opposite tactic. The European controllers insisted on the reduction of governmental expenses, including the army's. Naturally enough, the Turkish-speaking rulers chose to economize by retiring many officers, mostly Arabic-speaking, at half pay. Of those Egyptians with a natural receptivity to Egyptian nationalism, Arabic-speaking officers were at the top of the list. Therefore, this action brought into harmony the role of ideological interests of these officers and created in them a high revolutionary potential. Furthermore, a colonel from within their ranks, Ahmed Arabi, quickly demonstrated leadership qualities which seemed to include a charismatic potential. As will be seen, the British accommodated perceptually by picturing Arabi as a half-savage, crassly ambitious charlatan. John Marlowe, whose *Cromer in Egypt* was published in 1970, describes Arabi gratuitously as an "arrogant and illiterate braggart,"[2] and this is a faithful representation of the view Arabi's British contemporaries had to hold if they were to be comfortable with their treatment of him. But regardless of his personal characteristics—and no one should envy the biographer of so controversial a figure—Arabi was of momentous importance in this story.

In September 1881, the army, led by its Arabic-speaking officers, demonstrated and compelled the khedive to accept a new government led by Sherif Pasha and under the influence of Arabi and his fellow officers. Very quickly the British and French found themselves in an utterly ridiculous position. The happily casual, inexpensive, and unobtrusive control scheme they had unwittingly constructed had totally collapsed. A government based on the informal liberal, religious, and nationalist coalition had been created, and a process of increasing disregard for the European bureaucrats who sat uncomfortably in their midst had been set in motion.

Some well-informed Englishmen, such as the unabashedly imperialist Cairo correspondent of the *London Times,* consistently denied the significance of the Egyptian national movement; but English Liberals of the radical school had looked on the movement as significant and of great political benefit to Egypt. Now they were being compelled to recognize the problems Egyptian nationalism was generating. As will be seen, their need to accommodate this perceived nationalism and British interests led to an alteration in their perception of the nationalists, and in particular of Arabi. But that process of accommodation was slow, and much agonizing was necessary before the Liberal government could alter its view sufficiently to decide to occupy Egypt, even temporarily. Historians are often harsh in their judgment of Gladstone's vacillations, but his indecision is thoroughly understandable in view of this conflict between ideology and influence.[3]

When the military demonstration that forced a change in government occurred, the British suddenly understood the extent of their weakness inside Egypt. Therefore, through Vice-Consul Cookson, they directly threatened Arabi:

I represented to Arabi Bey in the plainest terms the great risk which he and those with him incurred by the menacing attitude they had assumed. I told him that, if they persisted in assuming the government of the country, the army must be prepared to meet the united forces of the Sublime Porte and of the European Powers, both of whom were too much interested in the welfare and tranquility of Egypt to allow the country to descend, through a military government, to anarchy. Arabi Bey answered that the army was assembled to secure by arms the liberties of the Egyptian people. I answered that the Khedive and Europe could not recognize a barely military revolt as the expression of the will of the Egyptian people.
[But] . . . the attitude of Arabi Bey to me personally was most courteous and he used expressions of friendliness to Europeans generally, and to England in particular, to whose efforts for the liberation of slaves he alluded, as showing that she ought to sympathize with the Egyptians in their attempt to obtain liberty.[4]

It was apparent that France would not agree to the sending of Turkish troops, that neither power would tolerate the unilateral intervention of the other, and that a joint intervention was unlikely unless the two governments felt a very clear challenge from Arabi and the new government. That challenge was not forthcoming. Arabi demanded only that there be a new government, that the minister of war be Arabic-speaking, and that the army be expanded to 18,100 men. In a long dispatch sent September 23, Sir Edward Malet, the British agent in Egypt, placed the blame for the demonstration on the stupidity of the khedive's brother-in-law, who as minister of war had provoked the officers by ordering a key regiment out of Cairo.[5] There was as yet little sense of urgency, and the European powers did not go beyond dispatching a symbolic man-of-war to Alexandria and sending a message to the khedive assuring him of British-French backing in his efforts to restore discipline to the army. As Cookson's reaction to Arabi suggests, it was still possible to view Arabi ambivalently.

The new government in Egypt represented a fundamental change, but its leadership was anything but radical. They could not afford to be, for Arabi and the army needed the support of other coalition elements. Sherif Pasha represented the liberal constitutional faction within the Turkish-speaking community, and he moved quickly to gain the support of Arabic-speaking landowners by convoking and offering increased power to the landowner-dominated Chamber of Notables. In addition, the new regime could count on the support of the liberal Moslem leadership. Far from being monolithic, the regime was an uneasy alliance of conservatives and moderates, cosmopolitans and nationalists. A radical program would have destroyed the alliance.

There was understanding among the British of this pluralism. Sir Auckland Colvin, the British controller, wrote on September 19:

The army is elated by what it has achieved, and its leaders are penetrated with the conviction that their mission is to give Egypt liberty. The Notables, who are in large number in Cairo, though they have taken into their own hands the right to ask for an extension of civil liberties, and deny the officers any right of petition or of interference in the matter, are at one with them in the desire to obtain some solid concessions. All is being done in an orderly and even exemplary manner: but the chance of any final settlement depends:—

(1) On the army dispersing to the several quarters assigned to it.
(2) On the moderation shown by the Notables in their demands.
(3) On the tact and firmness of the Ministers in dealing with the army and the Notables . . .

I do not think it is at all my duty to oppose myself to the popular movement, but to try rather to guide and to give it definite shape. So long as the financial position of the country, or the influence of this Control, is not likely to be affected by concessions made to the Notables, I believe I should be very foolish to express any hostility to their wishes. It is in this sense that I propose to act, and to advise Charif Pasha when the matter is ripe for discussion.[6]

Lord Cromer looked at Colvin's memorandum years later and made this comment: "Sir Auckland Colvin rightly judged the situation. Sherif Pasha was the nominal Prime Minister but Arabi, as Sir Edward Malet said, was the 'arbiter of the destinies of the country.' "[7] Colvin's own book, written years later, evinces not the slightest awareness of the political pluralism and the "popular movement" he saw in 1881.[8] Cromer and Colvin, as major imperial officers in British-occupied Egypt, saw an Egypt close to the imperial image; indeed, Colvin's view was far more nearly ideal typical than Cromer's. When they looked back to pre-occupation days, they simply reinterpreted the situation, but at the precrisis moment British officials did understand that the Sherif regime was one of considerable diversity.

The process set in motion was at first one of erosion rather than confrontation. The Europeans were very uneasy about Arabi's demand for an expanded army. This underlined too clearly the almost absurd weakness of the European control, dependent for enforcement on the very elements that it most feared. But the issue that moved the situation toward confrontation finds its parallel whenever a parliament seeks to make its influence on the decisional process meaningful: the right to vote the budget. The Chamber of Notables asked for this right, but only for that portion of the budget which was not to be used for servicing the debt. Even so, the British and French rejected the demand on the grounds that the Egyptians would overspend and soon would place demands on the portion administered by the European controllers.

In November 1881, Leon Gambetta became premier of France. Gambetta favored a policy to restore some of France's lost grandeur, and in the three months of his premiership he played a vital role in hastening the crisis in Egypt. He suffered from none of the ambivalence toward self-determination that the English Liberals experienced and favored a tough policy. In the view of many Englishmen, Gambetta "was quite prepared for, if not anxious to provoke, an Anglo-French occupation."[9] In any event, Gambetta suggested what has been called the Joint Note to the Egyptian government, and the British Foreign Secretary, G. G. Leveson-Gower, second earl of Granville, agreed. The note, which both the British and French consuls in Cairo delivered, asserted "that the English and French Governments consider the maintenance of His Highness on the throne . . . as alone able to guarantee for the present and the future good order and general prosperity in Egypt."[10]

In *ex post facto* reporting of this eipsode, Cromer regards it as a key factor in making occupation inevitable. He quotes a telegram of Sir Edward Malet to Lord Granville:

The communication has, at all events, temporarily alienated from us all confidence. Everything was progressing capitally, and England was looked on as the sincere wellwisher and protector of the country. Now, it is considered that England has definitely thrown in her lot with France, and that France, from motives in connection with her Tunisian campaign, is determined ultimately to intervene here.[11]

The *London Times* correspondent, on the other hand, reported a wildly enthusiastic reception in Egypt, and the *Times* said editorially that "the successful prosecution of the joint policy of the two countries in Egypt is largely dependent on M. Gambetta."[12] There is indeed every reason to suspect that Cromer's analysis exaggerated the impact of the note out of all proportion in an effort to depict the crisis of a few months later as French-generated.

There was at the time a widely circulated rumor that Arabi was seeking to depose the khedive. The rumor was serious enough that British friends of Arabi had published in the *Times* a statement ostensibly by Arabi. In it, he accepted existing Egyptian relations with the Ottoman Empire but said any effort to tighten Ottoman control would be resisted; he expressed "loyal allegiance to the person of the reigning Khedive" but said there would be no restoration of the despotic regime; he recognized the services of England and France to Egypt but asserted the temporary nature of the arrangement; and he said the "National Party has confided its interests at the present time to the army" because it alone could protect Egyptian liberty but asserted that when that situation passed, "the army will abandon its present political attitudes."[13] This statement was designed to counter a dangerous perception developing in both England and France of the nature and motives of the National party and its leader. The Joint Note reflected that perception.

In any event, there is nothing to indicate that the British were any more interested than the French in granting budgetary approval rights to the Chamber of Notables. This was the critical issue that led to the collapse of the Sherif government and the broad coalition which had ruled Egypt since September. More conservative elements among the Arabic-speaking landowners and religious leaders were clearly uncomfortable with the now solidly nationalist regime,[14] but open opposition was difficult for any politician: Popular support was too great, and army control was too strong.

At the end of January the Gambetta regime in France was overturned, and his forward policy reversed by the successor regime of Charles Louis de Freycinet. From then on, the British were the consistent initiators of interventionist policy in Egypt. Granville made clear his reluctance to engage in unilateral intervention, his unwillingness to consider unilateral French intervention, and his preference for the least of the evils, Turkish intervention.[15] But the French refused to consider Turkish intervention, and de Freycinet did not see sufficient cause for joint Franco-British intervention.[16] A decision to accommodate to the nationalist regime was apparently not seriously considered. Given this situation, a major confrontation was probably unavoidable. The dual control of the British and French was by now little more than a collecting agency for servicing the debt. Yet the Egyptian government was careful not to provoke the British in either of the two areas which would have given any easy justification for unilateral intervention: default on the debt or a threat to the security of the Suez Canal. Short of such a provocation, the British could not easily justify the coercive force necessary to give substance to the threats made implicitly or explicitly since September 1881. Thus, the British position remained humiliating.

Confrontation was likely whenever the nationalist regime attempted to reduce further the power of the khedive and the badly weakened Turkish-speaking elite. The ruler and the conservative Turkish-speaking landowners were Britain's sole allies now, and weakening their position further would simply add to the British sense of impotence. The first confrontation issue that developed was natural. Turkish-speaking officers were relegated to positions of little influence in the army, and many had been retired. That they would wish to reverse this situation was certain, and they were likely to take action to give substance to that wish. It was also probable that Arabic-speaking officers would expect such action and perceive signs of it which had no basis in reality. In any event, forty of the

Turkish-speaking officers were charged with conspiracy against Arabi, convicted, and sentenced to banishment to the Sudan.

When asked to countersign the sentences, the khedive called Sir Edward Malet to his palace and asked for his advice. "I replied that there were moments when one must face the unknown, and that I thought that if His Highness desired to maintain his reputation as a civilized Prince he should on this occasion refuse to sanction a sentence which by his own showing, and in general opinion, was contrary to the principles of justice and humanity."[17] Malet fully understood the seriousness of his advice, for he described the objections of his French colleague, M. de Sinkiewicz, in these terms: "My colleague is no doubt influenced by a strong desire to avoid a rupture between the Khedive and the Government which might in its turn lead to the necessity of intervention."[18] This supposition was proved correct. Premier de Freycinet, obviously acting to foreclose a British demand for Turkish intervention, suggested the sending of ironclads to Alexandria.[19] Granville responded that he would favor sending a three-nation commission, and "under the present urgent circumstances, I should have been ready to accompany it with a threat of Turkish intervention."[20]

The results of this maneuver were totally predictable: a major effort to consolidate power by the nationalists and, in particular, Arabi and his military colleagues. The khedive had followed British advice, and the result was a serious loss of influence for the court and for the Turkish-speaking elite. Marlowe states flatly that the ministry sought to convoke the chamber for the purpose of deposing the khedive,[21] but that view is not reflected in the diplomatic correspondence. Malet and Sinkiewicz met with Arabi, who said that he had no desire to depose the khedive, "but that in the event of an Anglo-French squadron arriving he could not guarantee public safety."[22] On the contrary, the nationalist regime continued to behave moderately. But the British had passed their point of no return. Malet pleaded with Granville to instruct him on the means to halt the rapid deterioration of the khedive's position. Malet said this could be done by compelling the present ministry to resign and be replaced by a new Sherif Pasha premiership, but he made clear his conviction that Anglo-French threats must be backed by credible means of coercion.[23] His reading of the situation led Malet to make explicit his demands in what was later in Commons described as an ultimatum. Malet delivered the following demands to the president of the Council of Ministers:

1. The temporary retirement from Egypt of his Excellency Arabi Pasha . . .
2. The retirement into the interior of Egypt of Ali Fehmy Pasha and Abdullah Pasha . . .
3. The resignation of the present Ministry.[24]

The president of the council accepted this note, and his action led to Arabi's resignation as minister of war. The army demanded his reinstatement, and even conservative Arabic-speaking notables and religious leaders were compelled to make official requests for his return. Some army officers called for the khedive's deposition,[25] but this appears to have been more bargaining than a serious request since the demand was not repeated. The khedive reinstated Arabi and thus accepted a titular role in the decisional process. He had little choice: The Anglo-French threat, despite Malet's pleas, lacked teeth. Granville appealed urgently to all interested European powers to agree to Turkish military intervention, but again without effect.[26]

Premier de Freycinet at this point proposed that a conference on Egyptian affairs be convoked immediately. He was reported to have said, "There can no longer be any reasonable hope of a pacific solution through the moral influences of the French and English squadrons and the good offices of the two Agents at Cairo."[27] The British immediately accepted the proposal only to find that the sultan of the Ottoman Empire was reluctant to agree. Granville remarked to the Turkish ambassador impatiently that were there to be Turkish obstruction "it would be difficult to find arguments to meet the pressure that would be put upon us to take immediate and independent action in consideration of the pressing nature of the circumstances and the engagements under which we lay."[28] The Turks now comprehended, as did de Freycinet, the extent of British agitation and dispatched a commissioner, Ibrahim Dervish Pasha, to Egypt. But the British were not to be denied a conference. They told the Turks that one would take place in Constantinople regardless of their opposition.[29]

Two developments which were to spark the occupation had become obvious by early June. First, the Egyptians, confronted with an allied squadron, began constructing and repairing batteries in the Alexandria harbor. The British, through the Turks, induced them to stop.[30] But both countries had entered a twilight zone of armament maintenance and construction that would spark the bombardment of the Alexandria fortifications. Second, the temper of the Arabic-speaking Moslems and of the European residents of Alexandria was such that any minor spark could create a conflagration. The spark flamed on June 11, 1882, in the form of a petty quarrel between Greeks and Arabs. By the time it was over, many Europeans and a handful of Moslems had been killed.[31] Admiral Frederick Seymour was given orders to protect British citizens even if he must land troops.[32] A month later the admiral was given instructions to fire on Egyptian fortifications if the Egyptians persisted in constructing them.[33] On July 11, 1882, Seymour opened fire. The first step in the occupation had begun.

Prevailing World View

When Granville reluctantly gave Admiral Seymour blanket authority to take action against Egyptian fortifications, he told him to invite French participation.

But, when informed of Seymour's intention to begin bombardment, the French squadron weighed anchor and sailed for Port Said rather than risk involvement.[34] Later, when de Freycinet asked the French Chamber's approval for funds for joint action with the British to protect the Suez Canal, he was overwhelmingly defeated. Five days earlier the House of Commons had voted 275 to 19 in favor of funds for that expedition.[35]

As partners in the dual control in Egypt, Britain and France had been equally humiliated by Egyptian nationalism. Furthermore, French interests in Egypt were in many ways greater than those of the British. No French interest, however, compared with the British interest in the Suez Canal. But evidence that in these months the British really did perceive a threat to the canal is sparse; and only when intervention was almost certain did British rhetoric begin to focus on Suez.

An explanation for this differential in British and French responses to an identical challenge emerges when the prevailing world views of the two peoples are compared. For France, 1882 was only a little more than a decade after the French humiliation at the hands of a newly born Germany. French perceptions of Germany in 1882 still approximated the enemy image—a monolithic, highly rational foe with evil designs. Gambetta was driven by a desire to restore to France a sense of confidence and grandeur, but his early replacement by de Freycinet reflected his isolation in this response. For most Frenchmen all policy had to be calculated in terms of its meaning for Franco-German relations. Intervention in Egypt could easily produce a German-Ottoman combination that could threaten French interests in Africa and Europe. The price was intolerably high.

In sharp contrast, the English in 1882 perceived no serious threat from any European power. This was even more true in 1882 than it had been in 1876. The British perceived the Congress of Berlin of 1876 as a great diplomatic victory. Taylor argues, in fact, that this belief in the long run weakened Britain, "for it led the British public to believe that they could play a great role without expense or exertion—without reforming their navy, without creating an army, without finding an ally."[36] In 1876 the Balkan crisis and the possible demise of Turkey had given Britain serious cause for concern, but in 1882 a Russian threat to Constantinople and the straits was not perceived. Only in Central Asia, where the inexorable Russian advance persisted, was the sense of threat to empire severe.

Gladstone in 1879 gave full expression to this happy British world view. In a speech on November 25 he outlined six "right principles of foreign policy." The keystone was the idea of a Concert of Europe "to keep the Powers of Europe in union together. And why? Because by keeping all in union together you neutralize and fetter and bind up the selfish aims of each."[37] The need for allies was not perceived because no serious threat was perceived. The other principles suggested as well the range of perceived opportunity: The second was to preserve peace, "especially to the Christian nations of the world"; the sixth was that "there should be a sympathy with freedom, a desire to give it scope, founded not only on visionary ideas, but upon the long experience of many generations within the shores of this happy isle"; and the fifth was liberty: "Liberty is what I wish to defend, and I care not who is the assailant. . . . My mottoes are 'Hands Off' and 'the soil for the people.' "[38]

As has already been suggested, these latter three principles are not to be disregarded as determinants of British policy, for they symbolized values which were of great importance to one section of the British political elite, values with which policy had to be reconciled. They were of little importance to Liberal Whigs such as Spencer Cavendish, Marquess of Hartington, and to liberal-minded Conservatives,[39] but there is nothing to suggest that these leaders perceived the tranquility of Europe after the Congress of Berlin as offering an opportunity for expanding the empire. On a general level, both policy and verbal behavior of British elites suggest little perception of threat to England and the British Empire and little perception of opportunity for expansion.

Among interest groups, the same generalization holds true. Commercial interests seem to have perceived little threat and little need for government support in opening up new commercial opportunities. As was true in 1876, the antislavery advocates saw opportunity for government support in their mission to gain control over regions where the slave trade was substantial. But policy discussions rarely refer to this pressure, and the influence of this group must be judged as minor.

Given the low perception of threat and of opportunity, the mapping of world views consists of clusterings around the complex center. Indeed, were it not for the view of Egypt, figure II.3 would be a classic case of a parametric value at its lowest rating. Later I will depict differentiated views, but here only the prevailing view (PV) of Egypt is mapped. The position at which the prevailing view is placed reflects the image of Egypt at the time of the intervention. A coalition liberal and antiliberal regime at the moment sees Egypt in virtually the ideal typical imperial image. As will be discussed below, this discordant view became a disturbance which was to produce significant general strategy change in the system of foreign policy aims. The antislavery movement's view (A) of Africa is mapped as well.

Motivational System—General

Commenting on the Britain of 1882, Taylor concluded that "British policy was conditioned solely by extra-European interests."[40] Before the year was over, and largely because of the Egyptian misadventure, anger and hostility were being expressed toward France, and the beginnings of an enemy perceptual image were to be seen. But prior to the occupation of Egypt, the British sense of a need to defend herself and her empire was nowhere intense. There was some nervousness about Russian advances in Central Asia which were perceived as a threat to India and the life line to India, and within a few years this would lead to some forward activity in Afghanistan. But in 1882 there was little interest in expanding influence

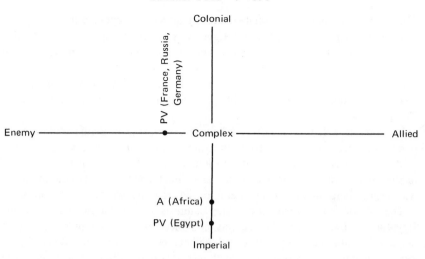

Figure II.3. British Prevailing World View, 1882

in any direction for whatever reason. The Gladstone election in 1880 has been described as one in which the articulate British public had expressed its will in foreign affairs, "the only one fought on issues of foreign policy until the election of 1935."[41] As seen earlier, the policy proposals to which they responded were couched in ideological terms and reflected a serene confidence in British security. There was emphasis on Christian nations, and there was a clear suggestion that British culture was something for others to emulate. But the thrust was on peace, freedom, and self-determination. Since they were the filters through which policy had to be seen, the impact of ideology on that policy was substantial. This point was clearly manifest in Egypt, where although peace, freedom, and self-determination ultimately all fell victim to British policy, a concern for these values long delayed British action.

The contention here, therefore, is that British motivations in 1882, when contrasted with those of 1876, reflect a downgrading of defense as the motivating force in British foreign policy.[42] It is proposed that the general motivational system of 1882 appeared as follows:

A. Defense
   National grandeur
B. Trade: exports and imports
   Ideological messianism
C. Religious messianism
   Cultural messianism
   Bureaucratic vested interests

The argument for placing national grandeur in the same category as defense will be developed later. The occupation of Egypt was of prime importance for British foreign policy in 1882, which anticipates the proposition that prestige was a prime motivating force in that policy. This, of course, is not to deny the importance of defense. But the case is strong that whatever threat was perceived in Egypt grew out of the Egyptian milieu and had little to do with a sense of direct threat from any European power.

Indistinguishable from the overall defense factor is that of British trade. British policy reflected no serious activity in expanding opportunities for British commerce, but it was strongly committed to defending existing trade. In most cases, as in Suez and in India, the threat to trade was indirect, and the thrust of the challenge was felt far more on the fringes of empire, where trade was of less importance.

The addition of bureaucratic vested interests is also based largely on the Egyptian and Indian cases. Bureaucrats, convinced of the civilizing role they were playing but also certainly concerned with career security and advancement, included many who saw British national interest as demanding a forward policy to protect the empire against developing threats. This point, too, will be further developed.

General System of Aims

A comparison of the system-of-aims outlines in this chapter and chapter 8 will indicate first the inferential judgment that British foreign policy system values in 1882 as in 1876 were status-quo. Despite Gladstone's expressed concern for freedom and national self-determination, British policy did not bear the mark of an ideological crusade. As the motivational system indicates, ideology had been upgraded in the judgment of British motives in 1882 as compared with those of 1876, but it is not reflected on the most fundamental level, that of system aims.

The outline does reflect the judgment that a general strategy change in the British system of aims had occurred since 1876, but it was of minor importance. In chapter 8 the primary parametric value determinant of 1876 was proposed to be a perception of threat from the development of a hostile combination of powers in Europe which is of such low intensity that no polarized allied-enemy perceptual syndromes appear. Largely as a result of the Congress of Berlin, this perception of threat was replaced by a low-intensity perception of opportunity. The inferred parametric value determinants of 1882 are therefore: (1) a perception of opportunity for British diplomatic leadership in creating a Concert of Europe which would preserve the peace from disturbances resulting from a conflict of petty selfish interests; (2) a perception of threat from Russian expansion southward toward India and the imperial life line of moderate intensity and a threat of low intensity from French expansion of control in Egypt; (3) a perception of opportunity to advance freedom and national self-determination among other peoples; a perception of opportunity to serve as a civilizing force in areas where Englishmen instruct local officials; a low-intensity perception of threat to British imperial trade and economic interests abroad; and (4) a perception of threat to the dignity of the British Empire and its officers from native anarchic forces. As compared with 1876, this represents a change, though again of no more than moderate importance, in perceived opportunity to spread British political values to other peoples and in a perceived threat to British dignity from native agitators.

These changes can be seen represented primarily in division A of the outline. There the opportunity to bring lasting peace to Europe, especially as perceived by Gladstone, is spelled out. Division B reflects confidence in the permanence of the features of the Congress of Berlin and also declining fear of French imperialism. Division C reflects the increased emphasis on ideological messianism, bureaucratic interests, and prestige as compared with 1876 and the decline in concern for the beleaguered Christians of the Balkans.

I. Preserve the peace, well-being, and security of the British people and safeguard the British Empire
   A. While avoiding entangling alliances, work for a Concert of Europe, to preserve the peace and influence the status quo in Europe
      1. Preserve the Franco-German status quo
      2. Counter polarizing tendencies such as that of the League of Three Emperors and the Triple Alliance
      3. Maintain the Balkan and Ottoman status quo as developed in the Congress of Berlin
   B. Defend the empire and the imperial life line from Russian or French threats
      1. Preserve the Near East status quo which inhibits a Russian southward advance
      2. Prevent Russian expansion southward toward India from engulfing Afghanistan
      3. Counter any French move to gain further control over Egypt and the imperial life line through the Suez Canal
   C. Satisfy the foreign policy–related demands of the British people
      1. Maintain and protect from native agitation a colonial bureaucracy capable of administering the British Empire efficiently and well
      2. Maintain a foreign service bureaucracy capable of administering and directing British foreign policy
      3. Maintain armed forces capable of providing for the defense and security of Great Britain, the empire, and the imperial life line
      4. Defend and advance the interests of British industry and commerce on the high seas, in the empire, abroad, and at home
      5. Defend the dignity and enhance the prestige of the British nation, in particular against native agitation

6. Accept as a special mission the defense and encouragement of moves abroad in the direction of freedom and national self-determination
7. Advance civilized values in Africa and the Orient, particularly through talented British officials; work to eliminate the slave trade

In 1876 the disturbance most likely to effect general strategy change was that in the Balkans. By 1882 that disturbance had passed, and its passing produced the general strategy change noted above. Now the most threatening disturbance was internal agitation in Egypt. Most directly threatened were C.1, British administrators in Egypt; C.4, the interest of British bondholders in Egypt; and C.5, the prestige and dignity of the British nation, because of the humiliating position in which Britain was placed by the Egyptian nationalists. But it was well understood that an energetic countering of those threats would generate hostility from the French and Russians and thereby intensify the perceived threat from those two powers to the empire. This, in turn, could produce a general strategy change which would be reflected both in imperial defense policy and in Britain's ability to work for a Concert of Europe and to avoid entangling alliances within Europe.

Prevailing Situational View

British perceptions of the situation in Egypt from September 1881 to July 1882 were strikingly diverse. Some were stable throughout the period, while others changed sharply as the Egyptian crisis intensified. Looking at role, ideological conviction, and historical progression, however, the perceptions of each group were fully comprehensible.

Most consistent were the views of Englishmen resident in Egypt and dependent on the British presence for the security of their livelihood. An eloquent and sophisticated example of this group was the correspondent of the *London Times* in Cairo. His was a thoroughly imperial point of view, as has been seen in the description of the previous period. In 1882 he spoke of Ahmed Arabi and the Khedive Tewfik with the confidence of profound conviction. Arabi, true to the agitator image found in the ideal typical imperial view of local nationalists, was an ignorant, self-seeking, military adventurer—certainly not a sincere nationalist. Tewfik, on the other hand, almost the WOG in the ideal typical imperial image, was fine, courageous, and popular, however deficient in English competence. Typical was the following description in the *Times*:

In the first place, Arabi Bey, stripped of the kind of sentimental, "saviour of society" reputation he has obtained is nothing more than a colonel of a regiment who has twice broken through all the rules of military discipline in the most flagrant manner. . . .

I state my conviction that 99 out of every 100 Egyptians are content with the guidance of their Khedive, their Ministers and the Controllers, and do not want any fresh leaders, however patriotic they may be.[43]

Gambetta's no-nonsense attitude was popular among Englishmen in Egypt, and the Joint Note was applauded as a sign of the Europeans' growing willingness to be tough. The aim of the nationalists was clear enough—absolute power. Writing of the Turkish-speaking officers' trial, the *Times* correspondent remarked, "It cannot be doubted that the real motive of the trial was to clear off a large number of dangerous rivals";[44] the possibility of their guilt was apparently never considered. When the khedive refused to countersign the sentence, "the attitude of the khedive is applauded without exception by all classes, even infatuated followers of Arabi, agreeing that in the last few days he has thrown off the mask and shown himself in his true colours as an ignorant and ambitious fanatic."[45] Furthermore, no real reason was seen to take Arabi seriously. His nationalist regime was viewed as absurdly weak, as nothing more than a handful of agitators who, in a setting in which there was no public opinion, had no one to appeal to. "It is universally believed that the arrival of a Turkish Commission, supported by a handful of troops, would cause the bubble to burst in days."[46]

Confronted with undeniable evidence of popular support for Arabi, the *Times* correspondent had no difficulty in bringing perceptual accommodation:

As for popularity with the masses, that is in Egypt entirely a matter of success. I have sometimes spoken of Arabi as hated. I was wrong. With some few doubtful exceptions, the average Egyptian does not love or hate. At every turn in recent events native opinion regarding Arabi has undergone a change. Did he seem to be succeeding—he was the saviour of the nation. Did he receive a check—that same nation howled at him with the foulest abuse. I admit that Tewfik is unpopular in this sense. So is England, so is France, and so will Turkey be, if she allows herself to be snubbed.[47]

The moral, of course, was clear. All the native understands is force. Dervish Pasha, the Turkish commissioner, understood this, and when a group of Arabi's supporters began complaining to him of European behavior, he cut them short. "The result was precisely what might have been expected by all who knew the Egyptian nature. They cringed, professed themselves his slaves, and stated that they existed in Egypt only to obey his orders."[48]

When the European response was weak, the pattern was as expected. "The position of Europeans and especially of the English and French who remain has become intolerable; not from fear of immediate danger, but from the extreme contempt and insult with which they are treated."[49] But when the response was forceful, the other side of the pattern prevailed. When Admiral Seymour gave the Egyptians his ultimatum, the *Times* response was ecstatic:

We have but to show ourselves prepared to use force, and we shall obtain all we want, possibly without having to use it.

Supported by 15,000 troops ready to land from two sides in Alexandria, the risk would be reduced to nothing, and the loss to property not so great as is incurred by each day's delay.[50]

When the bombardment was followed by the burning of Alexandria, the *Times* correspondent was enraged. He knew where to place the blame: "The fires in the town were undoubtedly the work of the soldiers, at the direct instigation if not of Arabi himself at least of . . . his prominent supporters."[51] But he did admit amazement at the Egyptian resistance to the bombardment. "Their perseverence in resisting was contrary to all received opinion. . . . The resistance made, as a matter of endurance, would do credit to any gunners in the world."[52]

Equally consistent on the opposite side was Sir Wilfrid Blunt. Blunt has been dealt with badly by historians of this period. Marlowe refers to him as "the Egyptian nationalist and sympathizer and propagandist."[53] Robert L. Tignor warns his readers that Blunt was "a pro-Egyptian observer whose evidence must be treated with great caution."[54] Tignor's admonition is correct, of course. Blunt had the deepest affection for Egyptians, and he saw the Arabi movement as a fundamental manifestation of Egyptian political identity. This was his reality view, and he accommodated events to it. He saw, for example, a solid case for the contention that the forty Turkish-speaking ex-officers had indeed plotted against Arabi.[55] But this acceptance of the case with little evidence is no more suspicious than the rejection of the case by other observers with no more evidence, and Tignor does not warn us about them. Possibly some future historian will discover whether there was such a plot, but his findings will be academic. Men acted on their perceptions at the time, and the prevailing perception, that is, the one on which policy makers in Britain acted, was not Blunt's but one closer to that seen in the *London Times* correspondent's writings. The propensity to downgrade Blunt does, however, reveal the value frame of those who do so.[56]

Blunt maintained his perceptual construct of Arabi and the Egyptian national movement even when his beliefs made him vulnerable to the charge of treason. Yet he saw Arabi and Egypt through very English eyes. He described Arabi as follows: "A typical fellah, tall, heavy-limbed, and somewhat slow in his movements, he seemed to symbolize that massive bodily strength which is so characteristic of the laborious peasant of the Lower Nile. He had nothing in him of the alertness of the soldier."[57] One senses throughout a certain disappointment in Arabi's failure to measure up to a British ideal. But Blunt's view of the national movement was highly favorable. "The National movement of 1881 was essentially a fellah movement having for its object the emancipation of the fellahin."[58] His description of the reaction to the September 1881 army demonstration was polar to that of the *Times*:

The three months which followed this notable event were the happiest time, politically, that Egypt has ever known. . . . Throughout Egypt a cry of jubilation arose such as for hundreds of years had not been heard upon the Nile, and it is literally true that in the streets of Cairo men stopped each other, though strangers, to embrace and rejoice together at the astonishing new reign of liberty which had suddenly begun for them.[59]

Blunt's description of the Joint Note and its importance also diverges sharply from that of the *Times* correspondent, but in this case, his perception is close to that of the British agent, Sir Edward Malet, and of Lord Cromer. His picture of Gambetta as an ultraproud French nationalist coincided with the prevailing view, but he added another point: "He was besides, through his Jewish origin, closely connected with the *haute finance* of the Paris Bourse, and was intimate with other capitalists who had their millions invested in Egyptian Bonds."[60] Blunt consistently saw a greater role for the bondholders in generating British and French policies than did other observers. He frequently noted the importance of the Rothschilds as part of a Jewish extended family able to exert substantial influence in London as in Paris. In the case of the Joint Note, he remarked, "The effect of Gambetta's menace to the National Party was disastrous at Cairo to the cause of peace."[61] He saw polarization developing: "Arabi . . . gained immensely in popularity and respect and for many days after this I hardly heard anything from my Egyptian friends but the language of Pan-Islamism."[62] With the Egyptians adamant, he felt a French intervention was inevitable. "Indeed, I think it is not too much to say that Gambetta's resignation on 31st January alone saved Egypt from the misfortune, even greater perhaps than what afterwards befell her, of a French invasion avowedly anti-Mohammedan and in purely European interests."[63]

Blunt saw a sudden shift of attitude among the British in Egypt. "Following Colvin's lead they had all gone over like sheep to ideas of intervention, for be it noted that it was now no longer French intervention that was talked of, but English, and at once in English eyes the immorality of aggression had been transformed into a duty."[64] Blunt saw this shift very much in terms of bureaucratic vested interests: "Malet and Colvin had committed themselves at the time of the change of Ministry in February to an attitude of uncompromising hostility to the Nationalists, and any solution of the crisis which would leave these in power they knew would mean their own disgrace."[65] Blunt therefore considered Malet's ultimatum thoroughly in line with this bureaucratic position. Blunt recognized as well a clear connection between the British drift toward intervention and the difficult Irish question.[66]

With regard to the crucial question of the Egyptian threat to the Suez Canal, Blunt is very specific. He presents a detailed case which purports to show that even when British tactical plans for landing at the canal in order to advance on Cairo were clear, Arabi was hesitant about blockading the canal:

His hesitation was due to French influence. M. de Lesseps had arrived at Alexandria towards the end of July and having learned something of the English design of using the Canal for an attack on Egypt, became alarmed for its safety, and he had gone on to Port Said and set himself to work to prevent, as far as in him lay, this design of appealing to Arabi's sense of honour.[67]

Blunt's perception, therefore, is of willful behavior on the part of individual Englishmen, particularly Colvin, Malet, and Seymour. They produced the momentum for British occupation once Gambetta had fallen, and with Gambetta's political eclipse any real threat of French intervention ended. He saw both the threat of anarchy and the threat to the council as essentially mental inventions for justifying behavior that was dictated fundamentally by bureaucratic and economic (bondholder) vested interest.

Blunt's perception of Colvin as bitterly hostile to the Egyptian nationalist movement is confirmed by Colvin's book, *The Making of Modern Egypt*. Of the Egyptian officers Colvin states flatly, "In September, as in February, the programme of the officers aimed almost exclusively at their own interests." On Egypt, he quotes Lord Milner approvingly: "a nation of submissive slaves, devoid of the slightest spark of the spirit of liberty." Then he adds, "Egypt may one day shake off her immemorial past, and show herself capable of self-restraint, self-respect, and self-government. But no one in 1882 whose eyes were not obscured could believe that Mohammad Sami and his troop were Washingtons or Hampdens, or that the hour of Egyptian emancipation had struck."[68] The attack on Sami, a Turkish-speaking ally of Arabi's, rather than on Arabi himself, is significant. Colvin and others in the colonialist British wing saw Sami as a sinister gray eminence and doubtless an agent of the sultan."[69] Presumably the "docile" Egyptians could not conceivably produce a true leader. In contrast, Blunt has this estimate of Sami:

I find he is one of those who first planned the National movement as long ago as in Ismail's time. He suffered a great deal for his liberalism yet stuck to his principles. Several leaders of the party, Nadin, Abdu, and even Arabi, confess that they owe their power to his help and constancy.[70]

Alfred Milner, who was to spend many years in the British bureaucracy in Egypt and returns to this story as a central actor in the 1921 period, is another typical representative of British imperial perception. In 1882 he wrote of Egypt: "And this country, which the common efforts and sacrifices of all the Powers had just dragged from the verge of bankruptcy, was now threatened, not with bankruptcy merely, but with a reign of blank barbarism."[71] His picture of Arabi and the National party was consistent with his view of Egypt: "The object which the Egyptian National party had in view—the original and sound objects—were not to be achieved by the feeble agitators who led, or by the ignorant populace who composed it."[72]

Lord Cromer's account of these events, one of the most detailed, demonstrates far greater detachment than that of Colvin or Milner. The reader may recall the suggestion in part I of this book that men vary sharply in what can be called a detachment quotient. Men such as Cromer and Salisbury may have a first-intensity attachment to the British nation and yet be far less likely than most British nationalists to move away from a complex image when Britain is perceived to be threatened. Such individuals appear to be less inclined toward affective responses. Cromer's perceptions are clearly in the imperial category, but well removed from the ideal typical imperial image. He gives a highly differentiated picture of nationalist moderates and shows little tendency to view the Egyptian national movement as an insignificant monolith directed by sinister men with foreign support. He argues that the Turkish-speaking elements of the alliance were doomed to eventual replacement. In their place would be (1) "the mass of the fellaheen population who were sunk in the deepest ignorance"; (2) "a certain number of small proprietors, village Sheikhs, Omdehs, etc. . . . who, in point of knowledge and governing capacity were but little removed from the fellaheen"; (3) "the Copts, whose religion would deny them any influence"; and (4) "the hierarchy, consisting principally of the Ulema and the El-Azhar Mosque." The latter would be "by far the most important and influential of the four classes. . . . The corruption, misgovernment, and oppression which would have prevailed if the influence of this class had become predominant would probably have been greater than any to which Egypt had been exposed at previous periods." In summary he wrote:

Is it probable that a Government composed of the rude elements described above, and led by men of such poor ability as Arabi and his co-adjutors, would have been able to control a complicated machine of this nature? Were the Sheikhs of the Al-Azhar Mosque likely to succeed where Tewfik Pasha and his ministers, who were men of comparative education and enlightment, acting under the guidance and inspiration of a first-class European Power, only met with a modified success after years of patient labour? There can be but one answer to these questions.[73]

Cromer consistently argued that the nationalists could have been manipulated had their importance been estimated accurately. He blamed the British government and Gladstone specifically for misperceiving the nationalists as a purely military force at the time the Joint Note was issued.[74] As will be shown, Cromer was in error on this point. His error had its complement in his view of Colvin, onto whom Cromer consistently and erroneously projected his own large view of Egyptian society. Nevertheless, and in spite of a greater ability to detach, Cromer's view was that to be expected from a man whose great reputation was gained in the bureaucracy. Far from seeing bureaucratic self-interest as precipitating the intervention, as did Blunt, he saw a picture close to its opposite and reflecting a semi-imperial image:

A few able Europeans, like Sir Auckland Colvin, by the exercise of tact and judgment, by encouraging the civil elements of Egyptian society, and by the exhibition of some sympathy with reasonable native aspirations, might possibly in time have acquired a sufficient degree of moral control over the movement to have obviated the case for armed intervention.[75]

Cromer's perception of Gambetta's role in Egyptian history was close to Blunt's:

During the short time M. Gambetta was in office, he exercised a decisive and permanent influence on the future course of Egyptian history. . . . When he assumed office, the Egyptians entertained confidence in the intentions of England and France, especially in those of England. . . . When he left office England and France were alike mistrusted by the Egyptians. The ascendancy of the military over the national party was complete. Any hope of controlling the Egyptian movement, save by the exercise of material force, had well-nigh disappeared.[76]

In fact, the most that could be argued was that the note had hardened the determination of the nationalists that the Chamber of Notables should indeed be allowed to vote the part of the budget not earmarked for debt liquidation. But that demand, if acquiesced in, would have diminished the influence of the dual control. Bureaucrats in Cairo at the time, whose view Cromer reflects, saw increasing military domination. This is a natural perceptual accommodation, given the deteriorating British position. As the conviction hardened that Egypt was entering a period of military dictatorship, other aspects of the situational view changed. Arabi was to be made a part of the half-enemy, half-imperial view of Turkey, and Blunt was to be seen as toying with treason: "Not only did Arabi receive encouragement from the Sultan, but the advice of English sympathizers with the nationalist course tended to consolidate the union between the military and civil elements of the movement."[77]

Cromer shared, in part, the prevailing view of the Turkish-speaking ex-officer plot—"There does not appear to have been a shadow of trustworthy evidence to show that the charge of conspiracy was true"—but he again demonstrated a detachment not shared by his fellow bureaucrats. "Like most ignorant men, Arabi was very suspicious," he wrote. "The conspiracy to murder him merely existed in his own imagination."[78] That supposition may or may not be accurate, but it could not be held by those who perceived a clever, if barbaric and cruel, plot by Arabi to destroy the remaining Turkish-speaking influence. If Arabi perceived a plot to murder him, the trial was totally understandable, and no broader purpose needed to be suggested.

Nor did Cromer stress the danger to the canal as the immediate threat. Following the delivery of the Joint Note, Egypt passed into the control of a mutinous military group which could not conceivably govern but was too strong for any internal force to deal with.

When it became apparent that some foreign occupation was necessary, that the Sultan would not act save under conditions which were impossible of acceptance, and that neither French nor Italian co-operation could be secured, the British Government acted with promptitude and vigour. A great nation cannot throw off the responsibilities which its past history and its position in the world have imposed upon it.[79]

Although the bondholder image on the one hand and Blunt's on the other remained constant in the 1881–1882 period, that of British officials in Cairo altered sharply and rapidly. The perceptual migration was away from the complex pole toward the imperial pole. By June 1882, some British officials held views as close to the imperial ideal typical image as those of the bondholders.

The view of this situation was considerably different in London. On February 3, 1882, after Gambetta's fall, the *London Times* published a letter from Blunt in which he attempted to explain Egyptian resentment of the dual control: "In Egyptian eyes it shares the vice of all paternal arguments based on ideas of the infinite incapacity of the ruled and the infinite wisdom of the rulers."[80] The *Times* approved editorially of the letter, and it further noted the rapidity of the process later to be called growth in political awareness: "Those who a few years ago knew nothing of politics, except from the visit of tax-gatherers, are beginning to notice and discuss politics." But it also asserted that military rule had begun in Egypt and that British policy had to be guided by the fact of Egypt's geopolitical position, not "by abstract considerations of the beauty of Parliamentary institutions."[81] By May 30, the *Times*'s position had moved in the imperial direction: "From the very outset we have held that Arabi Pasha so far from being a national leader was a mere military adventurer."[82] In fact, the *Times* had had a very different opinion of Arabi earlier, but after the Alexandria riots it saw the nationalist as even more evil: "The Egyptian National party—that is to say, every would-be robber and cut-throat in the country."[83] By now, "there must be no mistake made as to the duty they impose on our Government. Measures must be taken at once to bring the Egyptian anarchy to an end. It is not time now for diplomatic trifling."[84] The *Times* was explicit about the reason for action:

As far as the interests of the bondholders are concerned, it may be measured by the heavy fall in Egyptian securities which took place yesterday in Paris; as far as the interests of the European dwellers in the country are affected, it may be estimated by their almost complete exodus and by the total collapse of their enterprise in which they were engaged. . . . But the primary interest of all, so far as England is concerned—that of the Canal and its traffic—is placed in no less jeopardy than the rest.[85]

The most interesting aspect of parliamentary involvement in the affair was the lack of interest until after the ultimatum calling for Arabi's exile had been given the Egyptian government. On March 13, 1882, a debate took place, and Sir George

Campbell stated the radical position emphatically. He said that Egypt was passing under European administration and suggested that Egyptians would probably prefer to be ill governed by their own people: "When we interfered with foreign countries, we said it was for the benefit of the Natives, but there was a good deal of hypocrisy in that. It was the interests of the money lenders of this country and of France that had prevailed in the case of Egypt, not the interests of the Natives."[86] He was answered by Goschen, who had represented the bondholders in 1876; but neither Goschen nor any other member argued the bondholder case. Rather, they chose to focus on good government.

By May 1882 the same perceptual progression seen among the bureaucrats and in the *Times* was discernible in Parliament. The Irish and a few Radicals continued to see the national movement as respectable. Sir Wilfrid Lawson argued against intervention as leading to a heavy expenditure of blood and money; F. H. O'Donnell saw the national movement as genuine and respectable, and his remarks reflected no trace of the imperial view: "It was forgotten that there was at present an active, intelligent, widely-spread and ably-conducted Mohammedan and Arabic Press, as well served with correspondents and educated writers, in proportion to the state of their civilization and education, as the Press of any part of Europe."[87] O'Donnell was to hold that position through the summer, but he was only one of nineteen members of Parliament who did so.

The Liberals were on the defensive. The ultimatum had been issued and was ignored. The fleet was at Alexandria and was ignored. Salisbury echoed the sentiment of many when he said:

It would undoubtedly be a very humiliating thing to withdraw the Fleet, but to leave it there to look on helplessly and passively while British menaces are being disregarded and British policy frustrated—while the work which British industry had laboriously built up during long years and at great expense are being destroyed, and while British subjects are being slaughtered is a lower and still deeper depth of humiliation.[88]

Two themes other than humiliation appeared with frequency: a view of an aggressive France and a view of paramount British interests. Both points are included in a statement by Joseph Cowen summarized in Hansard:

England, unlike France, was not seeking conquest. All that she required was to maintain her road to the East. He was prepared to go any length for the maintenance of that highway. He would fight for it if it was essential. France was seeking quite different ends. She was striving to assert her supremacy along the whole of the Northern Coast of Africa. It was her undisguised aim to make the Mediterranean, as far as she could, a French lake.[89]

Within the cabinet the perceptual split was sharp. The Whigs, with Spencer Crompton Cavendish, Lord Hartington, as their spokesman, did not see any receptivity to liberal ideas in the East and consistently held the imperial image of the Egyptian national movement. The Radicals, on the other hand, were ideologically predisposed to see and applaud the Egyptian national movement.[90] Both clearly transferred perceptions of the Irish situation to that of Egypt.[91] On January 4, 1882, Gladstone wrote Granville: "I am not by any means pained, but I am much surprised at the rapid development of a national sentiment and party in Egypt. . . . 'Egypt for the Egyptians' is the sentiment to which I would wish to give scope."[92]

By June 1, 1882, Gladstone was telling Commons that Arabi Pasha "has completely thrown off the mask,"[93] thus using the very phrase of the Cairo correspondent of the *Times!* This perceptual alteration came in the face of continuing humiliation, threats to British lives and property, growing popular excitement, and deep division within the cabinet. Hartington and the Whigs were threatening to resign. As the situation deteriorated, the Radicals gradually moved to the perceptual picture of the Whigs, but reluctantly and with anguish. One member, John Bright, resigned when Seymour bombarded Alexandria.[94] Blunt, comparing Bright and Gladstone, made a shrewd observation: "Bright, when he saw he had betrayed his principles by consenting to it, 'went out and wept bitterly'; Gladstone stifled his remorse and profited as largely as he could by the popularity which war always brings to the Ministry that makes it."[95]

To illustrate this rapid perceptual migration, perceptual maps of two momentary situational views are proposed below. Figure II.4 is the map at the time of the Joint Note. Figure II.5 is the map at the time of the invasion. In both, the prevailing view (PV) is shown, along with the views of bondholders (B), Radicals like Gladstone (R), British officials in Cairo (O), Whigs (W), and anti-imperialists like Blunt (AI).

Situational Motivational System

Earlier in this chapter I made the point that European control of Egypt was based on cooperation with one segment, and a largely discredited segment, of the Turkish-speaking governing elite. At the same time, the foreign presence and the destruction of the complex control system set up by Ismail stimulated the growth of an Egyptian national movement which could not be controlled by the reactionary wing of the ruling elite. Therefore the Europeans, in particular the British and French, were in a vulnerable and essentially humiliating position. They insisted on playing a determining role in Egyptian decisions but had no means of compelling Egyptian acquiescence. The Egyptians at no point produced a challenge dramatic enough to allow for a popularly supported nationalistic response on the part of the Europeans. Instead, as outlined earlier, the Europeans progressively added to the drama of their humiliation—finally insisting on the exile of the leader of the

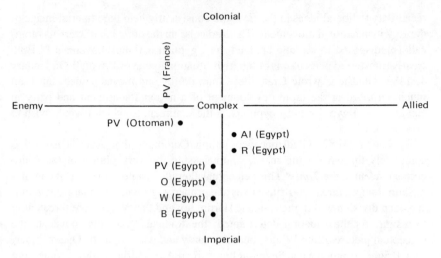

Figure II.4. British Perceptions at the Time of the Joint Note

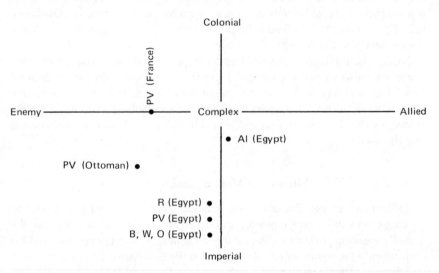

Figure II.5. British Perceptions at the Time of the Invasion

national movement and supporting that demand with the symbolic presence of a naval squadron. When that too was ignored, the absurdity of the European situation demanded a policy change. But then the French and the British chose opposite policies. The French seemed ready to accommodate to Arabi's leadership,[96] but the British precipitated an open conflict which resulted in their occupation of Egypt.

Put in other terms, internal developments in Egypt made an alteration of the imperial arrangement unavoidable. To maintain the degree of influence in Egyptian decision-making that had evolved by 1879, the two powers would have to create a major coercive instrument. The price of doing so would be very high. As the leaders of both states clearly recognized, the highest price to be paid would be an altered relationship among the European powers, and the French feared this far more than the British did. The two great powers were being humiliated equally. The public of Britain responded by supporting intervention; the public of France opposed intervention. This was true in spite of one of the few incontestable points that has emerged here: the bondholding public in France was far more influential in French policy toward Egypt than was the bondholding public in England in English policy. Part of the explanation undoubtedly lies with the greater imperial interest of Britain in Egypt. But a far more important aspect of the explanation of the response differential was to be seen in the two prevailing world views.

In the British world view, there was significant perception of neither threat nor opportunity. The French, on the other hand, perceived a serious threat from Germany, which in French eyes approached the ideal typical enemy image. Consequently, perception of Egyptian developments had to accommodate to general perceptions of the German threat. The Paris correspondent of the *London Times* reported on June 10, 1882:

The boldest Frenchmen do not feel sure that once in Egypt they will not be confronted by the Porte, and that behind the Porte there will not be Germany and Austria. The fear may seem absurd, but it exists, and exists both among those who reason and those who are too terrified to reason. This is why . . . the national feeling is with M. de Freycinet.[97]

The proud and sophisticated Georges Clemenceau congratulated the French government on avoiding involvement in the Alexandrian bombardment. Cromer describes Clemenceau's reaction:

Speaking with a manifest suspicion of the policy and intentions of Germany, he said that it appeared to him that endeavors were being made to get the French forces scattered over Africa, and that, as Austria had been so pushed into Bosnia and Herzegovina, so France had been pushed into Tunis, and was now being pushed into Egypt.[98]

Both quotations suggest the supposition of evil intent, extraordinary rationality, and monolithic decisional process which marks the ideal typical enemy image. With such a price in mind, the French were far less inclined than the British to brood over their humiliation and to seek to avenge themselves by striking at Arabi and his colleagues. Perceptions of an Arabi who could be worked with were a natural perceptual accommodation.

The authors of *Africa and the Victorians,* speaking of Gladstone say that "the only real solution, as the Prime Minister had said, was to come to terms with Arabi and the nationalists. Time after time indeed the Liberal government tried to do so on a basis of concessions to the Chamber of Notables, but the French objected to the slightest delegation of authority to the Egyptians."[99] During Gambetta's sixty-six days, French intransigence was certainly perceived, although it is by no means certain that the perception was accurate. But if this was true before and after Gambetta, it does not appear in the diplomatic correspondence or in the recorded memories of British bureaucrats. On the contrary, at the time of the army demonstration, the French consul general, Baron de Ring, was perceived to be of the same mind regarding the nationalist officers as Blunt. He was in a position to use his official position to intrigue with these nationalists, and he did. The khedive, in fact, requested his replacement.[100] Then, following Gambetta's fall, Malet and Colvin were obviously the initiators of a policy of hostility toward the nationalists.

Fears were constantly expressed that if the British did not move into Egypt, the French would. Yet French behavior after Gambetta was more often annoying to the British because the French would not support British proposals for intervention.[101] This is not to say that the verbalized fears of French occupation of Egypt were insincere; on the contrary, they appear to have been believed deeply. What it suggests instead is that in the perceptual accommodation needed to justify intervention, something more than wounded pride had to be seen. This was developed by constructing a distant French threat, one that would flow from Egyptian anarchy. In the motivational system, defense may well have been a derivative of national grandeur, but by July 1882, defense was certainly a primary determinant of interventionist policies.

Nor did the estimate of an Egyptian progression toward anarchy have much evidential support prior to the Alexandria riots of June 11. And these, it could well be argued, occurred in a situation shaped by a British refusal to accommodate to the nationalist regime. The nationalists sought to increase the size and improve the quality of the domestic coercive institution, the army. The dual control stood in the way because of a belief, explicitly and frequently stated, that it would result in military dictatorship—a most unlikely prescription for anarchy. The authors of the "anarchy" perception were men whose vested interests, bureaucratic and economic, would suffer if the nationalist dictatorship materialized. To prevent this, European intervention seemed necessary, and the "anarchy" symbol was a good one for manipulating in particular the British government and opinion-formulating elites. As has been seen, stressing the threat to British economic interests would have damaged the case.

The threat to the canal, the perception of which was one of the strongest aspects of the prevailing situational view in June and July of 1882, was even more a derivation.[102] As we have seen, even after the invasion began, Arabi understood how vital it was not to use the canal to threaten Europe. The threat, though certainly perceived in July 1882, was based on deductions, especially those flowing from the important assumption of an anarchic trend. In the case of the bombardment of Alexandria, there is some evidence of conscious precipitation of conflict. Thomas George Baring, first earl of Northbrook, a supporter of Hartington's, has been quoted as telling Gladstone, "If we want to bring on a fight we can instruct B. Seymour to require the guns to be diminished. My advisors do not think they will do much harm where they are."[103] Blunt reports conversations which suggest that Hartington was indeed consciously manipulating the situation.[104]

In the progressive perceptual alteration, the central determining factor was an increasing sense of humiliation. This was a common explanation at the time in France. *Union*, for example, editorialized: "Public opinion in France is becoming more and more unfavorable to incurring any danger on account of Egypt, and at present it is only national amour propre which is opposed to a policy of abstention."[105] The Paris correspondent of the *Times* quoted a French observer to the effect that the British could not empathize with Egypt sufficiently to comprehend the national movement: "Hence no understanding is possible, and somebody has to be exterminated in order to solve the question. It is just now Arabi, because the British policy has been such that the honour of England is pledged to Arabi's disappearance from the scene. Everybody acknowledges this."[106]

The sense of humiliation predisposed Englishmen to accept a hostile perception of Arabi and the national movement. They had a ready-made image from bureaucrats and Englishmen resident in Egypt whose vested interests had been seriously threatened. The role of the *Times* correspondent in providing such an image cannot be underestimated in a day in which the *Times* was so widely and carefully read by the opinion-formulating elite. This perception carried a dynamic of its own. Men could seriously accept the proposition that these adventurers were leading Egypt toward anarchy and hence a probability of European intervention—and that would be a clearly intolerable development.

Gladstone's gradual acceptance of the imperial image was essential for initiating the occupation decision. His ideological predisposition, as has been seen, was in the opposite direction. Furthermore, his image of his own divinely ordained role of bringing about a Concert of Europe predisposed him to accept a perception of an Egypt with no need of an intervention which could damage the prospects for success in Europe. Then, too, his fairly well-crystallized nonimperial view of Ireland and the best policy response to it predisposed him to see a parallel in Egypt. The factors that led to his anguished choice of the imperial picture would appear to be, first, his vulnerability to the charge of allowing England to be humiliated and, second, his deep desire to stay in power and preserve his cabinet. To do this he had to move toward Hartington's imperial policy, and that in turn strongly predisposed him to accept a perception of Egypt that would justify the interventionist policy.

For Gladstone, for Radicals in his cabinet and in Parliament, and for the liberal and anticolonialist public, a further perceptual development was necessary. They had to be able to see that British intervention would be "good" for Egypt, that it would bring Egypt cultural and political values which the liberal anticolonialists admired in England.

The inferred situational motivational syndrome is now seen as follows:

A. National grandeur
   Defense
   Bureaucratic vested interests
B. Economic investments abroad, security
   Domestic personal power
   Military vested interests
   Participant excitement, public
C. Cultural messianism
   Ideological messianism

Specific Policy, Expectations, and Response

The general outline of the preferred specific policy was clear by January 1882. The dual control would be preserved, and European influence in Egyptian decision-making would be maintained as it had been prior to September 1881. Since this was unacceptable to the Egyptian ministry, coercion would have to be applied. But much exploring would be necessary to develop the coercive instrument to achieve this purpose. There were serious objections to every perceived alternative. Gladstone's cabinet preferred, as had Disraeli's, to work through the Ottoman Turks and to make credible a threat of Turkish military intervention. This was far from an ideal solution since it would add seriously to the problem of maintaining European decisional influence in Egypt, a province of the Ottoman Empire, should an occupation by Ottoman troops become necessary. But in the British view the potential for conflict in a joint Franco-British intervention was far greater, and the damage to English relations with all of Europe would be severe were there to be a unilateral British intervention.

French opposition to the Turkish alternative, however, was paralyzing. The French feared both the danger to French North Africa posed by an expansion of Ottoman influence and the extraordinary opportunity this development would offer Bismarck's Germany. For months, British policy was focused on convincing both Turkey and France of the utility of the proposal. As seen in the introduction to this chapter, both powers moved in this direction only when they understood that continued foot-dragging would lead to a unilateral British intervention. But the European Conference proposed by France and held at Constantinople, in spite of Turkish nonparticipation, very soon emerged as incapable of furnishing leadership to provide the necessary coercion. And the Turkish response of sending commissioners to Egypt was foredoomed. The Turkish commissioners understood how local control could be constructed, but that required some accommodation with Arabic-speaking Egyptian elements, and the British had moved far beyond the point where that was possible. Turkish willingness to send a military force came too late.

Thus, specific policy came to be a series of interventionist steps beginning with the bombardment of Alexandria harbor and ending with the military occupation of the country. Those steps were taken, not as the execution of a phased plan, but on a strictly *ad hoc* basis. The British, with broad consensus, expected this policy to lead to European hostility, especially in France, and these expectations were fully realized.

After the occupation, the specific British policy goals remained generally the same: Egyptian repayment of the debt to Europeans and a maintenance of control that would guarantee repayment and domestic stability with as little damage to Britain's relations with Europe as possible. But there was no thought of a return to the status quo ante. Recognizing that Anglo-French rivalry was now greater than before and that even the earlier rivalry had led to internal paralysis, the British decided to establish in its place "an informal British suzerainty."[107] In an effort to alleviate European hostility, the British would agree to a rapid withdrawal from Egypt and the canal, both of which would be neutralized by European agreement. The expectation was that a stable and independent government (with the help of British advisors) could be created within a year or two, making possible a British withdrawal.[108] It was a hope more than an expectation that the promise of a speedy withdrawal would satisfy Europe, especially France.

Events demonstrated quickly that neither expectation would be fulfilled. France insisted on a definite date of withdrawal and, failing to receive this, "renewed its liberty of action in Egypt."[109] Deep enmity followed and, in the scheme used here, this can be described as a disturbance which altered the prevailing world view substantially, producing a general strategy change.

Internally, the British hoped and expected to set up an Egyptian regime which would carry out extensive reforms, maintain its relationship with a British bureaucracy, and create a sufficient popular consensus to provide the necessary stability for a British withdrawal—all within an outside limit of two years. Frederick Blackwood, first marquis of Dufferin, was sent to Egypt to prepare a report about how this was to be done, but it was couched in such generalities that Cromer suspected that Dufferin himself did not believe in it.[110] Through whom would the British work, and what kind of coercive instrument would be set up? The British turned first to Riaz Pasha and the Turkish-speaking conservatives, but this class had demonstrated time and again its inability to make the minimal reforms necessary to create a consensus even at an acquiescent level. They then turned to liberal Turkish-speaking elements under Sherif, but this group had to satisfy its followers' insistence that they be regarded as patriotic leaders. Although they were responsive to a reform program, they could not maintain their position and acquiesce in the surrender of the Egyptian empire. Obviously the British could not turn to the hostile Arabic-speaking elite. They therefore turned to Nubar, who had no native constituency but was willing to be the native executor of British policy. Such a regime had to satisfy the material wants of the people sufficiently to bring even minimal acceptance. At best, it would need a substantial coercive arm, and that had to be British. Thus, within a year and a half of the bombardment, a *de facto* colonial administration had been set up.

These developments were anything but sensational. Although they amounted to a substantial expectational failure, the failure was hardly noticed. The hope that withdrawal would be possible persisted until 1887, and even then the explanation for an implicit decision to establish a semipermanent imperial presence was French intransigence. Also unrealized were expectations of an Egyptian people so happily acquiescent in British tutelage that no British armed forces would be necessary; but no notice was taken of this forecasting failure either.

As was true of the British in Egypt in 1876, expectational nonrealization following the occupation of Egypt in 1882 did not result in perceptual adjustment. The same propositional explanation offered in the previous chapter appears to apply here. There it was proposed that any tendency to accommodate perception to the unexpected flow of events was countered by an intensifying perception of threat. The British feared French interference in Egypt, and this necessitated their remaining there. This sense of necessity apparently required their seeing an Egyptian population that desired British tutelage. Clear evidence to the contrary was filtered out.

10 / Summer 1887

Historical Narrative

There were Englishmen in 1882 who favored annexing Egypt to the British Empire and others who favored total withdrawal from Egypt. The official objectives, as incorporated in the instructions given Lord Dufferin, could be summarized as seeking a stable regime, improving administration, achieving greater social justice, and developing democratic institutions.[1] Actual policy lines that evolved in the early months of the occupation pointed to a somewhat different British objective for Egypt: to establish a regime that would be stable, friendly to the British, willing and able to stand by its financial commitments, and sufficiently independent of Britain to avoid annoying France and other European powers unduly. Reform, though sincerely advocated, appears to have been a derivative objective.

There is little doubt that with few exceptions the British were sorry to be in Egypt and anxious to withdraw. Furthermore, they were generally bewildered at finding themselves in Egypt. As noted earlier, for a short period a broad consensus existed around the perception that Arabi and his cohorts were opportunists and barbarians who were creating anarchy in Egypt and threatening the Suez Canal. A few months later the British public was aghast at the thought that Arabi would be executed, and there was general agreement that, whatever his faults, he had been a true Egyptian patriot. Officials and public alike needed to believe that the occupation would produce necessary reforms and lead eventually to a solidly based democratic regime. Anything less would call into question not only the wisdom but the morality of Arabi's overthrow.

Policy priorities suggested a very different thrust. The regime must be stable, but that goal would be difficult to achieve. Since the Arabic-speaking elite and their followers were outraged by the occupation, stability required that the most prominent of the Arab elite be imprisoned or exiled and the rest given to understand that any future revolutionary acts would be dealt with severely. But the regime could not be based primarily on coercion, which the British were well aware would necessitate a large occupation force that would invite the hostility and suspicion of France and other European powers. Direct colonial rule would

211

similarly generate European enmity. Consequently, a program of reform that would satisfy some of the material demands of the people was a practical necessity if popular acquiescence was to be produced. However, the problem of locating individuals and groups willing to front for the British was serious. As noted in the previous chapter, the reactionary wing of the Turkish-speaking elite would not cooperate to achieve the necessary reforms, and the reformist section of that elite insisted on British support for a defense of Egyptian imperial interests in the Sudan. The British turned finally to Nubar Pasha, who accepted a subservient role to a considerable degree but who represented no one. They were most fortunate in having Tewfik as khedive, for he gave the regime an aura of legitimacy and yet was generally loyal to British interests.

Dealing with French hostility was the most difficult single problem. The British occupation was a blow to the French sense of grandeur, already badly shaken by the defeat of 1870 and the loss of Alsace-Lorraine. The abolition of the dual control was a necessity if any governmental stability was to be achieved, and the British decided to pay the heavy price in terms of French hostility. France could hardly be mollified short of a British withdrawal from Egypt and acceptance of a substantial international voice in day-to-day Egyptian governmental policy. The British bureaucracy was loud in its protestations that no sound and consistent policies were possible so long as there was uncertainty regarding the length of the occupation and the possibility of an international veto of major policies. Nevertheless, the British government paid this price as well.

Nothing symbolized so well the limited British commitment in Egypt as did the decision to withdraw from the Sudan. The extension of Egyptian control in the Sudan had been a cherished policy of Mohammed Ali and his successors, in particular Ismail. But by 1882 a religio-political independence movement dedicated to restoring Islam had gained great force in the Sudan, focusing on the Mahdi, Mohammed Ahmed. The Mahdi owed his strength to his religious appeal among tribal leaders, and his followers fought with a determination and courage that astonished the British. A large Egyptian force commanded by a retired British officer, General William Hicks, was dispatched to deal with the Mahdi in September 1883. In November, Hicks was defeated and his force annihilated. Khartoum, the capital of Sudan, and the Red Sea ports were threatened. Baring, later Lord Cromer, responded by recommending the evacuation of all the Sudan except for one Red Sea port, and he was supported by the senior British officers in Egypt, Sir Frederick Stephenson and Sir Evelyn Wood. The British were to suffer other humiliating defeats in the next months in the Red Sea area, and Cromer's detailed account indicates that many British officers would have preferred a policy of reconquering the Sudan.[2] But Cromer remained true to his limited commission. He understood that the costs of reconquest were prohibitive, and his primary aim was to bring financial solvency to Egypt.

The Sudanese story took a bizarre twist with the selection of General Charles Gordon to execute the evacuation of the Sudan. Known to the public as "Chinese Gordon," this eccentric personality had become a British folk hero. He had been governor of the Sudan for the Egyptians from 1877 to 1879, prior to the occupation, and therefore knew the area well. His record in combating the slave trade there was, in fact, one of the reasons for his fame and popularity in England. He was, however, volatile, unpredictable, and temperamentally insubordinate. The stolid Cromer made clear his lack of enthusiasm for the appointment but made painful efforts to support Gordon's often wildly contradictory demands.

Shortly after Gordon's arrival in Khartoum on February 18, 1884, it became clear that an orderly evacuation of the Sudan would be extraordinarily difficult without the military support of a British relief force. Since the Gladstone government was violently opposed to any military adventure in the Sudan, it occurred to Gordon to establish a native authority in Khartoum which could provide enough stability to permit evacuation. He saw only one alternative to the Mahdi, and that alternative was ironic in the extreme. It was to reinstate as first minister Zobeir Pasha, an old enemy of Gordon's and a man known to the British public as a slave trader.

Gordon's first mission as governor of the Sudan had had two goals: The first certainly was to combat the slave trade; the second was to secure the Sudan for the Egyptian khedive. These goals were incompatible. Traditional rule in the Sudan was based on an ability to deal with fluid tribal alliances, religious leaders, and landowners, and the slave trade was a part of this intricate equation. Anyone attempting to maintain control without a large coercive force had to understand all the intricacies, including the interaction with the slave trade, and manipulate them carefully. Gordon's goal of eliminating the slave trade, if achieved, would have profoundly disrupted this traditional situation in the Sudan, since profits from the slave trade found their way into the pockets of all the traditional elites. The term cultural revolution is not too strong for the impact of Gordon's policy.

Since Zobeir was the supreme manipulator of the Sudanese traditional order, he was Gordon's natural enemy. Moreover, in one military clash with Gordon's forces, Zobeir's son was killed, and Zobeir was believed to hold Gordon personally responsible for this loss.[3] Zobeir might well also have held Gordon responsible for the rise of the Mahdi, for upsetting the traditional order destroyed the means by which such religious fanaticism had been contained.

This time Gordon had a different objective: to establish a minimum-cost control of the Sudan for the British-controlled Egyptian government. The time-proven recipe for such situations was to ally with and thereby strengthen a traditional control system. Imperial influence in classic indirect, formal colonial form is exercised in such a way as to restore the position of a traditional native elite which had been losing its ability to exercise control. In this case restoration of a traditional control system would inevitably have included the reinstatement of the slave trade, although surely with low enough visibility to avoid offending British sensitivities.

Gordon's proposal was rejected in spite of its appeal and of Cromer's support. The British public found it inconceivable that the antislavery hero Gordon could propose reinstating one of the most notorious exploiters of the slave trade in all Africa. This was a case of symbolic backfire. The "civilizing mission" argument had been the one used most to justify British policy in the area, and its use had limited the freedom of action of the British government. Thus, the one easy alternative for an orderly retreat had been rejected, but the British government could not bring itself to provide the coercive force necessary to protect Gordon's position.

Finally on August 8, 1884, Parliament approved the funds for an expedition to relieve Gordon and the Egyptian troops. But the expedition did not begin until October 5, 1884, five months after communications with Khartoum had been cut and the situation had become desperate.[4] Nile steamers with the first relief contingents came within sight of Khartoum on March 28, 1885, three days after Khartoum had fallen and Gordon and his forces had been killed. The public uproar in England was intense, and the demand for vengeance was heard everywhere. British honor had been sullied by a fanatical barbarian. Nevertheless, after the initial excitement, the decision to evacuate the Sudan was quickly confirmed.

Participant excitement, grandeur, and cultural messianism had all called for an imperial campaign into the Sudan, but the price would have been high in terms of European enmity and financial expenditures by both Egypt and Great Britain. There was some concern that the Mahdi would soon engulf Egypt, and therefore the defense factor was also operative. Resisting all these pressures, the British chose to meet this threat from within Egypt itself. The Mahdi died not long after, and the threat to Egypt and the imperialist imperative became decreasingly compelling.

The Sudan episode is a good test of British imperial motivations in Egypt. The situation was almost classic as a generator of an imperial adventure. However, defense concerns relating to Europe and bureaucratic vested interests in both Egypt and Great Britain might well have been adversely affected by intervention in the Sudan. Popular excitement soon subsided, and a status-quo policy stance was preserved.

The rhythm of administrative and service improvements carried out by British officials in Egypt is also revealing of motivation. Most important of British priorities was the creation of Egyptian financial solvency. Although it was customary to deprecate the interests of British bondholders in Egypt, the perception was widely held in London that foreign bondholders of other countries, especially the French, had great influence with their governments.[5] The assumption was that foreign intervention was very likely if Egypt defaulted on interest payments—and the British government could not tolerate foreign intervention. Therefore Egyptian finance was a major focus of British officials.

Even greater sacrifices were demanded of Egypt. The foreign community in Alexandria insisted on reparations for losses suffered prior to and during the occupation. From the beginning, the British felt the costs of their occupation should be borne by the Egyptians, since the Egyptians were profiting from it. This necessitated a renegotiation of the debt and its increase by £9 million. French obstruction made renegotiation difficult, but finally international agreement was obtained.[6] By 1889 solvency was achieved, thanks to the efforts of Cromer and his financial advisor, Edgar Vincent.

Since the British could not afford to antagonize the pasha class further, tax reform which would shift the burden from fellah to pasha was not feasible. Instead the focus was placed on increasing production through irrigation. The British rightly took great pride in this innovation. They transferred some excellent technicians from India, who with a minimal budget but much ability vastly improved irrigation. New areas were brought into cultivation, and in the Nile Delta a shift was made from seasonal to year-round production. Yield per acre also improved dramatically.[7]

Another British focus was on the Egyptian armed forces. English officers set about the task of making the Egyptian army into a defense force capable of meeting internal security needs and any attack from the Mahdi's forces in the Sudan. Their initial experience was depressing. Superior Egyptian forces would break and run on first contact with Sudanese tribal forces. But eventually the army was molded into a force which performed very well in disciplined units fighting with competent British officers in command.[8]

Putting the financial house in order, improving agricultural production as a means for increasing revenue, and providing for minimal defense needs—the three priority task areas of British officers in Egypt—reflect British interest in financial solvency and basic stability. In three other task areas commitment was low. Health received a small amount of budget assistance, and education was neglected. Administration of justice was of greater interest to the British, as would be expected given the objective of stabilizing the situation, but British behavior spelled out the marginality of concern with judicial and law enforcement reform. Interest was great enough for the government to assign two highly competent and strong-minded technicians to the Egyptian service. Clifford Lloyd was appointed under minister of interior and addressed himself to police, sanitary, prison, and municipality reform. Sir Benson Maxwell attempted to bring notions of British-Indian justice to the native courts. Egyptian official toes were inevitably stepped on, and Nubar Pasha became so exercised that he threatened to resign if the two Britons were not removed. The British government, confronted with a choice of greater commitment to judicial reform or acquiescence in a traditional justice which seemed to work, however unfairly by British standards, sent Lloyd and

Maxwell home.[9] Obviously cultural messianism was not a first-level British motivation in Egypt.

A reading of the books by Cromer, Colvin, and Milner leaves the reader in no doubt about the sincerity of their authors' interest in Egyptian reform. But the priorities they determined strongly reflected the low intensity of British concern with the colonial regime in Egypt. The budget was small, and the personnel and funds available were focused on projects which would produce stability at the lowest possible price.

For the British, the unhappiest consequence of the Egyptian misadventure was the alteration produced in their European relationships. As we have seen, French enmity was an immediate result, and it in turn led to a greatly improved bargaining position for Bismarck's Germany. Confronted with a Franco-Russian combination opposed to the British presence, Her Majesty's government looked to Germany, Italy, and Austria-Hungary for support. Without such support, dealing with the international community in Egypt would have been extremely difficult. But the price paid was high. The British had to look with approval on German colonial plans and become deeply embroiled in Africa south of the Sahara, and they were compelled to increase their diplomatic activity in Europe.[10] Aloofness from European affairs was a luxury the British could no longer afford.

On several occasions agreement with France on the terms of setting a three-and-a-half-year limit to the occupation and neutralizing of Egypt seemed possible. But each time the negotiations fell victim to negative French opinion and Bismarck's machinations.[11] In 1885 and again in 1887, the British turned to the Ottoman Empire for a solution. Formal Ottoman suzerainty still existed in Egypt, and the British continued to believe, as they had in the months before the occupation, that Turkey offered the cheapest way out of the dilemma. In 1885, Sir Henry Drummond Wolff negotiated a convention by which Britain and Turkey would each send a high commissioner to Egypt. Then, in 1887, Sir Henry was sent to Constantinople to see if another convention could be negotiated calling for a British withdrawal but granting the right to return should internal deterioration recur. The failure of his mission was the next climactic moment in this imperial episode. From 1882 to 1887 the British had tended to think of their occupation as a temporary annoyance. After 1887 most Britons understood that the occupation would last a long time.

Prevailing World View

On January 8, 1887, the *London Times* published an angry article written by its Rome correspondent. Annoyed by a description of French interests in Egypt printed in the Rome newspaper *Riforma*, he commented:

The *Riforma* has followed imperfectly the history of the Egyptian intrigue, and does not understand the reasons why France refused to cooperate with England in the suppression of the Arabi rebellion. The chief reason was that it was mainly fomented and sustained by the French agents, of whom Arabi was a tool, and the moral influences of France would have gone to pieces if she had attempted to undo her own work. For the same reason it is still impossible for France to participate except on conditions which England could not consent to, in the continuation of the work undertaken by England.[12]

This picture of France did not typify either British officialdom or British public journals, but it was found among Englishmen with substantial interests in Egypt and comes very close to the ideal typical enemy image. The *Times* correspondent in Paris stood at the opposite pole of British perceptions. He saw a France dominated by moderate men who were more than anxious to agree to British terms for Egypt, and he deplored the conclusion that the jingoist view typified French opinion.[13] His view approximated the ideal typical complex image far more closely. Parliamentary debates and official statements suggested that modal British perception was between these extremes.

As compared with 1882 there was a marked change in prevailing British perceptions. Gone was the basis for Gladstone's happy expectations of a Concert of Europe. In its place was suspicion of the motives of all European actors, German as well as French and Russian. Salisbury, a statesman with a high detachment quotient, remarked to Queen Victoria that his policy in the Mediterranean was designed to prevent the formation of a continental league which would seek to divide up the British Empire.[14] This perception led Salisbury to play the balance-of-power game. He negotiated what came to be called the Mediterranean agreement with Italy and Austria-Hungary to secure the Mediterranean status quo. This placed him in harmony with Germany through the Triple Alliance and helped safeguard the British position in Egypt. But reconciliation with France was Salisbury's long-term objective,[15] and his hope was that Britain and Turkey would sign a convention regarding Egypt that would please the French.

There was a considerably heightened perception of threat to the empire from a Europe which was turning to the sea and looking for colonies, but the perception was still far from intense. Modal perceptions were much closer to the complex pole than to the enemy pole, and no real differentiation of European states into friends and enemies had occurred. In the prevailing view, France, Russia, and Germany were all perceived in moderate enemy terms, with France and Russia only slightly closer to the enemy pole than Germany. The perceptual picture of Africa indicated a sense of opportunity only to deny that continent to other European powers.

Gladstone had comprehended intuitively the probability that intervention in Egypt would lead to conflict among European states which, in turn, would be expressed in the form of imperial rivalries in Africa. As prime minister, Gladstone tested this proposition, and the test produced impressive substantiating evidence. British intervention can be viewed as a disturbance in the French system of foreign policy aims. The French response to this disturbance, which was at the general strategy level of intensity, took the form of policy choices which became major disturbances for the British system of foreign policy aims. This was manifest in the form of a moderate migration of the British prevailing view in the enemy direction, especially concerning France but also with regard to the other major European powers. The change reflected an enhanced threat perception which would produce general strategy alterations for the British government. However, perception of threat from any single country was not intense enough to produce a sense of need for a major ally. Thus the parametric value was rising but was still relatively low.

The perceptual map (figure II.6), as compared with that of 1882, reflects the parametric value change. The view of Egypt remains relatively stable in its position along the complex-imperial line, but it shifts from the enemy-imperial quadrant to the allied-imperial quadrant. The prevailing view (PV), bondholder view (B), and Radical Liberal view (R) are illustrated.

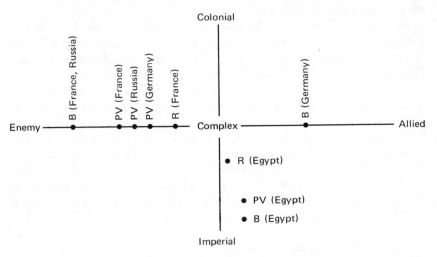

Figure II.6. British World Views, 1887

Motivational System—General

British motivation for expansion in 1887 was far more influenced by defense considerations than was true in 1876 and vastly more than in 1882. The Egyptian occupation had become a prime determinant of British policy elsewhere. The British wanted a stable, friendly, neutralized Egypt in which English involvement was not formalized. Yet few who knew Egypt were sanguine about that possibility. The pessimistic expectation was widely shared that the lack of a formalized British presence would lead to internal collapse.[16]

In 1886 a new crisis developed in Bulgaria, and once again the possibility of a

Russian advance to the Black Sea Straits haunted England. An Ottoman Empire bulwark against a Russian advance remained a British objective. But as the straits appeared more vulnerable and the Porte less reliable, the defensive need for Cairo was even more acutely perceived. In 1885 the Russians in Central Asia advanced to the border of Afghanistan after a victory over the Afghans at Penjdeh. The British perceived heightened threat to India.

The proposed general motivational system in 1887 is as follows:

A. Defense
B. Trade: exports and imports
   Bureaucratic vested interests
C. National grandeur
   Cultural messianism

The sharp downgrading of national grandeur illustrated in the Sudan case reflected the heightened perception of threat in the overall system. With a very low-intensity perception of threat, national grandeur could be far more determining of policy. Likewise, the disappearance of religious and ideological messianism as significant determinants of policy reflects the passing of the happy world view of Gladstone's Midlothian statements. Bureaucratic vested interests are sharply upgraded, however, because the colonial perception of British officials in Egypt was now readily accepted in London. With this perception, stability in Egypt could not be achieved by the childlike Egyptians or the venal Turkish ruling class. To leave Egypt alone would be to invite collapse, French intervention, and a major threat to the imperial life line. The alternative perception of Radical Liberals, to be illustrated below, was not shared by either Salisbury or the Liberal foreign minister, the Earl of Rosebery. Seeing an Egypt that could easily collapse into chaos, Salisbury's government endorsed the policy of demanding the right of reentry into Egypt. That demand, in turn, destroyed any possibility of French acceptance.

Cultural messianism remains in the system. The symbolic manifestations of this motive force were prominent in British rhetoric. As noted in the Sudan case, previous symbolic references to the slave trade strangely limited the freedom of action of the British government to expand its influence. But such limitations are the exception. Generally cultural symbol manipulation is the means for rallying public support for an imperial policy. Nor were cultural symbols manipulated crassly. Statesmen and bureaucrats really did believe that they were civilizing the natives, and this belief somewhat determined their behavior.

General System of Aims

My inferential judgment is that British foreign policy system values in 1887 remained status-quo in thrust. Although this was a period of expansion, the prime motive force for expansion was a perception of threat. The parametric value of the British foreign policy aims system was still low in 1887 but a good deal higher than it had been in 1882. In 1882 the primary parametric value determinant was "a perception of opportunity for British diplomatic leadership in creating a Concert of Europe which would preserve the peace from disturbances resulting from a conflict of petty selfish interests." By 1887 the primary parametric value determinant was a perception of threat. It should be noted, however, that this alteration, though significant, does not reflect a high-intensity threat perception. British modal perceptions did not polarize the enemy and allied categories, as would be expected in the presence of an intense threat perception. Rather, the threat perceived was of only moderate intensity, as is reflected by the system of aims outlined here. This alteration of the British foreign policy aims system was largely a consequence of developments in Egypt, and the case is a good example of the feedback process. British policy in Egypt generated French hostility and a negative policy response. French enmity in turn led to an enhanced British perception of threat and a sharply altered system of foreign policy aims.

The inferred parametric value determinants for 1887 are as follows: (1) a perception of threat from a Franco-Russian or even a general European alliance directed toward dismantling the British Empire; (2) a continuing perception of threat from Russian expansion southward toward India; (3) a renewed perception of threat to the Ottoman Empire from Russia because of Balkan disturbances; (4) a low-intensity perception of threat from France to the British position in Egypt; and (5) a perception of threat to the British position in Egypt from internal Egyptian forces. Gone were the perceptions of opportunity, present in the aims system of 1882, for advancing British ideology, cultural values, and religious values.

I. Preserve the peace, well-being, and security of the British people and safeguard the British Empire
   A. Manipulate the European balance of power to cancel out the effects of French and Russian enmity and Balkan disturbances, and to prevent an anti-British alliance from developing
      1. Cooperate with Italy and Austria-Hungary to maintain the status quo in the Mediterranean
      2. Maintain the Balkan and Ottoman status quo and obviate the dangers resulting from intra-Balkan flare-ups
      3. Effect a reconciliation with France and with Russia in order to reduce imperial rivalry
   B. Defend the empire and the imperial life line from Russia, France, or any combination of European powers
      1. Maintain the British position in an Ottoman Empire capable of resisting Russian southward expansion
      2. Prevent Russian expansion toward India from engulfing Afghanistan

   3. Gain French acceptance for British predominance in Egypt
   4. Assure equal opportunity for British interests in the Far East
 C. Satisfy the foreign policy–related demands of the British people
   1. Maintain and protect from native agitation a colonial bureaucracy capable of administering the British Empire efficiently and well
   2. Maintain a foreign service bureaucracy capable of administering and directing British foreign policy
   3. Maintain armed forces capable of providing for the defense and security of Great Britain, the empire, and the imperial life line
   4. Defend and advance the interests of British industry and commerce on the high seas, in the empire, abroad, and at home
   5. Defend the dignity and enhance the prestige of the British nation
   6. Advance civilized values in Africa and the Orient, particularly through talented British officials; work to eliminate the slave trade

These changes are reflected primarily in division A of the outline. A complete change has occurred since the 1882 representation. In place of generating a Concert of Europe for peace, there is the primary aim of manipulating balance-of-power forces to safeguard the empire and to prevent renewed Balkan disturbances from leading to a deterioration of the British position in an Ottoman Empire bulwark against Russian expansion.

Division C reflects the declining interest in spreading British ideology, culture, and religion. All of these factors are downgraded as compared with 1882.

As in 1882, British policy in Egypt was the disturbance most likely to effect general strategy change in this system of aims. The Drummond Wolff negotiations in Constantinople were designed to achieve A.3, a reconciliation with France; B.3, French acceptance of British primacy in Egypt; and B.1, continued British influence predominance in a strong Ottoman Empire. Success for this policy would reduce perception of threat. Failure would almost certainly result in enhanced perception of threat and hence a significantly different system of aims.

Prevailing Situational View

Situational perceptions of Englishmen in Egypt crystallized in 1882, as described in the previous chapter. There had been little alteration by 1887. Most bureaucrats and the English community in Alexandria had a perception of Egypt that closely approximated the ideal typical imperial image. Their reactions to the Drummond Wolff negotiations were therefore entirely predictable: great nervousness as they progressed and great relief when they finally failed.

Once again the Egyptian correspondent of the *Times* serves as an articulate example of the imperial view. He wrote that the British bureaucrats in Egypt, "in many cases taken from easier and more congenial employment in England or

India, are employing their best years in the ungrateful task of benefitting a foreign country amid the indifference of the natives, the hostility of the Europeans, and the inadequate support of their own Government."[17]

With regard to the terms of the Drummond Wolff convention, his responses were predictably negative. Of the proposal to neutralize Egypt on the model of neutral Belgium he wrote, "It is difficult to understand the meaning of the term as applied to a country admittedly unable to govern itself and without force sufficient to maintain order."[18] He quoted Nubar Pasha on a Belgian form of neutrality: "It is eminently desirable providing you import the Belgians."[19] Concerning a five-year limit for British occupation (later reduced to three years) he wrote:

There is possibly something to be said in favour of an immediate retirement, which, though fatal to the country, might satisfy Turkey and France, or in favour of fixing a date extending over a generation, which plan would secure the time required for giving the new system a fair trial. But it is difficult to conceive anything more certain to upset all possibility of success than the definition of a short term.[20]

Twelve months will not elapse before there come about a military revolt, an exodus of the Europeans, and a financial collapse.[21]

When news of the collapse of the negotiations was received, he wrote:

By Englishmen and those friendly with the English it has been received with satisfaction. The general opinion is that it leaves England with a freer hand, and annuls all the promises made by the Gladstone Government. There exists an earnest hope that the English Government will now carry out a strong policy which will enable it to build up a stable Government, which had been hitherto impossible owing to the continual opposition of certain Europeans supported by their Consuls.[22]

He clearly held the picture of a childlike people who need tutelage, respond to discipline, and are being civilized by a dedicated colonial administration. Left to themselves, local agitators would soon produce anarchy, disarray, and a reversion to barbarism. His views closely paralleled those of the colonial officers who ruled in Egypt. All looked on the failure of the Drummond Wolff negotiations with satisfaction.[23]

The *London Times* felt the civilizing mission as deeply as did Cromer. Speaking of the irrigation improvements in Egypt, the *Times* editorialized: "The duty is the same for an Arab Khedive and his English protectors as for a Pharaoh or a Ptolemy. . . . Though they have not the burning desire of the Pharaohs to leave monuments of their grandeur on its surface, they feel as keen a sense of the responsibility attaching to all guardians of that strange land to turn its gifts to their full and proper use."[24] Naturally enough the *Times* was delighted with Drummond Wolff's failure:

To name . . . a date under any conditions whatsoever is a distinct injury both to English and Egyptian interests, to counterbalance which we gained at most a very dubious formal recognition of the legality of our position in Egypt and our right to reoccupy in case of serious disturbance. Our own belief is, and always has been, that this recognition would not be found in practice worth the paper it is written upon.[25]

A very different picture emerged in the parliamentary debate following the failure of Drummond Wolff's mission. A comparison of that debate with those of the summer of 1882 points to some striking differences in the decisional process. In the summer of 1882, only the Irish deputies were outspokenly opposed to the occupation; Radical Liberals were hardly to be heard from, thus reflecting the role of public excitement and the sense of wounded dignity. In the summer of 1887, the turnout for the debate was meager,[26] reflecting a low level of public interest, but most of the speeches reflected deep dissatisfaction with the British role in Egypt. Nor was discontent limited to the Liberal side of the House. Conservatives also lamented the policy of drift in Egypt, and the imperial image was hardly to be found. Far from glorifying the civilizing role of British officials in Egypt, most speakers agreed with Sir George Campbell, who said: "I . . . strenuously maintain that Egyptian administration is overmanned by British officials, that it is paying too much in regard to them, and that we are not taking the necessary steps to bring about an administration by purely Egyptian officials."[27] Only one speaker, Lord De Lisle, expressed an opinion close to that of the ideal typical imperial:

I think our duty imposes upon us the necessity of remaining in Egypt, . . . with us the term "duty" is synonymous with the cause of civilization and freedom. . . . Although they are a dark race, and are intellectually and physically our inferiors, I do not wish to be understood to mean that so long as the country is in the hands of Europeans they cannot do a good deal in the way of government.[28]

For his remarks concerning race he was severely taken to task by subsequent speakers.

Regarding the role of France, Sir George Campbell reflected the Radical Liberal view when he said:

It seems to me that a great error has been committed by Her Majesty's Government in not trying to make terms with the French Government before attempting to arrange with the Sultan. The French Government—not only one Government, but successive Governments—showed every disposition to meet us in a friendly spirit on this subject, and they have gone so far as to say that on certain terms they would be willing to consider the right of reentry on our part.[29]

This detached, neutral view of France was not shared by Conservative speakers. R. C. Munro-Ferguson typified their view when he said: "France in times past has been giving us more trouble than all the rest of the world together; and until France is prepared to show a changed feeling—and I do not see any sign of that at present—it is impossible to talk of our being able to maintain that hearty understanding with her which we all wish to maintain."[30] R. W. Hanbury came closest to the ideal typical enemy image. Envisioning a brilliant, highly rational strategy on the part of Russia and France, he said: "The two countries which derived the greatest advantage from our occupation of Egypt are France and Russia, who, I believe, do not wish us to leave because by staying there we are creating distrust in the minds of Turkey, and affording an opportunity to France to occupy the New Hebrides, and to Russia to work her will in Bulgaria."[31]

Liberals in 1887, unlike 1882, had words of praise for Arabi and Egyptian nationalism. Irish deputies shared their image. John Dillon found much agreement to his statement that "there is not a single reform that has been instituted by the English Government which was not part of the programme of Arabi Pasha, and which he was not in the process of carrying out when you committed that most outrageous thing recorded in English history—namely, the bombardment and burning of the town of Alexandria with no excuse under the sun."[32]

Radical Liberals claimed that the British motive for being in Egypt was satisfaction of the demands of the bondholders. No one had a kind word for the creditors. But Sir James Ferguson asserted that even if British creditors were disregarded, "other Powers would not also disregard them."[33] He advanced the government's own estimate of motive: to provide a secure and stable Egypt which would not be occupied by any other European power. Sir Richard Temple pleased Conservatives by saying that Britain was in Egypt only because of "duty,"[34] but only De Lisle spelled out "duty" as meaning a civilizing mission. James Bryce gave the most sophisticated explanation: "I believe we are in Egypt . . . simply because having made certain improvident engagements, engagements which we should not make again . . . we have never yet been able to see our way clear to get out of the country."[35]

As figure II.7 illustrates, these perceptions add up to an imperial image among those with a vested interest in the occupation, an anti-imperial, complex image among those with the most deeply felt liberal ideology, and an image inclining toward the imperial for the majority of interested citizens.

Situational Motivational System

When the British occupied Egypt in 1882, their prevailing situational view was of an Egypt moving toward anarchy and unable to defend the Suez Canal. There was real danger of intervention in Egypt by a European power, and France was by far the most likely. The picture was not cynically contrived to bring approval for occupation; rather it justified occupation in the minds of those executing the policy. Those making British policy had a view of the situation derived from

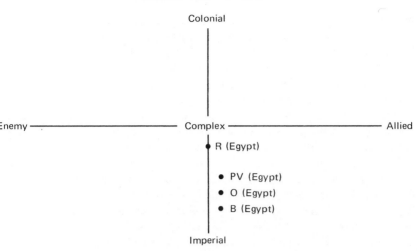

Figure II.7. British Situational Views, 1887

wounded dignity, threatened bureaucratic and economic vested interests, and personal power interests of Gladstone and his cabinet, rather than from solid evidence. Even though the base of politically conscious Egyptians was narrow in 1882, the nationalist ministry was probably the first Egyptian government in the history of that ancient state to be at all broadly based. It was informally led by a leader with charismatic qualities and supported by an army fully capable of providing internal security. Furthermore, by the summer of 1882 it was evident that France was ready to overlook the humiliation it had suffered at Arabi's hands and to accept the nationalist ministry as the legitimate government of Egypt. But men act on their perceptions of the situation, and by July 1882 the British saw anarchy and a threat to the canal.

Ironically, the British intervention made a self-fulfilling prophecy of their prevailing situational view in 1882. The Egyptian nationalist movement was decapitated by the exile and imprisonment of its leaders; and, as has been described before, the British were unable to provide the necessary control by working through either wing of the Turkish-speaking elite. By 1887 the British were acting through two men who closely approximated the ideal typical WOG image, Nubar Pasha and the Khedive Tewfik, and the regime had no Egyptian base of support. A British withdrawal at that point would almost certainly have been followed by a period of anarchy.

If the British had withdrawn, economic vested interests would probably have been severely threatened, and they would have sought a remedy from their government. But in the governmental decision to negotiate a neutralization of Egypt and a date for British withdrawal in return for an agreement to the right of reentry, the economic vested interests, now including the factor of trade, appear to have played very little role. A probable explanation for their passivity was given by the *Times* Egyptian correspondent. Describing the virtual indifference of the European community in Egypt to the Drummond Wolff negotiations, he wrote, "first that there was no probability of the English Government being able to carry out its expressed intentions; secondly, that if it did so it would be compelled to return and the occupation would be a permanent one; thirdly, that if it did not return another Power would certainly take England's place."[36] In other words, the investors' perception of threat to their interests was of low intensity, and in the situational motivational system it has been downgraded to the third level.

The most important consequence of the decision to occupy Egypt was the development in France of a deep enmity toward Britain. Some Englishmen perceived a flexible and accommodating France in 1887 and others a bitterly hostile and cunningly clever enemy France. It is typical of the process of perceptual accommodation that those Englishmen who wished to leave Egypt saw an accommodating France and those who wished to establish a permanent colony in Egypt saw an enemy France. Both had supporting evidence. As reported both by the *Times* Paris correspondent and by Sir James Ferguson, the government spokesman, the French Foreign Ministry in 1887 would have liked to agree on a settlement not too far removed from the Drummond Wolff proposals.[37] However, hostile French opinion was powerful enough that the Foreign Ministry appears not to have had full control of its representatives in Cairo and Constantinople. The French consul-general in Cairo, Count d'Aunoy, was quoted as announcing to the colony there, "I will not allow to be endangered the important interests which are confided to me, and I count on the patriotic cooperation of the colony to assist me in my task." The *Times* correspondent fumed: "The spectacle of the representative of a Great Power appealing to his fellow-subjects to assist him in systematic opposition to the Government to which he was accredited would be sufficiently undignified, even if these subjects were not, as in this case, mainly composed of the Government's officials."[38]

The full dimensions of this lack of control are to be seen in a démarche given to the sultan by the French ambassador in Constantinople. Several versions of his note were published. The following appeared in the *Times* and, judging from Sir James Ferguson's comments in Parliament, was close to the original.

If this ratification be given, the French Government will direct its attention to the safeguarding of its own interests, prejudiced as they will be by the rupture of the equilibrium in the Mediterranean, and to this end will take the measures which it may deem necessary. In the contrary case—that is to say, if your Imperial Majesty should not ratify the said Convention, the French Ambassador is authorized by his Government to give to your Imperial Majesty the absolute and formal assurance that the French Government will preserve and guarantee your Imperial Majesty from the consequences, whatever they may be, which may arise from the non-ratification of the Convention. . . . It is only the disinterested policy of

France which can safeguard the Ottoman Empire in view of the encroachment and ambitious desires of England.[39]

Anger and bitterness in France were real. Unlike 1882, the British in 1887 had reason to feel threatened by France in Egypt, in Turkey, and in Europe. Defense, therefore, was a major determinant of British imperial behavior in Egypt. It is important to compare the British in Egypt in 1882 to the British in the Sudan in 1885. In both cases wounded national dignity was clearly apparent, but in the Egyptian case the wound to dignity became a central factor in creating a perceptual base for intervention. In the Sudan the British swallowed their pride much as the French had done in Egypt in 1882. Obviously Egypt was vastly more important for Britain than was the Sudan, and the picture was more complicated. But I would propose that the British perception of threat from France was a major factor in their willingness to swallow pride, just as French perception of threat from Germany had been the basis of their refusal to intervene in Egypt. The motive for national grandeur is therefore downgraded in 1887 to the third level.

In contrast to economic vested interests in Egypt, the British officials who very self-consciously controlled general Egyptian policy felt frustrated and unhappy from 1882 to 1887. The basis of their frustration was the necessity to include the international community in Egypt and the representatives of the major powers of Europe in their decisional process. In a letter of October 28, 1882, Cromer spelled out this frustration to Lord Granville:

> There is one obstacle which stands in the way of almost every move forward, and that is the necessity of consulting every Power in Europe before any important steps can be taken. . . . Would it not be possible to issue a Circular to the Powers explaining our difficulties, and saying that we did not propose to consult them any more on each detail, but that, when we had put matters straight, we should ask them to accept the settlement *en bloc*, and that we should then at once withdraw our troops?
>
> Give me 2000 men and power to settle matters between the English and Egyptian Governments, and I will guarantee that in twelve months there shall not be a British soldier in Egypt, and that the country is put in such a position as to render it very improbable that any Egyptian question will be raised again for many years to come at all events.[40]

The factor of cultural messianism by 1887 was even more important than in 1882. British officials attached to the Egyptian government quite naturally perceived theirs as a civilizing role of great benefit to the natives. Supporters of the occupation in England felt similarly, not hypocritically, but through a natural perceptual accommodation. The factor of cultural messianism is particularly difficult to weight in a motivational scale because it is usually derivative. Unsympathetic observers tend to dismiss it as a process of rationalization, but the perception that they are bringing civilization to a people is important for the morale of the interested public and for the sense of dedication of colonial officers.

Therefore, cultural messianism was part of the predispositional base of British policy in Egypt. I give it a second-intensity rating in the situational motivational system. Ideological messianism, however, has been dropped from the system. Formal but decisionally meaningless Egyptian governmental institutions were set up, as will be described later, but the officials in British decisions in Egypt pointedly ignored them. The establishment of liberal democracy in Egypt appeared to be an even more distant goal.

Military interests were developing slowly in Egypt. The military had been chiefly concerned with Gibraltar, Malta, and Aden, but their interest in Egypt, the canal, and the Red Sea coast would soon become intense.

As the low interest in Parliament suggests, public concern with the major turn in the imperial road represented by the Drummond Wolff negotiations was slight. The government could largely disregard the attentive public; and the factor of participant excitement, important in 1882, has been dropped from the motivational system of 1887.

The domestic personal power factor is retained in the motivational system. Salisbury was presiding over a weak cabinet, dependent on the imperialist-minded Liberal-Unionists for his survival. His cabinet contained both an Egyptian group and Gladstonians who wished to be rid of the Egyptian albatross. Survival demanded that Salisbury reconcile those views with his own conviction that Cairo's importance in imperial security increased as Turkey became a less easily manipulable and important imperial bulwark. The Drummond Wolff negotiations can best be seen in the context of a need to satisfy intensely competing interests.[41]

The inferred motivational system for 1887 is therefore as follows:

A. Defense
   Bureaucratic vested interests
B. Military vested interests
   Cultural messianism
C. National grandeur
   Economic investments abroad, security
   Trade: imports
   Domestic personal power

Specific Policy, Expectations, and Response

In the parliamentary debates concerning the Drummond Wolff negotiations, speaker after speaker asked to be enlightened about the exact nature of British policy in Egypt. Their bemusement is understandable. The British system of foreign policy aims was a maze of conflicting objectives, and the policy chosen for Egypt would affect every other aspect of British foreign policy. Any policy decision would have an important impact on the balance of power in Europe and hence on the British aims of maintaining the Mediterranean status quo through agreement with Italy and Austria-Hungary; on British influence with the Ottoman Empire and the course of events in the Balkans; and on the important objective of reconciling France and Russia. British policy on Egypt should strengthen the Ottoman Empire and bring French acceptance of British predominant interests in Egypt. Furthermore, that policy should take into account the position, morale, and effectiveness of British officials in Egypt; British capability for defending the imperial life line; British economic interests in Egypt; and the great civilizing task the British had undertaken there. In addition, since different members of the cabinet granted different priorities to these varied objectives, the policy adopted should reconcile their opposing recommendations.

Seen against this background, the Drummond Wolff negotiating terms appear to have been an extraordinarily skillful balancing act. The British were willing to accept a neutralized Egypt and to agree to a definite date for withdrawal from Egypt (the figure of three years was finally accepted). They hoped thereby to appease France and Russia and to please the other concerned powers. They hoped by negotiating in Constantinople with the sultan's government to please the Porte and maintain British influence with it. But what recourse would the British have if after they withdrew from Egypt the Egyptian government should collapse? In British eyes such an eventuality would threaten the imperial life line. The solution, the government thought, was to give Britain the right of reentry. A French acceptance of this right would meet the British need for French recognition of British predominance. In addition, the right of reentry would grant an impressive bargaining lever for a British-advised Egyptian government to use against domestic opponents and hence would grant some of the permanence needed for carrying out long-term planning in the civilizing mission. The British military was assured that the canal would remain in friendly hands, and economic vested interests could count on a government in Egypt favorable to them. The Ottoman Empire was given the same right of entry in the event of an anarchic situation—a provision designed to please the sultan and to maintain the dignity of the Ottoman claim to Egyptian suzerainty. And warring factions in the cabinet could agree: Neither the intervention nor the withdrawal advocates in the government would be really pleased, but the proposal was one both could live with.

Another advantage of the proposal was that even if it were eventually to fail, the British would have demonstrated their essential disinterest and lack of imperial aggressiveness. The French public would have its suspicions allayed.

Whether accepted or rejected, the Drummond Wolff proposals seemed to work toward the achievement of every major British foreign policy aim affected by Egyptian policy. The Porte's initial response was indeed favorable, and the convention was signed. But then Franco-Russian pressure was applied against the sultan's government, and ratification was delayed. The British government and Sir Henry again and again agreed to postponements of dates for Turkish ratification.

At last Sir Henry gave up and sailed for London. The convention was never ratified.

Expectations had never been high that, even with an Ottoman ratification, France would concede legitimacy to the British presence in Egypt, but the subsequent growth in French hostility was unexpectedly intense. It amounted to a major failure in British diplomacy and resulted in a general strategy change in the foreign policy aims system. The parametric value altered because of a threat perception which increased so substantially as to affect the entire aims system. Perceptions of France shifted substantially in the enemy direction, and the defense factor in the British motivation system became even more dominant. As will be seen, this resulted in an increasingly aggressive British imperial policy in the area.

Similarly, expectations of a steady or improved British influence position in Constantinople were not fulfilled. Perceptions of threat to the Ottoman Empire increased to the point that they too amounted to a general strategy alteration and a major change in the entire system of aims, particularly in granting an increasing importance to Cairo in British defense calculations.

A third expectational failure was in the area of Egyptian reactions. Far from being saddened by the failure of the Drummond Wolff negotiations, nationalistic Egyptians were delighted.[42] They saw the resistance in Constantinople to ratification of the convention as a sign of willingness in Islam to oppose the dictates of the imperial West. Nationalistic Egyptians could look to the Ottoman Empire as an ally in their struggle to reenter the decisional process of their country. Just how important this would be was apparent to the British only when Tewfik died and was succeeded by a son who did not conform to the WOG outline. At that point the British found themselves embarrassed much as they had been in 1881, when the native aspects of the control system suddenly failed.

These expectational failures all worked toward making the occupation permanent. Egypt was suddenly a vital center of imperial defense, and the British suddenly perceived an important enemy. If the British presence had to be expanded to keep Egypt under imperial control, then that would be done. For British officials in Egypt, long-term planning and major career investments now made a good deal of sense. The intensity of British imperial control grew sharply in 1887.

11 / Fall 1914

Historical Narrative

In the decade 1887 to 1897, Egypt was a prime determinant of British imperial policy and indeed of British foreign policy generally. Gladstone's unhappy prediction of ten years earlier that British involvement in Egypt would spill over into all of Africa proved correct. Anglo-French disagreement in Egypt pushed the French toward an alliance with Russia, and this in turn set the tone of British policy in Europe.[1] Yet to a late-twentieth-century observer, the most striking feature of this Anglo-French conflict is its low level of intensity. The perception of threat from a Franco-Russian alliance was real, particularly in the eastern Mediterranean, but the detachment with which it was viewed is noteworthy. As Salisbury remarked to the queen: "France is and always must remain England's greatest danger. But that danger is dormant as long as present strained relations exist between France and her two eastern neighbors. If ever France should be on friendly terms with them, the Army and Navy estimates would rise very rapidly."[2]

Juxtaposed against the perceptual ideal typical referents in this study, the prevailing view approximates far closer the complex than the enemy. Similarly, the prevailing view of Germany, Austria, and Italy—friends of England in her Mediterranean policy—was far closer to the complex than to the allied image. This is typical of a foreign policy system of aims in which the parametric value is of low intensity. Neither perception of threat nor perception of opportunity was sufficient to reduce perceptual detachment markedly. What should follow, then, is that the demands of decision makers concerned with foreign policy would be given low priority on resource allocation. Imperial expansion should thus proceed sluggishly. This was indeed the case. Ironically, this decade of extraordinarily important imperial expansion witnessed an imperial policy that attracted little public interest and placed only minor demands on the national budget.

Policy alteration can be seen as closely related to the three areas of expectational failure noted at the close of the previous chapter. Most important of these was the unexpectedly severe public hostility in France to British insistence on the right of reentry into Egypt. In 1876 there was a widespread expectation among the British foreign policy elite that chaos in Egypt would lead to French intervention. That

231

expectation persisted throughout the succeeding decade and was strengthened by the unexpectedly severe French public response. Therefore, since unilateral French intervention in Egypt was to be prevented even at the cost of war, British withdrawal from Egypt became increasingly unlikely. Verbal explorations of British evacuation of Egypt as a means for improving Anglo-French relations continued, but these explorations were desultory.

With this greatly increased sense of permanence of the British presence in Egypt came a heightened sense of Egyptian security needs. In 1889 Cromer, who previously had adamantly opposed any suggestion that the Sudan be defended, wrote Salisbury: "The establishment of a civilised Power in the Nile Valley would be a calamity for Egypt. . . . The savage tribes who now rule in the Sudan do not possess the resources nor the engineering skill to do any real harm. . . . The case would be very different were a civilised Power established in the Nile Valley."[3] The Italians, the Germans, and most particularly the French could not be permitted to gain any control of any part of the Nile Valley. That determination became a central British diplomatic thrust for the next decade, and until the Nile Valley was secured Egypt would remain a prime focus of British foreign policy.

The unexpected deterioration of British influence in Constantinople was likewise reflected in altered British policy. A Franco-Russian naval force in the area of the Black Sea Straits was suddenly perceived as a possibility, and British naval policy was not prepared for such a contingency. The British navy was superior to either the French or the Russian navies, but several years would be required to gain superiority over a combination of the two. The policy of bolstering Ottoman resistance to a Russian southward advance therefore had to be seriously reconsidered.[4] Thus, Anglo-French rivalry in Egypt had a circular impact on the ancient British aim of maintaining the Ottoman buffer against Russian expansion. A British naval threat against the Russians in the straits ceased to be credible, increasing the British policy shift of emphasis toward Cairo. This in turn resulted in further consolidating the Franco-Russian entente and thus further reducing British influence in Constantinople.

The third area of expectational failure was the unanticipatedly strong support among attentive Egyptian publics for Ottoman nonratification of the convention. The implications for British control were serious. Far from being destroyed by the exile of Arabi Pasha, the nationalist movement was strong and assertive. Yet given the imperial reality view held by British officials in Cairo, those implications could not be perceived. National movements are not perceived in the ideal typical imperial image, and none was perceived at this time by British officials in Egypt.[5] Yet the activity of the nationalists could not be denied. One device for taking note of the activity without granting those responsible the credit for being nationalists was to depict the movement as pan-Islamic.[6] This apparently was symbolically effective with British officials and hence could be viewed as a situational translation of the "agitator" image. Fear of pan-Islamic influence in India was surely at the root of this symbolic receptivity.

Cromer understood far better than his bureaucratic contemporaries the seriousness of the British control problem in Egypt. As mentioned earlier, he had an ability to detach himself from a situation and produce an analysis that was not entirely self-serving. He did not dismiss Arabi as contemptuously as did his contemporaries. Nor did he hold the WOG image of Egyptian collaborators as responsible men trying their best to emulate their imperial masters. Referring to the Turkish-speaking ruling class, the collaborating class, he once said: "The Egyptian Oriental is quite one of the most stupid . . . in the world."[7] This stupidity plus the fact that the class had been discredited became a major aspect of the rationale for remaining. Cromer was explicit on this point: "The real reason why the evacuation policy is well nigh impossible of execution . . . is based on the utter incapacity of the ruling classes in this country. . . . [They] are almost exclusively foreigners. . . . Now, all this class are detested by the people, and they are more disliked now than they ever were before."[8]

Yet one of these "foreigners," the Khedive Tewfik, was so useful to the British that even Cromer described him in the ideal typical WOG pattern. His position symbolized Ottoman and Islamic legitimacy, and he was therefore a major factor in a still rather casual control system. Unlike his prime minister, Riaz, he was not regarded by British officials as an example of the Egyptian Oriental, the world's "stupidest." Milner said of him, "He had not the qualities of a conqueror or a creative statesman. . . . But he had tact, patience, dignity, courage, self-possession, a genuine feeling for his people, a real sympathy with the new ideas of just, humane and progressive government." He was, Milner admits, "an invaluable link between the Europeans and the natives—a heaven-born mediator in that stage of transition through which Egypt was passing." Furthermore, this association with Britain and the great things the British were doing for Egypt was helpful in building support for the khedive from his not quite adult people. Milner continued: "The bulk of the people, conscious of their improved condition, but not very analytical of its causes, looked for an explanation of their prosperity and for an object of their gratitude, and they found it in the person of the Khedive. . . . So [it is] untrue . . . that the effect of British policy in Egypt has been to dwarf or undermine the influence of its native ruler."[9]

Milner understood the legitimating function of the Khedive Tewfik and was grateful for his help in making possible inexpensive control of Egypt. Tewfik had powerful Egyptian enemies. Mohammed Abdou, when asked his opinion of the khedive, said that since Tewfik "had joined the enemies of his religion at the time of war it was impossible for him to command the respect of the Egyptians . . . they did not wish for 'traitors with Egyptian faces and British hearts. . . . Egypt is not wanting in honorable men or men of capacity. But you insist on having those who will do your work; and no honest man in Egypt will work for the British government.' "[10] Abdou surely reflected the views of many in the intellectual, religious, and nationalist community. But for the Egyptian fellah, whose world remained traditional, the khedive occupied a position of unquestioned authority. The fellahin were controlled by their own unquestioning acquiescence in traditional authority and customs. Mild coercion and a certain satisfaction of material interests were sufficient to control those for whom the khedive was viewed as little more than a British agent.

Their dependence on the khedive was made painfully clear to the British in 1892, when Tewfik suddenly died and was succeeded by his son Abbas II. Cromer had been warned that Abbas "was likely to cause a good deal of trouble. He was sure to be surrounded by bad advisers. He would belie his oriental origin if he did not directly or indirectly encourage sycophancy in those around him."[11] But Cromer was supremely confident that he could make a good WOG of Abbas. Indeed, he seemed to relish the prospect of educating Abbas to an understanding of his proper role. While he recognized that "the young Khedive is going to be very Egyptian . . . I feel convinced that . . . I shall soon have him in my pocket without his knowing it or feeling the yoke."[12] But Cromer was wrong. Within a year Abbas's determination to reduce the British role was apparent, and he even had the effrontery to propose a prime minister of his own choice.

This independence, of course, could not be allowed. The perception of threat to British imperial interests, now crystallized around Egypt, was real even if of low intensity. Obviously a government that had paid the price of an unwanted Franco-Russian alliance rather than evacuate Egypt was not likely to allow an internal disintegration of its position. In terms of the British system of foreign policy aims, the primary determinant of parametric value was the perceived threat from France; and that perception of threat was intensifying. In this context, Abbas's noncooperation was a minor disturbance but one which had to be dealt with. The response would be at the situational policy level.

The independent stance of Abbas made the British realize how important Tewfik had been in keeping their control in Egypt so inexpensive. Although some politically sophisticated Egyptians had regarded Tewfik as having sold out his birthright, they were too few to disrupt British control. For the vast, acquiescent majority, the office of the khedive was the focus of legitimacy. Now that it was occupied by a man resisting rather than executing British orders, the khedivate was a problem for rather than support of British control. Sudden revolution was not a threat: Acceptance of the khedivate was habitual, not active, and the khedive had no means of mobilizing the passive, acquiescent Egyptian public. But Egyptians at the court and in the government for whom the khedivate was an active focus no longer passively acquiesced in British policy. Even the Legislative Council, whose members approximated the WOG model, showed signs of restiveness.[13]

Perceptual response on the local scene was predictable. Perception of threat to

British control having suddenly intensified, conspiracy suggestions fully in tune with an enemy-satellite image quickly appeared. Cromer telegraphed Rosebery that the young khedive was "in connivance with Turks acting on behalf of the Porte, and of the desposed Khedive, Ismail; that it was also pre-arranged with France and Russia, and that if it proved successful, would be followed by the wholesale dismissal of British officers in the Egyptian government."[14] Nor could these developments be seen as real evidence of Egyptian nationalism. Like Arabi, Abbas II had to be seen as purely self-interested. Cromer met the point directly in his book *Abbas II*: "The Khedive's patriotism, if genuine and directed in a healthy channel, deserved sympathy and respect. But was it genuine? Was it directed in a right channel? Did not the Khedive, and those who surrounded him, rather confound the terms Khedival and Egyptian which, in fact, were far from being synonymous?"[15]

The effect of the khedival stance on Egyptian nationalists was substantial and has been well described,[16] but in Cromer's account this extensive interaction between court and nationalists is not recorded. The demands of perceptual accommodation were such that he could only deny the existence of a nationalist movement and see in Abbas a "petulant boy" responding to imagined grievances.[17] After listing trivial complaints about British conduct, Cromer summarized his view: "Petty complaints of this sort were but the outward and visible signs of general discontent which had its origin in the fact that British troops were in occupation of the country, and that British civil and military administrators prevented the Khedive from doing what he liked, whereas he thought his will, however whimsical and capricious should invariably be law."[18] The writings of Cromer, Milner, and Colvin reveal perceptual alteration in the direction of—but far from reaching—the ideal typical enemy image relating to France, Russia, and Turkey. There was also a migration in the direction of the ideal typical imperial image pole regarding Egypt, and in this case the approximation was close.

A disintegrating colonial situation being exploited by Britain's primary enemies called for a major shift in policy. First the khedive had to understand that London supported Cromer fully and would not tolerate independence of the degree he was showing. In January 1893 the cabinet council sent Cromer the telegram he had requested. It stated flatly that "Her Majesty's Government expect to be consulted in such important matters as a change of Ministers."[19] But more had to be done. Abbas was, Cromer admitted, attracting support:

Every Pasha who had been deprived of his privileges or curbed in the exercise of his ill-used power, every fanatic Moslem who cursed the Giaour in his heart, every unsuccessful place hunter, every corrupt employee whose illicit gains had been curtailed by the British control, every feather-headed young Egyptian who thought himself of equal if not superior mental calibre to his British official superior, rallied round the foolish youth, who—probably without being fully aware of it—had raised the standard of revolt against Western civilization. . . . [But] in spite of all these outward and visible signs, the movement was in reality hollow and fictitious. The poor ignorant village sheikhs who, at the bidding of the Pashas, congratulated the Khedive on his resistance to the Englishmen, were all the time devoutly hoping that the Englishmen would stand firm against the Khedive and save them from a relapse into the abuses of the past.[20]

So it goes. The self-sacrificing, civilizing colonial officers were beset by self-seeking agitators who would deny the great civilizing contributions of colonialization to their childlike countrymen.

Nevertheless, the changed situation had to be accommodated. Previously acquiescent Egyptian bureaucrats and army officers could no longer be relied on. The coercive aspect of the control system had to be intensified. "The remedy was simple," Cromer wrote. "An increase of the British garrison would serve the double purpose of preserving public tranquility, which was seriously threatened, and of calming the troubled political waters by showing that local opinion had wholly misunderstood the attitude of the British Government." On January 19, 1893, he requested an increase of the garrison, and four days later the request was granted.[21]

Cromer also concluded that British control of the bureaucracy must be strengthened. The number of British officials in Egypt had grown only slightly prior to this crisis. Now, in a moment of near panic, he proposed "to take military possession of the Ministries of Finance, Justice and the Interior with instructions to the officers in command that the three Ministers who have been named without our consent shall not be allowed to enter."[22] This proposal was rejected from London, but the stage was set for an influx of British officials and a steady replacement of unreliable Egyptian Moslems with British officials and reliable Armenians and Syrians. Between 1896 and 1906 the number of British officials rose from 286 to 662.[23] By 1905, the Milner mission estimated, 28 percent of higher posts were occupied by Egyptians, 42 percent by British, and 30 percent by Armenians and Syrians.[24]

In 1896 the British were embarrassed by the ill-fated Jameson Raid in South Africa. To add to their discomfiture, the kaiser sent a telegram of congratulations to President Kruger of the Transvaal Republic. Salisbury interpreted this as a German attempt "to frighten England into joining the Triple Alliance," and the cabinet considered it "to be important in the present state of things to settle as many questions with France as possible."[25]

Enmity toward France due in large part to the conflict over Egypt was very costly for the British. It resulted in French support for Russia's drive southward toward the Ottoman Empire, Afghanistan, and India; it forced the British into a forward policy in East Africa; and it carried a dynamic which pushed Britain in the direction of the Triple Alliance. Nor did any really strong psychological obstacles stand in the path of improved relations. As Salisbury's suspicions of the kaiser's motives indicated, the British were psychologically far from being either allies of the Germans or enemies of the French. The perception of threat from the French to Egypt intensified in 1895, but that situational perceptual development must be seen in a broader world context.

The Italians had been attempting for some time to gain a territorial foothold in the Ethiopian area, but by 1895 their military situation had deteriorated and collapse appeared imminent. Salisbury was totally unsympathetic to the Italians, but he was concerned that the Ethiopians might be acting as agents of the French. If that were the case, an Ethiopian occupation of the Nile could be a serious threat to Egypt.[26] Furthermore, the French, after some hesitation, decided in November 1895 to send an expedition to the Upper Nile.[27] The British, taking advantage of a German desire to strengthen the Triple Alliance by encouraging a British diversionary effort in the Nile to help the Italians, countered in March 1896 with an advance up the Nile. Perception of threat from France was the ultimate and probably also the immediate cause of this British action. But as a result of the British move, Franco-British relations deteriorated further, leading in turn to an enhanced perception of threat from France. Temporarily, the members of the Triple Alliance and Britain began to perceive each other in terms slightly more congruent with the ideal typical allied image. All moves toward détente with the French failed, and the British for a time even dropped the goal of defending the straits. As the director of naval intelligence wrote: "The time . . . for jealously guarding the inviolability of the Dardenelles is passing away, and is not worth any important sacrifice now."[28] The shift to Cairo as primary security focus was complete.

British response to the kaiser's telegram to Kruger was indicative of the limits of this growing Franco-British enmity. In systems analysis terms, the parametric value was primarily determined by the perception of threat from France. However, that perception was of low intensity, and the claims on British resources from those concerned with foreign policy decision-making were weak. Furthermore, there were other less compelling yet important perceived threats. Decision makers concerned with the Ottoman Empire, Afghanistan, and India were unhappy with the added strength of the Russian bargaining position granted by the Franco-Russian alliance—an alliance perceived to be a consequence of Franco-Russian enmity over Egypt. Decision makers concerned with South Africa and many British diplomats in Europe were uneasy about German ambitions and therefore about a *de facto*, if low-level, British association with the Triple Alliance. In addition, the Far Eastern situation was beginning to take center stage. Conflicting Russian and Japanese ambitions and the increasing presence of the Germans were creating an ambiguous situation—one in which the French were more Britain's natural ally than her enemy.

The internal contradictions within British foreign policy had their parallel in the foreign policy of every other European power.[29] No single factor governed the interactive patterns of European diplomacy. In this larger context, Egypt was becoming a minor factor. Both Russia and Germany made it clear that their *de facto* allies in Egypt could count on no more than diplomatic support for their positions.

This was a highly unstable system of foreign policy aims in which any number of disturbances threatened to produce a general strategy change. Confronted with these disturbances, British decision makers found increasingly onerous the diplomatic strait jacket imposed on British diplomacy by Franco-British enmity. Yet the British perception of threat to vital imperial interests from the French remained real, and the general strategy change could actually occur only if that perception were altered or if some other perception of threat or opportunity became even more intense and therefore overriding as a basic determinant of the boundaries of major foreign policy lines.

Among French diplomats there had always been strong sentiment for resolving the conflict with Britain over Egypt,[30] but their freedom of action or decisional latitude was restricted by their sense of French public anger at the British. However, in the French foreign policy aims system the perceived threat to the dignity of the nation inherent in British policy in Egypt was not the primary parametric value determinant. Perceived threat from Germany in Europe and to French interests in the Far East were far more important. Therefore, the outcome of the crisis over the Upper Nile was easily predictable. One historian argues that "the French hurried on the Marchand expedition in order to get Egypt settled before the Eastern question blew up."[31]

The Anglo-French military confrontation on the Nile in 1898 did have a surrealistic flavor to it. On July 10, 1898, following a sixteen-month journey, Captain Marchand and a handful of men arrived at Fashoda on the Upper Nile. The French public was delighted. But in March 1898, the British, fearful of French-Ethiopian collusion in the Sudan, authorized the reconquest of the area. Military operations against the Ethiopians were unexpectedly difficult and costly, but eventually the British were victorious.[32] The commander of the British forces, Lord Kitchener, then requested the additional resources necessary for the reconquest of the Upper Nile, and the British government reluctantly acquiesced. The meeting between French and British forces that took place at Fashoda on September 19, 1898, was symbolic of the difference in resolve. "Kitchener had an army," while Marchand "had seven Frenchmen marooned by the banks of the Nile; Salisbury had a united government; Delcassé had a tottering ministry; Britain had a navy ready for war; France had a pack of legal arguments."[33]

The resulting crisis reflected public excitement but an official sense of the absurd. Having established their presence on the Upper Nile, the British proposed that Marchand be recalled and that British suzerainty in the Nile Valley be formally recognized. But the British ambassador in Paris reported a stiff reaction from Minister of Foreign Affairs Théophile Delcassé: "All France would resent such an insult to the national honour as is involved in the proposal to recall M. Marchand and to treat the French occupation of Fashoda as an unjustifiable act. He [Delcassé] could not think that it is wished in England to go to war over such a question, but France would, however unwillingly, accept war rather than submit." The British ambassador believed that Delcassé was not bluffing.[34] French policy was clearly dictated in major degree by a public sense of having suffered yet another blow to national dignity. But in Britain this policy produced a perception of threat severe enough to flavor overall British policy. The diplomatic formula for conflict resolution was obvious: salve the French sense of honor and reduce the British perception of threat. An initial compromise suggestion, that of allowing the French a minor presence in a Nile Territory, seemed to have been reasonable. Queen Victoria, no shrinking violet in imperial policy, opposed "a war for so miserable and small an objective,"[35] but the hard-line members of the British cabinet were quite willing to go to war rather than make even the smallest concession.

Events broke the impasse. Marchand's expedition had to withdraw simply to survive, and the drama of the confrontation was thus sharply reduced. With this development, the interest of the French public waned, and in November 1898 the French government sent Marchand *ex post facto* instructions to evacuate. On March 29, 1899, the Anglo-French declaration was put into effect which included French acceptance of their total exclusion from the Nile Valley.

The death of the Khedive Tewfik and the Anglo-French declaration were two events of great importance for the British in Egypt in the period 1887 to 1914. The first produced immediate and highly visible changes in the British presence and style, while the second had little immediate impact. But in systems analysis terms, the first was of relatively minor, situational-level importance, the second extremely important for British imperial policy at the general strategy level.

With the realization that Abbas II would not serve as the legitimating agent for the British presence and gross policy control, the British established a different type of control system—one which relied far more on direct coercive instruments. This produced alterations in British motivation for being in Egypt. British personnel increased numerically, each with an important role vested interest in his Egyptian assignment, so both the bureaucratic and military vested interest motivational factors became more important. But the prime determinant of British policy in Egypt remained perceptual. Perception of threat from France was sufficient to justify increased expenditures once the local exigencies were apparent.

The Anglo-French declaration of 1899, on the other hand, was a concrete reflection of a general strategy level change. Frenchmen, not without a residue of bitterness, were now reconciled to British occupation of Egypt. French policy henceforth would not challenge that occupation, and consequently the prime determinant of British foreign policy aims would no longer be a fear of French intentions. Profound changes in the international system necessitated full British attention. Even before 1899, the developing conflict in the Far East was a disturbance of system-shattering importance. Likewise, South Africa carried with it a constant threat of international involvement. After the final flare-up and resolution of Franco-British conflict in Egypt, British policy was allowed a fair degree of autonomy.

With the sudden elimination of a strongly perceived threat from France to the British position in Egypt, the situational motivational system changed in both structure and importance. British determination to remain in and maintain substantial control of Egypt suddenly weakened. The first-intensity motivational factor for being there had been defense, and now that factor had lost some of its saliency. The added saliency of the bureaucratic and military vested-interest factors could not compensate for the loss of saliency for defense.

The disappearance of the perception of threat from France in Egypt removed the central obstacle for Franco-British rapprochement. In 1904 good relations were formalized in the Anglo-French agreement, and from that point on threat from France ceased to be a major factor in the overall British foreign policy system of aims.

In accordance with the theory advanced here, the British perceptual response with regard to Egypt should have been a move away from the ideal typical imperial image. As long as a fear of French intervention was serious, the motivation for tightening British control was strong. With the removal of that threat, the strength of the motivational force declined. British officials in Egypt, whose role interests demanded at least the maintenance of British control at the current level, should have continued to see Egypt in a way that would approximate the imperial image. But for those officials in London who had to weigh many demands on resource allocation, perceptual alteration should have been in the direction of the complex image. Actual alterations in perception followed these anticipatable patterns.

In the ideal typical imperial image, it will be recalled, the existence of nationalist leaders in the colony is denied: When the activities of men claiming to be nationalist leaders are undeniably visible, these men might be classified as agitators. Similarly, the need for benevolent and self-sacrificing tutelage from the imperial power is called for if the childlike local populace is to move toward civilization. In 1905, Harry Boyle, Cromer's like-minded Oriental Secretary, argued for the policy of employing many Englishmen in Egypt. He asserted:

Experience showed that native officials, considered as a class, however gladly he might welcome or intelligently receive the advice and instructions of his English superior, had not reached either the stage of intellectual development which would enable him to carry out these instructions with efficiency, or of moral courage enough to face the terrors of unsupported responsibility. . . . Hence it is that the backbone of the Egyptian administrative body has been strengthened in recent years by a comparatively large number of young Englishmen, carefully selected for their character and attainments.[36]

Alfred Milner, writing in 1906, was still asserting that "the native population is childlike and dependent."[37] And Cromer wrote in 1907, his last year in Egypt: "It is essential to show that British policy in Egypt . . . is not liable to be influenced, nor the British occupation disturbed, by any passing wave of local opinion."[38]

But in London a very different view was articulated, not only by Wilfrid Blunt,[39] but also by liberal journals such as the *Manchester Guardian* and by liberal politicians, the most noteworthy of whom was James Robertson. The picture of reality of this group reflected an empathy with Egyptians seeking to bring about the realization of the national self-determination ideal. In fact, these two sharply opposed views of reality were found throughout the imperial episode. The rhythm of the relative importance of one compared to the other is directly related to the centrality of the situational policy concerning Egypt to overall general strategy lines. When the Egyptian situational policy was central, as in 1882 and 1897, the imperial view easily prevailed. But after 1897 the Egyptian situational policy lost its importance, and the anti-imperialist view came to attract more and higher-level adherence than previously. Following the defeat of Arthur Balfour and the Conservatives in 1906, men whose value predisposition was in the anti-imperial direction assumed control of the British government, and British policy in Egypt came to reflect the impact of the anti-imperial view.

The Egyptian setting for which the altered policy was being formulated reflected the pluralism of society, the passivity of the fellahin mass, and the growing strength of Egyptian nationalism. Although British policy neglected such areas as education which would have accelerated social transformation, the population was becoming more aware of the modern world and Egypt's humiliating position in it. The new awareness owed much to the spillover of modern ideas from educated Egyptians to friends, relatives, and acquaintances. With encouragement from the British, awareness would have grown much more rapidly, but even without it, awareness grew substantially and resulted in an ever expanding core of dissatisfaction within the politically aware community.

By identifying with nationalism, Abbas II electrified this important though still relatively small section of the population. Members of the traditional elite, both Turkish and Arabic-speaking, who had viewed the nationalists with alarm, now had little choice but to enter into a *de facto* alliance with them. To have opposed the khedive and cooperated with Cromer would have opened them wide to the charge of disloyalty and even treason. The British were left in the uncomfortable position of having to rely on those elements—Syrian and Armenian—which identified least with Egypt and were for the most part seen as foreign Christians.

The community of interest of these *de facto* Egyptian allies embraced only the negative objective of opposition to British control. There were three identifiable alliance systems among the nationalists. First was Abbas II, his court, and his allies. The newspaper *al-Muayyad*, edited by Ali Yusif, became the spokesman for this group, which included many members from the Turkish-speaking upper class.[40]

A second group formed more or less around the Islamic reformer and veteran of the Arabi movement, Sheik Mohammed Abdou. This group was reformist and moderate. It saw an Egypt sorely in need of long tutelage, and some within it could bring themselves to praise aspects of the British rule. Most noteworthy of those associated with this group were Saad Zaghlul, soon to be Egypt's great national leader, and Ahmed Lutfi al-Sayyid, a brilliant political thinker and publicist. From this group was to come the Umma party, later to be the core of the great Wafd party.

In the late nineteenth and early twentieth centuries, the man who most captured the imagination of Egyptian nationalists was Mustafa Kamel. Heavily influenced by the ideas of French civilization, especially the Enlightenment, Kamel was the personification of liberal nationalism in Egypt. His group was to found the Watani party. His newspaper, *al-Liwa*, had a circulation in 1900 estimated at ten thousand.[41]

Al-Sayyid has written that "the Khedive's connections with the nationalist movement rendered it suspect to Cromer. He was convinced that Abbas had manufactured the whole movement for his own ends, and that it was spurious. To the very last he never admitted that there was a spontaneous nationalist movement in the country, with a desire to see the British occupation at an end."[42] Cromer's own writings tend to confirm that view, but following the disappearance of the French threat, some of his actions were not in accordance with his statements. Cromer could not be indifferent to charges from London that he was hopelessly authoritarian and not preparing Egyptians to take over their own affairs. Nor, with the disappearance of the French threat, could he deny that the costs of the British occupation of Egypt appeared excessive.

Cromer's response would undercut both of these criticisms, but it could not have occurred to one holding an imperial view of Egypt. His tactic could only have been perceived by one who saw a differentiated Egyptian political elite. He in effect allied himself with one of the three groups, that of Abdou, and sought to isolate and eliminate the other two. He thereby achieved a cheaper means of control and one that gave the appearance of preparing Egyptians for self-government.

Abbas was his great personal enemy, and Kamel's movement was the most threatening. Cromer therefore turned to the most tractable of the three, the Umma party, and made some important concessions. He established a cordial and supportive personal relationship with Mohammed Abdou and appointed Saad Zaghlul to be minister of education. These acts may have been no more than a personal response, since Cromer liked Abdou and had appointed Zaghlul at the request of Zaghlul's father-in-law, the WOG prime minister, Mustafa Fahmy. Still, when responding to the charge of indifference to training Egyptians to handle important positions, he referred explicitly to his appointment of Zaghlul and added, "Of course it is anticipated that we shall go further in the direction of pushing the natives. I am quite prepared to do so, but I shall not be in too great a hurry. I want to see how the present experiment works."[43]

Viewed in control terms, Cromer's overtures to the Umma group was extremely shrewd. With the disappearance of the French threat it was unlikely that Cromer could succeed in any bid for a substantial increase in the allocation of resources for Egypt, and an increase would have been necessary to control the burgeoning Egyptian nationalist movement by coercive means. Cromer's strategy was to disarm an important section of the nationalist movement by granting them some influence and official favor. The movement was further weakened when the relationship between Abbas and the Mustafa Kamel wing of the movement deteriorated as the latter became increasingly aware of the antiliberal and antire-form attitude of the khedive.

Possibly the British presence in Egypt could have stabilized for a time, but eventually the inherent conflict of interest between Egyptian nationalism and British colonial control would have produced a crisis. The crisis erupted prema-turely as a result of an incident called the Dinshawi affair. It involved a group of British officers out shooting pigeons near the village of Dinshawi. Since pigeons were part of the livelihood of the community, the "sport" was viewed with something less than sympathy by the villagers. When a barn caught fire during the hunt, the villagers blamed the officers and attacked them verbally. A gun went off, wounding a woman, and this sparked physical violence. All the officers were beaten. One, suffering from a concussion, ran for help and fell dead from sunstroke. An Egyptian peasant who tried to help him was assumed by British soldiers to have killed him. The soldiers beat the peasant to death.

Fifty-two villagers were arrested, but no action was taken against either the officers or the soldiers. A special tribunal was established consisting of five judges: three were English; one, Butros Pasha Ghuli, was an outstanding repre-sentative of the Coptic community; and the other, Fathi Bey Zaghlul, was the brother of Saad Zaghlul. Four men were sentenced to death and publicly hanged, two were sentenced to imprisonment for life, six for seven years, three for one year and fifty lashes, and five for fifty lashes.[44]

Egyptian nationalist response to the incident and the sentencing was one of outrage. Newspaper articles and public statements by political and religious leaders made Dinshawi a national symbol and a symbol of the arrogance of British imperial rule. Yet, for all its vehemence, the public response was ignored or played down by many people, British and Egyptian.

Cromer's comment reflected a sharp drift toward an imperial view: "I do not believe that this brutal attack on British soldiers had anything directly to do with political animosity. It is, however, due to the insubordinate spirit which had been sedulously fostered during the last year by unscrupulous and interested agitators."[45] It did not occur to Cromer that British behavior in the Dinshawi affair would convulse Egyptian public opinion. How could it, if public opinion was no more than nascent?

More puzzling but probably ultimately revealing was the willingness of Butros Ghuli and Fathi Zaghlul to participate in the sentencing. Butros Ghuli's role symbolized the dilemma of the Egyptian Coptic community. The Copts were better educated and higher achieving than their Moslem neighbors, so that they had a special interest in the kind of rapid change associated with a modernist national movement. But the Copts were little attracted to Kamel, just as two generations later they were little attracted to Nasser. Egyptian nationalism was a particular problem for Egypt's Copts. As inheritors of an ancient civilization they were attracted; but as a small minority vulnerable to oppression from governments responsive to Moslem opinion, as a nationalist regime would surely be, they were repelled. That Butros Ghuli would enrage the sensitivities of Moslem nationalists argues that he did not anticipate such a reaction and that he underestimated significantly the force of Egyptian public response. Butros Ghuli later became prime minister, but he was assassinated by a man who listed the Dinshawi case as one of his grievances.

Fathi Zaghlul's willingness to be associated with the sentencing of his countrymen also tells much about the Umma, the moderate wing of the nationalist movement. Having agreed to collaborate with the British, leaders of this faction had gambled on their ability to ride the British horse until they were firmly in the Egyptian government saddle. A rapid development of nationalist public opinion would make this strategy difficult to follow. Therefore Fathi Zaghlul, like Cromer and Butros Pasha, had a vested interest in a slow growth of Egyptian public opinion. Like them, he accommodated perceptually to the Dinshawi affair by not anticipating public outrage. Umma was able to recover from the affair, but Fathi Zaghlul was not. He was scorned and ridiculed from that point on.[46]

Liberal opinion in England shared the outrage of Egyptian nationalism. The British prime minister, Sir Henry Campbell-Bannerman, received Mustafa Kamel in London. And the foreign secretary, Sir Edward Grey, certainly no crusading anti-imperialist, publicly complained of the "want of public spirit" on the part of some British officials in Egypt.[47]

Cromer finally realized the seriousness of the assault on his policies. But in his own mind he was sure of the causes of the attack, and they did not include his underestimation of Egyptian nationalism: "They arise entirely from the supposed sympathy in England with the ultra-opposition here." He told Grey, "To suppose that, while the occupation lasts, we can leave the extremely imcompetent Egyptians to do what they like about local affairs is madness."[48] Cromer now followed the pattern expected of one holding an image close to the ideal typical imperial who sees little or no public opinion. Public disturbances are perceived, as they were by Cromer, as resulting from the activities of a few local agitators with an assist from their sympathizers among the public of the imperial power. In his farewell speech upon resignation in 1907, he made clear his view of Egyptian preparedness for democracy: "I shall urge that the wholly spurious and manufactured development of parliamentary institutions should be treated for what it's worth and . . . let me add that it's worth very little."[49]

His successor, Sir J. Eldon Gorst, was Cromer's own choice. Yet Gorst, an ambitious career officer, understood that he must provide stability in Egypt without asking for additional resources. Lacking Cromer's ego investment in the imperial view of reality, Gorst held an entirely different situational view. His statements and actions indicated a desire to establish a real rather than a formal indirect colonial system. He called for granting Egyptian officials far greater real authority, for reversing the trend of replacing Egyptian officials with Englishmen, and for allowing an Egyptian educational system to develop and grow.[50] He coupled this with a decision to set up an alliance between the British and the most conservative of Egyptian elite groups, those most closely associated with the court. Such an alliance would further separate the court from Mustafa Kamel but would place a heavy strain on the *de facto* alliance Cromer had engineered with the Umma moderates.

Many British officials were intensely hostile to the direction of change. Their view of Egypt, highly congruent with their career interests, was similar to Cromer's. Gorst had the support of London, however, and his views were to prevail. London perceived that the Cromer policy could only result in a higher allocation of resources to Egypt, and there was no longer a perceived need to grant high priority to control of Egypt. Gorst understood his mission to call for a reduced, not an enhanced, British presence.

However, the costs of this change in direction were soon apparent. As would be expected, the shift in policy resulted in a dramatic alteration in the attitude of Abbas II, who now supported British policy.[51] But Mustafa Kamel did not. Attacks on the new alliance between the British and conservative Egyptians appeared regularly in the press and placed an added strain on Umma-type moderates, representing especially Arabic-speaking landowners and moderate religious leaders. Not only were they uncomfortable with the court, but they had to demonstrate nationalist credibility in the face of strong attacks from the nationalist press.

Faced with escalating criticism, the discredited prime minister, Mustafa Fahmy, resigned in 1908. The new government was an implicit effort to maintain center-right support for the regime. Gorst was able to persuade Butros Ghuli to become prime minister, Saad Zaghlul remained in education, and other Egyptians and moderate nationalists were brought into the government.[52] This was a classic response pattern, one to be repeated countless times by American diplomacy in the

Cold War: to seek stability by encouraging governments to place moderate and technically competent men in positions of authority.

With the Umma-type leaders accepting British largesse, the field was clear for the Watani party of Mustafa Kamel to reap the harvest of popular discontent. Advancing beyond their professional-intellectual base, al-Watani leaders began appealing to students, an emerging labor element, and more radical Moslem leaders.[53] Mustafa Kamel died suddenly in 1908. His successor, Mohammed Farid, was a less appealing leader, but Watani continued to be the focus of nationalist discontent. Gorst turned to modest coercion and had enacted a tough but difficult to enforce press law and a criminal deportation act. These annoyed without sufficiently repressing undesirable activity.

Matters came to a head in 1910. Butros Ghuli was assassinated, and the General Assembly refused to agree to a government request to extend the Suez Canal concession for forty years (from 1968 to 2008). These two acts carried important messages for both the British and cooperating Egyptians. For the British, they indicated the need for a sharp shift to coercion as a control device, and they discredited officials like Gorst, who advocated an inexpensive, indirect, colonial control system. The symbolic expression "liberalizing" for this policy is in part a misnomer. What it amounted to was a scheduled transfer of power to conservative and technocratic elites who could provide a stable regime with minimal British expenditures. Gorst's difficulties demonstrated that this "liberalized" regime would have to be given considerable coercive support if it was to survive.

In chapter 5, I described the process by which situational-level policy change occurs. When expected results from a policy are not realized, the prevailing situational view will change, not because of altered analyses but because new personnel with different situational views replace the old. This pattern was followed in Egypt in 1910. The government replaced advocates of indirect colonial control (Gorst and his supporters) with advocates of far more direct colonial control (followers of Cromer). Gorst was replaced by Kitchener, whose imperial view of Egypt and Africa had long before ossified.

For the Egyptians, the measure was the same one they had not quite understood at the time of the Dinshawi affair: A nationalist public opinion existed which had to be dealt with. As Kitchener was soon to demonstrate, nationalism could still be quieted, at least temporarily, by fairly simple suppression. But Egyptians who cooperated with imperial officers in such suppression would risk being eternally discredited. Both Copt leaders and Umma leaders received this message. So did the court. Particularly to be avoided was an already growing Moslem-Copt enmity. Consequently, all these leadership groups began to seek to recoup their threatened position. That they were able to do so, indeed that Saad Zaghlul was able to become the charismatic leader of anti-British Egyptian nationalism, supports the conclusion that the nationalist force at this time, though rapidly expanding, was still only a veneer of the population.

In any case, the messages received reinforced British and Egyptian predispositions. This was 1911, and World War I was soon to begin. With it came a British
determination to pay the price necessary to stay in Egypt. But the war merely
postponed an inevitable British decision: either increase the strength of British
coercive control in Egypt or accept a sharp decline in influence.

Kitchener happily reestablished official enmity between the British and the
court, repressed the nationalist leadership, and acquiesced reluctantly in a deterioration of relations with Zaghlul and the Umma group. His policies were direct
and simple. He sharply reduced the authority of the court, thereby regaining
effective administrative control, and initiated some energetic public works programs designed to recapture public support. With regard to the nationalists, he
attempted to isolate and destroy those he saw as extremists and to attract the
support of those he saw as moderate and constructive. The leaders of Watani were
imprisoned or exiled. Both Mohammed Farid and the popular nationalist Abd
al-Aziz Shawish were exiled. Kitchener succeeded in destroying the Watani party
as the primary focus of Egyptian nationalism.

To maintain the support of moderates and especially the Umma party, he
supported strengthening the legislative branch of the Egyptian government by
amalgamating the Legislative Council and the General Assembly into a new
Legislative Assembly. Still with only advisory powers, the new legislative body
was to be elected, and the property qualifications for the electorate gave a strong
advantage to the landowner-dominated Umma.[54] But Umma leaders, especially
Saad Zaghlul, were not so easily controlled this time. They accepted their
enhanced position but used the Legislative Assembly as a rostrum from which they
could lay claim to nationalist leadership. This role in turn could only lead them
toward progressive opposition to the British presence; to do less would have been
to risk their newly achieved leadership. Thus, the base for confrontation was laid,
but the confrontation itself was to be put off until after World War I.

Prevailing World View

In December 1914 the British government proclaimed Egypt to be a protectorate of the British Empire. Abbas II was deposed and was succeeded by Husain
Kamil Pasha, now granted the title of sultan. The proclamation ended the anoma-
lous suzerainty relationship Egypt had had with Constantinople and abruptly
changed Anglo-Egyptian relations.

Internal developments in Egypt and direct Anglo-Egyptian relations had shown
a declining, not an enhanced, British control, and this dramatic shift in policy
reflected a general strategy change in British foreign policy aims. With startling
suddenness, British perception of threat from Germany had become intense and
highly determining of the entire flavor of foreign policy aims. Even a few days
prior to the beginning of the war against Germany on August 4, 1914, the world

view of the British press was remarkably lacking in either enemy or allied perceptual characteristics.[55] Within hours a world-view transformation occurred, and a picture of Germany congruent with the ideal typical enemy image had appeared.[56]

As it related to Egypt, this perceptual transformation focused on a long-standing British fear: the exploitability of Islamic hostility to British imperialism. As noted frequently, the classic agitator in the imperial syndrome was one who stirred fanatical religious hostility. It was, then, only natural for the British to assume that an aggressive, monolithic, and highly rational German leadership would see the opportunity afforded by Islamic hatreds. To counter this, the British Foreign Office in November stated publicly:

German intrigue cannot influence the loyalty to Great Britain of the 70 million of Moham-medans in India and the feeling of the Mohammedan inhabitants of Egypt. They must look with detestation on misguided action under foreign influence at Constantinople, which will inevitably lead to the disintegration of the Turkish Empire, and which shows such forget-fulness of the many occasions on which Great Britain has shown friendship to Turkey. They must feel bitterly the degeneration of their coreligionists who can thus be dominated against their will by German influences, and many of them realize that when Turkey is pushed into war by Germany, they must dissociate themselves from a course of action that is so prejudicial to the position of Turkey itself.[57]

The statement is revealing of British assessments of the Egyptian Moslem. The British assumed that those who might be attracted by appeals from Constantinople to join a holy war would lose their enthusiasm if a case were made that Germany was behind the appeal. In fact, the section of the Egyptian public most receptive to the appeals of Constantinople was the pro-Watani professional and intellectual class. Members of that public were most hopeful that German support for Turkey could produce a combination that would defeat the British. Watani leaders worked actively in Constantinople to persuade the Turks to accept more, not less, German assistance. The statement suggests the familiar inability on the part of British officers to perceive the importance of public receptivity to anti-British colonial appeals.

Although there had been little to indicate a British view of an elaborate German conspiracy in Egypt prior to World War I, by December 1914 history had been reconstructed to accommodate it. The *London Times*, for example, gave this picture of Egyptian leaders:

After the Turkish Revolution of 1908, a pro-Turkish "Nationalist" party [the Watani] arose which preached and practiced sedition. The Khedive Abbas Hilmi did little to discourage, if he did not actually encourage the movement. Fortunately the Anglo-French agreement of April 1904 had changed French obstruction into hearty cooperation and deprived the seditious party of support they might otherwise have secured. German agents laboured, however, to foment trouble and ultimately influenced the Khedive himself . . . who had latterly thrown in his lot with Turco-German intrigues.[58]

The prevailing world view in Britain in fall 1914 was, for the first time, one of general polarization. A war of unprecedented danger had developed, and the German foe was perceived in terms approximating the ideal typical enemy image. Britain's allies now approximated the ideal typical allied image. Egypt returned from the decreasingly imperial image of a few years earlier to a near ideal typical imperial image. But the Ottoman enemy, weak as it was, was seen as acting under German orders, a style later generations would describe as satellite. This is mapped in figure II.8.

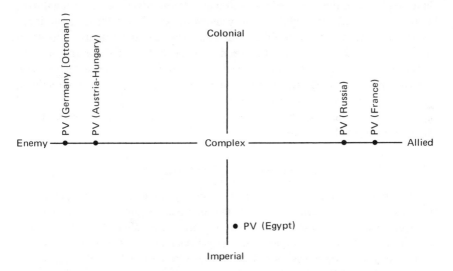

Figure II.8. British Prevailing World View, Fall 1914

Motivational System—General

The general motivational system for British foreign policy in 1914 bore scant resemblance to that of 1887. In 1887 there was little perceived threat or opportunity for British foreign policy decision makers. Consequently, although defense was placed alone in the first-intensity category, the most important observation was the relative lack of importance of foreign as compared with domestic policy, reflecting a low parametric value. In other words, those concerned with foreign policy could not make a strong case for significant priority rating in resource allocation. By late fall 1914, perception of threat to British interests in Europe, the Mediterranean, the Middle East, and the Far East was acute. Foreign policy demands on resources were given top priority and were unlikely to be denied.

The proposed general motivational system for 1914 is as follows:

A. Defense
B. Military vested interests
   Trade: exports and imports
C. Bureaucratic vested interests
   National grandeur

Defense of Great Britain, the empire, and the imperial life line were uppermost in the minds of those making policy. The particular direction of that policy would reflect the role-determined perspective of the responsible military and civilian bureaucracy, and the proposed motivational system reflects this decisional role. Comparing this with the motivational system proposed for 1887 (page 219), it can be seen that the changes reflect the sudden importance of the military in decision-making. Cultural messianism has been eliminated from the system of 1914 because it was of such minor importance compared with the defense factor that it does not qualify for a significant rating. The factor of national grandeur is retained, but at a low-intensity level, again because it is far less important than survival itself. However, as always, it is deeply interactive with defense and certainly affected decisional direction.

General System of Aims

The sudden outbreak of war and the consequent intense threat perception produced a general strategy level change of great magnitude. The result was convulsive change in both general and specific aims, although system values remained essentially status-quo. The motivational system indicates that the primary motivating force was indeed defense of Great Britain and the empire.

In 1887 the inferred parametric value determinants were seen as moderate- to low-intensity threat perceptions, primarily from France and Russia. By the late fall of 1914, Russia and France had both been seriously wounded by the German assault. A party urging a separate peace existed in Russia, and any perception of threat from Russia to India or to the imperial life line had vanished. Perception of threat to British Mediterranean interests from France persisted but was of very low intensity. In their place was a perceived threat from Germany to the British position in Europe and to the empire. Some German threat was seen to India and to British communications and oil interests in Iran, but the focus of threat to the imperial life line was in the eastern Mediterranean and on the high seas.

To contain this threat, both force and diplomatic maneuvering were required. Their thrust was directed at buoying up the alliance to deal with the German threat in Europe. The declaration of war against the Ottoman Empire ended the long era in which British diplomacy made the survival of the Porte a central strategic objective. The trend of focusing on Egypt as the mainstay of the imperial life line had been under way since the 1800s, and it now reached its logical conclusion. Without clearly planning it, British strategy came to rest on Egypt, the Arabian peninsula, the Mesopotamian area, Iran, and Afghanistan as the region that must remain under British influence. The Ottoman territory to the north of this line could be bargained away in exchange for the maintenance of the Entente. As a consequence, a series of bewildering, ambiguous, and self-contradictory agreements was negotiated with the Russians, the French, the Italians, the Greeks, the Zionists, and several sets of Arab leaders. Britain was to pay heavily for these maneuvers after the war, but their short-term objective was achieved: The British gained preeminence in the region then the focus of imperial security. For Egypt this amounted to the establishment of a protectorate. In Arab areas British preeminence was established in the Hejaz, in the rapidly expanding Saudi Arabian regime, and in the area to be known as Iraq. In Iran, the British gained formal preeminence in the former neutral zone designated in 1907 and—more important—virtual indirect, nonformal colonial control of the country.

The general strategy line constant of satisfying the foreign policy–related demands of the British people, represented in division C of the system-of-aims outline, reflects the changed situation. In response to the strongly felt threat perception, there had to be a major upgrading in priority of the demand for additional resources by the defense, colonial, and foreign policy bureaucracies. The increase in particular of the decisional influence of the defense bureaucracy is reflected in the motivational system. Downgraded substantially was the factor of cultural messianism seen in the system of aims as a low-intensity interest in continuing Britain's civilizing mission.

I. Preserve the peace, well-being, and security of the British people and safeguard the British Empire
   A. Contain and defeat the armed forces of the Central Powers in Europe
      1. Bring to bear overwhelming military force on the western front to halt and defeat the attack on France
      2. Bring Italy into the conflict as an ally of the Entente
      3. Keep Russia in the war to force Germany to fight on two fronts
      4. Protect the Serbian front with Austria-Hungary by developing an alliance with Italy, Greece, and Rumania and countering the Central Power pressure on Bulgaria
      5. Bring maximum American cooperation in meeting the German challenge in Europe and on the high seas
   B. Defend the empire and the imperial life line from Central Power assault in the Mediterranean, in South Asia, and on the high seas
      1. Utilize the partitioning of the Ottoman Empire to achieve diplomatic objectives for dealing with the Central Power threat in Europe

2. Secure the British position in Egypt, the Arabian peninsula, the Persian Gulf, and Afghanistan from German-Ottoman assault
3. Consolidate the above position in anticipation of any postwar challenge from France and/or Russia
4. Defeat and destroy the German naval challenge to British shipping
5. Protect British interests in the Far East from Japanese expansion

C. Satisfy the foreign policy–related demands of the British people
  1. Maintain and expand British armed forces capability for dealing with the Central Power threat and for consolidating a postwar position
  2. Maintain and expand a foreign service bureaucracy capable of achieving new and vital diplomatic goals
  3. Maintain and expand a colonial bureaucracy capable of establishing firm stability in the British Empire in the face of German-inspired agitation
  4. Protect and support British commercial interests and industry necessary for the successful prosecution of the war
  5. Defend the dignity and the prestige of the British nation
  6. Protect and defend the rights of European peoples to national self-determination and sovereignty
  7. Continue the civilizing mission in Africa and the Orient

Prevailing Situational View

The trends in the British situational view concerning Egypt from 1887 to 1914 have been described in the historical narrative section of this chapter. We found that a sharp alteration in situational view developed in London away from the imperial toward the complex image. My proposition was that this alteration was a manifestation of the sense of security concerning the imperial life line through the canal after the 1904 Anglo-French agreement. By 1914, however, the pendulum had already begun a strong swing back to the imperial view, owing initially to the failure of the so-called "liberalizing" policy of Gorst and then to the early success of the Kitchener program of coercion against the nationalists mitigated by institutional reform and an expanded public works program. The *London Times* spoke in typical imperial terms when describing the Kitchener summary report on finances in Egypt: "These matter-of-fact documents, taking absolutely for granted all the marvels which British rule has wrought in Egypt and the Sudan and rising to a note of enthusiasm only when they anticipate further reforms in the near future, might well stand as an epitome—complete because of the very unconsciousness—of the British genius in ruling subject peoples."[59]

Blunt expressed great skepticism regarding Kitchener's rule when he wrote, "Every foolish autocrat in history who has sowed the seeds of revolution that brought his throne to the dust has boasted of the 'firm' and 'strong' hand. The despot's role is, after all, the simplest of all roles to play."[60] However, the anti-imperialists were generally silent. No serious objections to Kitchener were raised in Parliament that year.

The Kitchener-sponsored reform of the legislature and relaxation of press control were favorably noted by imperial-minded writers. But a danger signal that year was not perceived. As noted above, Cromer had successfully disarmed one section of the nationalists (the landowner-based Umma party) and like-minded moderates by his friendliness to Mohammed Abdou and by appointing Saad Zaghlul as minister of education. Kitchener hoped to continue this policy, and the property requirement for voting allowed a heavy Umma representation in the Legislative Assembly. Saad Zaghlul became its vice-president, but he immediately also became the spokesman for the nationalist opposition to the British presence. The imperial mind could not see this as the natural move of a politician who believes that he must oppose an unpopular regime which has exiled or jailed the most prominent nationalist leaders. Instead, Zaghlul was perceived as an ingrate and an irresponsible agitator—at best an obstructionist. As the *Times* correspondent noted, "The conduct of the Assembly is disappointing to the hopes reposed in the new Assembly, especially in the case of Saad Zaghlul, from whom a better lead was expected and who certainly missed his opportunity yesterday. It is evident that the Assembly differs little from its predecessor and does not yet realize that the first duty to representative institutions is to respect the decision of the majority."[61] The *Times* reported later, when Kitchener coupled his financial report with a warning to the "obstructional" element, that Egyptians received both the report and the warning favorably.[62] However, in July, again commenting sadly on obstructionism, the *Times* allowed itself some speculation as to cause: "The delegates when in committee have shown themselves moderate, sensible, and practical-minded, yet no sooner have they come into the open Assembly than in many instances these good qualities have disappeared like lightning." Astonished by this behavior, the correspondent did not consider the possibility that it reflected the boundary-setting role of public opinion. Noting that "the Oriental has always been regarded as a model of quiet dignity and one whose respect for those placed in higher social positions was most profound," he speculated that obstruction in the legislature was a consequence of "the spread of education or the increased contact with Europe and Occidental life" which had produced "a change in temperament."[63]

Complicating this picture of a benign colonial administration tutoring a grateful but as yet immature population with only an occasional agitator, was the rapidly developing perception of external threat. We have seen how the reconstructed view of Watani suggested that it was involved in intrigue with the Germans. By June, the *Times* was printing alarmed reports of and warnings to Turkish agents operating in Egypt.[64] When Britain declared war against Turkey, concern mounted over the perceived ability of Turkey to agitate through religion. The statement initiating war read in part: "Recognizing the respect and veneration with which the

Sultan in his religious capacity is regarded by Mahomedans in Egypt, Great Britain takes upon herself the sole burden of the present war without calling on the Egyptian people for aid."[65]

But perceptual accommodation of the imperial and the enemy view necessitated characterizing Egyptians such as the Watani leaders and Abbas II as virtually enemy agents and in no way considering them as representatives of the Egyptian people. The people were happy with the British regardless of such changes in policy as the break in relations with their old allies, the Ottoman Turks. If the *Times* did not consider Egyptian nationalists to be representative of the people, it had no difficulty in finding its own spokesmen. It quoted a police officer whose views it saw as typical of "the huge conservative majority of the Moslems in Egypt": "Why should we want the Turks here? All orderly people know how it was in Ismail Pasha's days when the Turks were masters. All who have been to Turkey say that everyone is always being sent to prison there, and that their fellaheen are always being oppressed, whereas here there is enough work and food for everyone, and the English, thank God, are not mad like the Young Turks, who must go stirring up trouble everywhere."[66] Given such support, there was little to fear internally. As a British businessman in Egypt was reported as saying, "We do not fear the Turk or a native rising. If some rowdy natives tried to stir up a row, the fire brigade could settle them with a hose pipe."[67]

The prevailing situational view in this period of intense threat was also the view of most individuals concerned with British policy in Egypt. Only the anti-imperialists such as Blunt diverged, and in 1914 there were few of these. The perceptual map is shown in figure II.9, which includes the prevailing view (PV) and the view of the anti-imperialist (AI).

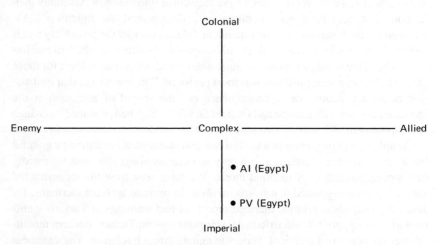

Figure II.9. British Situational Views, Fall 1914

Situational Motivational System

If 1911 had been the time chosen in this study to illustrate alteration in the British imperial presence in Egypt, the primary motivational factor might well have been inferred as bureaucratic vested interests. Although sense of threat to the security of British interests in Egypt had declined since Fashoda, the stability of the British position in 1911 was deteriorating as a result of internal political developments. The nationalist movement, though small, was growing so rapidly that moderate leaders such as Saad Zaghlul continually found themselves lagging behind. The British dilemma was whether to strengthen control sharply or to accept a situation in which demands for withdrawal could escalate.

The choice made was that favored by the Cromerites within the bureaucracy: strengthen control. Kitchener applied coercion against the court and Watani nationalists while appealing to the broad public through public works and education programs. He offered Umma-type nationalists increased influence in partnership with the government. His scheme appeared on the surface to be working, and even the anti-imperial author M. Travers Symons concedes that Kitchener's administration could claim popularity.[68]

But evidence such as Saad Zaghlul's drift into active opposition suggested that this success was only temporary. The elements supporting a more radical nationalist program were too numerous this time to be controlled by removing their leaders. However, before the approaching crisis appeared, external events produced a general strategy level change in the foreign policy aims system of Britain, and the impact was felt strongly in Egypt. Now no real consideration could be given to the option of withdrawal. Egypt was not directly threatened, even though Turkish troops were just across the Sinai, but Egypt's position was a vital link in the imperial life line. As the *London Times* editorial stated on August 2, 1914, Serbia was attacked as part of a calculated policy,

because [it] is the chief obstacle to the Austro-German advance toward the Mediterranean and to the establishment of complete German control of the Balkans, the Dardanelles, Asia Minor, and of the land and sea routes to Egypt and India.

It is not a question of Servia, nor of Russia. It is a question of isolating England in order that when isolated she may be compelled to submit to German dictation. It is a question of destroying the security of the Mediterranean through which England's route to Egypt and India and the bulk of her food supplies pass.[69]

The *Manchester Guardian* complained when a protectorate was declared over Egypt, but there was no real parliamentary opposition. The anti-imperial position so loudly advanced four years earlier had virtually disappeared. The imperial image of reality was more congruent with the actions defense interests were compelling the British government to take.

In the inferred situational motivational system, therefore, only one factor, that of defense, will be placed in the first-intensity category. Were Britain to lose this war, the days of imperial greatness would be over. Egypt was vital, and no real thought could be given to any notion of withdrawal.

This aim coincided with the vested interests of both the Foreign Office and the military bureaucracy. The Cromerite imperial situational view reflected these interests and was equally congruent with defense needs. Since British decisions were being made by the London defense bureaucracy and the military and foreign policy bureaucracy in Egypt, the motivational system should include military and bureaucratic vested interests at the second level of intensity.

Those involved in making decisions concerning British policy in Egypt described their policies in terms of the civilizing mission of the British Empire, and they certainly believed they had improved the quality of life in Egypt immeasurably. For this reason, the factors of national grandeur and cultural messianism are included at the third level of intensity. The assumption here is, as it has been throughout this study, that symbolic expressions are not simply rhetorical but in part determine policy.

It is much more difficult to discover explicit evidence of any significant role for commercial interests in the decision to formalize the British position in Egypt. Occasional complaints of a lack of governmental sensitivity to commercial interests did appear in print. For example, the *Times* had given voice to a complaint of the British commercial community in Egypt earlier in 1914. It reported a major oil discovery on the shores of the Red Sea but suggested that the government should be more concerned. It is "in the interests of the British nation that any such oil fields shall be properly developed and worked, and not simply left as 'reserves' for the future. Whether the Colonial Office is properly alive to this duty, whether even it is properly advised or equipped for the purpose, is by no means certain."[70] Direct evidence of active participation by commercial interests in the British decisional process as it related to Egypt is rarely found in any period. I have included economic vested interest factors in previous situational motivational systems because of policy behavioral evidence that these interests had been internalized by political leaders and bureaucrats. Stated more negatively, policy makers seemed to understand that if they were not sensitive to British commercial interests, pressures from those interests would soon develop. During World War I, however, I see little manifestation in official decisions of a concern for commercial interests. For this period the economic factor has been eliminated altogether from the inferred situational motivational system which follows:

A. Defense
B. Military vested interests
   Bureaucratic vested interests
C. National grandeur
   Cultural messianism

Specific Policy, Expectations, and Response

After the initial confusion that engulfed the British foreign policy aims system following the shock of World War I, an aims system developed whose central and overwhelming purpose was to win the war. Policy toward Egypt was outlined by this central objective and the strategy for achieving it. Ottoman suzerainty had to be erased and the British presence formalized. Only two alternatives were considered: annexing Egypt and declaring a protectorate. There was an annexation party in London, but British officials in Egypt were strongly opposed.[71] Annexation would intensify control problems and, further, run counter to the situational view that had developed over the years: Egypt required a prolonged period of tutelage before national adulthood could be reached; but though prolonged, the period of occupation was to be temporary. Of concrete and immediate significance, if annexation were proclaimed, Egyptian cabinet officers and senior administrators could not remain in office without losing all claims to national legitimacy. This truth was comprehended by British officials in the field. In London, preference for a clear, unambiguous annexation policy was possible largely through innocence.

Expectations of officials in London and in Egypt were that the Egyptian people would welcome the new Egyptian sultan, Husain Kamil, and that the British would have no more than minor control problems in Egypt. These expectations were in part fulfilled. Control problems were not serious during the war. Nationalist leaders apparently realized the British could not afford to see their control challenged as long as the German threat was real. But expectations of achieving any genuine popular acceptance for the new regime were not fulfilled. Following the war, a popular demand for real independence appeared with a force and suddenness to shock even those of Blunt's persuasion. This expectational failure was much too dramatic not to lead to profound perceptual alteration once the defense-related necessity for maintaining control of Egypt had lost its force.

12 / Winter 1921

Historical Narrative

On November 4, 1920, a debate took place in the House of Lords in which one question at issue was independence for Egypt. Could it be that what Cromer called the "extremely incompetent Egyptian" and the "stupidest of Orientals" would be granted independence? Surely the Cromerites, the imperial hard-liners, would suffer near apoplexy at the hint of such a suggestion. Yet the strongest statement made in the Lords that day was made by a leader of the imperial hard-liners, Lord Salisbury, who said:

People in this country who were principally concerned felt as if we were approaching a period of disintegration. . . . The idea that we were to abandon the Egyptian peasantry, or the people of the Sudan, or our responsibility to the British Empire because an American statesman who had lost the confidence of his own country invented the phrase self-determination was a conclusion against which every statesman would rebel.[1]

This undramatic statement reflected an acceptance of the inevitable by the imperialist-minded. In the winter of 1921 the British government announced its intention to abolish the protectorate and grant Egypt what amounted to quasi independence. Only a few years earlier such a proposal would have astonished even Wilfrid Blunt and been inconceivable to anyone to the right of him on imperial issues. Yet in 1921, the objections were few and as moderate as the above remark.

As late as 1918, Sir Francis Reginald Wingate, soon to be high commissioner for Egypt, had favored outright annexation of Egypt into the British Empire.[2] His view, like those of Kitchener and Cromer, was that Egypt was in need of a long tutelage before independence in any form should be considered. The establishment of a protectorate amounted to official acceptance of that position. What converted the Egyptians in only a few months into a people fully capable of running most of their domestic affairs? Surely it had not been their experience during the war: Supplies had been requisitioned, forced labor hardly distinguishable from the corvée had been general policy, and Egyptian landowners had been compelled to shift from cotton production to the growth of foodstuffs for the allied military.[3] Yet somehow in British eyes the Egyptians had been transformed by 1921.

Other dramatic perceptual alterations have been noted in this study, but none compares in dimension to this one.

Prevailing World View

My analytic assumption is that perceptual alterations of this dramatic dimension reflect a major general strategy level change in the foreign policy aims system. The latter change is assumed to occur in response to an alteration in perception of threat or opportunity. Obviously such an alteration was occurring in Great Britain in 1921. World War I had ended, and Britain's German and Russian competitors had both sued for peace and were much weakened. France, though victorious, had seen a greater deterioration in her naval strength than had Britain. Imperial rivalry between the two countries persisted, but in general they could be thought of as friends. Italy had been humiliated in the war and was not perceived to be a serious rival.

Verbalizations regarding the British position in Egypt continued to mention imperial defense, but such remarks were nonspecific and seemed to refer to some future eventuality. In a note signed by Field Marshal Edmund Allenby to Sultan Fuad, in 1921, the Egyptian government was reminded that a major purpose of the British presence was to safeguard Egypt from foreign intervention and that this purpose was "as powerful now as in the past."[4] In response the *New Statesman and Nation* editorialized:

What hostile power is baring its teeth at us in the Mediterranean or the Red Sea? Is it Japan, or America, or France, or Bolshevik Russia? Or is it the Senussi tribesmen whom we have found we can dispose of with a couple of aeroplanes? The fact is that once you turn the pompous abstractions of this letter into concrete questions, the whole notion of a threatened attack appears in its childish absurdity.[5]

Even the *London Times* could muster only one perception of threat in 1920–1921, and it concerned the alleged preference of Egyptian students for a German education. The *Times*'s Cairo correspondent remarked:

There is little doubt that the sojourn in Berlin is part of a well-conceived plan for the propagation of pro-German, possibly of Bolshevist doctrines in the Near East, in which the notorious Sheikh Abdel Aziz Shawish, who is said to be living sumptuously in Berlin, is taking part. . . . It is highly probable that some, if not all, of these candidates for German diplomas will return as active pan-German or Bolshevist agents and will constitute a serious danger, not only to their own country but also to the peace of North Africa and the Middle East.[6]

The article is a curious amalgam of past and current fears. Shawish, the much maligned Watani leader, had earlier been labeled a German agent; now the old threat was being updated. Despite a great deal of agitation in Egypt, this was the only suggestion of foreign sponsorship published that year in the *Times*. Most descriptions of Egyptian dissidents bore the marks of detachment, that is, no conspiracy theories and a differentiated description of opposition elements.

During that same period, the *Times* carried daily articles describing Bolshevik forces in Russia as starkly evil, but the threat seen to emanate from bolshevism was not spelled out in terms of specific manifestations such as in Egypt. The *New Statesman and Nation* attacked Winston Churchill for seeing the Bolshevik menace everywhere. In an article on British policy in Egypt it accused him of being "one of the chief mischief makers in this country. His contempt for public opinion, his vanity, his ignorant terror of Russia, have wasted life and money."[7]

The map of various world views in England in 1921 (figure II.10) differs sharply from that of 1914. Not only have enemies and allies disappeared, but the prevailing view (PV) regarding Egypt had migrated toward the complex pole. Although an imperial back-bench group (I), of whom Winston Churchill was the most colorful spokesman, still saw enemies and colonial peoples, the overall perceptual change was dramatic. The anti-imperialist view (AI) is also shown.

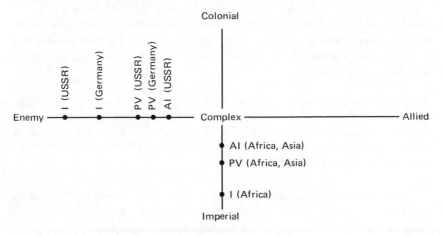

Figure II.10. British World Views, 1921

Motivational System—General

The perceptual alteration among Englishmen concerning Egypt was consistent with general trends. The Boer War and the imperial image that accommodated British norms and imperial expansion were barely a generation in the past, yet they seemed to be part of another age. Mighty Britain, the greatest of world powers, was accommodating to a decline in relative power. Anti-imperial attitudes in England and a perception of the colonial world in which national movements are seen, public opinion described, and national leaders recognized can be identified throughout the nineteenth and early twentieth centuries; and occasionally this image was characteristic of the prime minister, as it was of Gladstone, and of broad sections of the most attentive public. But never had such a view been as widely held as after World War I. The *New Statesman and Nation*, rarely in tune with the majority, could claim with some confidence that not "one man in a hundred in this country cares a brass button today about the number of red splotches on the map of the world and . . . not one in ten thousand is willing to pay for adventures to increase them."[8]

But the *New Statesman and Nation*, week after week, warned its readers that the military would not acquiesce in this fact and that adventurers such as Winston Churchill had an image of empire that could bring disaster:

The British Empire, if it is to play the high part, which it can and ought to play, will have to purge itself of certain vicious ideas inherited from the past. The most vicious of these ideas is that we can hold together half Asia and Africa by force. The British Empire will not play its part—indeed, it will not continue for long to exist—as a military empire. And there are none who are preaching a more disastrous doctrine to-day than the professional soldiers and their civilian abettors.[9]

Opposing rhetoric from conservative journals such as the *Times* in no way paralleled the stridency of these remarks. On the contrary, they too began to see national movements in colonies where they had not seen them before. National movements, in fact, seemed suddenly to be materializing everywhere. For those such as Lord Salisbury who were particularly bemused by this phenomenon, a satisfactory explanation seemed to be that local agitators received great encouragement from Woodrow Wilson and his softheaded followers.

I am not arguing that a primary drive now flowing from British motivations was to dissolve His Majesty's empire. Rather, I am saying that in England at this time there appeared implicitly a comprehension that the costs of perpetuating the empire as it had been would henceforth be greater than the British public was willing to pay. Those for whom national grandeur was of great primacy might be willing to pay the price of maintaining the empire undiminished; possibly Winston Churchill was one such man. The military bureaucracy, swollen and with its decisional latitude expanded by the war, would have a strong role predisposition to maintain the empire. But policy behavior suggests that even with the motive force of national grandeur expanded and with military vested interest approaching the first-intensity category, the drive was not sufficient to prevent retrenchment.

The decline in perception of threat resulted in a low parametric value for the foreign policy aims system. Defense remains in the first-intensity category of the motivational system. Verbalizations suggest that British decision makers were very much concerned with potential threat even though they admitted the lack of current threat. But foreign policy had lost importance. This is reflected in the sharp decline of the priority claim the foreign policy bureaucracy could make on the national purse.

The proposed general motivational system for 1922 is as follows:

A. Defense
   Military vested interests
B. Trade: exports and imports
   National grandeur
C. Bureaucratic vested interests

Given the parametric value decline, the higher standings of military vested interests and national grandeur were less significant than would otherwise be the case. Concomitantly, it is significant that the position for bureaucratic vested interests is static as compared with the proposed general motivational system of 1914. This implies a relative decline in the input intensity from the foreign policy–related civilian bureaucracy. Similarly, the continued second-intensity rating for trade argues for the conclusion that the actual policy impact of commercial elements was in decline. Both points, it must be admitted, are made with insufficient evidence and, in fact, are based largely on the evidence seen in the situational experience in Egypt.

General System of Aims

In sharp contrast to 1914, the general system of aims proposed here for 1921 is based more on perception of opportunity than on perception of threat. But the opportunity perceived is less to satisfy an economic, ideological, or other vested-interest motive than to produce a system that would form the basis for a long era of peaceful cooperation. Thus, the entire first division of the proposed system of aims relates to a peace settlement that will set up international institutions for the peaceful settlement of disputes and will accommodate competing national and imperial interests in such a way that the defeated peoples reenter a peaceful and democratic system. The major cacophony in this division arises from two perceptions of threat: one from a revitalized and remilitarized Germany bent on revenge, the second from the consolidation of power in Russia by a Bolshevik regime. Placing these concerns below the general strategy level reflects the assumption that neither perception of threat was sufficient to set the tone for the general aims system.

I. Preserve the peace, well-being, and security of the British people and the peoples of the British Empire
  A. Work for the creation of an effective collective security system of peaceful, democratic states
    1. Establish and develop international institutions that can provide collective security and international cooperation, the foremost of these being the League of Nations
    2. Seek to establish international agreements concerning arms control
    3. Effect a peace settlement with Germany that will result in a peaceful, democratic, cooperative regime
    4. Effect a peace settlement with regard to the former Austro-Hungarian Empire and Ottoman Empire that will conform with the principles of national self-determination and will reduce international rivalry
  B. Provide for the security of the peoples of the British Empire and the imperial life line
    1. Effect a disposition of German and Ottoman imperial possessions in Asia and Africa in a manner that conforms to the security interests of the British Empire and that is least likely to result in imperial rivalries
    2. Continue efforts to provide for the well-being of peoples under British control and to prepare all such peoples for eventual self-rule
    3. Effect a settlement in the Far East that protects imperial trade and prevents domination by a single power
    4. In Egypt and the Middle East, safeguard the imperial life line and imperial commercial interests with the least possible British imperial presence
  C. Satisfy the foreign policy–related demands of the British people
    1. Maintain British naval and military forces at a level consonant with imperial security needs
    2. Maintain British foreign service and colonial service sufficient for the achievement of foreign policy and colonial policy goals
    3. Encourage and support British commercial interests overseas and safeguard British home industry and commerce from unfair foreign commercial practices
    4. Defend the dignity and prestige of the British nation and empire
    5. Support the liberal democratic form of government and humanitarian interests of all peoples and advance the principle of self-determination
    6. Proceed with the civilizing mission for peoples under British control

At the system aims level a change has been proposed concerning the empire. For the aims system of 1914 the proposed wording was "safeguard the British Empire." For 1921 this has been changed to "preserve the peace, well-being, and security of the peoples of the British Empire." The change reflects a conclusion that a changed relationship within the empire had been accepted in which imperial control was reduced and focused more on achieving the kind of consensual acceptance that existed in England. This change is spelled out at the general strategy level in division B and below that in terms of specific policy. This division, too, develops the notion that the disposition of former colonies of the defeated powers be made in such a way as to increase imperial security and to reduce the potential for exacerbated imperial rivalry. The division reflects as well the systemic change toward reducing control costs and accepting a consonant reduction in degree of control.

As was suggested in the discussion of general motives, this picture of sharply reduced perception of threat should increase the relative influence of domestic pressure groups in the determination of foreign policy. A low-intensity threat or opportunity perception, seen in system terms, is reflected in a parallel parametric value reduction for the foreign policy aims system. Translated, this means an analytical representation of the weakened bargaining position of foreign policy decision makers in laying claim to resource allocation. Thus, the aspect of general foreign policy reflected here in the C division, the foreign policy–related demands of the British people, should be more important than those in the other division. But there would be, as well, sharp alterations of relative influence of groups associated with different goals within the C division. For example, in 1914 overwhelming priority was given to the general goals associated with containing and defeating the Central Powers. This goal therefore set the tone for the entire aims system. Within the C division it meant that top priority would go to the goal of creating and maintaining British military capability sufficient to achieve this task. Or, in bargaining terms, it meant that the relative influence of the military bureaucracy was extraordinary.

With the defeat of the Central Powers and the consequent elimination of the general goal associated with an intense perception of threat from them, the new goal lacked the importance that an intense threat perception could grant. But a huge military bureaucracy remained, and its essential bargaining position had disappeared. The British military bureaucracy quite naturally perceived a situation in which it would play a continuing role. That led to a view of reality, as described earlier, that included a high potential for a revived German threat and for a developing threat from the Russian Bolsheviks. However, as the system of aims just outlined reflects, I conclude that for the British polity generally, the prevailing view, this threat perception was below the general strategy level. It is depicted instead as a minor disturbance leading to specific foreign policy goals in the A division. Nevertheless, the military bureaucracy did have a strong enough voice to have its influence represented in the motivational system at the highest-intensity level.

In discussing the Egyptian situation, I will argue that the colonial bureaucracy did not succeed in maintaining comparative influence. Instead, its relative influence sharply declined vis-à-vis the military.

A decline in parametric value generally will be reflected in declining influence for the foreign policy and defense bureaucracies relative to that of public vested-interest and ideological pressure groups. But in Britain after World War I, reduced bureaucratic influence did not have its counterpart in a relatively enhanced influence position for commercial interests. At least there is little evidence that significant pressure was placed on the government for particular policy objectives desired by the commercial community.

There is, however, evidence that ideology became a more important determinant of British policy. There were two thrusts, neither reflecting any degree of organized activity, but suggesting rather a public response to the manipulation of symbols by politicians. First, there was a concern for British prestige, and the symbol manipulation in this case was successful to a significant degree. In a period of imperial decline some men, such as Winston Churchill, were determined to reverse the trend and struck a responsive chord within the general public and within officialdom. The motivational system proposed for this period reflects this conclusion in placing national grandeur at the second-intensity level.

The second set of symbols manipulated with some success were those of national self-determination. Imperial advocates assessed the fixation on self-determination as the major determinant of the British imperial retreat in Egypt and elsewhere. My conclusion is that the imperial retreat, which was real enough, was overwhelmingly the result of an implicit understanding that the costs of imperial maintenance would be rising in geometric progression. To pay this added cost, the British public would have to have felt some overriding need, such as a perception of threat could provide. It felt no such need. By clothing the imperial retreat in the garb of national self-determination, Englishmen could make a virtue of necessity. But I conclude that the interest in advancing self-determination as an end lacked the kind of intensity it must have to qualify as ideological messianism. For that reason I do not give ideological messianism even a third-intensity rating in the motivational system.

Prevailing Situational View

Today Saad Zaghlul is little remembered in Egypt or abroad, yet he played an extraordinary role in Egyptian history. His countrymen are more likely to recall favorably Mustafa Kamel, and this is understandable. Zaghlul's relations with the colonial master were ambiguous, while Kamel's were reasonably pure. Mustafa Kamel was a true son of the Enlightenment; Zaghlul was more willing to compromise liberal and national values.

In 1921, conservative Englishmen saw Saad Zaghlul as the epitome of the unreasoning, mindless colonial agitator. His career suggests a different image —one of almost litmus-paper sensitivity to the Egyptian political climate. For a wife he chose the daughter of Mustafa Fahmy, an upper-class, Turkish-speaking WOG, and gained the social access essential to his political career. He gravitated naturally to moderate, conservative elements in the reform movement rather than to the nationalist purist wing. Cromer astutely recognized him as a powerful potential ally in a mutually advantageous working relationship. Zaghlul apparently sensed the thinness of the veneer of the liberal nationalist movement and yet saw a basic popular receptivity to the nationalist appeal. He watched the purist nationalists of Watani suppressed and forced into exile by Kitchener. Then he took full advantage of the position in the Egyptian legislature that his past collaboration had granted him to assume sponsorship of the nationalist appeal.

By the close of World War I, Zaghlul had become the spokesman for nationalist resentment. As a long-time member of the top Egyptian political elite, he moved easily among lesser politicians whose attacks on the British were timid and rare. Among sophisticated nationalists of the Watani persuasion he was suspect, but they could hardly fault his rhetoric or the adamancy of his position. For the student element, who had heard much of Zaghlul and little of Watani leaders, he was Egyptian nationalism personified.

Saad Zaghlul was hardly a free agent. On the contrary, his career brilliantly mirrored the boundaries within which the successful politician could act. Osmond Walrond, a British intelligence officer and influential adviser to Lord Milner, paints a WOG-like picture of Zaghlul and of the Wafd party which formed around his leadership that is understandable given earlier British experience with Zaghlul. He described Zaghlul and Wafd as "well disposed to us" and said "it was an evil day when they were first dubbed 'Nationalist.'"[10] But the remark simply reflects a memory of long-time friendly collaboration and fails to recognize the Zaghlul who sensed that such overt collaboration was no longer allowed him. To retain his position as unquestioned spokesman for Egyptian national aspirations, he had to follow a narrow and clearly delineated path.

The agony of British adjustment to the changed situation in Egypt can best be viewed by looking at policy response to Zaghlul. The episode that first revealed the changed situation occurred in November 1918, when a delegation led by Zaghlul called on the British high commissioner, Sir Francis Reginald Wingate. Their objective was to have Zaghlul and others named part of an official Egyptian delegation to the Paris peace conference to negotiate for Egyptian national self-determination. Zaghlul at the time held no official position, but both Sultan Fuad and the prime minister, Hossein Rushdi, supported the Zaghlul representation.[11] London's response was to reject the proposal summarily and to rebuke Wingate for having given any official countenance to its claim.

The Foreign Office, led by Arthur Balfour and George Curzon, was anything but receptive to the notion of extending the spirit of the Fourteen Points to Egypt.

Nor was there real disagreement with that position among British representatives in Cairo. Wingate had favored annexing Egypt outright rather than continuing with the anomaly of a protectorate status.[12] Why, then, should Wingate have given the slightest official encouragement to Zaghlul?

From 1876 through World War I, officials in London advocated a softer line than did British officials in Egypt. After World War I this pattern was reversed, and London consistently took a harder line toward Zaghlul than did Cairo. Furthermore, Wingate, Allenby, and Milner were each much tougher in attitude when in London than in Cairo. Finally, each of these officials, as well as many lesser bureaucrats, vacillated between a tough and an accommodationist stance.

There was a manifest rhythm to the vacillation of British officials in Cairo which can be typified by the example of Milne Cheetham.[13] Cheetham had been a senior official in Egypt since 1911, and in 1919 he was acting head of mission. As late as February 1919 Cheetham's reports were fully in tune with the imperial view. According to him, the agitating Zaghlul was steadily losing what little real popularity he once had and the situation was fully under control. When London refused to allow Zaghlul to attend the Versailles conference, Zaghlul responded by forcing a confrontation with Egypt's Sultan Fuad, ostensibly the head of government. Cheetham's recommendation to London, in harmony with his imperial view, was to be tough and forceful: arrest and deport Zaghlul. London agreed and Cheetham expressed confidently the expectation that, with the removal of the primary agitator from the scene, peace and stability would be restored. But his expectations were not realized. Demonstrations and strikes erupted everywhere. Now, instead of seeing an agitator with a veneer of support, Cheetham said what was happening was "nationalist in the full sense of the word."[14] He recommended some conciliation of Egyptian opinion, even including the acceptance of the demand that a nationalist delegation be sent to Paris. This recommendation was rejected, and Cheetham was told to concentrate on restoring law and order. A few days later Field Marshal Allenby, supposedly a hard-liner, reached Cairo to head the British mission. No sooner had he arrived than he too reversed his position and seconded Cheetham's recommendation.

There is an easy explanation for this rhythm, and it is suggested by a summary of Milner's remarks to the House of Lords following his mission to investigate the situation in Egypt:

That we could maintain our position in Egypt by our own strength, he had not the slightest doubt but the danger which at one time seemed to threaten was that we should find ourselves maintaining it against the wishes of the Egyptian people, and with a constant spirit of discontent and revolt on their part against what they might regard as an alien foreign yoke. His belief was that a course of action was possible which would enable us to ensure all that we needed in Egypt, including the maintenance of order and progress of which we ourselves were the authors without involving ourselves in permanent hostility with the Egyptian nation.[15]

In other words, in 1920 the English could remain in Egypt with undiminished control only if they were willing to allocate much more extensive resources. But they could nevertheless remain in Egypt without an increase in price by reducing the degree of control. There is no question that Britain could have retained or enhanced its overall degree of control. Soviet Russia, in a similar situation at this time with local nationalism in her Asian empire, chose to pay the additional price required. But the disappearance of a perception of immediate threat to British imperial interests made unnecessary the retention of the degree of control that had existed in Egypt during the war years, and there was no real likelihood of an increase in resource allocation for the purpose of maintaining tight control. The perceptual response to this fact can be seen in Milner's accommodation to the new situation.

The problem is easily stated: British officials in Egypt were anxious for London's approval and yet fully aware of their inability to pressure London into making a heavier commitment of resources. They were naturally inclined to see a situation in which they could exert a maximum of control given their resource allocation. They had accepted an imperial image of Egypt and in noncrisis moments were true to that image. But when a crisis developed, they advocated policies far more congruent with a complex image. Thus, in periods of quiescence a Wingate could see a climate favorable to annexation, a Milner could see reasons for long-term tutelage, and a Cheetham could see a decay of support for Zaghlul. But when disorder threatened to get out of hand, the imperial lens was dropped, and a differentiated view of Egyptian politics came into focus, one which allowed for internal political maneuverings to effect the best possible compromise. When this seemed to necessitate cooperation with Zaghlul, he was perceived as receptive to cooperation. When the British position was stable, officials sought to isolate him from more conservative establishment politicians and perceived him as a vainglorious, irresponsible agitator.

Of course it should not be expected that all officials would respond similarly. I have argued that variations in response should flow from different identity value intensities, different political values, and idiosyncratic socialization differences. Elie Kedourie indicates that in Cairo the accommodationist view was advocated strongly by Allenby's deputy, Sir Gilbert Clayton,[16] and there were sharp disagreements among the British in Egypt. But role is a vital determinant of perception, and the harmony of views in Cairo is more apparent than is the range.[17]

Egyptian politicians were painfully aware of this patterned response from the British. Both Sultan Fuad and Prime Minister Rushdi expressed their wish that the British establish a consistent interventionist policy.[18] Without it, neither could be sure of how much he should compromise with the nationalist movement. Again and again, like other conservative Egyptians, they were the victims of British vacillation. The WOG role is a difficult one. Typically in Egypt and other areas in which the British sought inexpensive colonial control, the WOG was a member of the conservative upper class. His role interests called for an alliance with colonial officers who would grant a certain protection to the traditionalist's vested interests in return for his cooperation. But as nationalism gained increasing currency, he was in constant danger of losing all vestiges of his nationalist legitimacy as a result of his cooperation. As this occurred, his ability to maintain control declined. With the decline in his ability to maintain control, the value of his alliance for the colonial officers suffered a parallel decline. The colonial officers, therefore, were confronted with the choice of either expanding their alliance, and in the process adding to their control problem, or increasing the strength of their coercive instruments. Since the latter option was not available after World War I, the British were compelled to take the first option. This amounted to a net loss for the WOG leaders, and their disappointment and bitterness ("after all we have done for them") were understandable. Rather than lose all, they too had to make their compromises with elements of the nationalist counterelite.

During the period 1920–1923, British officials and Egyptian politicians were settling into a new relationship. Even with the great asset of a charismatic leader who could personify nationalism for the awakening mass, the Egyptian movement was not sufficiently strong to compel the granting of real independence. Yet it was too strong to ignore. Both British officials and Egyptian WOGs had to make their accommodations to it.

In the previous chapter, quotations from Lord Milner's book, *England in Egypt*, were cited to illustrate a view of reality approximating the ideal typical imperial image. Now that same Lord Milner was about to confound his critics by recommending a modified form of independence for Egypt. When he did so in the Milner mission report, published in 1921,[19] the *New Statesman and Nation* remarked, "It is a curious irony that the man who was known twenty years ago as the archpriest of the old cult, is now the protagonist of liberty."[20] Milner himself thought it not at all strange. He wrote in the preface to the 1920 edition of his book:

The view has been expressed in some quarters that any relaxation of British control over the administration of Egypt would be an abandonment of the objects which we have been hitherto pursuing in that country. Nothing can be further from the truth. The establishment of Egypt as an independent state in intimate alliance with Great Britain, so far from being the reversal of the policy with which we set out, would be the consummation of it.[21]

The contrast between Milner's *England in Egypt* and the Milner mission report is so great that the two together can stand as a classic illustration of perceptual accommodation to a changed situation. In his preface to the thirteenth edition of his book, published at approximately the same time as his report, Milner argued that there was, in fact, no contradiction. It is quite true that *England in Egypt* calls for tutoring Egyptians for independence, but it was for an independence in the far distant future. All Milner did perceptually was to shrink the temporal factor. Having done this, he was able to give a picture of Egyptian politics and nationalism with few of the imperial manifestations. Egyptians are now fully adult; their political movement is respectable by British standards, and highly differentiated; they continue to need a British presence but primarily because of the legacies of past imperial rule: the conflicting European claims, the capitulations, the unfairly favored cosmopolitan community, and the ever present potential for imperial conflict over the Suez Canal. New times call for a treaty between two friends with deep mutual interests to replace the old superior-subordinate relationship.

The Milner mission report is not without bitterness and ambivalence. Nationalism need not have surfaced in the negative, agitating manner the Milner mission saw when it visited Egypt in 1920. Certainly, had the wisdom of the British been allowed to prevail it would have been much different.

The evolution of a sane and moderate spirit might have been regarded with sympathy and interest, and, indeed, the late Lord Cromer had hopes that it might be turned to good account. But unfortunate political rivalries among the Western Powers led it from the first to assume an anti-British colour. The Nationalists were alternately encouraged and opposed by the ex-Khedive for his own personal aims. Their ranks were swelled by the members of a thoroughly dissatisfied civil service, who regarded the presence of the British as a bar to promotion, and who were further discouraged by a system of selection which made it possible for the influential to secure the preferment of relations and dependents. The increasing number of the students who look only to State employment as a reward for the often real sacrifices made in order to qualify for it, and who regard their prospects of obtaining any appointment as diminished by the competition of the foreigner, made them a ready instrument for such propaganda in the provinces.[22]

Of course, the British did share some of the blame. But according to the report, this was largely because of the preoccupation with winning the war—a result important for Egypt itself.[23] And mistakes were made by individuals, for example, Milne Cheetham's major error in recommending Zaghlul's deportation.[24] In sum, though, the British role in Egypt was most beneficial, and Egypt's preparation for a degree of independence was a result of that role.

The report regrets that there was nastiness in the nationalist agitation and much ingratitude. Nationalist leaders recognized the opportunity presented by Wilson's Fourteen Points: "Those in Egypt who had anticipated, and would at one time even have welcomed a German and Turkish victory, now found a favorable opportunity for shifting their ground. This section now claimed that by contributing morally and materially to the victory of the Allies Egypt had herself been instrumental in throwing off all that was left of the Turkish yoke."[25]

The treatment of the Milner mission in Egypt was rude but still instructive:

We had not been many days or even hours in Cairo before we had ample evidence of active and organized antagonism. Telegrams poured in announcing the intention of the senders to go on strike as a protest against our presence. Many of these were dispatched by school boys and students, but others came from public bodies, such as Provincial Councils, a few from government officials, and a considerable number from corporations or communities of greater or less importance. We received in all 1,131 such messages during our stay, while only twenty-nine telegrams of welcome.[26]

The mission did not dismiss the importance of its negative reception, as it easily could have. In an earlier period the Egyptian reaction would have been seen as the work of a handful of self-seeking agitators, probably in collusion with either the French or the Turks. Now public opinion was looked at in a cold, detached, and probably reasonably accurate way:

It has been said that "every Egyptian worth his salt is at heart a Nationalist." This is only true of the educated and semi-educated classes, who constitute less than 10 per cent of the fourteen million inhabitants of Egypt. It would be meaningless as applied to the 92 per cent of illiterates and especially to the fellahin, who are two-thirds of the whole people. The turbulent crowds of the great towns may indeed be easily worked up to excitement by political catchwords, which they vociferate without understanding. But the fellahin, as a body, are normally very indifferent to politics.[27]

The fellahin response concerned the Milner mission, as it had many Englishmen before. Whatever the agitators may say, the argument went, the fellahin profited from and were perfectly satisfied with British rule. Therefore the fact that unrest "should have spread to the fellahin and should have led to outbreaks of savage violence among a class which has derived such immense benefits from the British Occupation, needs explaining."[28] Milner's explanation is again mainly the inadvertent injustices resulting from the war. "But it is idle to hope that the comparatively satisfactory attitude of the peasantry will long be maintained, if our relations with the middle and upper classes of their countrymen continue as strained as at present. Nationalism has, for the time being at any rate, established complete dominance over all that is vocal and articulate in Egypt."[29]

The report is generally detached, and it took a cool look at the alternatives for Britain. Would it be possible for Britain to remain in Egypt?

It might seem at first sight as if we had no choice but either to abandon our position in Egypt altogether, or to maintain it by sheer force, in the teeth of the general and ever-increasing hostility of the Egyptian people. But a closer study of the problem led us to take a more hopeful view. From many and intimate conversations with representative Egyptians, including some who were commonly regarded as extreme Nationalists, the conviction was borne in upon us that they were not so intransigent and certainly not so anti-British as the frantic diatribes of the press might have led us to suppose. The broad banner of Nationalism was seen to cover many shades of opinion, and, above all, most notable differences of temper and of aim.[30]

The report's view of Egyptian nationalism exactly parallels the view held by Blunt and like-minded Englishmen from the 1870s. Such a view was congruent for men with no role interest and with a value system which predisposed them to an anti-imperial view of reality. That the one-time spokesman for a polar view of Egypt should now embrace this anti-imperial perception is in no way the result of conversion. In 1921, Milner probably would have expressed as much contempt for the Blunts as he had in 1890. But he came to accept their view of reality in 1921 because it then concurred with British interests. With such a view of reality, a political strategy could be developed which would accommodate to the price Britain was willing to pay for the maintenance of some control in Egypt.

Yet in 1921 the Milners owed something to the Blunts. Just as Gladstone in 1882 for a period of months accepted the imperial view of reality which had been so nicely articulated within the pages of the *London Times*, Milner now accepted the anti-imperial view of reality which had been articulated long and well by Blunt and by the Radical faction in Parliament. In both cases the exigencies of the moment called for policy responses that were highly congruent with situational views with which the policy maker was thoroughly familiar. In neither case was any note taken of the fact that the policy maker had quietly dropped his own reality view and adopted that of despised political enemies. In neither case is there any real evidence of discomfort in adopting the new view or even of any awareness of the radical nature of perceptual alteration. The parallel with Lyndon Johnson in March 1968 concerning Vietnam is exact.

I have abstracted the Milner mission report at some length because it articulates so well the prevailing view. It illustrates the sharp migration of the prevailing view from a position close to the ideal typical imperial image to a position much closer to the ideal typical complex image. Those die-hards in London who persist in seeing Egypt in the imperial image are now far distant from the prevailing view. This picture is mapped in figure II.11.

Situational Motivational System

The most striking alteration in the foreign policy aims system of 1921 from that of 1914 is the change in parametric value. This change has been reflected in the extraordinary perceptual change described in the previous section, and it is manifest in the policy adopted for Egypt. But the foreign policy motivational factors considered salient changed little, and the systems construct for 1921 resembles closely that for 1914. As Allenby wrote in his letter to Sultan Fuad, "Egypt lies upon the main line of communications between Great Britain and the King's dominions to the east. The whole territory of Egypt is indeed essential to

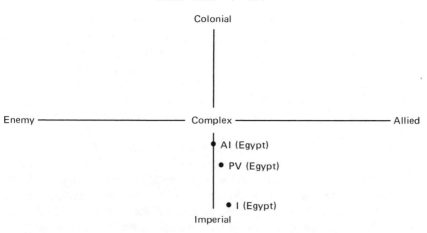

Figure II.11. British Situational Views, 1921

those communications, since the fortunes of Egypt are inseparable from the security of the Suez Canal Zone."[31] Although no immediate threat to this communications line was perceived, vulnerability to future threats was seen. Not even the anti-imperialist *New Statesman and Nation* was willing to deny British general defense interests in Egypt.[32] As was true in the general motivational system, the factor of military vested interests is upgraded to first-level intensity, reflecting the continued major decisional role of the swollen military bureaucracy immediately following the First World War. Egypt figured high in the world view that prevailed among the military. Specifically, the military advocated a large British presence in Egypt, and not just in the canal zone as Egyptian nationalists preferred. It could not, however, present a strongly plausible case for any particular contingency necessitating a major military presence. And considering the weakness of the case advanced, the military was surprisingly successful in achieving its objectives.

However, bureaucratic vested interests as a factor for the maintenance of a major British presence are placed at the second-intensity level. British civilian personnel in Egypt were much more accommodating to the nationalist pressures in Egypt than were the military. They acquiesced in a reversal of the policy inaugurated by Cromer of steadily expanding the bureaucratic positions available for British personnel. Now Egyptians were replacing Britons, and with the full cooperation of British officials.[33] They were able to get from the Egyptian government an agreement to protect the rights of British civilian employees of the Egyptian government.[34] The Cromerite position of a decade earlier had no prominent spokesman among civilian officials after 1920.

There is evidence of concern for the protection of British commercial interests in Egypt sufficient to grant a third-level intensity rating to economic vested interests. Far more apparent was an appreciation of threat of intervention in Egypt in support of foreign commercial interests. That threat is part of the defense motive of Britain. As Allenby's letter stated: "The prosperity of Egypt is . . . important . . . not merely because Great Britain and Egypt are each other's best customers, but because any serious danger to financial or commercial interests in Egypt invites the intervention of other Powers and threatens her independence."[35] Nevertheless, this factor appears to be important enough to argue for a third-intensity rating for the security of trade and economic vested interests.

With the move toward granting greater independence, we have seen that the British proclaimed the completion of the tutelary process. Thus, the factor of cultural messianism no longer figures significantly among motivations. The factor of national grandeur is also downgraded. Egypt is ready for independence, and Great Britain can take great pride in that fact; henceforth what happens in Egypt is far less the responsibility of Great Britain. Still, given the low level of interest in Egyptian policy, the factor of national grandeur deserves a third-level intensity rating.

The system, then, is inferred as follows:

A. Defense
   Military vested interests
B. Bureaucratic vested interests
C. Economic vested interests
    Export and import trade
    Security of investments
   National grandeur

Specific Policy, Expectations, and Response

With the publication of the Milner mission report in February 1921 and the declaration of intent to abolish the protectorate, the general lines of British policy in Egypt became clear. But that policy was to remain curiously ambivalent. It amounted to a decision to reduce substantially the British decisional role but not to eliminate it, and the Milner report provided the key to that decision. By cooperating with one segment of the Egyptian political elite, the British could maintain a sufficient decisional role to safeguard British interests. Just what that segment of the elite would be in terms of its representative nature was never to be made clear. The British could not satisfy the demands of Watani purists for complete independence, or of Zaghlul and Wafd for substantial independence. But they could and did satisfy the demands of both the court and the conservative, largely Turkish-speaking, landowning element, members of which later formed the Liberal Constitutional party.

In accordance with the Milner report, a treaty relationship would replace the protectorate. Egypt would be independent and would have a constitutional monarchical form of government. British troops would remain to protect Egypt and the imperial life line. Egypt would retain a British financial adviser and judiciary adviser. Representation abroad would be permitted, but Egypt's foreign policy must conform to that of Great Britain.

The expectation was that this treaty relationship would be acceptable to a sufficient section of the Egyptian political elite to allow for a stable regime and a cooperative, symbiotic relationship between the two countries. But the expectation was based on an overly sanguine picture. Most important, expectations of a formalized, clear, cooperative relationship were not to be realized. From the beginning the British underrated the intensity of opposition. Milner understood that Zaghlul would not accept his recommendation, but he hoped that the respected moderate leader, Adly Pasha, would accept the proposals and would provide a rallying point for more moderate nationalists.[36] Although Adly did agree to head the Egyptian government, the limits of his ability to make concessions became apparent in the course of prolonged negotiations in the summer of 1921. He was unwilling to agree to a settlement that would require British bayonets for enforcement.

The debate within the British government that followed the failure to negotiate an agreement with Adly tells much of British motivations. British officials in Egypt, well aware of the difficulty of maintaining order and of the minor commitment the British government was ultimately prepared to make to retain a position in Egypt, were inclined to make the necessary concessions to the Egyptian leaders. Some advocated British withdrawal and discounted the notion that foreign troops would replace the British.[37] Within the Foreign Office the possibility of annexation or of the maintenance of the British presence by force was mentioned, but in general the necessity for making concessions was accepted.[38] The initiative for finding a tolerable alternative was left to the British in Cairo, and the acceptable formula came to be one advocated by Lord Allenby. It called for a unilateral declaration of the end of the protectorate and of a bilateral relationship not sharply different from that included in the Milner report. London reluctantly accepted this proposal and it was put into effect on February 28, 1922.

In retrospect, the solution appears remarkably harmonious with the needs of the situation. No Egyptian government could accept the limitation of Egyptian sovereignty implicit in the Milner proposals, but these proposals reflected very closely the manifestation of British foreign policy aims as they applied to the declining British imperial position. The foreign policy decisional community could not agree to abandon the British position in Egypt; neither could they count on enough support from the public to rule by bayonet. The Allenby solution allowed for an ambiguity that made even the British, stereotypically the pragmatists, nervous; yet it met the requirements of the situation.

In the years following, British interventions in the Egyptian decisional process were occasional and of varied intensity. Allenby expected that a constitutional regime would be best for Egypt and that it would accept the Anglo-Egyptian relationship. In that expectation he was to be disappointed. When elections were reasonably free, they were won by Wafd, which had one overriding program: to rid Egypt of the restrictions on her sovereignty. Since the British were not prepared to grant this, the election results had to be annulled. Typically this was done by an alliance embracing the British, the court, and conservative political leaders. The pattern reflected the contradiction in the British situational view and the determining quality of British foreign policy aims which sought to maintain the remnants of the empire. But the imperial decline was fundamental and had to be reflected in altered policies toward Egypt. In 1956 these would finally lead to a termination, not only of imperial control, but of any hope for control in the future.

13 / Fall 1956

Historical Narrative

In January 1924, elections were held in Egypt. The Wafd party won overwhelmingly, electing 190 of 214 members of the Chamber of Deputies. Saad Zaghlul became Egypt's first constitutional premier. With such overwhelming support, the Wafd's position seemed invulnerable. Yet eleven months later, in November 1924, Zaghlul resigned and the Wafd fell from power. The immediate reason was the assassination in Cairo of Sir Lee Stack, commander of the Egyptian army and governor general of the Sudan. Allenby seized the occasion to make demands on the Egyptian government that no nationalist prime minister could accept.

Writing many years later in his memoirs, *Full Circle*, Anthony Eden expressed contempt for and disgust with the Wafd.[1] His assessment was typical of imperialist Englishmen, who had hoped for an inexpensive and secure control system in Egypt. Much the happiest arrangement would have been for the popular Wafd party and Saad Zaghlul personally to have accepted the limited sovereignty of the imposed solution and to have pursued a policy of domestic reform and development. John Marlowe, who has written extensively on the British rule in Egypt, laments that Zaghlul was not enough of a statesman to see the potential of this role.[2] But these expectations were unrealistic, and when they failed the British could only feel that the adolescent Egyptian government was refusing to live by the advice of its mature imperial advisers. In fact, it would have been impossible for the Wafd to accept that kind of a relationship. Saad Zaghlul had an acute ear for the politically expedient. Considering his long history of close association with the British, there is no reason to believe that he refused to accept the British partnership because of nationalist purity. Far more reasonable is the explanation that this sensitive politician understood the limits imposed on his freedom of action by the nationalist membership of the Wafd.

William Riker assumes that political parties, like national governments, pursue a minimal winning coalition. A party composed of diverse interests that proves capable of winning a substantial electoral victory will shed some of its component parts. Logic argues for Riker that there is little point in seeking to reconcile more interests than are necessary for political victory. Yet in the Third World a common phenomenon is what Gabriel Almond calls the dominant, nonauthoritarian party.[3] Parties of this type can win overwhelming victories in politically free elections without shedding unnecessary component groups, even though a high price is paid for their continued association. The PRI in Mexico, Congress in India, the National Front in Mossadegh's Iran, and the Wafd in Egypt are examples. Surely there is no single explanation for the phenomenon of maintaining a coalition far larger than that required to win in a free election, but in the case of the Wafd there is an easy explanation. Even with a coalition including left nationalist students, centrist bureaucrats, professional and business leaders, and conservative, Arabic-speaking landowners, Wafd could not stay in power. The influence exerted by the British, by Turkish-speaking landowners, and by the court of Fuad and later Farouk, expressed in a variety of combinations, could deny office to the Wafd in spite of its often demonstrated ability to win elections. An account of how this was accomplished is beyond the scope of this study, but the history of the Wafd party, its great strength and shocking humiliations, must be understood by anyone seeking to explain modern Egypt.[4]

The death of the Wafd followed the military coup of 1952. In the course of its life, the image of the Wafd in Egypt evolved from that of 1919—an organization dedicated to the resurrection of an independent Egypt deserving of world respect—to that of 1952—an organization dedicated to the self-serving interests of its leaders and ready to compromise even with imperial representatives in order to achieve power. The fate of liberal democracy in Egypt was closely tied to that of the Wafd, and when both disappeared in 1952, few lamented their passing. British responsibility for the tragedy is, I believe, substantial, entirely inadvertent, and ironical. The irony lies in the British view of their own role. Their form of control in Egypt after 1922, which I call indirect, nonformal colonial, was perceived in Britain as gentle tutelage. The Egyptians would be pushed and guided in the direction of responsible and democratic self-government. Yet in the British foreign policy motivational system for Egypt that I advance, cultural messianism and ideological messianism are not included. This reflects my conclusion that "tutelage" was not a serious British objective in Egypt. Low-cost control for the purposes of defense, trade, and grandeur is closer to the heart of British policy. If the Wafd had been willing to accept a modest British military presence and British policy advice in a few areas, such as foreign policy, British support for the party would surely have been forthcoming.

Any such cooperation by the Wafd was, of course, out of the question. The party's overwhelming early electoral victories were obviously an endorsement of the single real issue that the Wafd raised: the demand that the British leave and grant Egypt real independence. For Egypt's politically participant population, this was the most salient issue; and politicians such as Saad Zaghlul and his successor, Mustafa el-Nahas, had no alternative but to advance that issue. In doing so they could mobilize a coalition that embraced virtually every Arabic-speaking elite element. But when they won the election, the British could not really grant them the authority to carry out their program. From 1919 to 1936 the Wafd was an electoral giant united around one highly salient but negative issue. In 1936 Nahas Pasha, then leader of the Wafd, compromised on that issue, and the deterioration of the Wafd image proceeded rapidly after that.

From 1921 until 1936 the Egyptian political process reflected the degree of imperial control most congruent with British foreign policy aims. It was a difficult and uncomfortable management problem for the Englishmen responsible for administering British imperial interests in Egypt. It called for manipulating Egyptian politics by playing one center of power against another, with the court, the Wafd, and conservative political leadership the most important power foci. By the early 1930s, however, system disturbances which would compel a basic pattern disruption were apparent. There were two primary disturbances, one internal to Egypt, the other external, that is, in the international system.

Internally, Egypt was experiencing the process which Westerners, somewhat ethnocentrically, call the growth of political awareness. Typically, this involves an altering of identity focus from the parochial to the national. An individual who thought of himself primarily as a member of a village community begins increasingly to think of himself as a member of a national community. As he does so, national affairs become of more concern and interest to him, although he may or may not develop a sense of having some ability to influence them.

Political community identity is rarely simple. Most individuals identify in varying intensity with a number of politically relevant communities. As the individual develops an identity with a national community, he is most unlikely to cease identifying with those politically relevant communities which were traditionally important to him and to his ancestors. The nation is simply an additional community to whose interests he must accommodate. If his attachment to the national community is sufficiently intense to lead him, in a case of perceived threat to the nation, to risk sacrificing life or career for it, he is said to be a nationalist. But he may also be willing, under similar circumstances, to risk the sacrifice of life and career for family, tribe, regional community, and religious community. In each case in which such a sacrifice is conceivable, the identity attachment is assumed to be of first-degree intensity. Some individuals, therefore, will identify with a number of politically relevant communities at a first-degree intensity.

In Egypt the political communities which had probably attracted a first-degree identity intensity prior to the 1920s were local village, town, city, Egypt, and Islam. For rare individuals an attachment to the Ottoman community was that intense, but behavior suggests that for most an identity with the Ottoman community was of low intensity. In the late 1920s, and increasingly in the 1930s and 1940s, there began to appear an increasingly intense identification with the Arab community, a nascent Arab nation. The cultural impact of Arabs on Egypt was obviously profound, having given the Egyptians their language and, for most of them, their religion. Why the people of Egypt began increasingly to identify with the Arab community at this particular time is something of a mystery. Two influences seem apparent. First, Egypt shared with other Arabic-speaking peoples the humiliation of Western imperialism. The appearance of Zionism in Palestine was a particularly dramatic manifestation of Western imperial control. Even more than the European colonizers in North Africa, European colonists in Palestine appeared to threaten the yearnings of Arabic-speaking peoples for national self-fulfillment. The unity of Zionism and Western imperialism seen by Arabic-speaking peoples is a perceptual phenomenon of major importance. The Arabic-speaking Egyptian easily empathized with the Arabic-speaking Palestinian and, as Egyptian behavior from 1948 on indicates, identification with the Palestinians in Egypt was sufficiently intense to lead Egyptians to make major sacrifices on their behalf.

The second influence was that of Islam. As political awareness penetrated deeper into the Egyptian population, it reached broad sections of the population whose faith was simple and intense. Public opinion interviews produced evidence that for many of these newly aware, no clear distinction was made among the terms "Egypt," "Arab," and "Islam." In the nineteenth century, those individuals who were described as nationalists tended to have in mind clear distinctions among these terms, and they clearly preferred "Egypt."[5] By the 1930s politicians and political writers reflected an understanding that the identity concerns of the newly politically aware were different. They paid much greater attention to Islam,[6] and concerns for Arab affairs intensified. One manifestation of the latter phenomenon was a rapidly developing rivalry between Egypt's leaders and the conservative oligarchy which ruled, in partnership with the British, in Iraq. Egypt was being drawn into Arab politics.

The control problem for Britain manifest in the growth of political awareness in Egypt was serious. Already the British had seen how difficult it would be to control the Egyptian democratic process, with its strange mixture of the modern and traditional. This difficulty intensified as Egypt appeared more and more to be part of the Arab world. In 1930 the problem looked as if it might solve itself. With the support of King Fuad and British troops, Bakir Sidky Pasha seized control. The Sidky dictatorship, with its conservative, landowning, and in part Turkish-speaking base, was easily compatible with British interests. But Sidky was an exceptional leader, and when he became ill the tenuous nature of his one-man control became apparent.

Coincidentally, external developments were having a convulsive impact on British foreign policy aims relating to Egypt. By the 1920s tendencies of extreme aggressiveness were apparent in Japan and Italy. But it was not until Germany manifested these tendencies that perception of threat in Britain was sufficient to produce a parametric value alteration in the foreign policy aims system. By 1936 change on that level was occurring, and with it came an alteration of the entire British world view, including the view of Egypt.

The Sidky dictatorship had come to an end because of the health of the dictator more than because of opposition to his dictatorship. Nevertheless, an altered relationship between the Egyptian successor government and the British was inevitable. British interest in Egypt was intensifying as the world situation changed, and a more energetic British role in Egyptian political affairs was a certainty. A strong and stable regime that would be comfortable with the British role would be ideal, and British-Wafd cooperation was most likely to produce such a government. Strangely enough, Nahas Pasha, the leader of the Wafd, was willing to cooperate. The immediate result was new and reasonably free elections won by the Wafd. Then the new Wafd government prepared to negotiate a treaty with the British.

Egypt emerged from the negotiations for the Anglo-Egyptian treaty of 1936 with symbolic victories: The title of the high commissioner was changed to ambassador; Egypt was supported for admission to the League of Nations. And there were real changes as well. The "capitulation" system which had allowed for gross discrimination in favor of foreign residents of Egypt was to be terminated; British troops were gradually to be withdrawn to the canal zone and Sinai; and the Egyptian government would gain full control over its own security forces. In twenty years the question of an end to the occupation would again be raised.

Although the treaty represented a granting of additional sovereign rights to Egypt, the relationship remained an indirect colonial one. It is easy to see why Nahas Pasha, with his hunger to lead a Wafd government, accepted the agreement. A more sensitive politician, a Zaghlul, would have understood the high price to be paid. The most politically attentive and nationalistic of Wafd supporters felt betrayed.

Histories of the young officers who executed the July 1952 coup exemplify this sense of betrayal. As a result of the Anglo-Egyptian treaty of 1936, Egypt would have a national army under Egyptian control, and the way was open for young, lower-middle-class Egyptians such as Gamal Abdel Nasser to begin a career in the officer corps. Ironically, the young men attracted to the army were those who saw betrayal in the agreement. Typically, they were members of the Wafd in secondary-school days who became disillusioned with the party and its politicians after the agreement. They sought alternatives in the Young Egypt political group, with its national socialist tendencies, or in the Moslem Brotherhood. These groupings appeared to such young men as ideologically more pure, their nationalism unsullied.

A further consequence of the treaty was equally damaging to the Wafd. Now that their single unifying issue—an intransigent demand for independence—had been removed, the great diversity of interests in the party was revealed. In the past the British could be blamed for the failure of the Wafd to execute a legislative program. Now that excuse was eliminated. The result was a splintering of the party and further disillusion on the part of those who sought democratic reforms. Within months Wafd again fell from power, this time because of severe internal problems.

I mentioned earlier that by 1952 the Wafd had gained a reputation for being little concerned with Egypt and much concerned with the self-interests of its leaders. I also ascribed some responsibility, albeit inadvertent, to the British for this development. The basis for this ascription is that the British, because of their need to exercise some control in Egypt, had to exclude the Wafd from power. This resulted in a Wafd that was able to preserve a broad coalition around one negative issue. It also resulted in a Wafd in which there was programmatic paralysis beyond that one issue. Traditional landowners and socialist intellectuals had entirely different ideas about social and economic policy. Hence, when the Wafd did come to power no real program could emerge. Individual leaders of the party, however, made full use of their position for their own personal profit. An image of corruption, lethargy, and even hypocrisy naturally developed.

The British were thus denied a strong cooperative government in Egypt, and a succession of weak rightist regimes in close alliance with the court followed one after the other. Internally Egypt was developing toward a revolution, as the steady growth of Young Egypt and the Moslem Brotherhood illustrated. The Wafd remained the uncomfortable home for the liberal intelligentsia, but dark rumors of corruption and incompetence surrounded its leadership. Rightist splinter groups from the party, in particular the proindustrialist Saadists, were frequently leading members of government coalitions. The Wafd remained a declining buffer against revolution but offered little leadership. The internal situation was deteriorating but did not yet threaten stability.

Externally, however, the threat to Britain was perceived to be intensifying, and British determination to strengthen control in Egypt grew stronger. After World War II broke out, Egypt found itself between an invading Italian army in Libya and the Vichy French regime in Syria; and threat to British control of the Suez communications life line was seen as extremely serious. When Erwin Rommel took command of the German army in North Africa, the possibility of a German occupation of Egypt assumed realistic proportions. Egyptian politics reflected the change in circumstances. Farouk and his premiers asserted their neutrality, and much of the populace supported Rommel.[7] Miles Lampson, the British ambassador, feared the formation of a pro-Axis government.

Then an event occurred that the British had no right to expect: Nahas Pasha expressed his willingness to head a pro-Allies Egyptian government. This government would not actually declare war on the Axis but would agree to a strong British presence. When Farouk refused to appoint Nahas premier, Lampson was more than willing to force the king's abdication. The palace was surrounded by tanks, and the abdication agreement was read to Farouk. The king capitulated and the Wafd, the great Egyptian nationalist party, accepted power wrenched from the palace by British bayonets.

Nahas agreed to accept power with reservations that were apparently sufficient to persuade him that his patriotism was not tarnished and that the liberal element of his party would not defect. The liberals had no place to go, although a few established a weak and isolated splinter party. In the eyes of Egyptian nationalist youth, however, the Wafd politicians seemed to be so hungry for the emoluments of power that they allied themselves with the devil. It is difficult to disagree with Peter Mansfield's conclusion that this event marked the beginning of the end for the Wafd and for Egypt's experiment with democracy.[8] The beneficiaries were again the basically antidemocratic organizations such as the Moslem Brotherhood. But, as events were to show, the most important consequence of Nahas's act was the extreme disillusion of a group of young Egyptian officers. For Gamal Nasser and his friends, all faith in the democratic process was lost.

Overt British support enabled the Wafd to stay in power for two years, despite sensational corruption and helplessness in dealing with inflation. But by 1944 the probability of an Allied victory in the war was generally accepted, and there was no longer any direct threat to British interests in Egypt. Once again general strategy level change began to occur in the British foreign policy aims system. As was true a generation earlier, at the close of World War I, Egypt appeared in British perceptions as decreasingly important to foreign policy objectives. Reflecting this change in priorities, Miles Lampson, by then Lord Killearn, ceased his interventions for Nahas, and almost immediately the Wafd government fell.

The Wafd leadership seems belatedly to have understood its great mistake. It could not collaborate with the British and yet maintain its claim to be the spokesman for Egyptian nationalism. The party therefore made a sharp turn toward nationalistic intransigence. At first the British appeared willing to agree even to extreme nationalist demands. In 1946 the British were prepared to agree in principle to a future evacuation of their troops from Egypt. However, a broad consensus behind this decision failed to develop. While the end of World War I had brought a general perception of decreased threat, many Englishmen perceived a real and ominous threat soon after World War II, from the Soviet Union. Winston Churchill and many of the military bureaucracy saw the evacuation of Egypt as the height of folly.[9] Nevertheless, in 1946 the government of Clement Attlee negotiated the Sidky-Bevin agreement with an Egyptian government headed by ex-dictator Sidky Pasha which provided for the evacuation of Egypt by 1949. It was ambiguous on the question of the Sudan, however, and Egyptian nationalists were adamant in their insistence on some form of Egyptian control over the entire Nile Valley. British military and colonial bureaucracies were equally adamant, and the agreement was never ratified. The Wafd party and the Moslem Brotherhood had achieved such popular success with the Nile issue that no Egyptian government could compromise. Neither, apparently, could a British government.

From 1946 to 1952, Anglo-Egyptian relations deteriorated. The Wafd did not regain its hold on the young nationalists, who had given up on it, but it retained sufficient strength to win another sweeping electoral victory in 1950. The conservative landowner leaders of the Wafd had to pursue a nationalistically uncompromising position in order to retain nationalist support. Nothing serious was done to bring about needed economic and social reforms, and disaffection continued. The violence of the anti-British line being pursued by the Wafd, Young Egypt, the Moslem Brotherhood, and others encouraged direct harassment of British forces in Egypt. In 1951 a Wafd government unilaterally abrogated the 1936 treaty Nahas had negotiated. The British refused to recognize this abrogation, and a direct confrontation followed. In January 1952, Egyptian police and British troops battled in Ismailia, and fifty policemen were killed. The next day riots swept Cairo, and major sections of the city and much foreign property were burned.

This was a classic impasse. The two major motivating forces behind British immobility were perception of threat from the Soviet Union (defense) and a reluctance to accept the loss of control over the old imperial life line (grandeur). As Anthony Eden's *Full Circle* makes clear, there was the deepest resentment in London of what was seen to be American encouragement of the Egyptians in their adamancy.[10] But Egyptian political leaders had no decisional choice. The Wafd could not again retreat on a nationalist issue, and after it lost power following the burning of Cairo, successor governments understood that their freedom of action on the issues of a new Anglo-Egyptian treaty was narrowly restricted. King Farouk's insensitivity to these developments merely added to the overall paralysis.

The situation was redefined in July 1952. A military coup in that month brought to power a military junta soon to be dominated by Colonel Gamal Nasser. Farouk was compelled to abdicate, and control over Egyptian affairs passed into the hands of men determined to maintain a tight hold. Egyptian democracy was dead, and the once great Wafd party was soon to be outlawed. The coup also ended the old power triangle of court-Wafd-conservative politicians which allowed the British easy manipulative potential and hence cheap control. A new and vital factor appeared in the form of close relations established by the American government with the new regime. Miles Copeland's *Game of Nations* is probably the most authoritative account of the minor American role in the coup and the favorable response of many in the American bureaucracy to the junta.[11] The American desire to see the conclusion of an Anglo-Egyptian treaty which would terminate the occupation was painfully apparent to the British.[12] And the junta's early declaration of willingness to allow the Sudanese to decide on the future Egyptian-Sudanese relationship removed the chief obstacle to a settlement.

Nevertheless, the British were most reluctant to leave Egypt. Anthony Eden believed that the evacuation should be premised on conditions that would give

Britain immediate use of a well-maintained base in the event of war and the continuous use of Egypt by the Royal Air Force. He called for Egyptian participation in a Middle East defense organization that would in effect make Egypt an Anglo-American ally. In return Egypt would be given economic aid by the United States and Britain.[13] According to one authority, the British wished to keep seven thousand servicemen in Egypt to maintain the base and man the depots.[14]

The junta found these terms unacceptable. As Colonel Nasser said, memories of British imperialism were too fresh for Egypt seriously to consider joining a Middle East defense organization. Such a course would have been suicidal for the new government.[15] It had already compromised on one issue that had been a focal point of Egyptian nationalism—Sudanese independence. Asking more of the junta demonstrated Eden's own imperialist disregard of Egyptian opinion and the limits a public places on even dictatorial political leadership. This point is usually comprehended when dealing with cultures not regarded as inferior, but it is rarely understood when "civilizing" or "modernization" is thought to be necessary.

Eden saw American behavior somewhat at variance with that of a good ally. In the days prior to the coup, Eden had quoted approvingly a remark made to the American ambassador to the United Kingdom, Walter Gifford: "It was unfortunate that the United States Government found such difficulty generally in the Middle East in giving Her Majesty's Government support in the only way in which the Oriental understood the word."[16] And at the time of his negotiations with the junta, Eden quoted the British ambassador to Cairo as saying that "American policy in general seemed to be conditioned by a belief that Egypt was still a victim of British 'colonialism.'" Eden added his own view that Americans were "influenced by a desire to reach a quick solution almost at any cost and by a pathetic belief that once agreement was reached, all would be well."[17] Already apparent for Eden and his government was the motivational force of grandeur, manifest in an extraordinary reluctance to depart and a deep suspicion that British departure was an aim of Britain's closest ally in one realm but rival in another, the United States.

The stage was being set for an initial British humiliation. The British and the Egyptians could not approach each other's minimal conditions, negotiations were broken off, and attacks resumed against the British military in the canal zone. But, lacking the support of either their American ally or opposition Labour party leaders, the Conservative government finally resumed negotiations. An agreement was reached by which the British would evacuate within twenty months. Egypt did not join a Middle East defense pact but did agree to a British return to Suez in the event of an attack on an Arab state or Turkey. The Royal Air Force had to be satisfied with overflight rights and landing facilities rather than joint air defense. Freedom of navigation of the canal was reaffirmed. British influence was no longer at or near the colonial level, and in Britain there was a brooding resentment against both the Egyptian regime and the Americans for compelling Britain to surrender that influence. As events would show two years later, that resentment was deep and compelling.

Control of events passed from British hands at this point, in October 1954, and was not to return. The British tried to come back in the fall of 1956 and, had they been successful, might well have attempted to reimpose a nonformal, indirect colonial control. The effort to return was made during the Suez crisis, and British and French forces actually occupied part of the Suez Canal zone. But they were humiliated, and that is the final moment of the British imperial presence in Egypt. The failure of the Suez campaign destroyed the illusion, still strong in Egypt, that Britain was one of the great powers.

Control of events in Egypt from 1954 to 1956 was largely in the hands of a strong Egyptian government, that of Gamal Abdel Nasser. But Egypt was already asserting its leadership in an Arab world that was undergoing profound change. Intra-Arab conflict involved competing identity interests and competing attitudes regarding the speed and direction of social and economic change. The Egyptian position in this conflict was one of giving leadership to forces working for a loose association of Arab states and for fairly rapid and state-assisted economic and social change.

The demands of this role involved Egypt, probably more than its leaders wished, in the Arab-Israeli conflict. For many Arabs throughout the Arab world, Nasser was the real and the symbolic leader of the Arab nation. Nasser thus had a clear choice. He could limit his support for the Palestinians to the rhetorical, as traditional Arabs in leadership positions almost always did, and thereby surrender any aspirations to lead the Arab nation. Or he could more actively oppose Israel. Nasser's choice was the latter, although the anti-Israeli strategy he followed seems to have been at the minimal level necessary to retain his Arab leadership role.

The decision to claim for himself and for Egypt leadership of the Arab world set clear bounds to Nasser's freedom of action. It pulled him steadily toward renewed confrontation with Israel, and confrontation with Israel involved him in the Soviet-American Cold War, now just beginning to crystallize in the Arab world. The Suez crisis of 1956 resulted from the interaction of conflicts which developed on many levels, including the intra-Arab, the Arab-Israeli, and the Soviet-American Cold War. British and French involvement in that crisis must be seen in this context. Their own concerns were real enough but in the context appear atavistic remnants of another age. France was furious with Nasser for giving support to Arabs in Algeria who were seeking to complete French expulsion from North Africa. Britain was attempting to hang on to some influence in Egypt and was resentful at being excluded from the mainstream of events there. The French and British concerns were sufficient to make the Suez crisis into one of the most spectacular events of the post–World War II era.

On February 28, 1955, the Israelis raided an Egyptian military outpost in Gaza and decimated it. That event is often pointed to as a great turning point in Arab-Israeli relations.[18] Egypt was humiliated, and Nasser's position both in Egypt and in the Arab world necessitated a vigorous response. Those who see the Gaza raid as making inevitable the Suez crisis develop a strong case, but that case rests on the premise that Nasser was prepared to acquiesce in the existence of Israel. Some Israelis, including Prime Minister Moshe Sharrett, acted as though they accepted that premise, but other Israelis clearly did not.[19] Foremost among these was David Ben Gurion, Israel's first prime minister, who came out of retirement to deal with the problem of continuous Arab raids, mainly from Jordanian soil, against Israel. Ben Gurion's assumption that a series of violent reprisals against the Arabs would bring a halt to the raids reveals an image of the Arabs that is closer to the imperial than to the enemy pole. If Nasser is seen as an agitator-type leader in a country with little public opinion and little nationalism, the tactic of massive reprisals is entirely reasonable. Like many imperialist Englishmen before him, Ben Gurion felt that the only thing the Oriental understands is force.

The thesis of this study is that conflict must be seen as it was viewed by the participants. Indeed, the term "misperception" can be an analytic red herring. An individual's perception of the situation is the product of experience, values, and temperament. His inability to communicate with another individual with different experiences, values, and temperament is a product of their holding competing and largely unquestioned reality views. In conflict situations, such as the Arab-Israeli, in which value conflict involves deeply held national values, reality views will differ starkly. Only the rare individual whose own national values are threatened will be able to perceive a foe whose responses are equally determined by fear. Instead, more typically, the two contestants, responding to fear, will each see a reality calling for policies to deal with an aggressive foe—policies which will reinforce each other's perceptions of threat.[20] The Arab-Israeli dispute followed this pattern. A circularity of events continually reinforced threat perception for each side. After Gaza, the Egyptian army directly sponsored fedayeen raids against Israel, and the Israeli army retaliated.

In the Cold War arena, the Arab-Israeli conflict had exceptional accidental war potential. The Middle East was a focal point of Cold War competition. Soviet-American interference in the affairs of the Arab states, Iran, and Turkey was extensive and in some cases involved complicity in the overthrow of regimes. Endemic in this Cold War behavior, involving as it did covert diplomatic cooperation with competing groups, was a serious control problem for the two great-power actors. Operating indirectly and exercising influence over decision-making to a minor degree, the two "superpowers" were far from deserving the title of "colonial master." Yet each of the great powers saw the other's third-country collaborators as satellites and, as the term implies, without individual freedom of action. This perceptual phenomenon characterized the Arab-Israeli conflict generally.

Exercising minor control, in fact, each of the superpowers was perceived to be calling the policy tune for its client government.

There is a striking historical irony here. By 1957 American policy was defined in terms of the Eisenhower doctrine, a classic construct of the enemy image.[21] It offered protection to Middle Eastern states threatened with aggression from the Soviet Union or states controlled by it. As specific policy demonstrated, the Egyptian and Syrian regimes were seen as Soviet-controlled. Yet in 1956 this image had not yet crystallized. Had it done so, there is every likelihood that the United States would have supported the British, French, and Israelis in the fall of 1956. But in 1955 and 1956 the developing Arab-Israeli conflict was still seen partially in terms of imperial liberalization and competing national aspirations.

However, the Eisenhower administration's tendency toward the classic enemy view, in which Egypt would be seen as the satellite of the Soviet Union, was strong even in 1955 and 1956. After the Israeli Gaza strip raid, the Nasser government made urgent representations to the American government to provide them with arms. The request posed an impossible problem for any American administration. The foreign and defense bureaucracies favored the request, but no American regime could supply arms for a deadly enemy of Israel's without paying an extraordinary domestic political price. The response was to put off answering the request rather than to reject it. Inevitably, as the circular raid-counterraid process continued in the Arab-Israeli conflict, an exasperated Egypt began to look elsewhere for arms. They found the Soviet Union sympathetic, and Soviet negotiators suggested making an arms delivery agreement with Czechoslovakia.

The shock of this agreement did not lead Dulles and Eisenhower immediately to classify Egypt as a satellite. On the contrary, Dulles responded favorably to a suggestion that America improve its bargaining position by helping to finance the great Aswan Dam, which was expected to increase Egypt's hydroelectric production and arable acreage. But many American legislators, reacting to fears of Jewish constituents, saw the situation in more classical enemy terms.[22]

Dulles was pursuing a difficult and unpopular policy, and he expected the Egyptians to understand and appreciate the price he paid for his willingness to stand up to hostile congressional response. He was thus deeply angered when Nasser, in the natural progression of his third-force neutrality views, recognized the government of Communist China. Furthermore, the Egyptians sought to improve their position in financing the Aswan Dam by allowing rumors to persist of a Soviet counteroffer to build the dam. Dulles's annoyance became strong enough that he decided to withdraw the American offer. In the meantime, the Egyptian government had decided to accept the American terms. When the Egyptian ambassador went to tell the State Department of his government's agreement, he was told of the withdrawal of the offer. In a public statement, Dulles questioned the ability of the Egyptian government to meet the terms of the agreement, considering the costs of the Czech arms agreement.[23] Nasser viewed this as a gratuitous insult and retaliated by nationalizing the Suez Canal Company.

At this point, the Eden government became deeply concerned. Britain would have participated with the United States in financing the Aswan Dam. Before telling the Egyptians of his withdrawal of the Aswan offer, Dulles informed the British of his intentions, but he did not consult with them. Britain was still the lesser ally. When Nasser announced the nationalization of the company, however, he twisted the lion's tail, and the British government moved onto center stage.

France joined her voice with that of her old imperial rival. Although French interests were primary in the Suez Canal Company, French hostility toward Nasser antedated the nationalization. France had endured one humiliation after another since World War II. First, her allies compelled her to evacuate Syria and Lebanon. Then, after prolonged and anguished struggling, France had to accept defeat in Indochina and to surrender western leadership there to the United States. In North Africa, Morocco and Tunisia had wrenched independence from France, and in 1956 Algeria was attempting to do so as well. In each of these cases, France felt that the United States was anything but supportive. This was true even in Algeria. American relations with Egypt were good, particularly on the intelligence level, and Egyptian intelligence was deeply involved in support of the Arab rebellion in Algeria. The French military in particular yearned for the opportunity to halt this Egyptian aid. Now there was a possibility of eliminating the Nasser regime altogether.

But Eisenhower and Dulles were not yet ready to apply the Mossadegh formula to Egypt and plot Nasser's overthrow. Their foreign policy and defense bureaucracies argued that an American-sponsored coup would encourage the Arabs to rally even more closely with the Soviet Union.

In the weeks that followed, while the French and British made military preparations, Dulles tried frantically to regain control of the situation. His tactic was to delay any precipitous action by the British and French with arguments that compromise was possible. The British and French did not want to act without American participation, and Dulles knew this. Again and again the British and French were led to believe they could expect American support for military action if the compromise efforts failed. But nothing materialized. Finally in exasperation, Eden joined French and Israeli leaders in planning an assault on Egypt in October 1956, which he hoped would lead to a new and more cooperative regime.

Prevailing World View

1956 was mid-Cold War, yet there were substantial differences between the prevailing world views of Britain and the United States. During the extensive parliamentary debate on British policy in Suez, Aneurin Bevan said:

Profound changes are taking place in Russian society. I believe that there are deep divisions among Russian leaders. I do not believe that the Russian Government are any more monolithic than are the Government sitting on those benches opposite. . . . I believe that these developments obey a tempo which attends upon world events just as much as upon events in Russia itself. If the world enabled Russia to relax, in other words, if moderate elements in Russia can find in the world a congenial condition in which to press themselves, they will do so.[24]

The United States in 1956 was just emerging from the Joseph McCarthy period, and no American political leader could have survived an expression of views similar to Bevan's. While it is certainly true that Bevan's image of the Soviet Union was on the extreme complex side of the enemy-complex scale of those speaking in these debates, none of the participants is very close to the enemy pole. In extended debates, not one MP advanced the image of a Nasser acting out a minor role in an overriding international communist conspiracy.

Typical of the Tory Suez backbencher world view is that of R. T. Paget, who remarked:

It is for the Russians to choose whether they will go on as they are, causing mischief around the world, being smart, stirring up trouble for us as we stir up trouble for them, or whether they will come in where they would always be welcome, into the concert of the world, to join with us in the demand that Egypt . . . should come before the world in judgment.[25]

Newspaper responses were in this pattern as well, with the Bevan-Paget images marking the limits of the enemy-complex range. Perception of threat from an international communist monolith or even from Moscow and Peking was not intense.

Once the invasion of the Suez area had been launched, however, the Labourites expressed fear of the consequences to the East-West balance in the Middle East. Kenneth Younger's lead-off speech in the debate on November 8, 1956, was typical of many Labourite remarks when he asked of the Eden administration:

Did they foresee the massive Soviet political intervention in the Middle East? Did they for instance foresee that within a single week the Parliament of Jordan, so lately their special Ally and Protege, would be passing a resolution of thanks . . . to the Soviet Union. Did they foresee the growing flood of arms into Syria? . . . Had they thought of the threat of volunteers from Russia?[26]

In *Full Circle*, Eden indicates that the possibility of Soviet volunteers and further intervention was one of the imponderables the British and French confronted prior to their invasion.[27] Since they were not deterred, apparently the risk was not considered great. In fact, the only clear evidence of a view of the Soviet Union that approximates that of the ideal typical enemy image appears in Eden's communications to Eisenhower. For example, on October 1, 1956, Eden wrote Eisenhower:

You can be sure that we are fully alive to the wider dangers of the Middle East situation. They can be summed up in one word—Russia.

    There is no doubt in our minds that Nasser, whether he likes it or not, is now effectively in Russian hands, just as Mussolini was in Hitler's.[28]

But this was not the general tone of Eden's account. Significantly, he prefaced the above quote with this contradictory remark: "The future of the canal was of little practical concern to Russia, but the Soviet Government saw an opportunity to fish in troubled waters and fish they did."[29]

The British image of the United States that emerges is consistent with this picture. I have theorized that intense threat perception is reflected in views of enemy and ally which approximate the ideal typical images. The enemy image of the Soviet Union, as has been seen, is far from the ideal typical pole. Likewise, the United States is viewed with a detachment more congruent with the complex image than with the allied image. Indeed, for some Tory backbenchers the United States is better seen on the enemy-complex line. On August 2, 1956, Lincoln Evans asserted: "The history of the Middle East of the last ten years is one of the constant undermining of British interests, authority and prestige by our American friends in that part of the world."[30] Viscount Hinchingbrook, Earl of Sandwich, another of the Suez bloc, complained bitterly of the Americans: "Shame on that country, now, shame, I regret to say, on the country which gave my mother birth that she should be behind us by days or even months in our endeavors jointly with the French to do for the Old World what she so successfully has done in the New."[31]

As this latter quote suggests, the image of the United States as ingrate or competitor is out of the Cold War context and much more in the regional context. Those speakers who placed the United States in the Cold War context described American policy more as weak and uncertain. Herbert Morrison said, "American policy has been hesitant, rather wobbling, and not exactly sufficiently cooperative with the policy of the United Kingdom."[32] When the events of Suez were unfolding, and an open break became possible, the image of the United States in Tory eyes returned to that of uncertain, misguided ally.

Labour added estrangement of the alliance as part of the unnecessary price the government was paying. Historic socialist suspicions of American policy appeared after the event, but Labour's image of the American ally was fairly benign. Anthony Wedgwood Benn, for example, said: "Of course there are oil interests in America, but do not let us ignore the many people in the United States today who regret our action for reasons quite unconnected with the folio of shares which they may have on Wall Street."[33]

Thus we may conclude that perception of threat from the Soviet Union was significant but not so intense that all local situations would be viewed in terms of that threat. Although the enemy image of Nasser held by most Tories and by many Jewish MPs approached the ideal typical, the projection was not Stalin into Nasser but rather either Hitler or Mussolini into Nasser. Britain's ally in the crisis, France, was described by Suez-bloc Tories in terms approximating the allied ideal typical image. This strongly suggests that an aggressive world communism was perceived, but a sluggishly aggressive one, and that the Middle East crisis was viewed almost totally out of the Cold War context by the Tory backbenchers and only slightly less so by those in opposition to Eden's policies.

The proposed map of British world views is drawn in figure II.12, including the prevailing view and the views of the Tory back bench (BB) and of Labour (L) typified by Bevan.

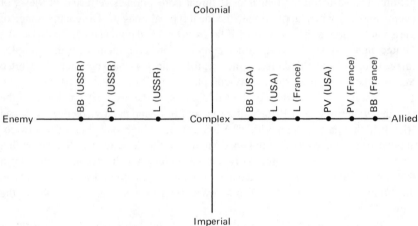

Figure II.12. British World Views, 1956

Motivational System—General

If Britain following World War I was compelled to accommodate to a relative decline in its world power position, few doubted that Britain must still be viewed as a power of the first rank. Now, following World War II, the British were confronted with much evidence that the world saw them in a second power rank. Admittedly, Britain was a permanent member of the United Nations Security Council, but so were France and the Republic of China. Indeed, British behavior in the Suez crisis strongly suggests a second-rank status to which the Tory back bench could not accommodate. The dramatic announcement that Britain could not be responsible for the defense of Greece, the abdication of responsibility in Palestine, an acceptance of the American lead in the Far East and in Europe itself, the solicitation of American financial support—the list could be extended—all add up to *de facto* acceptance of a secondary position.

Two themes running through parliamentary speeches concerning the Suez crisis symbolized British difficulty in accepting their altered world power status. One theme was the granting of independence to India and Pakistan. Confronted with yet another imperial retreat, Labour and Tory MPs alike were reminded of the trauma of surrendering imperial control of the Indian subcontinent. Again and again reference was made to the beneficence and grace of the act. No one spoke of necessity. The other theme was a restrained sense of outrage that America, with so little experience in and understanding of the Middle East, should be achieving decisional primacy in the area.

The most important of British motivations was undeniably defense against a strongly perceived threat from world communism centered in Moscow. British defense appropriations, membership in NATO, and willingness to maintain a substantial defense outlay testify to concern about the Soviet Union. But the yearning for a revival of British power was present, and the Suez episode is probably its clearest post–World War II manifestation. Even so, there was no thought of returning to a great imperial past. Describing the goals of the Tory backbenchers who formed the Suez group, Leon Epstein wrote, "What the Suez group said it wanted was not the restoration of the Empire of 1900, but instead the resumption of a frustrated development of that Empire into a Commonwealth of nations under British leadership."[34]

The secondary role they played in the Cold War allowed the British to avert their eyes from that conflict: It was America's responsibility and, if anything, the Americans were too much aware of it. Yet when in Suez this absent-mindedness led to the disruption of the Anglo-American alliance, the shock waves compelled a return to the priority goal of resisting the communist advance. The British system of foreign policy aims was a conglomerate of Cold War objectives, atavistic imperial objectives, and objectives related to the British need for economic recovery.

After World War I the British search for commercial outlets was surprisingly sluggish, but in the post–World War II period extreme economic need produced a British willingness to sacrifice at home in order to capture foreign markets. In many instances, grandeur and foreign trade motives closely interacted. The debates on Suez revealed how deep had been the impact of the nationalization of the Anglo-Iranian Oil Company in 1951; it even symbolized the threat to a major source of foreign exchange in an area traditionally subject to British imperial influence. Herbert Morrison, whose memory served him badly, referred to his own experience with Mossadegh in Iran. He compared Suez to "another case in which one Government—if it were a Government, which is very doubtful, but more likely it was one man—unilaterally decided that an agreement which had been freely entered into between his country years before and the Anglo-Iranian

Oil Company should be repudiated." Morrison went on to describe how he had taken the case to the International Court of Justice and won his point.[35] In fact, oil was nationalized by Mossadegh's conservative, royalist predecessor, Husain Ala, and the International Court denied jurisdiction, as Iran contended it should. Anger, bitterness, and contempt for profound nationalist stirrings in Iran, as in Egypt—all are reflected in this perceptual response to challenges to British grandeur and commercial interests within the ranks of the traditionally anti-imperialist Labour party.

The influence of the British military bureaucracy was also strong throughout the Cold War. They gained a major decisional role as the group with chief responsibility for providing the British share in the defense against a perceived communist advance. In the Suez crisis, their influence was apparent in the deep concern expressed over the possible loss of the old imperial life line and the need for a base in the eastern Mediterranean, as well as in activities to achieve a British-sponsored Middle East defense alliance.

In marked contrast, the civilian foreign policy bureaucracy was rapidly losing influence. The Colonial Office was being decimated by the rapid progression toward independence of colonies which only a few years earlier were expected to remain colonies for generations to come. The Suez crisis reflected some influence from this element. But it is significant that Eden did not reveal to his Foreign Office bureaucracy the fact of his collusion with France and Israel in October 1956. Kennett Love asserts that Eden understood this policy would not be received favorably within that bureaucracy.[36]

The motivational system can thus be depicted as follows:

A. Defense
   Economic vested interests: trade and overseas investments
B. National grandeur
C. Military vested interests

General System of Aims

As has been true for each of the moments examined in British imperial involvement in Egypt, in 1956 her foreign policy aims were essentially status-quo. Each of the guidelines for that categorization was clearly met. The prevailing nation-state system was accepted; a high priority was placed on the peaceful settlement of disputes; and Great Britain was not seeking to add to its overall world influence. The British did hope to avoid accepting too headlong a decline in their influence, but the inexorable fact was that their relative capability was in rapid decline, and even the most skillful use of the British leverage position could do no more than delay the inevitable accommodation to a lesser leadership role. As the following discussion will argue, neither Labour nor the Conservatives were prepared to accept the dimensions of this decline. But among the Conservatives there was one bloc, the Suez group, which was far less able to accommodate to Britain's declining power position than the rest. They envisioned an altered but still brilliantly influential British Empire. Had their moment of control of British policy endured longer, the first-level aims representation would have had to incorporate revitalizing and revamping the British Empire. But the failure of British policy, dramatic and humiliating as it was, indicated that for the first time in this study reference to the empire qua empire should be dropped as an expression of system aims concern.

The system of aims representation outlined here has five divisions. Each flows from a major foreign policy determinant which in the analytic scheme is translated in terms of perceptions of threat and opportunity which determine the decisional process direction. The inclusion of five divisions for 1956 contrasts with the usual three or four, reflecting a conclusion that there were four primary perceptual determinants of behavior, in addition to the compound of perceptions of threat and opportunity judged to be of second- or third-level importance and represented in the fifth umbrella division.

As has been noted, the major determining perceptions are a strongly perceived threat to Great Britain from world communism; a perceived threat to the survival of civilization implicit in the thermonuclear weapons systems of the United States and the Soviet Union; a strongly perceived threat to the already much reduced British world influence position; and an umbrella perception of opportunity to strengthen and stabilize the British economy through a foreign economic program.

The proposed translation into aims terms of these determining perceptions of threat and opportunity is given in the system-of-aims outline. Specific policy aims are ordered under each umbrella heading. A brief glance at this system of aims should suffice to indicate the extraordinarily delicate balance among them. They are not glaringly contradictory, but the difficulty of maintaining harmony is such that any serious crisis could develop into an unmanageable disturbance. There is, in fact, a basic, though implicit, contradiction in the system of aims. Perceived threat from international communism leads to a set of aims each of which is premised on the necessity of establishing a subordinate and complementary relationship with the United States. However, the perceived threat to the British influence position is attributable not to international communism, but rather to an overall power potential base decline. Indeed, the frustrations resulting from this decline are likely to produce resentment toward that same vital ally, the United States.

I. Preserve the peace, well-being, and security of the British people, including those of British dependencies
   A. Contain international communism centered in Moscow
      1. Complement American military deterrence strategy

      a. Coordinate British weapons systems with those of the United States

      b. Cooperate with the United States in developing effective military alliances

      c. Give military assistance to states newly independent or soon to be independent, such as Iraq and Malaysia, where there is a traditional British military presence

  2. Work for noncommunist stability and friendliness toward Britain in Third World states

      a. Provide economic and technical support in areas of traditional influence

      b. Through symbol manipulation, especially on a covert level, support noncommunist pro-British regimes

      c. Through overt and covert diplomacy, defend and strengthen noncommunist pro-British regimes

B. Avoid thermonuclear war

  1. Play a restraining role in the alliance with the United States to curb adventurist tendencies among American leaders

  2. Provide leadership in efforts to stimulate arms limitation agreements

  3. Cooperate with the United States in stabilizing accidental war areas

      a. Among divided states, give particular attention to stabilizing the German situation

      b. Take major responsibility for settling accidental war situations in Kashmir and Palestine

  4. Support and encourage international organizations, especially the United Nations

  5. Work for development of international law and encourage jurisdictional growth in the International Court of Justice

C. Maintain British world influence

  1. Provide leadership for the political cooperation of the British Commonwealth

  2. Provide leadership for close relations with Western Europe while avoiding either isolation or loss of sovereignty

  3. Maintain close and supportive relations with friendly Third World regimes in areas of traditional British influence

D. Restore British economic health

  1. Encourage health and growth of export industries and overseas investments which provide needed foreign exchange

  2. Work for mutually beneficial economic relations with the Commonwealth

  3. Work for mutually beneficial economic relations with countries of Western Europe

4. Work for world trade agreements which provide for nondiscrimination against British trade
5. Make energetic use of overt and covert diplomacy in Third World areas to protect existing investments and gain new commercial contracts

E. Satisfy the foreign policy–related demands of the British people
  1. Maintain British naval and military forces sufficient to play a complementary role in military deterrence of communism
  2. Maintain a foreign policy bureaucracy consonant with world leadership demands
  3. Support and encourage British commercial interests overseas and safeguard British home industry and commerce
  4. Defend the dignity and prestige of the British nation
  5. Support the principles of liberal democracy, national self-determination, and humanitarianism abroad
  6. Help Israel achieve security and permanence in the Middle East

The Suez crisis had enormous symbolic importance for a declining Britain. For close to a century the Suez had been a vital link in the imperial life line. The 1954 agreement by which the British accepted evacuation was not a total surrender; there was a sense that British control could be reestablished when the situation called for it. Now even that illusion had faded. Worse still, they had been expelled by a leader who appeared to many Englishmen to be of the same agitating variety against whom the British had intervened seventy years earlier. Nothing could better symbolize a decline which had yet to be psychologically accommodated.

Ironically, the Soviets were having parallel difficulties with another people who yearned for real independence, the Hungarians. But there was no British empathy with the suppression of the Hungarian challenge. Rather, the Soviet action reminded the British of the threat from world communism centered in Moscow. Thus, the two main thrusts of British foreign policy aims came to a climax simultaneously. The resulting disturbance was therefore a major one that was felt even at the system aims level.

Prevailing Situational View

The persistence of a polarized situational view concerning Egypt is one striking feature of this study. There were always Englishmen who viewed Egypt in imperial image terms and others who saw a respectable nationalist movement. But in 1956 there were two striking variants, one for each of the polar groups.

It might be expected that anti-imperialists in the Labour party would extend to Egypt the kind of Blunt-like situational view that was clearly seen in the *New Statesmen and Nation* articles quoted in the previous chapter. Indeed, it might be expected that the 1952–1956 era in Egypt would be seen by anti-imperialists as the final triumph of an eighty-year struggle for national self-fulfillment. Nasser, as he emerged from obscurity within the junta, could easily have been seen as the legitimate successor of Arabi, Mustafa Kamel, and Saad Zaghlul; in Egypt many saw him that way. But these expectations were rarely realized. Michael Adams, writing in the *Manchester Guardian*, followed expectations, but the *New Statesman and Nation* in particular did not.

The explanation for this expectational failure is not at all self-evident. In the 1920s Egypt was clearly Egyptian. In the 1950s Egypt was to a degree Arab, and the degree of Arabness was probably growing. From the days of World War II, Egyptians had played a major role in Arab affairs, and the entire Arab world was engaged in a fierce and consuming battle against Western imperialism. Egyptians, therefore, were leading a movement that would further erode the British Empire.

Arabs, like other peoples, tended to see their struggle in stereotypical terms. The ideal typical image that by 1956 was approximated by nationalists throughout the Arab world was the indirect, nonformal colonial image. In their eyes, Western imperialism was seeking to keep the Arab world in raw-material-producing subserviency. Furthermore, they were doing this by working through Arab reactionary leaders who profited enormously from the relationship financially and in personal power. In this view of reality, the reactionary Arab leaders were thought of as near traitors, while their opponents exemplified patriotic purity. Examples of the near traitors were Nuri as-Said, the first among Iraqi oligarchs, and Abdullah, king of Jordan.

Egypt's leaders were seen as being closer to the patriotic end of the spectrum. King Farouk had been compelled by British tanks to agree to a pro-British government, which led nationalists in Egypt to see some hope even in him. The Wafd, having learned a bitter lesson, tried desperately and with some success to rid itself of the onus of collaboration with the British in World War II. When the coup of 1952 occurred, it was seen more as American than as British-inspired.[37] And the United States had not yet been written off as the senior partner of the Western imperial conspiracy. Nasser's performance at Bandung in 1955 and his association with Third World leaders who symbolized anti-imperialism began to place him in the position of symbolic leader of not just Egyptian but Arab nationalism.

This should have posed no problem for Labour anti-imperialists, who viewed such rulers as Nehru, Sukarno, and U Nu as leaders of national self-fulfillment movements. Nasser could have been seen in this tradition. But in Labour eyes, Nasser was not a Nehru bringing dignity to the highly diverse Indian people, nor even an ambitious Bismarck-like prince unifying the Arab people. Nasser had written a book, *The Philosophy of the Revolution*,[38] which was read very differently, depending on the perceptual predisposition of the reader. Those who empathized with anti-imperial forces in the Arab world, Africa, and Islam saw the book as a yearning for a role of bringing liberation to the peoples embraced by those three circles. Those who found nationalist movements in the Third World threatening saw the book as the *Mein Kampf* of a lesser Hitler. Most leaders of Labour saw this latter picture.

Hugh Gaitskell, the leader of Labour in opposition in 1956, said:

We cannot forget that Colonel Nasser has repeatedly boasted of his intention to create an Arab empire from the Atlantic to the Persian Gulf.

The fact is that this episode must be recognized as part of the struggle for the mastery of the Middle East.

It is exactly the same that we encountered from Mussolini and Hitler in the years before the war.[39]

Projecting Nasser into Hitler was a most natural perceptual phenomenon. As discussed in chapter 4, a major perceptual pattern is the projection of a current threat into a parallel threat of the recent past. Hitler was very much in men's memories in 1956. The image of Nasser-as-Hitler or Nasser-as-Mussolini seemed to appear in every other Tory speech during the crisis and was a determining image for Anthony Eden. But so was it for many in Labour.

For Tories this historical projection was congruent with their political projection. Nasser symbolized "revolution" and "left," and for Tories these were negative symbols. But for Labourites the two projections were contradictory. "Revolution" and "left" were to them favorable symbols with which they identified. Therefore, Labourite perceptions of Nasser and Egypt were unstable. At first Nasser appeared to be a Hitler and Arab nationalists his fascistic followers, but that picture soon changed.

It is the misfortune of Arabs in the post–World War II world that they alone of Third World peoples seeking national dignity lacked the friendly encouragement of liberal anti-imperialists in the Western world. The Eleanor Roosevelts were willing to give time and money to any other national awakening. But the Arabs were not only fighting the British and French imperialists, they were fighting Zionism.

Arab perceptual accommodation to this double foe is easily described. In their eyes imperialism was a triple alliance of Western capitalist leaders, Arab reactionary elites, and Zionism. After all, they argued, Zionism had been imposed on the Arab world gratuitously by British imperialists in 1917, even as they began to impose their own imperial control east of Egypt. And Britain had made undeniably clear its preference for traditional Arab leaders. Furthermore, covert but widely known contact had been made between Israeli leaders and King Abdullah. Evidence was sufficient to reinforce the Arab perception of a *de facto* alliance among Western imperialists, Israelis, and Arab reactionaries.

But in the liberal world, much as in the Jewish community itself, Hitler's genocide had been unbearably traumatic. Sympathy for the Jewish people was deepened by the realization that Hitler's genocide was an expression of the worst in the Christian West. Anti-Semitism was something everyone encountered, and its ugliness only strengthened liberal resolve that never again should the Jewish people be made to suffer.

But how was one to accommodate this resolve to the fact of Arab national awakening? Weren't the Arabs as well entitled to liberal sympathy? Weren't they as well victims of the West? Perceptual accommodation to this contradiction was made by the modal liberal anti-imperialists by not seeing the Arab national yearning. A Bao Dai in Vietnam was easily recognizable to this group as an imperial creation. But Arabs whose history was similar, such as Nuri as-Said and King Abdullah, were seen as the real Arab patriots, not Nasser or the leaders of the then ideologically democratic and socialist Arab Baath party. The latter were seen as fascists or as agitators.

In the early weeks of the Suez crisis an enemy image of the Arab revolutionaries was most commonly held by British liberal anti-imperialists. However, when Israel invaded Egypt and the British-French collusion with Israel was increasingly suspected, perceptual ambivalence on the part of Labour became manifest. There were few kind words for Nasser at any time from Labour MPs, but as the crisis progressed he began to be recognized as a symbolic leader of Arab nationalism. The statement of Alfred Robens was typical: "The use of force might easily overthrow Nasser. It would not destroy Arab nationalism and it would not destroy the rising feelings of people of this kind for independence and for freeing themselves from what they call imperialist domination."[40] K. Zilliacus was even more to the point: "The Government. . . . do not want a settlement with President Nasser; what they want is a bash at Arab nationalism personified by President Nasser."[41]

Perceptual alteration went much further after the actual invasion of Suez and the self-evident, *de facto* collusion of Britain, France, and Israel. Wedgwood Benn expressed the altering view thus:

The problem of the Middle East is not one problem. It is a complex of problems. It is the problem of bitterness between Jew and Arab. It is the problem of ex-dependent peoples becoming independent. It is no good, people, my hon. Friends included, saying that there is no anti-colonial issue in the Middle East, because that just is not true. . . .

Although Colonel Nasser is not a democrat—he was not elected by the majority of the people of Egypt—let it be remembered that for many years we imposed the Government of Egypt upon the people of Egypt. What speeches were ever made by hon. Members opposite particularly when a British ambassador sent tanks to the palace as happened during the war. . . .

We did not care, because it was our Government of Egypt and was doing what we wanted. . . . If we are to excuse Israel—and I am not attempting to do so tonight—on the grounds that she was given a feeling of insecurity and was insupportably tempted and tortured by her enemies, the charge lies with the Government Front Bench. They never gave Israel the security which would enable her to resist the temptation to attack.[42]

On November 8, 1956, George Wegg went even further regarding Israel: "I think that the people of Israel have made a terrible mistake. They have become caught up with the Machiavellian, corrupt decadence of, above all, the French. . . . For in sorrow I must say that I regret that after 2,000 years of wandering, of the ghetto, the concentration camp and the gas chamber, the Jewish people have learned nothing."[43]

Jewish Labour MPs did not follow this perceptual progression. Perception of threat to Israel was too intense to allow an accommodation of the anti-imperial view which was rapidly becoming the predominant Labour view. Harold Lever put it this way:

Let me assert right away that I deny that there is any legal or moral authority for the view that the fact that Israel has crossed her own frontiers into Egypt is any kind of proof that Israel is an aggressor within the meaning of the United Nations Charter, or within the meaning of international law. . . .

The only yoke that the Egyptian people need to throw off to achieve some sort of prosperity is not the yoke of the party opposite but the yoke of a little clique of scoundrels, the military junta, who are channelling all Egypt's resources in support of their own need, ambitions and war like aims.[44]

No symbolic leader is perceived here.

Maurice Edelman was more extreme. He declared passé the "Marxist dogma that the emergence of the sovereign State as a reaction against feudalism was progressive." At least it should not be applied here and "the Egyptian dictator must not be allowed to get away with aggression, because that would be merely the beginning of whole series of aggressions."[45]

The deviance of the Jewish Labour MPs is instructive. It is further evidence of the heavily determining role political community identity plays in world view. This variable seems to explain the difference in perceptual development between a Wedgwood Benn and a Maurice Edelman. Hugh Gaitskell, whose wife was Jewish, was more ambivalent. His initial address on the Suez crisis compared Nasser and Hitler and was filled with references to the ill treatment of Israel by Egypt. But on October 31, 1956, following the Israeli invasion, he demonstrated an awareness of Arab perceptions. Of Israel he said sadly, "If they are looked upon as simple 'stooges' of Britain and France, a kind of advance guard of Western imperialism, then any prospect of a peaceful settlement with the Arab states is gravely endangered."[46] As this quote indicates, much of Labour by the end of the crisis was operating with a situational view that approximated the ideal typical complex image. Temporarily, at least, the deep concern for the Jewish people of Israel did not deflect Labour from a sympathetic view of a people in the process of casting off Western colonial rule.

The Conservative press and members of Parliament, despite the *de facto* alliance with Israel, evinced little real concern for Israel. There is no verbal evidence to suggest that the Conservative modal view of the situation was much affected by chagrin over Hitler's genocidal policy. Moshe Dayan, in his *Diary of the Sinai Campaign*, indicates his own and Ben Gurion's suspicions of their British ally in the last month before the Israeli-British-French attack.[47] When Iraqi troops entered a Jordan deeply fearful of an Israeli attack on October 14, 1956, Dayan thought the British "are happy at the opportunity—and are perhaps creating it—to show the Arabs that their being with us on the same side of one political front, the Egyptian, is not due to their love of Israel, and does not mean their abandonment of the Arabs on the other fronts of the Arab-Israeli conflict."[48]

Verbal evidence strongly supports Dayan's analysis. The imperial image can still be recognized in Conservative statements, and Conservative remarks toward the Arabs indicated little empathy but much sympathy. The Conservative feeling for the Arabs was paternal and affectionate; it was Nasser who was evil, and his people would be overjoyed to be rid of him. As Sir Thomas Moore said:

A few weeks ago, the Prime Minister said that our quarrel was not with the Egyptian people, but with Colonel Nasser. He was right. The Egyptians are a kindly, friendly, simple, though emotional people and once they realise this man Nasser is a menace to their peaceful existence and to their future happy relations with the Western nations, they will turn on him and throw him out.[49]

Speaker after Conservative speaker referred to this theme: Allow the Egyptian people some freedom of choice and they would turn to good and responsible leaders. And who would these leaders be? Julian Amery, a leading member of the Suez group and son-in-law of Harold Macmillan, showed some detailed knowledge of Egyptian political history and concluded that the Wafd and Nahas Pasha were the real representatives of Egypt.[50] In 1942, presumably, they proved that.

Indeed, if this were not the prevailing view, the British tactics made very little sense. Labourites asserted again and again the view that British tactics would rally the Arab world to Nasser and solidify his position of leadership. That reaction is of the type one expects from a people who are proud and sensitive to questions of national honor. Obviously the Conservatives could not hold such a view. Their view allowed them to expect that an outright invasion by Western imperial powers in alliance with the Zionist state would lead the Egyptians to turn against the leaders opposing the invasion and toward leaders who would collaborate with the invaders. Such expectations are in harmony with the ideal typical imperial image.

It is also congruent with the imperial view of reality to see an overly permissive attitude toward colonial regimes as likely to lead to serious trouble. Orientals understand and respect strength. Anthony Fell saw the Middle East this way:

Most people would agree that our failure to be strong at Abadan, and quickly strong, led to a deterioration of our reputation in the Middle East, and that that led to an agreement with Egypt which was not in every way the sort of agreement to which those who had respect and love for the Sudan were entirely favourable. That agreement eventually led to the with-drawal of our troops from the Suez Canal. Who can say that Nasser would ever have grabbed the Canal if British forces had not been withdrawn.[51]

But it was more than a colonial agitator who had to be dealt with firmly but fairly; it was an evil man who did what he did "primarily to enhance the prestige of Nasser and to discredit Britain in the Middle East." Major Patrick Wall said: "If Nasser gets away with this act, British prestige, which has suffered many blows since the war, will be completely eliminated from the Middle East. Our friends will fall away from us and Nasser will, I believe, have a very good opportunity of creating his dream-empire which will stretch from Casablanca to the Caspian."[52]

In opening the Suez debate, Anthony Eden focused attention on the vital role the Suez Canal plays for Great Britain: "As the world is today, and as it is likely to be for some time to come, the industrial life of Western Europe literally depends upon the free navigation of the Canal as one of the great international waterways of the world."[53] The sanctity of agreements was also stressed. But by the fall of 1956 the canal was functioning as well as it ever had under the Suez Canal Company management. Nasser had unequivocally agreed to abide by the 1888 convention guaranteeing free navigation, with the caveat that its terms could not apply to states at war with Egypt, that is, Israel, with which there was an armistice but not a peace treaty. Conservative speeches gave lip service to Eden's points; the focus was on prestige, influence, and the anti-British dynamics of the situation.

A representation of the situational view is probably best made by viewing the crisis in July and then again in October 1956 (see figures II.13 and II.14). This permits a description of the rapid migration of the Labour view (L) and indicates as well the views of the Tory back bench (BB) and Jewish MPs (J).

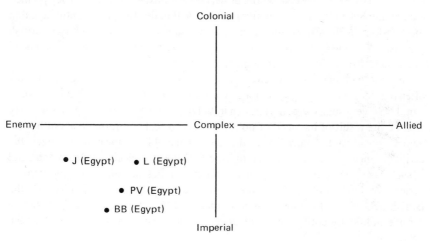

Figure II.13. British Situational Views, July 1956

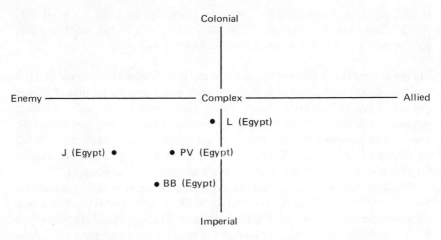

Figure II.14. British Situational Views, October 1956

Situational Motivational System

This examination of the Suez crisis leads to one inescapable conclusion: As much as was said in Parliament about the defense of the imperial life line and the vital economic stakes Britain had in the Suez, the first-intensity motivational factor was national grandeur. In the final days, the Eden government congratulated itself on showing the need for an international peace force to be sent to the Egyptian-Israeli border area. The Labourite response was to liken their argument to that of a criminal who says he should be applauded for demonstrating the need for a police force. Labour MPs bore down on the Conservative case. They pointed out that the Suez Canal was functioning very well under Egyptian control and that the freedom of the use of the canal was threatened only by ill-advised British actions. They saw British policy as a vainglorious, romantic act that was intended to enhance British imperial prestige but in fact demeaned it.

I have argued that what appear to be "rationalizations" for a policy are in fact often real, not symbolic, motivations. The motivational factor of cultural messianism, I believe, usually appears after an initial imperialistic move. In genesis it may well be the result of the need of policy makers to feel comfortable about having gained considerable control over other men. Once it has appeared, however, the civilizing mission becomes an end in itself for important decisional elements, and in such cases I have consistently included cultural messianism in the motivational system. In the case of the 1956 intervention, though, the rationalizations for the British actions are far more symbolic than real. Prestige and Eden's desire to survive politically could not be advanced as the most important reasons for the action.

Seeing the Suez crisis as a matter of face alone was impossible for the leading decision makers. Accommodation called for constructing the image of a Middle Eastern Hitler who was determined to conquer the area, consume British commercial interests, and (possibly in alliance with the Soviet Union) destroy the British defense position in the area.

Had the factors of defense and trade been in the first-intensity category, it is unlikely that the British would have capitulated in the face of Soviet-American pressure and even more unlikely that such threats would not have been perceived by Labour. Defense is given a secondary rating only because of a generalized perception of threat from the Soviet Union.

The motivational system for 1921 included bureaucratic vested interests. By 1956 that factor had passed from the second-intensity category to a position that is too low to be incorporated in the third-intensity category. British advisers with any important official connections had departed, and the Foreign Office bureaucrats were obviously perceived as unsympathetic to the government's decision. Indeed, they were not even informed of the collusion.

Military vested interest is more clearly a factor. The concern of military leaders was manifest in the perceived need to retain bases in Egypt and, failing that, to gain some kind of access to the Suez in crisis periods. However, in the actual invasion of Egypt the military seems to have been the executor rather than the initiator of the decision; consequently, its influence has been placed at third-level intensity.

Likewise, concern for Britain's trade was certainly a factor, although direct involvement of commercial interests in Egypt is difficult to see. Labour argued that British policy would damage rather than protect economic interests, and this proved to be correct. The canal was blocked, and British commercial interests in Egypt were confiscated. But there is no reason to doubt that in the perceptual accommodation of leading decision makers, concern for trade had been an important factor. Economic vested interests are placed at the third-intensity level.

The motivational system is inferred as follows:

A. National grandeur
B. Defense
   Domestic personal power
C. Economic vested interests: trade and investments
   Participant excitement
   Military vested interests

Domestic personal power is included because it is inferred that Anthony Eden felt that his credibility, especially with the Suez group, was not sufficiently strong. He had been accused of wavering, indecisive, and unmanly leadership. Participant excitement is included on the lowest level because the ledger is mixed: Some of the attentive public was appalled, others deeply excited.

Specific Policy, Expectations, and Response

In October 1956, the Eden government decided that military force must be used in Suez without American support. Evidence is now overwhelming that the decision was made to act in secret collusion with France and Israel. The United States would not be informed.[54] According to the plan, Israel would suddenly invade the Sinai in an action that for some hours might appear to be a large retaliatory raid. When it became obvious that this was an invasion, Britain and France would issue an ultimatum calling for a cessation of all warlike activity, a withdrawal of all forces to ten miles from the canal, and an acceptance of the temporary occupation of this zone by British and French forces. Twelve hours would be given for an answer, after which offensive action would be taken. Egypt was expected to reject the ultimatum; Israel would accept. Then the allies would bomb and destroy Egypt's air arm, and the British and French would land troops in the canal zone.

The British expected that the Nasser regime would be ousted and replaced by a cooperative regime such as had come to power in 1942. The Arab regimes friendly to Britain would publicly condemn and privately applaud. The Soviet Union, preoccupied with Hungary, would limit its action to verbal denunciations. The United States, preoccupied with the 1956 election and unwilling to offend Israel and its closest allies, would unhappily acquiesce. Third World agitators would understand that the day of permissiveness was over and would become more quiescent. All these expectational assumptions are clearly implicit in the statements of governmental supporters quoted at some length earlier in this chapter.

Expectations implicit in Labour speeches were vastly different. Zilliacus anticipated the Eden government's objectives on September 22:

A full blooded expression of that policy is one which hopes to find a pretext, and the withdrawal of the pilots and the new Canal user's association lay the foundation for the pretext—for intervening with armed forces, reoccupying the Suez Canal and eventually Cairo, and overthrowing the Nasser regime and putting in a puppet Egyptian Government, after which the advocates of this policy believe that the Arab world would be overawed and frightened and, in some cases, secretly pleased at Nasser's downfall.[55]

He asserted that government policy rested on three assumptions: (1) "Arab nationalism is a negligible quantity"; (2) "our economy is strong enough to stand . . . [this] kind of adventure"; and (3) "the United Nations is pie in the sky." He concluded that "imperialism will not work. We are a third class power in that field."[56]

Labour speeches suggested an appraisal of the consequences of a use of force. They predicted that because of the strength of Arab nationalism, Nasser would be even stronger while British friends would be discredited; the Soviet Union would reap the harvest; the Western alliance would be shaken; the British economy would be troubled; and the United Nations would be weakened.

Labour expectations were fulfilled, and Conservative expectations were not. A description of the disturbance effects on the foreign policy aims system flows easily from the systems-of-aims outline. The convulsion that followed the Suez invasion reached to the system aims level. The invasion and collusion symbolized an effort to go beyond defending the status quo, and for an instant the Suez group's notion of creating a new empire seemed to be official policy. The new empire would be different in form and relatively less influential than that of the nineteenth century, but it would be much more influential than it had been since the Second World War.

The costs of the new policy soon became apparent. The cornerstone of British policy had been an alliance with the United States to contain aggressive communism, and that alliance was now in disarray. President Eisenhower, his reelection a virtual certainty, did not allow domestic politics to muffle his response. He and Dulles appeared to be outraged personally by the behavior of presumably close allies. The American government and the Soviet Union became uncomfortable partners in insisting through the United Nations on British and French withdrawal. The most serious immediate consequence was in British economic health, where essential American support and cooperation had been replaced by antagonism. British investments in Egypt suffered irremediably, and the climate for investments was less favorable in the Arab world generally.

The second consequence was a decline in British influence with friendly Third World regimes. The decline was particularly apparent in governments subject to popular pressures in favor of neutrality. Friendly Arab regimes and leaders were in serious trouble, and the possibility of communist inroads was enhanced. The Soviet Union had threatened to use atomic weapons against London and Paris if the two governments persisted in their invasion. Although the threat was probably not taken seriously, the British and French did withdraw, granting the Soviet Union a major propaganda victory.

A third consequence appeared in the area of avoiding thermonuclear war. The British weakened rather than strengthened the United Nations and enhanced rather than reduced the accidental war potential in the Arab-Israeli conflict.

In the fifth division of the outline, relating to the satisfaction of foreign policy–related demands of the British people, virtually every element was adversely affected. The reputation of the military was damaged, the foreign policy bureaucracy was by-passed and thus lost prestige, commercial interests suffered, the norm of self-determination was violated, and ultimately British prestige was seriously reduced.

Zilliacus had been proved correct: Britain lacked the power to engage in the Suez brand of imperialist response. Had the power base been sufficient, there would have been a similar convulsion, and virtually every foreign policy aim would have been altered. Arab nationalism would have been offended, but a show of great strength could well have added to the influence of a British friend such as Nuri as-Said in Iraq. When the United States played a major role in the overthrow of Dr. Mossadegh in Iran, Iranian nationalism was deeply offended, but the successor regime has had great and stable influence.

In this case, however, there was no possibility of a new aims system developing around an essentially imperialistic motivational system. British power was not sufficient to support it. What occurred, therefore, was a general strategy change that accommodated an acceptance of declining influence. The price that must be paid to maintain influence, much less increase it, was greater than British decision makers could pay. As a result of Suez, the British role in the internal politics of Third World regimes lessened; there was a *de facto* acceptance of decline in Commonwealth unity and importance; and the British responded much more favorably to the appeals of a European confederation that would reduce the range of sovereignty. On the military level there was a frank recognition of dependence on the United States. At the level of avoiding thermonuclear war, there was a reduced assessment of British ability to alter American policy and an acceptance of a subordinate role in the German and Arab-Israeli accidental war situations.

The Suez crisis thus played a major if inadvertent role in the accommodation of British foreign policy aims to a second-rank power potential.

Conclusion: The British in Egypt

This has been a brief look at a moment, the British moment, in the imperial history of Egypt. My purpose was to illustrate the frame of analysis developed in part I and to see if descriptive insights would flow from an application of the frame. In the process of doing this I gained new respect for the problems of the historian. Although I spent many months with documents, biographies, newspaper and journal articles, parliamentary debates, and secondary sources, I came to understand that the subject matter could consume a lifetime. Also I discovered many areas in which the frame could be improved. Yet I do believe that the perceptual-motivational approach has major potential for comparative analysis. The case illustration offers verification for the assumption that perceptual patterning in political analysis is feasible.

The case illustration has the limitations of any case study. Although the episode is important in the history of modern imperialism and has been the object of diverse interpretations, it is not at any point an example of aggressive imperialism. No Hitler or Alexander the Great appears among British policy makers. There is no strong drive to expand trade or investments inordinately. In fact, there is little in the history of the British in Egypt that confirms Hobson's central thesis, much less Lenin's. The only factor producing an aggressive response is national grandeur, and that factor is of prime importance only twice—and then for no more than a few weeks in each case.

I had expected bureaucratic vested interests to be a more important motivational factor than they turned out to be. My conclusion now is that a large bureaucracy with a strongly perceived threat to its interests cannot prevail for long without a much broader perception of threat or opportunity. This suggests the proposition that in the declining days of the Cold War, the huge bureaucracy that developed to conduct the Cold War in the United States and the Soviet Union will not be able long to stem a tide of disengagement if mutual fear declines. It suggests as well the broader conclusion that the psychological milieu of decision-making in foreign policy must be a prime focus for analytic attention. Do important sections of a public perceive a great threat to or opportunity for something valued highly? If so, decision makers will adjust their world and situational views to accommodate a sense of threat or opportunity. If not, the foreign policy decision makers will lack the ability to make the kind of heavy claim on resources that an assertive foreign policy requires.

In figure II.15, the situational motivational systems inferred for each of the periods examined are juxtaposed. I do this to represent pictorially the rhythm of British policy in Egypt. The technique is described as comparative statics and is one way that systems analysis can be used to look at change.

The defense and national grandeur factors are inferred as most important. In five of the six periods (all but 1956), the system reflects a British policy that apparently seeks to maintain British relative influence. In 1882 the matter of face was important enough that national grandeur was given a first-intensity rating. But the overall parametric value in 1882 was not high, and national grandeur did not mirror anything like massive public excitement. In 1956, in contrast, the parametric value was moderately high. The motivational system inferred for that year mirrors the force behind a convulsive effort to reverse British decline from great-power status. These two periods, 1882 and 1956, mark the bounds of Britain's position in a changing world. In 1882 Britain adopted a policy of expanding the empire rather than accept any decline in relative influence. In 1956 Britain made a last move, romantic and nostalgic, as a great imperial power. Her humiliation indicated that her moment as the great imperial power of the Arab Middle East had already passed.

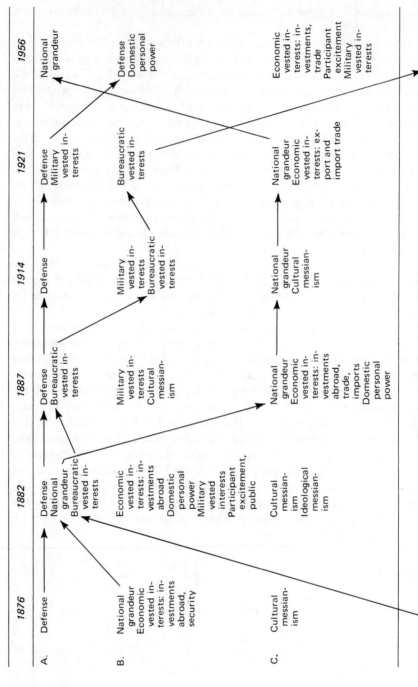

	1876	1882	1887	1914	1921	1956
A.	Defense	Defense National grandeur Bureaucratic vested in- terests	Defense Bureaucratic vested in- terests	Defense	Defense Military vested in- terests	National grandeur
B.	National grandeur Economic vested in- terests: in- vestments abroad, security	Economic vested in- terests: in- vestments abroad Domestic personal power Military vested interests Participant excitement, public	Military vested in- terests Cultural messian- ism	Military vested in- terests Bureaucratic vested in- terests	Bureaucratic vested in- terests	Defense Domestic personal power
C.	Cultural messian- ism	Cultural messian- ism Ideological messian- ism	National grandeur Economic vested in- terests: in- vestments abroad, trade, imports Domestic personal power	National grandeur Cultural messian- ism	National grandeur Economic vested in- terests: ex- port and import trade	Economic vested in- terests: in- vestments, trade Participant excitement Military vested in- terests

Figure II.15. Situational Motivational Systems

PART III
Conclusion

14 / Eliminating the Perceptual Basis of Conflict

Two themes have run through this book, one analytic and the other normative, that are associated with complementary purposes. The first purpose is to construct an analytic frame for describing a government's foreign policy. The description includes an estimate of the predispositional base of foreign policy and a description of foreign policy aims. Aims are ordered in a systems frame designed to point to the centrality of some aims and the derivative quality of others. The approach throughout is one of perceptual analysis, and the entire scheme rests on the assumption that perceptions fall into discoverable patterns. These patterns, once described, are the tools used to infer the predispositional base, or motivations, of policy. In this final chapter, rather than summarize the scheme, I intend to point to directions of refinement for the perceptual approach in international relations.

The second purpose is to begin to explore the possibility of eliminating the perceptual basis of conflict. This requires first of all a description of how conflict is perceived—the first purpose of this book. But there must be as well some preliminary suggestions as to how to go about dealing with the perceptual basis of conflict. In the second half of this concluding chapter I will offer three suggestions and will return to a look at the role academics might play in this endeavor.

Conflict in Value and Perceptual Terms

Every conflict has both value and perceptual bases, and a central analytic task is to infer the relative mix. My strategy for accomplishing that task is to compare the motivational system inferred for a particular government with responses by others to that government's policies. For example, if the motivational system inferred would produce a status-quo policy thrust but others are responding to it as if the policy thrust were essentially imperialist, I infer that the conflict is primarily perceptual in base. However, another approach for inferring relative mix could be to look at perceptual rhythm over time. There is always, I believe, a time lag between the development of value conflict and the perception of that conflict. A typical rhythmic pattern is seen in both the Soviet-American Cold War and in the Anglo-French rivalry in Egypt. A threat to deeply held, politically relevant values is perceived slowly; but once perceived, it leads to policy responses that produce counterresponses from the target actor which will reinforce the perception of threat. Symbolic representation of the conflict in the form of metaphors, such as that of falling dominos, may well prolong the life of threat perception even when the target government's response does not conform to hostile expectations. Perceived threat declines slowly. This pattern can be represented as in figure III.1.

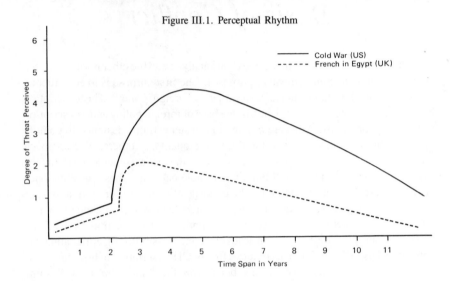

Figure III.1. Perceptual Rhythm

Such a pattern is likely to appear in a conflict situation such as the Cold War or the British-French rivalry in Egypt in which the perception of threat is a more important determinant of conflict than is value conflict. Case studies of a variety of different conflict types might well reveal entirely different rhythmic patterns.

A major problem in dealing with the relative mix of value and perceptual bases of conflict became apparent to me in the case illustration. In two of the moments looked at, 1882 and 1956, the motivational factor of national grandeur was judged to be of considerable significance in determining policy response. Yet the verbal evidence for that judgment was weak. Symbolic representations of a conflict are likely to be in terms with which the participants can be comfortable. The British in 1882 and 1956 were no more willing to describe their motivation in terms of a response to wounded vanity than were Americans in Vietnam in 1972. Rather, the symbols chosen were those conjuring up defense needs and, to a lesser extent, a beneficent and civilizing mission. To what extent, then, did the symbolic translations affect the motivational system? My conclusions were different for 1882 than for 1956. In both cases the symbolic translation accompanied policies which stimulated hostile responses from third countries. In 1882 the hostile response from France was sufficient to reinforce a perception of threat to the British imperial life line which had, in the initial stages, every mark of being perceptually contrived. In 1956 a Soviet threat to bomb London was so lacking in credibility that the perception of great threat to British interests in the canal could not be sustained.

In both cases there was strong verbal and decisional evidence of defense as prime motive. For 1882 I judged defense as a first-intensity factor, but for 1956 I judged the defense motive in the situation of Egypt as derivative and fragile. The differential in judgment was based on the extent to which later policy continued to reflect a concern with defense. The difficulty is that the manner in which a conflict is represented may well lead to an altered motivational basis of that conflict. This is the old problem of deciding when something that began as simply symbolic becomes real.

World View Determinants

When I began this study I was well aware of the importance of perception of threat to or opportunity for something highly valued as a determinant of world view. But as I developed the ideal typical perceptual patterns and began looking seriously at mapping problems, I realized that there are two other essential determinants of world view: perceptions of capability distance and perceptions of cultural distance. Also, I had assumed that the patterns associated with perceived opportunity would be similar to those associated with perceived threat. My case study convinced me that entirely different patterns result, depending on which of the four factors are involved and in what mix.

An obvious direction of refinement for anyone using this kind of approach is to construct additional ideal types. I am convinced that ideal types have exceptional analytic utility in perceptual analysis. In order to deal with an almost infinitely complex reality, man simplifies, and he tends to simplify in situationally deter-mined patterns. The ideal types represent the extreme point of particular simplify-ing tendencies. Taking the complex pole as reality in all its complexity and the other ideal typical poles as the end results of particular simplifying tendencies, potential scales for mapping suggest themselves.

Furthermore, I am tempted to conclude that the ideal types approximate indi-vidual metaphors and that in constructing additional ideal types some obvious individual metaphors may be of real help. The "enemy" is similar whether an individual or a collective. The enemy ideal type is thus the extreme perceptual tendency when there is a perception of threat from a state of comparable culture and capability. The "ally" is a friend, and the allied ideal type is the extreme view of another state of comparable culture and capability whose support is necessary in dealing with a perception of threat or opportunity. The tendency is likely to be stronger if the response is to threat rather than opportunity. The imperial ideal type is the extreme perceptual tendency when an opportunity is perceived involving a state perceived to be inferior both in culture and in capability (although that *opportunity* may be to make use of the state in order to deal with a *threat* from another state). The metaphor here is the "child." Conversely, the colonial ideal type indicates a perceptual tendency direction when a state is perceived as superior in culture and capability. In this case either perceived opportunity or threat pushes the viewer toward the colonial ideal type. A leader classified by those with an imperial view as a WOG and a leader classified as an agitator will share the colonial image even though the WOG hopes to enhance his influence position with the aid of the colonial officer and the agitator sees a threat to his influence position from the same officer. The individual metaphor is the "master."

Since most of my work was with American policy in the Cold War and British policy in Egypt, the five ideal types I have worked with seemed sufficient. Yet there were many cases in which mapping within the four quadrants allowed by the five ideal types was not really satisfactory. There are in particular two types of situations that are of vital importance and must be handled with different ideal types. The first is a situation in which opportunity is perceived concerning a state of comparable culture whether or not there is a perceived capability distance. The best examples of this are found in the pre–World War II setting. Germany and Japan both attacked states of comparable culture and capability, and to do this they had to see a situation which allowed them a reasonable prospect of victory. My initial assumption was that the perceptual tendency in such a case would be in the imperial ideal typical direction. But the imperial view is one of a childlike people, incompetent, requiring tutelage, and requiring strict and tough discipline; and that is not how the Germans perceived the French. On the basis of preliminary efforts to abstract an ideal typical view when opportunity is perceived concerning a state of cultural comparability, I am ready to conclude that the base metaphor is that of the "degenerate individual." The view is of a people, once strong, but now softened by overindulgence and a loss of sense of purpose. Thus, even if there is comparability or even superiority in weapons systems, the expectation of success in a confrontation is reasonable.

Another type of situation is of historical importance, is important today, and is likely to be even more important in the near future. That situation exists when a threat is perceived from a state which is superior in capability but inferior in culture. Here I believe the base metaphor is that of the "barbarian"—the very word used by ancient Rome and China. The barbarian is without compassion and without public opinion except for a single-minded and brutal desire to conquer, enslave, or kill. The discovery of intellectuals among the "barbarians" is always surprising. We have tended to take the description of Romans and Chinese at face value. But examples of this tendency today are Greece looking at Turkey—especially Greek Cypriots viewing the invading Turks—and, theoretically, Japan looking at China. I see strong tendencies toward this view in Israel, particularly looking at Syrians, now that estimates of Arab capability have been revised upward. However, I believe prior to the October 1973 war the enemy-complex-imperial quadrant was best for mapping Israeli perceptions of Arabs and that it is still the stronger tendency.

I doubt very much that a situation can develop in which an opportunity is perceived concerning a state seen as culturally superior but inferior in capability. "Cultural distance" is surely temporally defined. Today the indicators for the definition are exactly the ones the students of "modernization" have come up with. By and large they relate to a technical achievement and management efficiency. But my guess is that a state which lags technologically but sees the opportunity to expand will use, implicitly of course, different criteria for judging cultural distance. "They may be technologically advanced but they are an imitative people lacking in the spiritual and creative qualities that make for cultural greatness" is the variety of view I would expect in that situation.

Other ideal types should be constructed for situations of cultural comparability but capability distance where there is a perception of threat—the "bully"; and for situations of cultural comparability and capability distance in both directions when, as in the allied situation, there is need for help in dealing with perceived threat or opportunity—the "big brother" and the "little brother." Eastern European "satellites" of the Soviet Union are unlikely to see the kind of "master" that Third World "satellites" of the United States perceived during the Cold War period. Englishmen who saw Egyptians as pleasant "children" when they were allies in World War II did not see Danes that way.

Public Role

The perceptual approach applied to the role of the public in the determination of foreign policy may well lead to an upgrading of the estimate of its importance. My conclusion is that the public view is the prime determinant of the parametric value of a system of foreign policy aims. If a perception of threat is widely pervasive in a public, the foreign policy decision maker will be able to make a heavy claim on national resource allocation. If a perception of threat or of major opportunity is lacking in a public, the claim on resource allocation will be weak. Furthermore, because of their role interests, political leaders are far more likely to mirror the psychological mood than to give direction to it. Political leaders, whether in an open or closed society, can operate far more securely in an atmosphere of public consensus. Should a politically vital section of the public accept a competing world view and demand that policy conform to that view, as was the case in the United States during the Vietnam conflict, the response of the political leader is likely to be adaptation. He will, and usually nonconsciously, alter his world view to a point at which a policy is possible with which that important public group can identify.

It follows that a lack of public consensus regarding a threat or opportunity constitutes a general strategy level disturbance for the foreign policy aims system. This is the characteristic feature of American foreign policy in the late 1960s and early 1970s. The most useful approach for studying the public role is, I believe, to differentiate among and catalogue modal world views. If the distance from the prevailing view of a modal world view of a major public element is great, the expectation would be for uncertainty in foreign policy. If the modal views of all important public elements cluster near the prevailing view, foreign policy is likely to be stable.

Decision-Making

I consider this book at heart a foreign policy decision-making study. The motivational system construct is designed to abstract and suggest priority ratings for the most important determinants of the foreign policy decisional process. Both internal and external determinants are included, and the prevailing world view is really a description of the setting within which policy alternatives are perceived and decisions made. The approach goes well beyond the bureaucratic sets involved in particular decisions and seeks to identify the entire range of relevant public and private interests.[1] My vision of the decision-making process is one in which a great many bureaucratic sets, especially when operating routinely, formulate and execute policies which together give direction to overall policy. Neither the individual bureaucrats within a set nor those individuals with overall responsibility for policy will be entirely aware of policy direction or of individual roles in its generation. Rather, their focus is likely to be on the decisional demand of the moment. Indeed, it is likely that only the exceptional bureaucratic decision maker gives any serious thought to the overall directional thrust of foreign policy decisions, that is, is the thrust inclined in what can be called loosely a status-quo or imperialist direction? For the bureaucrats, these are givens. So are the most general outlines of foreign policy aims, for example, containment or rollback.

There is no real possibility, given such a picture, of tracing the path of a complex foreign policy decision. Interviews with direct participants can optimally give the researcher the participant's view of the situation in which an aspect of a problem was considered and alternatives debated, and that is important evidence. To get a full picture of the underlying process, however, the analyst must infer. My inferential device is a foreign policy aims system in which foreign policy objectives are arranged so that their genetic relationships are made clear. My assumption is that each objective is related to one or several of the main determinants of foreign policy, for example, to a perception of threat from the Soviet

Union. By juxtaposing all major policy lines according to derivation, a picture of foreign policy emerges that participants never see. Yet it is a picture that serves as a base for describing the kind of change that major disturbances create.

If the analyst focuses on decisional sets concerned with situationally specific policy, the conclusion may well be that the decisional process amounts to an involved bargaining process whose boundaries are set by style, organizational tradition, and particular task interests. Such a focus is undeniably valuable if the objective is to understand a particular decisional increment. For the study of the general foreign policy decisional process, however, it can be an analytic red herring.

For example, take an American AID mission in an African state. A focus on that bureaucratic element will lead the analyst to see the kinds of competition that occur within and between agencies concerned with that African state and its neighbors and also more broadly within AID. But, according to the foreign policy aims system I constructed for American policy in chapter 5, that mission is present in the African state first of all because of a perceived threat to the United States from the Soviet Union. A general strategy line of containing the Soviet Union was agreed to, and under the rubric of this strategy came the general policy line of providing for the noncommunist stability of developing countries. One of the specific policy lines designed to achieve that general policy objective was the granting of economic and technical assistance. Then the decision was made to put some low-priority AID programs in Africa and specifically in the state in the example. Now, as a consequence of developing trends spurred by the Vietnam involvement, the intensity of perceived threat from the Soviet Union has declined for many Americans. Reflecting this, Congress cuts funding for projects judged as marginal. The AID mission in the African state is closed by AID officials in response to budgetary cuts. Were the analyst to look exclusively at the world of the AID decisional set concerned with that African country, the termination of the program must appear arbitrary and capricious, especially if it had been accomplishing its specific tasks well. But seen in terms of the overall system of aims, cutting aid to the African country is easily explained.

Disturbances to the foreign policy aims system which ultimately lead to alterations in general strategy and even system values may originate in the domain of situational policy decisional sets. I gave several examples of this in chapter 5. But these disturbances develop when a situational-level policy decision leads to results that are not at all expected. In other words, the decisional set is suddenly ripped out of the comfortable context of the kind of routine decision-making that occurs in stable situations and is compelled to look at policy at least a step closer to the general strategy line of which they, only partially consciously, are an element.

The concept of expectation identification and expectational realization or nonrealization is central to this study. It is the concept used to describe and explain what occurs in the decisional process to produce change in foreign policy. The assumption is that even important environmental changes are reacted to most meaningfully when a bureaucratic set is confronted with responses to policies they are pursuing which do not conform to expectations. In part I, the decisional consequences of expectational failures in Vietnam were explored. In part II, the 1921 movement best illustrated the process of decisional accommodation to major environmental change. Further possibilities for using expectation are explored in this chapter.

Individual Decision Makers

Individual bureaucrats, members of public pressure groups, and citizens will vary enormously in world view. Yet individual variation within decisional elements must be ignored and the decisional element treated as a single modal individual. Otherwise the analysis will be unmanageable. The individual becomes, therefore, a manifestation of the role he plays. Without question some distortion results from this treatment, but the distortion is probably not too serious given the level of analysis. The same cannot be said of individuals who have ultimate decisional responsibility. They are far too important to be treated as manifestations of their role. They are the individuals who define the situation, and the manner in which they do so will determine the choice alternatives they can perceive.[2] An individual who sees the Soviet Union as unalterably imperialistic in basic motivation, for example, is unlikely to see policy alternatives that could nudge overall policy in the direction of détente.

A vital focus of foreign policy analysis, therefore, must be on the primary decision makers. Yet it is easy to see why analysts have been wary of that task. Richard Snyder et al., who recognized the vital need for a focus on individual decision makers, were inclined to move in the direction of personality typologizing.[3] That task thrusts the foreign policy analyst into a personality theory where most surely he would drown. My suggestion carries the risk of drowning as well, but I believe to a much lesser extent. I have concluded that there are three important questions to ask about these exceptional foreign policy decision makers. First, when perceiving a strong threat to or opportunity for the nation, is the individual inclined to view the situation in a way that approaches one of the extreme ideal typical images? Or is he likely to see the situation more in accord with the ideal typical complex image? Gladstone, for example, was inclined to see extremes. Salisbury rarely diverged in view from the complex image.

Second, is the individual inclined to adhere to a world view rigidly and to interpret all events, even the most unexpected, in such a way that he need not alter his view substantially? Or is he likely to be flexible and adjust his world view to conform to the dictates of a particular situation? The range here is very broad. Henry Jackson has frequently been my example of a man who is inclined toward rigidity in world view. William Fulbright has been an example of one who has adjusted his world view when events did not conform to his expectations. But Richard Nixon is an example of an individual who can operate with different world views defining several situations at the same time. Indeed, the phenomenon of operating in different situations with entirely contradictory world views is common. It reflects, I believe, the fact that salience of world view is low for many individuals.

In the next few pages, I suggest a list of indicators that correlate with these two tendencies. I believe they can be made operational and that a prediction can ultimately be made regarding an individual's probable perceptual inclinations. Crude typologizing of individuals according to these tendencies might be possible fairly soon, although more refined scaling is surely far in the future. To illustrate the kind of typologizing I envision, I have constructed figure III.2.

IMAGE STABILITY

		Rigid	Flexible
DISTANCE FROM COMPLEX IMAGE	Extreme	Henry Jackson Winston Churchill	Richard Nixon W. E. Gladstone
	Proximate	Dean Acheson Lord Cromer	Frank Church Lord Salisbury

Figure III.2. Proposed Typology of Individuals

A third question must be asked concerning the exceptional decision maker before turning to the indicators. In what kinds of situations and in what directions will an individual perceive a threat or opportunity? William Buckley and George McGovern may be equally devoted to the United States of America, but the external threats Buckley sees to his country are strikingly different from those McGovern sees. Some of the following indicators correlate with the direction of individual perceptual inclination *indicators*.

ROLE VALUES

Any individual whose decisional role is of vital importance will have, by definition, strongly held achievement values. His choices will have led him to a point of high status and of exercising considerable influence over others. For such an individual, who highly values achievement in terms of recognition and influence, role is certain to correlate in all three of the question areas. For example, if the individual holds high elective office, such as the presidency, role will necessitate his being sensitive to public attitudes. If there is considerable disagreement within the attentive public concerning foreign policy, it can be assumed the decision maker will see a reality picture which can accommodate to the need for a policy that will reduce disagreement. The factor of role in this case should disincline the individual to see extreme world views, should incline him toward flexibility in imagery, and should incline him to see threats and opportunities in nondoctrinaire directions.

Another individual, such as the secretary of defense, who represents a more homogeneous clientele with deep vested interests in foreign policy decisions, will be predisposed by his role toward very different perceptual inclinations. He will be more inclined toward an extreme view (the worst case often serves best the vested interests of his clientele), toward rigidity in view, and in a direction that argues for a heavy defense outlay whether the target is left or right.

The problem of dealing with role is complicated by the fact that most individuals who achieve the position of exceptional decision maker will play several roles. A decision maker who has a responsibility to his family for the well-being of family investments in the United Fruit Company, for example, is likely to see a reality which permits a policy that is at least not seriously damaging to United Fruit Company interests and yet balances individual career needs. New-left writers would surely see this role as of major importance in determining the direction of perceptual inclination (as they did in the case of John Foster Dulles, whose family did have such investments). I would tend to discount it. But in any case, operationalizing the role-value factor requires that all of the individual's major role commitments be considered.

POLITICAL COMMUNITY VALUES

Of political community identity values, that of nation is most important. My assumption is that the highly nationalistic individual will be more sensitive to threats to the nation in a particular situation than will a less nationalistic individual. Similarly, he would be predisposed to see opportunities for the enhancement of national grandeur and of the nation's economic and social welfare. On the other hand, an individual with dual loyalties or with loyalties to communities such as the Catholic church, which cross national boundaries, will see a reality that permits the construction of policy which accommodates the interests of all these communities. Therefore, a prime requisite for operationalizing this factor is the construction of an identity profile based on a study of the individual's choice patterns.

OTHER POLITICALLY RELEVANT VALUES

Another assumption of part I reinforced in the case study is that politically relevant values as a predispositional factor are best viewed in terms of symbolic projection. Any major foreign policy decision maker is likely to be on public record many times as having favored one of a number of possible alternatives in a policy decision. The sum of these choices should allow the analyst to place the individual on a number of value scales. After completing the case study, I concluded that three scales may prove predictive of most of the behavioral variance resulting from the factor of politically relevant values and therefore furnish the basis for operationalizing this factor. These are a progressive-conservative scale which measures how the individual responds to change; a scale ranking value placed on freedom of individual political expression; and a scale ranking value placed on freedom of individual economic and social expression.

In this area, choice rather than verbal behavior is the preferred evidence base. Any polity will have a prevailing symbol system, and defense of an alternative chosen will certainly be wrapped in modish symbolic clothing by anyone who has achieved significant decisional influence. In fact, diametrically opposed alternatives may well be given similar symbolic wrappings. But individuals will vary sharply in their willingness to accept change, to make sacrifices for political freedom, and to resist governmental welfare planning and restrictions of laissez-faire activity.

My contention is that individuals identify with governments abroad which are represented symbolically in a way that appears to parallel the individual's image of his own position on these scales. Similarly, an individual will project into the faction of another polity which can be described as occupying a parallel position on the scales. This is true even though in specific policy preference the individual may be closer to a different faction altogether, for he is less likely to be aware of specific issues that separate factions in their domestic policy than of the symbolic positioning of the faction. For example, an individual may look with favor on a government medical insurance program which parallels that advocated by a faction in another polity. But if that faction in its own milieu is considered to occupy a "radical" position and our individual in his milieu sees his position as "moderate," he is likely to project into the "moderate" faction in the foreign polity even though the policy programs supported by such moderates are, by the individual's domestic standards, far too conservative.

Of course these factors are all interactive. If a government perceived favorably by an individual allies itself with a frightening enemy, the individual will cease to view it favorably. An American in the 1930s who was suspicious of change, indifferent to human freedom, and strongly opposed to government planning and economic controls may well have viewed Franco's Spain favorably. But that view altered suddenly and sharply as a result of Franco's *de facto* alliance with Hitler.[4]

These projection patterns are important to identify for a simple reason: An individual with positive projections into the government of another state is predisposed to see opportunities for a close relationship and is predisposed not to see a threat even when evidence is substantial. Conversely, when the projection is negative, opportunity for an alliance will not be recognized, while a threat will be seen when evidence is meager. Politically relevant values, therefore, are important indicators of direction of perceptual inclination.

The intensity with which individuals hold political values is subject to wide variation. Some individuals are classified as apolitical. For them the decision that involves any politically relevant value is extremely rare. Others who have little interest in political values may yet value highly the personal exercise of influence and may achieve high political office. If, in making political choices, an individual manifests little ideological consistency, his political value commitment is probably not intense. My assumption is that this trait will incline an individual toward flexibility in world view. He may indeed hold different world views for different question areas simultaneously. When this is the case, the individual decision maker, in constructing a reality view which must accommodate diverse interests, can put aside the need to accommodate world view to his own political value system. Observers may be inclined to describe such a person as an "opportunist."

DETACHMENT QUOTIENT

In the case study I commented frequently on the range among individuals of what I called a "detachment quotient." Salisbury and Cromer, for example, appear to have been dedicated British nationalists and strong-minded proponents of ideological positions. Yet in their views of ally, enemy, and colony they always stayed close to the complex image of a target government and people. Cromer had great difficulty in accepting the growth of an Egyptian independence movement, but this was a manifestation of rigidity of view. Compared with his bureaucratic colleagues, he was a detached and objective observer.

I assume that this factor is separable from the next factor, affectivity, and that some individuals, for whatever reason, come to value highly the effort to strive for objectivity even in situations about which they have strong emotional feelings. Operationalizing this factor poses self-evident difficulties. "Detachment" suggests an end result more than an indicator, and most operationalizing notions that occur to me are implicitly tautological. What is called for is some means for discovering not only that an individual gives verbal evidence of placing a high value on objectivity but that in highly emotive situations he makes a major effort to be objective.

AFFECTIVITY

The popularity of the term "cool detachment" suggests a general conclusion that the quality of detachment is easier to achieve for the individual whose emotions are under tight control. Anger and gratitude, intense fear and trust expressed toward the government of another state are likely to incline an individual toward polarity of image. Furthermore, individuals given to strong affective responses are unlikely to surrender images easily. An affectively inclined individual can impose strong self-discipline and compel himself to look at all the relevant evidence, but when judgment is called for, he will have difficulty making a judgment that is not in tune with his affective response.

I believe it is important to distinguish carefully among affectivity, detachment, and value intensity. Too often affective responses are looked to as measures of the intensity with which values are held. But that is misleading. Affectivity is surely in part a temperamental characteristic, and affective responses accompanying choice patterns are therefore more revealing of temperamental variation than of intensity of value attachment. Similarly, the individual described as capable of detachment may in fact be inclined toward strong affective responses. But he may be inclined as well toward careful structuring of evidence. The two factors produce opposite tendencies in both distance and stability of world view.

EMPATHETIC ABILITY

Empathy is the ability to put oneself into the shoes of other actors. The naturally empathetic individual is likely to see motivational complexity and decisional differentiation. Simple conspiracy theories are unlikely to have much appeal. Nor will simple stereotypes such as the polar ideal typical images be part of the world view of empathetic individuals.

OPEN- AND CLOSED-MINDEDNESS

This factor is similar to empathetic ability. A closed-minded individual, likely to see simple motivations and elaborate conspiracies, is nonempathetic, but it need not follow that the individual judged to be open-minded is also empathetic. Although tolerance of differences and acceptance of change characterize the open-minded, a high empathetic ability is associated with a social sensitivity that a tolerant, accepting individual may not have. What is proposed here is that closed-mindedness is associated with a predisposition to see individual motivation in simple stereotypical terms. Open-mindedness should be associated with a predisposition to see individual motivation in complex terms. This factor could be operationalized on the basis of the kind of attributions made regarding individual motivation.

COSMOPOLITANISM-PAROCHIALISM

A cosmopolitan socialization in contrast to a narrow parochial socialization predisposes an individual toward the complex center of the perceptual field. It is difficult to accept simple stereotypical representations if one is acquainted with a broad diversity of individuals in a particular state.

EFFICACY

Individuals vary widely in their estimation of the ability of a person or government to alter major social, economic, and political trends. My assumption is that where that ability is believed to be sharply limited, the tendency is toward stability in world view. Individual decision makers with a low sense of efficacy are not likely to see a wide range of possible policy alternatives.

SELF-CONFIDENCE

Also inclining an individual toward a stable world view is confidence in his ability to comprehend a situation quickly and accurately. Conversely, the individual filled with self-doubt is more likely to surrender a reality view if his expectations are not unequivocally realized.[5]

Policy Science and Peace Science

The introduction to this study looked briefly at the teach-in phenomenon of the mid-1960s. I concluded that the teach-ins were described accurately by their critics. They were indeed emotional, one-sided, intuitively based, and usually lacking in well-informed judgments or solidly constructed alternatives. But they were as well a recognition by many academicians of the irrelevance of their work to policy. Peace science was a natural outgrowth of this concern, but peace science at the time of this writing is little more than a wish that the theoretical probings of analysts be relevant to policy. The task of adapting middle-range and macro theory to prescriptive usage is still mysterious. Here, too, we are at the beginning. My hope is that the areas for development identified in this study have prescriptive potential. I want, therefore, in this concluding section to spell out this potential as I see it.

Figure III.3 is a simple four-cell matrix reflecting perceptions of Soviet and Arab motivation by some American senators in 1973, constructed to serve as a focus for this discussion. Based on a brief survey of their verbal expressions and their policy

		SOVIET MOTIVATIONS	
		Active	Reactive
ARAB MOTIVATIONS	Reactive	Clifford P. Hansen	J. William Fulbright
	Active	Henry Jackson	Frank Church

Figure III.3. Perceptual Matrix

recommendations, four senators have been categorized, one for each cell of the matrix. The terms "active" and "reactive" refer to perceived Soviet and Arab motivations. The October war was by any definition an act of aggression in which Egypt and Syria were supported actively by Soviet arms. But the basic drive behind the attack is assessed very differently. If the observer sees the motivating force as essentially imperialistic, that is, primarily nondefensive, he is placed in the "active" column. If he sees the motivating force as essentially status-quo, that is, primarily defensive, he is placed in the "reactive" column.

Witnessing the same events in October 1973, these four senators perceived the situation in remarkably different patterns, as shown in figure III.4.

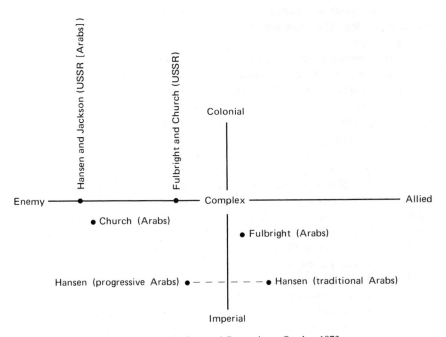

Figure III.4. U.S. Senators' Perceptions, October 1973

Senator Hansen occupies the Soviet-active, Arab-reactive cell. Others in that cell are individuals with role predispositions toward this reality view, such as oil company officials and Defense Department bureaucrats responsible for security interests in the Arab world. A view of the Soviet Union approaching the enemy image was therefore common. Perceived opportunity in the Arab world for trade and investments (oil) and for turning Arab regimes against the Soviet Union inclined many in this cell toward a view of the Arabs in the direction of the imperial image, but they differentiated between traditional and progressive Arab regimes.

Senator Jackson occupied the Soviet-active, Arab-active cell, a position he shared with Senator Hubert Humphrey, many Zionist activists, and military officials not assigned to Middle East affairs. Here the view of the Soviet Union was close to the enemy image, with Arab allies seen in a satellite-client relationship at the time of the war.

Senator Church shared the Soviet-reactive, Arab-active cell with most Senate doves on Vietnam. The image of the Soviet Union was not far from the complex, and Soviet cooperation with the Arabs, who were seen further along the enemy line, was viewed as a disappointing Cold War remnant.

Senator Fulbright occupied the Soviet-reactive, Arab-reactive cell. Senator Mark Hatfield occupied that cell with him, as did those officials who thought the Rogers plan, which would have called for close Soviet-American cooperation, was a good idea. They saw both the Soviet Union and the Arabs close to the complex image.

In three major areas there were important behavioral differences among the men occupying these four positions. First, they judged events in an entirely different way. For example, in late October 1973 the American and Soviet governments were able to persuade the Israeli and Egyptian governments to agree to a cease-fire. However, the Israelis were developing a major bridgehead across the Suez Canal and continued to do so after the cease-fire was to have taken effect. The Egyptian government asked for Soviet-American intervention to stop Israeli violation of the cease-fire. The Soviet government informed the American government of its willingness to do so bilaterally or unilaterally. At the same time the Soviet government took several actions involving the movement of troops and equipment which at the time of this writing have not been revealed. How should this Soviet behavior be assessed? Obviously those in the Soviet-active column would see it as far more threatening than those in the Soviet-reactive column. Placing American forces on nuclear alert, as was done, is sensible for the one group but an act of severe provocation for the other.

In my opinion, analysts have not dealt seriously enough with this problem of variation in world view. Any serious observer codes the conflict potential of an event, but the coding judgment for the occupants of each of the four cells has varied sharply. When area specialists are asked to do the coding, as is frequently the case, no real effort is made to correct for the world-view variation among the specialists. In the above example, I would have no difficulty in placing various Middle East specialists in each of the four cells, my own being the reactive, reactive cell. Judgments about the conflict potential of an event would vary, sometimes spectacularly. If specialists are not used, the problem is compounded.

The second major area of difference in policy-related behavior is the alternatives that will be perceived in dealing with a conflict. How serious an effort should be made to mobilize Soviet support for an Arab-Israeli settlement? Those occupying the Soviet-active column would be unlikely to explore alternatives here. Why give the Soviets a free ride on the road toward achieving their imperialistic objectives? Those occupying the Soviet-reactive column, on the other hand, would see Soviet-American cooperation as an alternative to be seriously explored. Why not give the Soviet Union the opportunity to associate itself with the United States in a joint effort to defuse a situation neither wishes to exploit?

Similarly, how serious an effort should be made to explore Arab willingness to agree to territorial accommodation with Israel? Those occupying the Arab-active column would see such explorations as appeasement. The Arab imperial appetite would be whetted. Those occupying the Arab-reactive column, on the other hand, would consider this kind of exploring central to conflict resolution. Arab suspicions of an Israeli aggressive purpose, supported by the United States, would be allayed.

Third, preferred policy choices vary in parallel fashion. Those sharing Senator Jackson's cell would naturally oppose any territorial concessions to the Arabs, would favor firm commitments to Israel, and would look with disfavor on opening the Suez Canal, a direct Soviet marine line to the Indian Ocean. Those sharing Senator Hansen's cell would naturally seek Israeli territorial concessions and other means of allaying Arab fears of Israeli aggression. But they would favor communicating to the Soviets, as the nuclear alert did, our determination to oppose their exploitation of the situation. Those sharing Senator Church's cell would oppose any serious effort to pressure Israel into making territorial concessions but would consider a joint Soviet-American guarantee of Israel's borders. Those sharing Senator Fulbright's cell would seek Israeli territorial concessions and a joint Soviet-American guarantee of Israeli-Arab borders.

The example is not atypical. It poses the kind of problems that peace science should and, I believe, can confront. The obvious first step is descriptive—an identification of a range of situational views. My example of Americans looking at the Arab-Israeli conflict is oversimplified for purposes of illustration. A really careful description would rely on perceptual mapping and avoid the distorting effect of placing diverse individuals in the same matrix cell. But clusterings do occur in the actual simplifying of reality in which all individuals engage, and the use of matrices in early stages of description can be clarifying.

In the more distant future, I see the possibility of adapting perceptual mapping to computerized foreign office use. With the exception of the complex, all of the ideal types I have developed or suggested are gross simplifications of reality. They are tendency positions that mark the extreme perceptual response of individuals who perceive threats or opportunities in a variety of situations. In the complex position, on the other hand, an extraordinarily complex reality view is held. I have contended that some individuals have come to value highly the ability to detach themselves from the tendencies to simplify. Such individuals, confronted with a latter-day Hitler, would see him as presiding over an extremely complex decisional process and depending on decisional elements, many of which oppose his aggressive purpose. The kinds of strategies for dealing with this new Hitler that would occur to the detached individual would differ in range and type from those advocated by other individuals who would see a simple enemy—evil, monolithic, and capable of devising elaborate conspiracies. The latter would favor, as did their World War II predecessors, a strategy calling for total defeat and total surrender. The former would see many possibilities of eliminating the Hitler without destroying half the world.

If this type of analysis were refined to the point that computer programs could be developed incorporating a wide range of perceptual tendencies, computers could become detachment agents. Foreign office practitioners could get the computer's assessment of the degree to which world leaders were diverging from the complex position and in what direction. This could offer strong evidence of motive. A leader responding to threat would reveal an image tending toward the evil enemy, the colonial master, or the barbarian. A leader responding to opportunity would reveal an image tending toward a child needing tutelage or a soft and degenerate adult.

I have argued that the various perceptual tendencies to simplify frequently become self-fulfilling prophecies. Seeing an enemy leads to responses that produce an enemy. Were it possible to program these tendencies, and were many foreign offices to use such programs, the end result could be self-denying prophecies. Where the basis of the conflict is predominantly perceptual, conflict resolution might well occur.

Diplomatic Probing

The diplomatic probe, as used throughout man's history, is in fact a test of an intuitively based and only partially explicated hypothesis. Most commonly, such probing is done so naturally that the diplomatic practitioner hardly recognizes the process as a probe. Virtually every conversation of diplomats engaged in their trade will involve nonexplicated explorings of motives, perceptions, and policy preferences. In only a few instances will such explorings be constructed formally and called probes. But the sum of the diplomat's testing gives a grasp of situational nuance that the analyst can only envy. Furthermore, the implicit frames used by diplomatic practitioners generally allow for a far more complex exploration of a situation than do the explicated frames of analysts.

Policy science application in this area, therefore, should be made with more than a little humility. What the foreign policy analyst can offer is the discipline of formal application. Only rarely will these decision makers recognize the fundamental nature of their differences. The probing they do naturally will be to test uncertainties at a low level of concern. Through whom in the Arab world is the Soviet Union working to achieve its nefarious objectives? To evaluate the validity of their strategic preference as compared with those of others with different base assumptions, the uncertainty that should be probed is whether the Soviet Union has these nefarious objectives. The foreign policy analyst can contribute in such a situation both by pointing out the assumptional differences that should be probed and by offering a formalized scheme for probing.

Constructing probes to test what amounts to differing propositions concerning motivations and policy aims is anything but a mechanical process. Elsewhere I have discussed at some length the range of types of probing that can be done.[6] If time permits, probes that do not involve policy commitment may be possible, but more frequently probes must be incorporated into policy with provision made for an alteration of policy direction if the probe results in unexpected responses. Whenever possible, several probes with different variable combinations should be made to test competing propositions. In all events, those doing the probing should spell out the responses to be expected if a particular proposition is valid. Unexpected responses, especially if a number of probes have been made, should lead to proposition revision. Expected responses, on the other hand, do not validate a proposition but can be considered as confirmatory. Further probing is always called for, since validation is never possible.

Strategic Planning

Assume in the October war example that Soviet foreign policy analysts have made a study of American world and situational views and have identified the four perceptual clusterings. Assume further that Soviet decision makers have concluded that optimal American policy from their point of view would follow were the reactive-reactive cell the prevailing view. Producing perceptual migration which would make the reactive-reactive view the prevailing view, therefore, becomes a central strategic objective.

In constructing a strategy to achieve such an objective, the concept of expectations has a utility parallel to its utility in diplomatic probing. The occupants of each cell have implicit sets of expectations of Soviet-Arab behavior. What the Soviet planners could do, therefore, is to advance policies and seek to enlist Arab cooperation in so doing that would disconfirm the expectations of the occupants of three cells but would conform to the expectations of the occupants of the reactive-reactive cell. Over time this could result in the kind of perceptual migration they wish both in the form of personnel change among American decision makers (those who had lost credibility would be replaced) and in an accommodation process on the part of remaining decision makers. Predictive failure results in a loss of credibility and a career setback. A sensitive careerist, therefore, is likely to alter his world and situational views (nonconsciously in large part) in the direction of those who had been predicting correctly and had thereby gained credibility. This may, and in important cases probably would, necessitate a focus on attentive public opinion.

The process of personnel change in a case such as this is likely to be role-related. Role constraints may well produce a certain amount of rigidity on the part of, for example, military planners. As repeated predictive failures reduce the credibility of the military planners, a president or secretary of state would likely turn more to, say, certain desk officers in the State Department whose predictions were consistently realized. Such a personnel alteration in a decisional units is one, possibly the major, means by which foreign policy motivation changes. In this case it would produce a decline in intensity of defense motivation reflecting a general strategy level change.

Therefore, my general suggestion is that strategic planning should focus on the range of world and situational views of a target polity. Through the use of expectations, perceptual alteration can be one of the most manipulable aspects of a target government's foreign policy.

Normative

Exploring possible directions for policy application of a scheme such as the one I have developed can be a healthy activity. It compels the analyst to investigate more carefully the scheme's utility for dealing with a chosen problem area, and he is likely to refine his scheme in a nonabstract direction. Unfortunately, to return to the theme of the introduction, many analysts who have serious pretensions in the area of policy science are little concerned with the political and societal implications of their work should their pretensions be realized.

In discussing policy implications and possible policy science developments of this scheme, I have spoken in terms of peace science. It is my hope that if aspects of the scheme can be developed in a prescriptive direction, these applications will be used for the purpose of reducing conflict. In fact, of course, this can be no more than a hope. Prescriptive theory which proves applicable to policy will be the property of a foreign policy bureaucracy and will be used for purposes considered appropriate by decisional units in that bureaucracy. Its contribution is to add to the manipulation potential of the bureaucracy.

The teach-ins of the mid-1960s were in part an agonized recognition of the role academic analysts had played in giving theoretical foundation to policies that much of the academic community had come to regard as repulsive. The concern was parallel to that of physicists who had given other bureaucrats the theory which made possible the construction and use of atomic weaponry. The remedy for the dilemma is anything but self-evident.

Many analysts, possibly most, are little concerned with this question. After all, the contribution an individual analyst can make to the manipulation potential of a bureaucracy is likely to be imperceptible. Yet for reasons outlined in the introduction, I believe the academic foreign policy analyst can play an important role in the policy arena. Given the esoteric nature of most problems in foreign policy, only in the academic community is there likely to be the expertise required for an understanding of problems that in any way approaches the understanding of the concerned bureaucratic elements.

My scheme may have some limited potential in this area. It is designed to help the analyst make explicit the assumptional bases on which decision-making rests. It also provides a frame for examining these assumptions in terms of a check list for evidential support. In the October war example, application of the scheme could bring an awareness of one's own and one's antagonist's operating assumptions. Such awareness, in turn, could lead to a different level of debate—one which focused on the competing cases for the assumptions rather than on the competing policy proposals which flow from hidden but profoundly different assumptional bases. The scheme could be used as well to construct strategies competing with the official one and even to explore competing basic objectives operationalized in strategic terms. Here, too, the purpose would be to persuade the official decision maker to engage in some energetic exploring of alternatives.

Experience offers little basis for optimism that a concerned bureaucracy will pay much attention to such challenges, even when carefully and skillfully constructed. Any really serious exploring of the problem of democratic control of foreign policy decision-making must be institutionally focused. Challenging prevailing assumptions may, indeed, be a central aspect of the problem of democratic control, and schemes such as this may offer the means for advancing competing assumptions. But much more thought must be given to the problem of developing institutions that can compel members of the bureaucracy to defend and to reexamine their operating assumptions.

Notes
Bibliography
Index

Notes

Chapter 1. Introduction

1. *New York Times,* May 19, 1965.
2. Stanley Hoffman, *Contemporary Theory in International Relations* (Englewood Cliffs, N.J.: Prentice Hall, 1960). See pp. 171–84 for Hoffman's proposals for analytic focus.
3. Careful studies of these and other of the more sensational activities of the CIA have not been made. David Wise and Thomas B. Ross sum up much of what is known about the Iranian and Guatemalan episodes in their journalistic *Invisible Government* (New York: Random House, 1964). Miles Copeland's *Game of Nations* (New York: Simon and Schuster, 1970) is an invaluable source for the Middle East. Copeland's memory may be fallible, but his book captures incomparably the spirit of the CIA's interventions. The 1957 Syrian intervention by the CIA is one of the most important keys to understanding Arab behavior and yet has barely been reported. Copeland is far better for earlier interventions. Patrick Seale, in *The Struggle for Syria* (New York: Oxford University Press, 1965), at least deals with the event honestly. Bradford Westerfield, in *The Instruments of American Foreign Policy* (New York: Crowell, 1963), uses the Syrian intervention as an illustration.
4. The theoretical foundations for the doctrine of graduated compellence are spelled out in Thomas Schelling, *The Strategy of Conflict* (Cambridge: Harvard University Press, 1960). The doctrine is advanced in his *Arms and Influence* (New Haven: Yale University Press, 1966).
5. See Townsend Hoopes, *The Limits of Intervention* (New York: D. McKay Co., 1969), esp. p. 80.
6. Louis Menashe and Ronald Radosh, *Teach-ins, USA* (New York: Praeger, 1967), pp. 139–51.
7. Ibid., pp. 110–11.
8. Ibid., p. 12.
9. Ibid., p. 131.
10. Ibid., p. 178.
11. William W. Kaufmann, *The McNamara Strategy* (New York: Harper and Row, 1964).
12. See a report on his views in the *New York Times,* May 11, 1970.
13. Murray Edelman, *The Symbolic Uses of Politics* (Urbana: University of Illinois Press, 1964).
14. Graham T. Allison, *Essence of Decision: Explaining the Cuban Missile Crisis* (Boston: Little, Brown, 1971).
15. Hoopes, *Limits of Intervention,* p. 224.

Chapter 2. Status-Quo or Imperialist

1. Hans Morgenthau, *Politics Among Nations,* 4th ed. (New York: Knopf, 1966), pp. 69–82.
2. Arnold Wolfers, *Discord and Collaboration* (Baltimore: Johns Hopkins University Press, 1962), p. 91.
3. William A. Gamson and André Modigliani, *Untangling the Cold War* (Boston: Little, Brown, 1971), pp. 22–24.

4. Fritz Heider, *The Psychology of Interpersonal Relations* (New York: Wiley, 1958), pp. 79–124.

5. Edward H. Carr, *The Twenty Years' Crisis, 1919–1939,* 2d ed. (London: Macmillan, 1946).

6. Hans Morgenthau, *Scientific Man vs. Power Politics* (Chicago: University of Chicago Press, 1946).

7. Inis L. Claude, *Power and International Relations* (New York: Random House, 1962), p. 37.

8. Morgenthau, *Politics Among Nations,* p.6.

9. Ibid., pp. 244–60.

10. William Riker, *The Theory of Political Coalitions* (New Haven: Yale University Press, 1962), p. 22.

11. Ibid., p. 229.

12. Writing under the title "Arguing About the Cold War," Morgenthau dismissed the focus of many writers he believed were preoccupied with ending the Cold War. He wrote, "That issue concerns techniques of diplomacy not its substance. For after the Cold War has ended, the struggle for the substance of power will continue" (*Encounter,* 28 [May 1967]: 37–41).

13. For an insightful discussion of the importance of this assumption, see Kenneth N. Waltz, *Man, the State, and War* (New York: Columbia University Press, 1959), esp. p. 21.

14. Henry Kissinger, *Nuclear Weapons and Foreign Policy* (New York: Doubleday, 1958). The quotations which follow are from the paper edition, which is abridged and much more sharply worded than the full text.

15. Matthews Josephson, "The Fantasy of Limited War," *Nation,* 185 (August 31, 1957):89.

16. James E. King, Jr., "Limited War," *New Republic,* 137 (July 1, 1957):20.

17. Kissinger, *Nuclear Weapons and Foreign Policy,* p. 44.

18. Ibid., p. 46.

19. Ibid., p. 52.

20. Ibid., p. 59.

21. Josephson, review of *Nuclear Weapons and Foreign Policy,* p. 90.

22. Robert Levine, *The Arms Debate* (Cambridge: Harvard University Press, 1963). This is a most impressive analysis.

23. Townsend Hoopes, *The Limits of Intervention* (New York: D. McKay Co., 1969), pp. 16–17.

24. "Mr. X" [George Kennan], "Sources of Soviet Conduct," *Foreign Affairs,* 25 (July 1947):566–82.

25. Kennan's views were expressed in a series of lectures published as a small book, *Russia, the Atom and the West* (New York: Harper, 1958).

26. See Thomas Schelling, *Arms and Influence* (New Haven: Yale University Press, 1960).

27. J. A. Hobson, *Imperialism: A Study* (London: G. Allen and Unwin, 1902), p. 106.

28. Carl Oglesby and Richard Shaull, *Containment and Change* (New York: Macmillan, 1967).

29. Ronald Robinson and John Gallagher with Alice Denny, *Africa and the Victorians* (New York: St. Martins Press, 1961).

30. For a good, concise discussion of these points, see Earle M. Winslow, *The Pattern of Imperialism* (New York: Columbia University Press, 1948).

31. Parker Thomas Moon, *Imperialism and World Politics* (New York: Macmillan, 1926).

32. Joseph Schumpeter, *Imperialism and Social Classes* (Cleveland: World, 1951).

33. Winslow, *Pattern of Imperialism,* p. 3.

34. Oglesby and Shaull, *Containment and Change,* p. 13.

35. Ibid., esp. pp. 72–84.

36. Robert W. Tucker, *The Radical Left and American Foreign Policy* (Baltimore: Johns Hopkins University Press, 1971).

37. Richard C. Snyder, H. W. Bruck, and Burton Sapin, *Foreign Policy Decision Making* (New York: Free Press, 1967).

38. Graham T. Allison, *Essence of Decision: Explaining the Cuban Missile Crisis* (Boston: Little, Brown, 1971).

39. Anthony Eden, *Full Circle* (Boston: Houghton Mifflin, 1960).

40. John Bartlow Martin, *Overtaken by Events* (New York: Doubleday, 1966).

41. Eden, *Full Circle,* p. 608.

42. For Goldwater's clear and integrated picture of communist interest, structure, and *modus operandi,* see *Why Not Victory?* (New York: McGraw Hill, 1962).

43. Oglesby and Shaull, *Containment and Change.*

44. For a thoughtful exploring of generational value change, see Ronald Inglehart, "The Silent Revolution in Europe: Intergenerational Change in Post-Industrial Societies," *American Political Science Review,* 65 (December 1971):991–1017.

45. In looking at behavioral responses to external interventions, I have proposed a similar notion of varied line drawing, a tolerance range of interference, in *Competitive Interference and Twentieth Century Diplomacy* (Pittsburgh: University of Pittsburgh Press, 1967), pp. 34–77.

Chapter 3. Motivation

1. John H. Herz, *International Politics in the Atomic Age* (New York: Columbia University Press, 1959), p. 8; and Hans Morgenthau, *Politics Among Nations,* 4th ed. (New York: Knopf, 1966), pp. 6, 37 n.

2. C. Wright Mills, *The Power Elite* (New York: Oxford University Press, 1956).

3. Richard C. Snyder, H. W. Bruck, and Burton Sapin, *Foreign Policy Decision Making* (New York: Free Press, 1967).

4. Alexander L. George and Juliette L. George, *Woodrow Wilson and Colonel House* (New York: J. Day Co., 1956).

5. William Riker, *The Theory of Political Coalitions* (New Haven: Yale University Press, 1962).

6. David Birch and Joseph Veroff, *Motivation: A Study of Action* (Belmont, Calif.: Brooks and Cole, 1966).

7. Abraham Maslow, *Motivation and Personality* (New York: Harper, 1954).

8. Harold and Margaret Sprout, *Foundations of International Politics* (Princeton: Van Nostrand, 1962), pp. 46–53.

9. This point is far from established, however. Certainly this expansion was a consequence of complex motivation, but authorities seem to agree that population pressure was a major part of motivation. See, for example, Claude Cohen, *Pre-Ottoman Turkey* (New York: Taplinger, 1968); and Harold Lamb, *The March of the Barbarians* (New York: Doubleday, 1940).

10. Paul R. Ehrlich, *Population, Resources, Environment* (San Francisco: W. H. Freeman, 1970).

11. For a study of population in international politics, see Katherine Fox Organski and A. F. K. Organski, *Population and World Power* (New York: Knopf, 1961). For an example of this type of expansion, see Frederick Merk, *Manifest Destiny and Mission in American History* (New York: Knopf, 1963).

12. See, for example, Fredrik Barth, *Principles of Social Organization in Southern Kurdistan* (Oslo: Brodrene Jorgensen, 1953).

13. For a comprehensive look at this subject, see J. H. Parry, *Trade and Dominion* (London: Weidenfeld and Nicolson, 1971). Also see John Strachey, *The End of Empire* (London: Gollancz, 1959).

14. This is done badly by Felix Greene, *The Enemy* (London: Cape, 1970), and far better by Harry Magdoff, *The Age of Imperialism* (New York: Monthly Review Press, 1969).

15. See the first issue of 1972 of the *Journal of International Affairs,* "The Military Industrial Complex: USSR/USA" (vol. 26). For a good collection of articles, see Sam C. Sarkesian, ed., *The Military Industrial Complex: A Reassessment* (Beverly Hills: Sage, 1972).

16. See particularly Greene, *The Enemy*.

17. Daniel Katz, "Nationalism and Strategies of International Conflict Resolution," in *International Behavior*, ed. Herbert C. Kelman (New York: Holt, Rinehart and Winston, 1965).

18. George Lichtheim, *Imperialism* (New York: Praeger, 1971).

19. See Harold Lamb, *The Crusades* (New York: Doubleday, 1945).

20. See Philip Khuri Hitti, *History of the Arabs*, 6th ed. (New York: St. Martins, 1956), pp. 139–46.

21. Howard Kennedy Beale, *Theodore Roosevelt and the Rise of America to World Power* (Baltimore: Johns Hopkins Press, 1956).

22. Barth, *Principles of Social Organization*, pp. 114–17.

23. George Vernadsky, *A History of Russia* (New Haven: Yale University Press, 1930), chap. 10; Alexander Kornilov, *Modern Russian History* (New York: Knopf, 1943), chap. 36.

24. See Glyndwr Williams, *The Expansion of Europe in the Eighteenth Century* (New York: Walker, 1966). Also see Ronald Robinson and John Gallagher with Alice Denny, *Africa and the Victorians* (New York: St. Martins Press, 1961).

25. "The White Man's Burden," published in the *London Times*, February 4, 1899.

26. Raymond F. Betts, Assimilation and Association in French Colonial Theory (New York: Columbia University Press, 1961).

27. Max Cary, *The Legacy of Alexander* (New York: Dial, 1932).

28. See in particular the use of such terms as "development" and "decay" in Samuel Huntington, "Political Development and Political Decay," *World Politics*, 17 (April 1965):386–430.

29. Robinson and Gallagher, *Africa and the Victorians*.

30. See the three "objects of support"—political community, regime, and authorities—in David Easton, *A System Analysis of Political Life* (New York: Wiley, 1965), pp. 153–219.

31. Barry Goldwater, *Why Not Victory?* (New York: McGraw-Hill, 1962).

32. Case studies would be helpful for identifying what the image might be at various points along a line or in cells in a quadrant.

33. Erich Fromm, *May Man Prevail* (Garden City, N.Y.: Doubleday, 1961).

Chapter 4. Perception

1. Hans Morgenthau, *Politics Among Nations*, 4th ed. (New York: Knopf, 1966), pp. 61–65.

2. Richard Snyder, *Foreign Policy Decision Making* (New York: Free Press, 1967).

3. Snyder, *Foreign Policy Decision Making*, develops the outlines of a frame within which bureaucratic roles can be examined. Graham Allison, *The Essence of Decision* (Boston: Little, Brown, 1971), deals as well with role determinants of bureaucratic behavior. For a case study addressed implicitly to the question of role determinants, see Robert J. Art, *The TFX Decision* (Boston: Little, Brown, 1968).

4. Despite a great many highly suggestive articles concerning foreign policy attitudes and based on survey research data, major revisions to overall assessments of the role of the public in foreign policy have not been made. An example of interesting essays on foreign policy attitudes is John E. Mueller, "Trends in Popular Support for Wars in Korea and Vietnam," *American Political Science Review*, 65 (June 1971):358–75. Kenneth Waltz has some useful observations on the subject in his *Foreign Policy and Democratic Politics* (Boston: Little, Brown, 1967), esp. pp. 274–86. But the basic studies remain Gabriel Almond, *The American People and Foreign Policy* (New York: Praeger, 1960); and James Rosenau, *Public Opinion and Foreign Policy* (New York: Random House, 1961).

5. A strange gap in the literature is a direct look at the impact of nationalism on foreign policy behavior.

6. Bernard C. Cohen, *The Political Process and Foreign Policy: The Making of the Japanese Peace Treaty* (Princeton: Princeton University Press, 1957).

7. Carl Oglesby and Richard Shaull, *Containment and Change* (New York: Macmillan, 1967).

8. In fact, press coverage was slight for so important a conflict, one which Onassis has described as the most serious of his life (Leonard Mosely, *Power Play: Oil in the Middle East* [New York: Random House, 1973], p. 312 n.).

9. There are two general accounts of Mossadegh's overthrow. One, best seen in David Wise and Thomas B. Ross, *The Invisible Government* (New York: Random House, 1964), is based largely on what was probably an official CIA leak to the Harknesses in their series on the CIA in the *Saturday Evening Post* in 1954 (Richard and Gladys Harkness, "Mysterious Doings of CIA," *Saturday Evening Post,* 227 [October 30, November 6, November 13, 1954]:19–21, 34–35, 30). The other, common in the revisionist literature, is simply inferred from the fact of American inroads into Iranian oil production.

10. The entire literature of so-called development deserves a careful look with the question in mind of the role of cultural messianism. In the development-decay dichotomy, the proposition should be explored that situations seen as typifying "decay" were in fact areas of perceived danger from Soviet inroads.

11. Americans for Democratic Action issues annual foreign policy statements on which this discussion is based.

12. This is a major theme of Arab propaganda. See Fayez Sayegh, *Zionist Colonialism in Palestine* (Beirut: Research Center, Palestine Liberation Organization, 1965).

13. For a study of American Zionist activities, see Marshall A. Hershberg, "Ethnic Interest Groups and Foreign Policy" (Ph.D. dissertation, University of Pittsburgh, 1973).

14. Psychological balance theory deals with this phenomenon. See Fritz Heider, *The Psychology of Interpersonal Relations* (New York: Wiley, 1958).

15. Perception is the most central analytic concept for this study. For a bibliographical reference to relevant sources in this conceptual area see Vivian J. Rohri-Wedge and Bryant Wedge, "The Role of Perception in International Politics," *International Studies Newsletter,* 1 (Fall 1973). As developed here, however, balance theory (Heider, *Psychology of Interpersonal Relations)* and cognitive consistency and cognitive dissonance have been most useful. See, in particular, Leon Festinger, *A Theory of Cognitive Dissonance* (Stanford: Stanford University Press, 1966); and Charles E. Osgood, George J. Suci, and Percy Tannenbaum, *The Measurement of Meaning* (Urbana: University of Illinois Press, 1957). Ralph White's articles on Vietnam (for example, "Misperception and the Vietnam War," *Journal of Social Issues,* 21 [1966]:103–22) and on the Soviet Union ("Images in the Context of International Conflict: Soviet Perceptions of the U.S. and the USSR," in Herbert C. Kelman, ed., *International Behavior* [New York: Holt, Rinehart and Winston, 1965]), are useful early translations of this focus in political literature. Kelman's book, especially his own essays, must be considered ground-breaking in this area. The essays of Ole Holsti, Dina Zinnes, Robert North, and Richard Brody in David Singer's *Quantitative International Politics* (New York: Free Press, 1968) are important for this approach. See also Ole R. Holsti, *Crisis, Escalation, War* (Montreal: McGill-Queens University Press, 1972); David J. Finlay, Ole R. Holsti, and Richard R. Fagen, *Enemies in Politics* (Chicago: Rand McNally, 1967); Robert Jervis, "Hypotheses on Misperception," *World Politics,* 20 (April 1968):454–79; Robert Jervis, *The Logic of Images in International Relations* (Princeton: Princeton University Press, 1970); J. G. Stoessinger, *Nations in Darkness: China, Russia and America* (New York: Random House, 1965); Kenneth Boulding, *The Image* (Ann Arbor: University of Michigan Press, 1956); Otto Klineberg, *The Human Dimension in International Relations* (New York: Holt, Rinehart, and Winston, 1964); and Erving Goffman, *Strategic Interaction* (Philadelphia: University of Pennsylvania Press, 1969). Issue no. 4, 1972, of *Daedalus* is devoted to the theme "How Others See the United States." The articles included are symptomatic of the lack of formal development in the approach.

16. Morgenthau, *Politics Among Nations,* pp. 235–49.

17. Milton Rokeach, *Beliefs, Attitudes and Values: A Theory of Organization and Change* (San

Francisco: Jossey Bass, 1968); and idem, *Nature of Human Values* (New York: Free Press, 1973).

18. Rupert Emerson, *From Empire to Nation* (Cambridge: Harvard University Press, 1960), p. 95.

19. Perception of threat and perception of opportunity are foci that serve the same analytic function in this question area as do the deprivation and gratifications foci for the much broader question with which Talcott Parsons is concerned. See Talcott Parsons and Edward Shils, eds., *Toward a General Theory of Action* (Cambridge: Harvard University Press, 1951).

20. This is a paraphrase of Kissinger's picture of the interaction.

21. Most usage of the term "WOG" is on a level of the American term "gook" and carries an implicit gross contempt. The "westernized Oriental gentleman" usage was one I found among the British in Iran in 1951–1952, the time of the quarrel with Iran over the nationalization of oil. With that usage there is exactly the right tone, respectable but not quite British, for the imagery and the imperial ideal type.

22. Archibald Paton Thornton, *The Imperial Idea and Its Enemies* (New York: St. Martins Press, 1959).

23. For a description of this "hidden hand" notion, see Richard Cottam, *Nationalism in Iran* (Pittsburgh: University of Pittsburgh Press, 1964).

24. Adam Ulam skillfully places the changing images of Tito in a setting perspective in his *Titoism and the Cominform* (Cambridge: Harvard University Press, 1952). He does the same for changing images in the Soviet setting in *The New Face of Soviet Totalitarianism* (Cambridge: Harvard University Press, 1963).

25. For a typically adulatory article, see *Time,* December 8, 1958, pp. 24–25.

26. *Time* describes Mossadegh differently depending on the period. In 1952 Mossadegh was the man of the year. The accompanying article was clearly hostile yet recognized Mossadegh's importance as a leader of a Third World country nationalism (January 7, 1952, pp. 18–21). After Mossadegh's overthrow and the consolidation of the shah's dictatorship, the mid-Cold War *Time* dismissal terms for Mossadegh were "fanatical, disastrous" (April 18, 1955, p. 42), "tear spouting" (September 8, 1958, p. 26), and "weepy, old" (June 9, 1961, p. 23). Then, as the Cold War waned, he became a "crusty old nationalist" (October 6, 1967, p. 32).

27. *New York Times,* August 9, 1953, sec. 4, p. 2; August 15, 1953, p. 14.

28. *New York Times,* January 28, 1963, p. 12; February 7, 1963, p. 6.

29. See the account in Marvin Zonis, *The Political Elite of Iran* (Princeton: Princeton University Press, 1971), pp. 65–66.

30. *New York Times,* May 12, 1957, sec. 4, p. 10: "This is a moment in which all who value the ideals of democracy and freedom can rejoice."

31. *New York Times,* April 26, 1957, ed. p. 24: "King Hossein in his brave struggle to control has made Jordan a symbol of what we consider necessary in the Middle East—independence, territorial integrity, freedom, sovereignty and no communist control."

32. This is in tune with the operating definition of Karl Mannheim, *Ideology and Utopia* (London: Routledge and Kegan Paul, 1935).

33. See Riley William Gilmore, "The American Foreign Policymaking Process and the Development of Post World II Spanish Policy, 1945–1953" (Ph.D. dissertation, University of Pittsburgh, 1967).

34. See Ole Holsti, "Cognitive Dynamics and Images of the Enemy: Dulles and Russia," in Finlay, Holsti, and Fagen, *Enemies in Politics,* pp. 25–96.

35. See John Bird, "The Miseries of Elder Benson," *Saturday Evening Post,* December 21, 1957, p. 19. The reference to Benson by his priestly title "elder" reflects the view that Secretary Benson, an apostle of the Church of Jesus Christ of Latter Day Saints, brought unity to his political and religious thinking.

36. See the conclusion for further development of his point.

37. Nixon's acceptance speech, Republican National Convention, Miami, August 8, 1968.

Chapter 5. Systems of Aims

1. Examples of underground publications are: *Khabar Nameh, Mojahed, Bakhtar Emruz,* and *Iran Azad.*

2. Morton A. Kaplan, *System and Process in International Politics* (New York: Wiley, 1957).

3. Kaplan, *System and Process,* p. 149. Kaplan says, "It is impossible to determine satisfactorily, within varying margins of error, what a system values, that is, the objectives of a system."

4. The definition of value closest to the one employed here is: "Normative standards by which human beings are influenced in their choice among the alternative courses of action which they perceive" (Philip E. Jacob and J. F. Flink with Hedva L. Shuchman, "Values and Their Functioning in Decision Making," *American Behavioral Scientist,* 5, no. 9, supp. [May 1962], pp. 6–34). The difference is in the reference to "normative standards." My preference is to define the choice pattern as "value" rather than that which predisposes the individual toward following the choice pattern. If the predispositional base is thought of as needs, many of which are nonconscious, the reductionist path would be in the direction of a need typology such as that provided by Abraham Maslow in *Motivation and Personality,* 2d ed. (New York: Harper, 1970). The difficulties and promise of such a focus in political science are apparent in Robert Lane's *Political Thinking and Consciousness* (Chicago: Markham, 1969). Jacob's later definition substitutes "principles" for "normative standards," but the reification problems are if anything more manifest. See Philip Jacob et al., *Values and the Active Community* (New York: Free Press, 1971), pp. 3–4.

5. Capability self-image is an essential aspect—but only one aspect—of an overall capability paradigm. For any dyadic relationship that paradigm should include, in addition to a capability self-image representation, representations for power potential, direct power manifestations, alter's image of capability, and bargaining system.

6. See Gabriel Almond, *The American People and Foreign Policy* (New York: Praeger, 1960). Subsequently, I have come to believe that the rhythm is somewhat different. Change is first accommodated at a specific policy level and much later at a general policy level. It may in fact be accommodated verbally before it is accommodated on the broadest decisional level.

7. This case is largely taken from my own reading of verbal behavior and policy choices in the area. A reader interested in the subject can get a picture of the setting and many of the events from Miles Copeland, *The Game of Nations* (New York: Simon and Schuster, 1970); Patrick Seale, *The Struggle for Syria* (New York: Oxford University Press, 1965); and Malcolm Kerr, *The Arab Cold War, 1958–1967,* 2d ed. (New York: Oxford University Press, 1967).

8. For some material on this episode see Charles Wheeler Thayer, *Diplomat* (New York: Harper, 1959); John S. Badeau, *The American Approach to the Arab World* (New York: Harper and Row, 1968); and Robert D. Murphy, *Diplomat Among Warriors* (New York: Doubleday, 1964).

9. A good illustration of this appears in Thomas Schelling, *Arms and Influence* (New Haven: Yale University Press, 1960), pp. 49, 52, 94. Schelling's writings are subject to the charge of being apolitical. This is a case in point. Writing years later, he continues to give an orthodox Cold War interpretation of this episode.

10. Townsend Hoopes, *The Limits of Intervention* (New York: D. McKay Co., 1969), p. 224.

11. George A. Liska, *Imperial America* (Baltimore: Johns Hopkins Press, 1967).

12. Herbert Hoover's address to the Republican National Convention in 1948 (*New York Times,* June 23, 1948, p. 8) was a brief but persuasive statement later to be billed as his Fortress America speech. Its persuasive quality makes all the more mysterious the lack of a broader appeal.

13. "Mr. X" [George Kennan], "Sources of Soviet Conduct," *Foreign Affairs,* 25 (July 1947):566–82.

14. James Forrestal, *The Forrestal Diaries,* ed. Walter Millis (New York: Viking, 1951).

15. For an account of the speedy assimilation patterns for both Christian and Moslem Arab-Americans, see Abdo A. Elkholy, *The Arab Moslems in the United States* (New Haven: College and University Press, 1966).

16. With further study I have concluded that the metaphoric translations given world views add to their durability. See my unpublished paper, "The Cold War Metaphor and Oil Diplomacy," presented at the International Studies Association Conference, February 1975.

17. The list of American Black politicians, including Stokes, who signed a pro-Israeli newspaper advertisement in 1971 reads like a Who's Who in Black politics.

18. Mobil and Standard of California published advertisements in 1973 that at least implied a foreign policy position preference.

19. During the month of Black September, 1970, the Soviet Union's response to vigorous American activity was on the surface passive.

20. William A. Gamson and André Modigliani, *Untangling the Cold War* (Boston: Little, Brown, 1971).

21. See my development of this subject in *Competitive Interference and Twentieth Century Diplomacy* (Pittsburgh: University of Pittsburgh Press, 1967), pp. 139–53, 189–203.

22. See part III for a further development of this theme.

Chapter 6. America in Vietnam

1. See text of U Thant's speech to this effect, *New York Times,* February 25, 1968, p. 24.

2. Townsend Hoopes, *The Limits of Intervention* (New York: D. McKay Co., 1969), p. 225.

3. For the text of the foreign policy statement see Myron Rush, *The International Situation and Soviet Foreign Policy* (Columbus, Ohio: Merrill, 1970), pp. 250–70. That this was in fact anything but a departure in Soviet foreign policy is a contention of Adam Ulam in *Expansion and Coexistence* (New York: Praeger, 1968).

4. For a good illustration of this, see Marshall D. Shulman, *Stalin's Foreign Policy Reappraised* (Cambridge: Harvard University Press, 1963).

5. See, for illustrations, Hoopes, *Limits of Intervention,* pp. 16–17. For textual verification see *The Pentagon Pagers,* ed. Senator Mike Gravel (Boston: Beacon Press, 1971–72).

6. For a well-articulated statement of this view, see Carl Oglesby and Richard Shaull, *Containment and Change* (New York: Macmillan, 1967).

7. See in particular the reporting of David Halberstam in the *New York Times.* The essence of these reports is included in David Halberstam, *The Best and the Brightest* (New York: Random House, 1972).

8. Pentagon Papers, vol. III, pp. 57–105, 511–55.

9. This is well argued in Halberstam, *Best and Brightest.*

10. Herman Kahn, *Thinking About the Unthinkable* (New York: Discuss Books, 1968).

11. William W. Kaufmann, *The McNamara Strategy* (New York: Harper and Row, 1964).

12. Thomas Schelling, *Arms and Influence* (New Haven: Yale University Press, 1960), pp. 69 ff.

13. See, for example, Barry Goldwater, *Why Not Victory?* (New York: McGraw Hill, 1962), pp. 49–50.

14. Since the Vietnamese conflict had become a multibillion dollar operation, its impact on the American economy and especially on defense industry was very great. It could be argued, therefore, that although there was nothing comparable to the vast oil investments in the Middle East, the economic implications of the Vietnam conflict were even greater. Indeed, writers of the left such as Carl Oglesby regard as self-evident the notion that the military-industrial complex thus became the prime determinant of policy.

The notion that the defense industry would act in a highly rational and monolithic fashion is in line with the most commonly noted pattern in this study. The left's perception of the domestic decisional process is in every respect parallel to the enemy image outlined above. Indeed, the parallel holds further. Perception of opportunity for continued expansion of American influence abroad and perception of great threat to the military-industrial establishment should the conflict in Vietnam be settled are assumed to exist. Empirical testing of these assumptions may be minimal, but that too is in line with behavior based on an enemy image. There was, after all, very little empirical testing of the Soviet monolith notion by American scholars in the 1960s.

The less process-oriented revisionist writers tend to see a great hidden hand directing American policy. The lack of empirical data supporting this notion is no proof that it is incorrect. The informality of the process inhibits empirical investigation. However, the proposition accepted here is that interest groups behave very much as nations do. The focus of concern is likely to be on specifics for both. Therefore, it is inevitable that a centralized oil industry with enormous investments in the Middle East would indeed perceive serious threat both in the Arab-Israeli conflict and in the growth of a social revolutionary Arab nationalist movement. Similarly, that industry is likely to perceive great opportunity associated with accommodationist Arab regimes such as those of Kings Faisal, Hossein, and Idris. That their perceptions in turn would color their entire situational view is only to be expected. It does not follow that big steel, which would suffer serious dislocations were defense-related contracts to be cut, would behave similarly toward the situation in Vietnam. On the contrary, those who expect big steel to behave in this manner grant to the steel bureaucrats truly extraordinary powers of rationality.

The expectation flowing from this proposition is that the steel bureaucracy would indeed be influenced, as are all others, in their perceptions of conflict by their vested interests. Thus, perception of opportunity for increased sales domestically and in foreign markets for a wide variety of customers would be accommodated to the world view. But the demands of those interests are most unlikely to result in a single broad perceptual pattern. The Vietnam situation would be likely to have vested-interest implications when severe reductions in defense spending for material relating to steel were involved. At that point the steel bureaucracy might very well find persuasive a picture of a highly aggressive international communist foe. But my conclusion is that until such a point is reached, the perceptions of the steel bureaucracy would vary sharply with each individual's ideological and nationalist predisposition and that there would not be a vested-interest crystallization of perceptions comparable to that of the oil bureaucracy concerned with the Middle East. The section of the defense industry most sensitive to the Vietnam conflict should be those under direct contract for producing war material. Here the vested-interest crystallization would presumably occur, and a perceptual response parallel to that of the military bureaucratic customers would be expected. But in the sum of American industry, this is a relatively minor element. And even there, if an industry under contract with the Defense Department also is attracted to the possibility of exporting increasing amounts of other products to Eastern Europe, the perceptual accommodation of the two interests would be unlikely to take the form of perceived intense threat from the Soviet Union. More likely, contradictory perceptions of the enemy would be neatly compartmentalized in the two areas.

15. For the Pittsburgh area peace movement, see Arnold H. Miller, "Perceptions and Recommendations of the Vietnam Peace Movement: A Case Study of Activists in Pittsburgh" (Ph.D. dissertation, University of Pittsburgh, 1969).

16. See President Johnson's remarks at a press conference, *New York Times,* November 2, 1967, p. 1.

17. This is well illustrated in Seymour Martin Lipset, "Doves, Hawks and Polls," *Encounter,* 27 (October 1966):38–45. See also Robert B. Smith, "Disaffection, Delegitimation and Consequences: Aggregate Trends for World War II, Korea and Vietnam," in *Public Opinion and the Military Establishment,* ed. Charles C. Moskos, Jr. (Beverly Hills: Sage, 1971).

18. See verbal evidence to this effect in William Zimmerman, *Soviet Perspectives on International Politics* (Princeton: Princeton University Press, 1969), pp. 229–41.

19. Miller, "Perceptions and Recommendations."

20. My survey of the *New York Times* Bantam edition of the Pentagon Papers indicated this shift. At the time of writing, Dorothy Donnelly at the University of Pittsburgh is making a careful survey of all documents in the Pentagon Papers to test this assertion.

21. Thomas Schelling, *The Strategy of Conflict* (Cambridge: Harvard University Press, 1960), pp. 24 ff.

22. The "Johnson doctrine" generally refers to the policy implicit in the "Declaration of Peace and Progress in Asia and the Pacific" at the Manila Conference in October 1966. For Johnson's own view of this, see Lyndon Baines Johnson, *The Vantage Point* (New York: Holt, Rinehart and Winston, 1971), p. 249.

23. It is difficult to make a strong case for or against electoral punishment or reward because of a candidate's Vietnam views.

24. J. William Fulbright, *Arrogance of Power* (New York: Random House, 1966). See McGovern's basic speech on Vietnam, *New York Times,* April 26, 1967, p. 9.

25. See text, *New York Times,* August 30, 1968, p. 17.

26. General Clay advocated sending an armored convoy through the blockade. See Eric Morris, *Blockade* (London: Hamish Hamilton, 1973), p. 97.

27. According to Sorensen this view had very little inside support, possibly that of only one member of the inner group. There was a good deal of outside support, however. An air strike had many more supporters, including Senator J. William Fulbright (Theodore C. Sorensen, *Kennedy* [New York: Harper and Row, 1965], pp. 667–718).

28. Henry Kissinger, *Nuclear Weapons and Foreign Policy* (New York: Doubleday, 1958).

Chapter 7. The Case Illustration in Historical Perspective

1. This is discussed in many of the works previously cited, especially Ronald Robinson and John Gallagher with Alice Denny, *Africa and the Victorians* (New York: St. Martins Press, 1961); and Archibald Paton Thornton, *The Imperial Idea and Its Enemies* (New York: St. Martins Press, 1959). See as well what is probably the best modern biography of Gladstone, Philip Magnus, *Gladstone* (London: J. Murray, 1954).

2. A study that describes well the entire panorama of Egypt's history is yet to be written. H. Wood Jarvis, *Pharaoh to Farouk* (London: J. Murray, 1955), for example, is not a serious effort to describe historical evolution. For background to this period, three works are easily read and useful: Tom Little, *Egypt* (New York: Praeger, 1958); John Marlowe, *A History of Modern Egypt and Anglo-Egyptian Relations, 1800–1953* (New York: Praeger, 1954); and Elizabeth Monroe, *Britain's Moment in the Middle East, 1914–1956* (London: Chatto & Windus Ltd., 1963). For a good history of Egypt see P. J. Vatikiotis, *The Modern History of Egypt* (New York: Praeger, 1967).

3. See, for example, Alfred Milner, *England in Egypt,* 5th ed. (London: E. Arnold, 1894), p. 73. For an excellent biography of Milner, see Edward Crankshaw, *The Forsaken Idea: A Study of Viscount Milner* (New York: Longmans, Green, 1952).

4. See Evelyn Baring, First Earl of Cromer, *Modern Egypt,* 2 vols. (New York: Macmillan, 1908); also his *Political and Literary Essays* (London: Macmillan, 1913); Milner, *England in Egypt;* Wilfrid Scawen Blunt, *Secret History of the English Occupation of Egypt* (New York: H. Fertig, 1967); also his *My Diaries* (London: Martin Secker, 1932).

5. Blunt, *Secret History,* pp. 318–21.

6. See chapter 4 for a full discussion of these points.

7. Morton A. Kaplan, *System and Process in International Politics* (New York: Wiley, 1957), p. 9.

8. Stanley Hoffmann, *Contemporary Theory in International Relations* (Englewood Cliffs, N.J.: Prentice Hall, 1960), p. 48.

Chapter 8. Fall 1876

1. See Henry Herbert Dodwell, *The Founder of Modern Egypt: A Study of Muhammad Ali* (Cambridge: Cambridge University Press, 1931).

2. For a remarkably good study see David Landes, *Bankers and Pashas* (Cambridge: Harvard University Press, 1958).

3. A. E. Crouchley, *The Economic Development of Modern Egypt,* pp. 137, 225, quoted in Ronald Robinson and John Gallagher with Alice Denny, *Africa and the Victorians* (New York: St. Martins Press, 1961), p. 81.

4. See John Pudney, *Suez: De Lesseps' Canal* (New York: Praeger, 1969), for a brief but inclusive history of Suez.

5. A. J. P. Taylor, *The Struggle for Mastery in Europe, 1848–1918* (Oxford: Clarendon Press, 1954), p. 235.

6. Lord Derby, letter to Lord Lyons, ibid., p. 233.

7. Taylor, *Struggle for Mastery,* p. 226.

8. Ibid.

9. Robinson and Gallagher, *Africa and the Victorians,* p. 83.

10. "Britain and the Eastern Question." The argument can be found in G. T. Garratt, *The Two Mr. Gladstones* (New York: Macmillan, 1936), pp. 141–69.

11. Taylor, *Struggle for Mastery,* p. 241.

12. Ibid., p. 235.

13. Robinson and Gallagher, *Africa and the Victorians,* p. 10.

14. Ibid., p. 8.

15. Vivian to Derby, February 18, 1877, *British State Papers,* vol. 68, p. 208.

16. For an excellent biography of Disraeli which makes this behavior comprehensible, see Robert Blake, *Disraeli* (New York: St. Martins Press, 1967).

17. Hansard, vol. 227, February 21, 1876, p. 586.

18. Ibid., p. 618.

19. Ibid., p. 638.

20. Derby to Lyons, March 25, 1876, *British State Papers,* vol. 70, p. 913.

21. Derby to Lyons, February 19, 1876, ibid., p. 897.

22. Hansard, vol. 231, August 5, 1876, p. 642.

23. Derby to Lyons, February 19, 1876, *British State Papers,* vol. 70, pp. 897–98.

24. Hansard, vol. 231, August 5, 1876, p. 617.

25. *London Times,* February 14, 1876, p. 10a.

26. Ibid., April 25, 1876, p. 8d.

27. Ibid., December 6, 1875, p. 6b.

28. Ibid., April 1, 1876, p. 7b.

29. Ibid., February 1, 1876, p. 6a.

30. Ibid., August 25, 1876, p. 8d.

31. Ibid., April 4, 1876, p. 10f; also Hansard, vol. 231, August 5, 1876, pp. 619–26.

32. *London Times,* November 21, 1876, p. 7a.

33. Ibid.

34. Ibid.

35. Ibid.

36. Ibid.

37. Ibid., April 10, 1876, p. 6f. May 10, 1876, p. 11c. This included a review of the British press.

38. Lyons to Derby, March 23, 1876, *British State Papers,* vol. 70, p. 912.

39. Derby to Cookson, August 2, 1876, ibid., p. 939.

40. Vivian to Derby, October 15, 1876, ibid., p. 939.

41. *London Times,* November 29, 1876, p. 7f.

42. See the discussion on a definition of imperialism in chapter 2.

43. This was made clear in the course of the Midlothian campaign; see Philip Magnus, *Gladstone* (London: J. Murray, 1954), pp. 259–327.

44. Vivian to Salisbury, August 22, 1878, *British State Papers,* vol. 70, p. 1006.

45. Vivian to Salisbury, August 22, 1878, ibid., p. 991.

46. Salisbury to Vivian, December 2, 1878, ibid., p. 1006.

47. Vivian to Salisbury, January 11, 1879, ibid., p. 1016.

48. Wilfrid Scawen Blunt, *Secret History of the English Occupation of Egypt* (New York: H. Fertig, 1967), p. 37.

49. John Marlowe, *A History of Modern Egypt and Anglo-Egyptian Relations, 1800–1953* (New York: Praeger, 1954), has a differential picture of Egyptian oppositionists similar to this (pp. 112–13).

50. Vivian to Salisbury, February 19, 1879, *British State Papers,* vol. 70, p. 1072.

51. Vivian to Salisbury, February 22, 1879, ibid., pp. 1031–32.

52. Vivian to Salisbury, February 26, 1879, ibid., p. 1036.

53. Lascelles to Salisbury, April 4, 1879, ibid., p. 1054.

54. Lascelles to Salisbury, April 7, 1879, ibid., p. 1057.

55. Salisbury to Vivian, April 25, 1879, ibid., p. 1074.

56. Vivian to Salisbury, May 19, 1879, ibid., p. 1081.

57. Hansard, vol. 331, August 5, 1876, p. 642.

Chapter 9. Summer 1882

1. For a penetrating analysis of identity change in modern Egypt, see Nadav Safran, *Egypt in Search of Political Community* (Cambridge: Harvard University Press, 1961).

2. John Marlowe, *Cromer in Egypt* (New York: Praeger, 1970), p. 62.

3. See, for example, A. J. P. Taylor, *The Struggle for Mastery in Europe, 1848–1918* (Oxford: Clarendon Press, 1954), pp. 288–89.

4. Cookson to Granville, September 10, 1881, *British State Papers,* vol. 73, pp. 1133, 1134.

5. Malet to Granville, September 23, 1881, ibid., p. 1145.

6. Note that the ministers were predominantly Turkish-speaking. Cited in Evelyn Baring, First Earl of Cromer, *Modern Egypt,* vol. 1. (New York: Macmillan, 1908), p. 207.

7. Ibid., p. 208.

8. Sir Auckland Colvin, *The Making of Modern Egypt* (London: Seely, 1906).

9. Marlowe, *Cromer in Egypt,* p. 60. This quote from Marlowe is fully in tune with contemporary British comments.

10. Granville to Malet, January 6, 1882, *British State Papers,* vol. 74, p. 367.

11. Cromer, *Modern Egypt,* vol. 1, pp. 214–53, esp. p. 251. Quotation from pp. 228–29.

12. *London Times,* January 20, 1882, p. 3a; January 24, 1882, p. 9a.

13. Ibid., January 3, 1882, p. 4e.

14. See the *London Times* for the period. Their Cairo correspondent quoted such men endlessly.

15. Granville to Lyons, January 30, 1882, *British State Papers,* vol. 74, p. 378.

16. Lyons to Granville, February 3, 1882, ibid., p. 380; April 29, 1882, ibid., p. 391.

17. Malet to Granville, May 2, 1882, ibid., p. 398.

18. Ibid., pp. 398–99.

19. Lyons to Granville, May 11, 1882, ibid., p. 401.

20. Granville to Lyons, May 11, 1882, ibid., p. 402.

21. Marlowe, *Cromer in Egypt,* p. 61.

22. Malet to Granville, May 15, 1882, *British State Papers,* vol. 74, p. 408.

23. Malet to Granville, May 23, 1882, ibid., p. 417.

24. Ibid.

25. Malet to Granville, May 28, 1882, ibid., p. 426.

26. Granville to Lyons, May 26, 1882, ibid., p. 423.

27. Lyons to Granville, May 30, 1882, ibid., p. 428.

28. Granville to Dufferin, June 2, 1882, ibid., p. 430.

29. Granville to Dufferin, June 6, 1882, ibid., p. 437; June 21, 1882, ibid., pp. 457–58.

30. Malet to Granville, June 21, 1882, ibid., p. 435.

31. Marlowe likes the figure of three hundred Europeans killed, but the acting British agent reported fifty. Marlowe, *Cromer in Egypt,* p. 62; Colvert to Granville, June 11, 1882, *British State Papers,* vol. 74, p. 439.

32. Granville to Lyons, June 12, 1882, ibid., p. 440.

33. Granville to Lyons, July 4, 1882, ibid., p. 479.

34. Ronald Robinson and John Gallagher with Alice Denny, *Africa and the Victorians* (New York: St. Martins Press, 1961), p. 110.

35. Ibid., pp. 116–19.

36. Taylor, *Struggle for Mastery,* p. 250.

37. W. N. Medlicott, *Bismarck, Gladstone and the Concert of Europe* (London: Athlone Press, 1956), p. 30.

38. Ibid., pp. 29–31.

39. Robinson and Gallagher, *Africa and the Victorians,* p. 91.

40. Taylor, *Struggle for Mastery,* p. 284.

41. Ibid., p. 268.

42. See pp. 163–64.

43. *London Times,* January 14, 1882, p. 8c.

44. Ibid., May 11, 1882, p. 9e.

45. Ibid., May 22, 1882, p. 7c.

46. Ibid.

47. Ibid., June 16, 1882, p. 5a.

48. Ibid., June 12, 1882, p. 5b.

49. Ibid., June 20, 1882, p. 5a.

50. Ibid., July 7, 1882, p. 5a.

51. Ibid., July 17, 1882, p. 5b.

52. Ibid.

53. Marlowe, *Cromer in Egypt,* p. 53.

54. Robert L. Tignor, *Modernization and British Colonial Rule in Egypt, 1882–1914* (Princeton: Princeton University Press, 1966). This is first-rate scholarship but a very sober book.

55. Wilfrid Scawen Blunt, *Secret History of the English Occupation of Egypt* (New York: H. Fertig, 1967), pp. 186–93.

56. Actually a number of biographers have been fascinated by this peculiarly British phenomenon. One, I believe, does the justice possible in a brief sketch: Thomas Assad, *Three Victorian Travellers* (London: Routledge, Kegan Paul, 1964). Blunt is included in Shane Leslie, *Men Were Different: Five Studies in Late Victorian Biography,* reprint ed. (Freeport, N.Y.: Library Press, 1967). A noninterpretive but detailed biography is Edith Finch, *Wilfrid Scawen Blunt, 1840–1922* (London: Jonathan Cape, 1938). Apparently his family was scandalized by his infidelities, and that theme preoccupies his grandson, Noel Anthony Scawen Lytton, Earl of Lytton, *Wilfrid Scawen Blunt* (London: Macdonald, 1961).

57. Blunt, *Secret History,* p. 106.

58. Ibid., p. 110.

59. Ibid., pp. 116–17.

60. Ibid., p. 139.

61. Ibid., p. 143.

62. Ibid., p. 145.

63. Ibid.

64. Ibid., p. 156.

65. Ibid., p. 211.
66. Ibid., p. 201.
67. Ibid., p. 300.
68. Colvin, *Making of Modern Egypt,* pp. 10, 14, 15.
69. Ibid., pp. 11, 12, 15.
70. Blunt, *Secret History,* p. 249.
71. Alfred Milner, *England in Egypt,* 5th ed. (London: E. Arnold, 1894), p. 16.
72. Ibid., p. 21.
73. Cromer, *Modern Egypt,* vol. 1, pp. 325–27.
74. Ibid., p. 226.
75. Ibid., p. 250.
76. Ibid., p. 247.
77. Ibid., p. 255.
78. Ibid., p. 263.
79. Ibid., p. 330.
80. *London Times,* February 3, 1882, p. 3b.
81. Ibid., p. 9b.
82. Ibid., May 30, 1882, p. 7a.
83. Ibid., June 12, 1882, p. 9b.
84. Ibid.
85. Ibid., June 20, 1882, p. 9d.
86. Hansard, vol. 267, March 13, 1882, p. 769.
87. Ibid., vol. 269, May 26, 1882, p. 1731.
88. Ibid., vol. 270, Lords, June 15, 1882, p. 1220.
89. Ibid., vol. 269, May 26, 1882, p. 1722.
90. Robinson and Gallagher, *Africa and the Victorians,* p. 91.
91. Ibid., p. 92.
92. Ibid., p. 97.
93. Hansard, vol. 269, June 1, 1882, p. 1781.
94. Robinson and Gallagher, *Africa and the Victorians,* p. 110.
95. Blunt, *Secret History,* p. 283.
96. Robinson and Gallagher, *Africa and the Victorians,* p. 109; Cromer, *Modern Egypt,* vol. 1, pp. 292–93.
97. *London Times,* June 10, 1882, p. 7b.
98. Cromer, *Modern Egypt,* vol. 1, p. 313.
99. Robinson and Gallagher, *Africa and the Victorians,* p. 104.
100. Cromer, *Modern Egypt,* vol. 1, p. 180.
101. Robinson and Gallagher, *Africa and the Victorians,* p. 106.
102. Ibid., pp. 110–19.
103. Afaf Lutfi al-Sayyid, *Egypt and Cromer: A Study in Anglo-Egyptian Relations* (New York: Praeger, 1968), p. 25. The quote is from Paul Knaplund, *Gladstone's Foreign Policy* (New York: Harper, 1935), p. 183.
104. Blunt, *Secret History,* p. 277.
105. *London Times,* June 29, 1882, p. 5a.
106. Ibid., July 7, 1882, p. 5a.
107. Robinson and Gallagher, *Africa and the Victorians,* p. 122.
108. Ibid., p. 125.
109. Cromer, *Modern Egypt,* vol. 1, p. 340.
110. Ibid., p. 341.

Chapter 10. Summer 1887

1. For an explication of official objectives see John Marlowe, *Cromer in Egypt* (New York: Praeger, 1970), pp. 69–75.

2. Evelyn Baring, First Earl of Cromer, *Modern Egypt* (New York: Macmillan, 1908), vol. 1, pp. 349–592; vol. 2, pp. 3–111.

3. Ibid., vol. 1, pp. 454–60.

4. Ibid., pp. 581–82.

5. Throughout the debates on Egyptian policy reported in Hansard, there are references to the influence French bondholders exert on French policy but no real verbal defense of the interests of British bondholders.

6. Sir Auckland Colvin, *The Making of Modern Egypt* (London: Seely, 1906), pp. 95–107.

7. Alfred Milner, *England in Egypt,* 5th ed. (London: E. Arnold, 1894), pp. 271–323.

8. Ibid., pp. 169–210.

9. Marlowe, *Cromer in Egypt,* pp. 97–99; Milner, *England in Egypt*, pp. 108–15; Colvin, *Making of Modern Egypt,* pp. 196–200.

10. Ronald Robinson and John Gallagher with Alice Denny, *Africa and the Victorians* (New York: St. Martins Press, 1961), pp. 160–209.

11. Ibid., pp. 142–55.

12. *London Times,* January 8, 1887, p. 5b.

13. For example, ibid., July 1, 1887, p. 5a; July 18, 1887, p. 5a; August 1, 1887, p. 3b; August 2, 1887, p. 3a.

14. A. J. P. Taylor, *The Struggle for Mastery in Europe, 1848–1918* (Oxford: Clarendon Press, 1954), p. 314.

15. Ibid.

16. Robinson and Gallagher, *Africa and the Victorians,* p. 265.

17. *London Times,* February 18, 1887, p. 5e.

18. Ibid., February 19, 1887, p. 7c.

19. Ibid., February 11, 1887, p. 5b.

20. Ibid., May 5, 1887, p. 5a.

21. Ibid., May 13, 1887, p. 5c.

22. Ibid., July 18, 1887, p. 5b.

23. Milner, *England in Egypt,* p. 152; Colvin, *Making of Modern Egypt*, p. 158; Cromer, *Modern Egypt,* vol. 2, p. 380.

24. *London Times,* July 14, 1887, p. 9e.

25. Ibid., July 18, 1887, p. 9b.

26. Hansard, vol. 319, August 20, 1887, p. 1292.

27. Ibid., p. 1258.

28. Ibid., pp. 1290–91.

29. Ibid., p. 1264.

30. Ibid., p. 1271.

31. Ibid., p. 1278.

32. Ibid., p. 1297.

33. Ibid., p. 1230.

34. Ibid., p. 1284.

35. Ibid., p. 1317.

36. *London Times,* May 18, 1887, p. 7c.

37. Ibid., August 2, 1887, p. 3a. Also see Hansard, vol. 319, August 20, 1887, p. 1330.

38. *London Times,* July 4, 1887, p. 6b.

39. Ibid., p. 5a.

40. Cromer, *Modern Egypt*, vol. 2, pp. 357–59.

41. See Robinson and Gallagher, *Africa and the Victorians*, pp. 259–65, for a full discussion.

42. *London Times*, July 18, 1887, p. 5a.

Chapter 11. Fall 1914

1. A. J. P. Taylor, *The Struggle for Mastery in Europe, 1848–1918* (Oxford: Clarendon Press, 1954), p. 325; and Ronald Robinson and John Gallagher with Alice Denny, *Africa and the Victorians* (New York: St. Martins Press, 1961), p. 266.

2. As quoted in John Marlowe, *Cromer in Egypt* (New York: Praeger, 1970), p. 137.

3. As quoted ibid., p. 138.

4. Robinson and Gallagher, *Africa and the Victorians*, pp. 272–73.

5. For descriptions of Cromer's view, see Robert L. Tignor, *Modernization and British Colonial Rule in Egypt, 1882–1914* (Princeton: Princeton University Press, 1966), pp. 102–03; Robinson and Gallagher, *Africa and the Victorians*, pp. 274–81; Marlowe, *Cromer in Egypt*, pp. 140–41; and Afaf Lutfi al-Sayyid, *Egypt and Cromer: A Study in Anglo-Egyptian Relations* (New York: Praeger, 1968), pp. 75–77.

6. Al-Sayyid, *Egypt and Cromer*, p. 90.

7. Ibid., p. 77.

8. Robinson and Gallagher, *Africa and the Victorians*, p. 281.

9. Alfred Milner, *England in Egypt*, 5th ed. (London: E. Arnold, 1894), pp. 165, 166, 164–65.

10. Al-Sayyid, *Egypt and Cromer*, p. 91.

11. Evelyn Baring, First Earl of Cromer, *Abbas II* (London: Macmillan, 1915), p. 9.

12. As quoted in Tignor, *Modernization*, p. 156.

13. Ibid., p. 167.

14. Al-Sayyid, *Egypt and Cromer*, pp. 108–09.

15. Cromer, *Abbas II*, p. 11.

16. Al-Sayyid, *Egypt and Cromer*, pp. 98–155. This book is vital for anyone interested in seeing a non-British perspective on this period.

17. Cromer, *Abbas II*, p. 11.

18. Ibid., p. 16.

19. Ibid., p. 24.

20. Ibid., pp. 34, 35.

21. Ibid., pp. 37, 38.

22. Marlowe, *Cromer in Egypt*, p. 164.

23. Al-Sayyid, *Egypt and Cromer*, p. 139.

24. As quoted ibid., p. 140.

25. As quoted in Robinson and Gallagher, *Africa and the Victorians*, p. 343.

26. Ibid., pp. 347, 349.

27. Taylor, *Struggle for Mastery*, p. 359.

28. As quoted ibid., p. 355.

29. Ibid., pp. 346–71.

30. Ibid., p. 353.

31. Ibid., p. 359.

32. Robinson and Gallagher, *Africa and the Victorians*, p. 363.

33. Ibid., p. 371.

34. As quoted ibid., p. 372.

35. As quoted ibid., p. 374.

36. Marlowe, *Cromer in Egypt*.

37. Milner, *England in Egypt*, p. 391.

38. Al-Sayyid, *Egypt and Cromer*, p. 182.

39. Wilfrid Scawen Blunt, *My Diaries* (London: Martin Secker, 1932), pts. 1 and 2.

40. Al-Sayyid, *Egypt and Cromer*, pp. 96–97.

41. Ibid., p. 159.

42. Ibid., p. 148.

43. Marlowe, *Cromer in Egypt*, p. 269.

44. Al-Sayyid, *Egypt and Cromer*, pp. 169–72.

45. Ibid., p. 172.

46. Ibid., p. 173.

47. Marlowe, *Cromer in Egypt*, p. 269.

48. Ibid., pp. 269, 270.

49. Ibid., p. 272.

50. Ibid., pp. 273–75.

51. Tignor, *Modernization*, p. 296.

52. Ibid., p. 298.

53. Ibid., pp. 297–307.

54. Ibid., pp. 314–18.

55. Taylor, *Struggle for Master*, pp. 325–26.

56. The North study of 1914 illustrates this remarkably rapid perceptual alteration. See Ole R. Holsti, Robert C. North, and Richard A. Brody, "Perception and Action in the 1914 Crisis," in David Singer, *Quantitative International Relations* (New York: Free Press, 1968), pp. 123–58.

57. *London Times,* November 2, 1914, p. 10e.

58. Ibid., December 18, 1914, p. 8e.

59. *London Times,* May 27, 1914, p. 7a.

60. M. Travers Symons, *Britain and Egypt: The Rise of Egyptian Nationalism* (London: C. Palmer, 1925), p. 29.

61. *London Times,* March 20, 1914, p. 7f.

62. Ibid., March 30, 1914, p. 7b.

63. Ibid., July 15, 1914, p. 7b.

64. Ibid., June 24, 1914, p. 7c.

65. Ibid., November 9, 1914, p. 7a.

66. Ibid., December 3, 1914, p. 8d.

67. Ibid., December 5, 1914, p. 6c.

68. Symons, *Britain and Egypt,* pp. 28–29.

69. *London Times,* August 2, 1914, p. 5b.

70. Ibid., April 29, 1914, p. 21a.

71. Sir Ronald Storrs, *The Memoirs of Sir Ronald Storrs* (New York: Putnam, 1937), pp. 150–51.

Chapter 12. Winter 1921

1. *London Times,* November 5, 1920, p. 6a.

2. Elie Kedourie, *The Chatham House Version and Other Middle-Eastern Studies* (New York: Praeger, 1970), p. 89.

3. Sir Valentine Chirol, *London Times,* May 25, 1920, p. 32a; Kedourie, *Chatham House Version,* p. 102.

4. Egypt No. 4 (1921), Cmd. 1404, *British Parliamentary Papers,* p. 10.

5. *The New Statesman and Nation,* 18 (December 10, 1921):277–78.

6. *London Times,* April 8, 1920, p. 10f.

7. *The New Statesman and Nation,* 16 (February 26, 1921):606–07.

8. Ibid., 18 (February 4, 1922):493–94.

9. Ibid., 17 (May 28, 1921):205–06.

10. As quoted in Kedourie, *Chatham House Version,* p. 128.

11. Ibid., p. 91.

12. Ibid., p. 89.

13. Ibid., pp. 100–13 (chapter entitled "Sa'd Zaghlul and the British").

14. Ibid., p. 104.

15. *London Times,* November 5, 1920, p. 6a.

16. Kedourie, *Chatham House Version,* p. 113.

17. In a study resting so heavily on perception analysis, note should be taken of the difference between my perceptions of this situation and of those of Elie Kedourie, whose study has been extensively relied on here. Kedourie is a brilliant, colorful, and persuasive analytical historian. But as is true of any analyst, his own perceptions reflect his values and life experience. Kedourie's picture of Arabs is exceptional. He differs sharply from historians such as George Kirk and John Marlowe, whose analyses always coincide with a generous view of British imperialism. He differs even more from men such as Blunt and this writer, whose analyses are in greater harmony with an anti-imperial view. He appears to combine an imperialist image of the not-quite-adult Arab with the enemy image of evil intent and conspiratorial demeanor. In the study referred to so frequently here, Zaghlul is an evil, far-from-genius collaborator of other (almost all) similarly motivated Egyptian politicians. British officers, who never quite understood this picture, are depicted with extraordinary frequency as being "out of their depth" in Egypt. This image of Arab reality is common enough among Israeli analysts, and Kedourie's socialization in the Jewish community in Baghdad may well have predisposed him to that image.

18. Kedourie, *Chatham House Version,* pp. 95, 101.

19. Egypt No. 1 (1921), Cmd. 1131, *British Parliamentary Papers.*

20. *The New Statesman and Nation,* 16 (February 26, 1921):606–07.

21. Alfred Milner, *England in Egypt,* 13th ed. (London: E. Arnold, 1920), pp. iv–v.

22. Ibid., p. 10.

23. Ibid., pp. 8–10.

24. Ibid., p. 14.

25. Ibid., p. 12.

26. Ibid., pp. 3–4.

27. Ibid., p. 15.

28. Ibid., p. 10.

29. Ibid., p. 16.

30. Ibid., pp. 16–17.

31. Egypt No. 4 (1921), Cmd. 1404, *British Parliamentary Papers,* p. 10.

32. See, for example, the issue of May 28, 1921 (vol. 17), pp. 205–06.

33. Egypt No. 1 (1921), Cmd. 1131, *British Parliamentary Papers,* p. 9.

34. Ibid., p. 25.

35. Egypt No. 4 (1921), Cmd. 1404, *British Parliamentary Papers,* p. 10.

36. Kedourie, *Chatham House Version,* p. 138.

37. Ibid., p. 148.

38. Ibid., pp. 147–78.

Chapter 13. Fall 1956

1. Anthony Eden, *Full Circle* (Boston: Houghton Mifflin, 1960), pp. 248–90.

2. John Marlowe, *A History of Modern Egypt and Anglo-Egyptian Relations, 1800–1953* (New York: Praeger, 1954), p. 264.

3. Gabriel Almond and James S. Coleman, *The Politics of the Developing Areas* (Princeton: Princeton University Press, 1960), pp. 40–42.

4. For such an account, see Peter Mansfield, *The British in Egypt* (New York: Holt, Rinehart and Winston, 1971).

5. For a close look at identity transformation in Egypt in this period, see Mahmoud Ismail, "Nationalism in Egypt Before Nasser's Revolution" (Ph.D. dissertation, University of Pittsburgh, 1966).

6. See Nadav Safran, *Egypt in Search of Political Community* (Cambridge: Harvard University Press, 1961), for some good illustrations of this.

7. See Mansfield, *British in Egypt,* chap. 24, for a good account of this.

8. Ibid., p. 278.

9. Ibid., pp. 285–86.

10. Eden, *Full Circle*, p. 255.

11. Miles Copeland, *Game of Nations* (New York: Simon and Schuster, 1970), pp. 57–90.

12. Eden, *Full Circle,* chap. 10.

13. Ibid., pp. 274–75.

14. Mansfield, *British in Egypt,* p. 307.

15. Kennett Love, *Suez, the Twice Fought War* (New York: McGraw-Hill, 1969), p. 274.

16. Eden, *Full Circle,* p. 264.

17. Ibid., p. 284.

18. Love, *Suez,* prologue. The picture of a Nasser who hoped very much to serve as the primary leader of the Arab world but who hoped at the same time to avoid further warfare with Israel is developed minutely by Love. I find far less convincing the counterargument advanced by Uri Ra'anan, *The USSR Arms the Third World* (Cambridge: MIT Press, 1969).

19. Michael Brecher, *The Foreign Policy System of Israel* (New Haven: Yale University Press, 1972).

20. This is essentially the pattern seen by William Gamson and André Modigliani, *Untangling the Cold War* (Boston: Little, Brown, 1971), for the United States and the Soviet Union.

21. For a good account of this, see Sarah L. Botsai, "The Eisenhower Doctrine: A Study of Arab-American Relations in the Evolution of Policy" (master's thesis, University of Pittsburgh, 1959).

22. This image is inescapable in Herman Finer, *Dulles Over Suez* (Chicago: Quadrangle, 1964). The study is an agonized one.

23. For careful studies with strikingly different perspectives of this period, see Love, *Suez;* Finer, *Dulles Over Suez;* Hugh Thomas, *Suez* (New York: Harper and Row, 1966); and Nadav Safran, *From War to War* (New York: Pegasus, 1969).

24. Hansard, House of Commons, vol. 559, November 8, 1956, pp. 391–92.

25. Ibid., vol. 557, August 2, 1956, pp. 1674–75.

26. Ibid., vol. 559, November 8, 1956, p. 273.

27. Eden, *Full Circle,* p. 598.

28. Ibid., pp. 555–56.

29. Ibid., p. 555.

30. Hansard, House of Commons, vol. 557, August 2, 1956, p. 1643.

31. Ibid., p. 1646.

32. Ibid., p. 1667.

33. Ibid., vol. 558, November 1, 1956, p. 1705.

34. Leon Epstein, *British Politics in the Suez Crisis* (Urbana: University of Illinois Press, 1964), p. 52.

35. Hansard, House of Commons, vol. 557, August 2, 1956, p. 1663.

36. Love, *Suez,* pp. 393, 434, 457, 473.

37. See Copeland, *Game of Nations,* for a believable account of this.

38. Gamal Abdel Nasser, *Egypt's Liberation: The Philosophy of the Revolution* (Washington: Public Affairs Press, 1955).

39. Hansard, House of Commons, vol. 557, August 2, 1956, pp. 1620–21.

40. Ibid., vol. 558, September 13, 1956, p. 181.

41. Ibid., p. 176.

42. Ibid., vol. 558, November 1, 1956, pp. 1703–06.

43. Ibid., vol. 559, November 8, 1956, pp. 357–58.

44. Ibid., vol. 558, October 31, 1956, pp. 1486–89.

45. Ibid., September 12, 1956, pp. 110–13.

46. Ibid., October 31, 1956, p. 1464.

47. Moshe Dayan, *Diary of the Sinai Campaign* (Jerusalem: Steimatzky's Agency, 1966), pp. 28, 58–59.

48. Ibid., p. 58.

49. Hansard, House of Commons, vol. 558, November 1, 1956, p. 1628.

50. Ibid., vol. 557, August 2, 1956, p. 1703.

51. Ibid., vol. 558, November 1, 1956, p. 1683.

52. Ibid., September 12, 1956, p. 49.

53. Ibid., vol. 557, August 2, 1956, p. 1610.

54. Love, *Suez*, pp. 433–76.

55. Hansard, House of Commons, vol. 558, September 12, 1956, pp. 126–27.

56. Ibid., pp. 127, 131.

Chapter 14. Eliminating the Perceptual Basis of Conflict

1. The approach therefore is much closer to Richard Snyder, H. W. Bruck, and Burton Sapin (*Foreign Policy Decision Making* [New York: Free Press, 1967]) than to Graham T. Allison (*Essence of Decision: Explaining the Cuban Missile Crisis* [Boston: Little, Brown, 1971]). It can be considered an effort to operationalize in a preliminary way aspects of Snyder's overall scheme, especially those concerned with the setting of a dispute and with "access." Allison's second and third models really apply to those aspects of decision-making where bureaucratic sets have a great deal of autonomy and decision-making is focused on problems which in systems terms need no more than simple equilibrium adjustment. More severe disturbances, those posing the more interesting problems, must be related to the overall situation. Snyder has outlined the task of the analyst in dealing with such disturbances. For Allison to deal with them would require a serious development of his first model and a means for relating the three models. Allison very well may have captured the essence of bureaucratic interaction in his second and third models, but it is doubtful that he looked at the essence of decision.

2. Ole R. Holsti, *Crisis, Escalation, War* (Montreal: McGill-Queens University Press, 1972), focuses on perceived alternatives.

3. Snyder, *Foreign Policy Decision Making*.

4. Riley William Gilmore, "The American Foreign Policy-making Process and the Development of Post World War II Spanish Policy, 1945–1953" (Ph.D. dissertation, University of Pittsburgh, 1967).

5. My concern here is similar to that of those doing operational coding. This approach differs in that (1) it relies less on verbal behavior and (2) it is focused on three narrowly delineated question areas rather than on general politically relevant behavior. See Nathan Leites, *The Operational Code of the Politburo* (New York: McGraw-Hill, 1951); Alexander George, "The Operational Code: A Neglected Approach to the Study of Political Leaders and Decision Making," *International Studies Quarterly*, 13 (1969):190–222; Ole R. Holsti, "The Operational Code Approach to the Study of Political Leaders," *Canadian Journal of Political Science*, 4 (1971):123–57; and David McClellan, "The Operational Code Approach to the Study of Political Leaders: Dean Acheson's Philosophical and Instrumental Beliefs," *Canadian Journal of Political Science*, 4 (1971):52–75.

6. Richard W. Cottam, *Competitive Interference and Twentieth Century Diplomacy* (Pittsburgh: University of Pittsburgh Press, 1967).

Bibliography

Part I

Allison, Graham T. *Essence of Decision: Explaining the Cuban Missile Crisis*. Boston: Little, Brown, 1971.

Almond, Gabriel A. *The American People and Foreign Policy*. New York: Harcourt, 1950.

Anokar, S. "Party Strategies and Foreign Policy: The Case of Finland, 1955–63." *Cooperation and Conflict*, 8 (1973):1–17.

Art, Robert J. *The TFX Decision*. Boston: Little, Brown, 1968.

Axelrod, Robert M. *Conflict of Interest*. Chicago: Markham, 1970.

————. *Framework for a General Theory of Cognition and Choice*. Berkeley: University of California Press, 1972.

Badeau, John S. *The American Approach to the Arab World*. New York: Harper and Row, 1968.

Barghorn, Frederick C. *Soviet Foreign Propaganda*. Princeton: Princeton University Press, 1964.

————. *The Soviet Image of the United States*. New York: Harcourt, Brace, 1950.

Barth, Fredrik. *Principles of Social Organization in Southern Kurdistan*. Oslo: Brodlene Jorgensen, 1953.

Bauer, R. A. "Problem of Perceptions and the Relations Between the United States and the Soviet Union." *Journal of Conflict Resolution*, 5 (1961):223–29.

Beale, Howard K. *Theodore Roosevelt and the Rise of America to World Power*. Baltimore: The Johns Hopkins Press, 1956.

Benjamin, R. W., and Edinger, L. J. "Conditions for Military Control Over Foreign Policy Decisions in Major States: A Historical Exploration." *Journal of Conflict Resolution*, 15 (1971):5–31.

Bernstein, S. J., and Reinharth, L. "American Foreign Policy Formulation: A Proposal for a Countervailing Positive Value Model." *Polity*, 5 (1973):415–24.

Betts, Raymond F. *Assimilation and Association in French Colonial Theory*. New York: Columbia University Press, 1961.

Boardman, R. "Conflict in Western Perceptions of Change: Two Profiles of China." *British Journal of Political Science*, 1 (1971):191–208.

Boseman, A. B. *Politics and Culture in International History*. Princeton: Princeton University Press, 1960.

Boulding, Kenneth E. *The Image*. Ann Arbor: University of Michigan Press, 1956.

————. "National Images and International Systems." *Journal of Conflict Resolution*, 3 (1959):120–31.

Brecher, Michael. *Decisions in Israel's Foreign Policy*. New Haven: Yale University Press, 1975.

————. *The Foreign Policy System of Israel: Setting, Image, Process*. New Haven: Yale University Press, 1972.

————. "Images, Process and Feedback in Foreign Policy: Israel's Decision on German Reparations." *American Political Science Review*, 67 (1973):73–102.

Brodin, K. "Belief Systems, Doctrines, and Foreign Policy: A Presentation of Two Alternative Models for the Analysis of Foreign Policy Decision Making." *Cooperation and Conflict,* 7 (1972):97–112.

Brody, R., and Page, B. "Hawks and Doves, Isolationism and Political Distrust: An Analysis of Public Opinion on Military Policy." *American Political Science Review,* 66 (1972):979–95.

Buchanan, W., and Cantril, H. *How Nations See Each Other.* Urbana: University of Illinois Press, 1953.

Burgess, P. M. *Elite Images and Foreign Policy Outcomes—A Study of Norway.* Columbus: Ohio State University Press, 1968.

Cantril, H., and Free, L. A. "Hopes and Fears for Self and Country." *American Behavioral Scientist,* 6 (1962), Supplement.

Carr, E. H. *The Twenty Years' Crisis, 1919–1937.* London: Macmillan, 1946.

Cary, Max. *The Legacy of Alexander.* New York: Dial, 1932.

Choucri, Nazli, and North, Robert. *Nations in Conflict.* San Francisco: W. H. Freeman, 1974.

Christiansen, B. *Attitudes Toward Foreign Affairs as a Function of Personality.* Oslo: Oslo University Press, 1959.

Claude, Inis L. *Power and International Relations.* New York: Random House, 1962.

Cohen, Bernard C. *The Political Process and Foreign Policy: The Making of the Japanese Peace Treaty.* Princeton: Princeton University Press, 1957.

Cohen, Claude. *Pre-Ottoman Turkey.* New York: Taplinger, 1968.

Copeland, Miles. *The Game of Nations.* New York: Simon and Schuster, 1970.

Cottam, Richard W. *Competitive Interference and Twentieth Century Diplomacy.* Pittsburgh: University of Pittsburgh Press, 1967.

————. "Foreign Policy Motivations." *International Studies Newsletter,* Preliminary Issue B (1973):52–60.

————. *Nationalism in Iran.* Pittsburgh: University of Pittsburgh Press, 1964.

DeRivera, J. *The Psychological Dimension of Foreign Policy.* Columbus: C. E. Merrill, 1968.

Deutsch, Karl W. *The Nerves of Government.* New York: The Free Press, 1963.

————, et al. *Political Community and the North Atlantic Area.* Princeton: Princeton University Press, 1957.

Druckman, D. *Human Factors in International Negotiations.* Beverly Hills: Sage, 1973.

Easton, David. *A System Analysis of Political Life.* New York: Wiley, 1965.

Edelman, Murray. *The Symbolic Uses of Politics.* Urbana: University of Illinois Press, 1964.

Ehrlich, Paul H. *Population, Resources, Environment.* San Francisco: W. H. Freeman, 1970.

Elkholy, Abdo A. *The Arab Moslems in the United States.* New Haven: College and University Press, 1966.

Fann, K. T., and Hodges, D. C., eds. *Readings in US Imperialism.* Boston: P. Sargent, 1971.

Festinger, Leon. *A Theory of Cognitive Dissonance.* Evanston, Ill.: Row, Peterson, 1967.

Finlay, D. J.; Holsti, Ole R.; and Fagen, Richard R. *Enemies in Politics.* Chicago: Rand McNally, 1967.

Flack, Michael J. "The Role of Culture in International Operations." Pittsburgh: University of Pittsburgh, GSPIA, 1967.

Forrestal, James. *The Forrestal Diaries.* Edited by Walter Millis. New York: Viking, 1951.

Frankel, Joseph. *National Interest.* New York: Praeger, 1970.

Free, L. A. *Six Allies and a Neutral.* Glencoe, Ill.: Free Press, 1959.

Fromm, Erich. *May Man Prevail.* Garden City, N.Y.: Doubleday, 1961.

Fulbright, J. William. *The Arrogance of Power.* New York: Random House, 1966.

Gamson, William, and Modigliani, André. *Untangling the Cold War.* Boston: Little, Brown, 1971.

Gati, C. "Another Grand Debate: The Limitationist Critique of American Foreign Policy." *World Politics,* 20 (1968):133–51.

George, Alexander. *Propaganda Analysis*. Evanston, Ill.: Row, Peterson, 1959.

———, and George, Juliette L. *Woodrow Wilson and Colonel House*. New York: J. Day Co., 1956.

Goffman, E. *Strategic Interaction*. Philadelphia: University of Pennsylvania Press, 1969.

Goldwater, Barry. *Why Not Victory?* New York: McGraw Hill, 1962.

Greene, Felix. *The Enemy*. London: Jonathan Cape, 1970.

Guetzkow, Harold. *Multiple Loyalties: Theoretical Approach to a Problem in International Organizations*. Princeton: Princeton University Press, 1955.

Halberstam, David. *The Best and the Brightest*. New York: Random House, 1972.

Halpern, Morton. "The Decision to Deploy the ABM: Bureaucratic and Domestic Politics in the Johnson Administration." *World Politics,* 25 (1972):62–95.

Heider, Fritz. *The Psychology of Interpersonal Relations*. New York: Wiley, 1958.

Herz, John H. *International Politics in the Atomic Age*. New York: Columbia University Press, 1959.

Hitti, Philip K. *History of the Arabs*. 6th ed. New York: St. Martins, 1956.

Hobson, J. A. *Imperialism, A Study*. London: G. Allen and Unwin, 1938.

Hoffman, Stanley. *Contemporary Theory in International Relations*. Englewood Cliffs, N.J.: Prentice Hall, 1960.

Holsti, Ole R. "The Belief System and National Images." *Journal of Conflict Resolution,* 6 (1962):244–52.

———. *Crisis, Escalation, War*. Montreal: McGill-Queens University Press, 1972.

———. "Individual Differences in 'Definition of the Situation.'" *Journal of Conflict Resolution*, 14 (1970):303–10.

———. "The Study of International Politics Makes Strange Bed-fellows: Theories of the Radical Right and the Radical Left." *American Political Science Review,* 68 (1974):217–42.

———; Hopmann, P. Terrence; and Sullivan, John D. *Unity and Disintegration in International Alliances*. New York: Wiley, 1973.

Hoopes, Townsend. *The Limits of Intervention*. New York: D. McKay Co., 1969.

Hueem, H. "Foreign Policy Opinion as a Function of International Position." *Cooperation and Conflict,* 7 (1972):65–86.

———. *International Relations and World Images*. Oslo: Oslo University Press, 1972.

Hugo, Grant. *Appearance and Reality in International Relations*. London: Chatto and Windus, 1970.

Huntington, Samuel. *Political Order in Changing Societies*. New Haven: Yale University Press, 1968.

Hyndman, J. E. "National Interest and the New Look." *International Journal*, 26 (1970–71):5–18.

Isaacs, Harrold. *Scratches on Our Minds: American Images of China and India*. New York: J. Day Co., 1958.

Jacob, Philip, et al. *Values and the Active Community*. New York: Free Press, 1971.

Jervis, Robert. "Hypotheses on Misperception." *World Politics,* 20 (1968):454–79.

———. *The Logic of Images in International Relations*. Princeton: Princeton University Press, 1970.

Johnson, E. A. J., ed. *The Dimensions of Diplomacy*. Baltimore: The Johns Hopkins University Press, 1964.

Johnson, Lyndon Baines. *The Vantage Point*. New York: Holt, Rinehart, and Winston, 1971.

Kahn, Herman. *Thinking About the Unthinkable*. New York: Discuss Books, 1968.

Kaplan, Morton. *System and Process in International Politics*. New York: Wiley, 1957.

Kaufmann, William W., ed. *The McNamara Strategy*. New York: Harper, Row, 1964.

Kelman, Herbert C., ed. *International Behavior: A Social-Psychological Analysis*. New York: Holt, Rinehart, and Winston, 1965.

———. "Societal, Attitudinal and Structural Factors in International Relations." *Journal of Social Issues,* 11 (1955):42–56.

Kennan, George. *Russia, the Atom and the West*. New York: Harper, 1958.

Kerr, Malcolm. *The Arab Cold War 1958–1967*. 2d ed. New York: Oxford University Press, 1967.

Kissinger, Henry A. *The Necessity for Choice.* New York: Harper, 1961.

Kleinberg, O. *The Human Dimension in International Relations.* New York: Holt, Rinehart, and Winston, 1964.

Knorr, Klaus, and Verba, Sidney. *The International System: Theoretical Essays.* Princeton: Princeton University Press, 1961.

Lamb, Harold. *The Crusades.* New York: Doubleday, 1945.

————. *The March of the Barbarians.* New York: Doubleday, 1940.

Lane, Robert. *Political Thinking and Consciousness.* Chicago: Markham, 1969.

Leites, Nathan. *A Study of Bolshevism.* Glencoe, Ill.: Free Press, 1953.

Levine, Robert. *The Arms Debate.* Cambridge: Harvard University Press, 1963.

Levinson, D. J. "Authoritarian Personality and Foreign Policy." *Journal of Conflict Resolution,* 1 (1957):37–47.

Lichtheim, George. *Imperialism.* New York: Praeger, 1971.

Liska, George. *Imperial America.* Baltimore: The Johns Hopkins Press, 1969.

McClelland, Charles A. *Theory and the International System.* New York: Macmillan, 1966.

Maddox, Robert J. *The New Left and the Origins of the Cold War.* Princeton: Princeton University Press, 1973.

Magdoff, Harry. *The Age of Imperialism.* New York: Monthly Review Press, 1969.

Mannheim, Karl. *Ideology and Utopia.* London: Routledge and Kegan Paul, 1935.

Martin, John Bartlow. *Overtaken by Events.* New York: Doubleday, 1966.

Maslow, Abraham. *Motivation and Personality.* 2d ed. New York: Harper, 1970.

Menashe, Louis, and Radosh, Ronald. *Teach-ins, USA.* New York: Praeger, 1967.

Merkl, P. H. "Politico-Cultural Restraints on West German Foreign Policy: Sense of Trust, Identity and Agency." *Comparative Political Studies,* 3 (1971):443–67.

Mills, Charles Wright. *Images of Man.* New York: G. Braziller, 1960.

————. *The Power Elite.* New York: Oxford University Press, 1956.

Modelski, George A. *A Theory of Foreign Policy.* New York: Praeger, 1962.

Moon, Parker Thomas. *Imperialism and World Politics.* New York: Macmillan, 1962.

Morgenthau, Hans. *Politics Among Nations.* New York: Knopf, 1967.

————. *Scientific Man vs Power Politics.* Chicago: The University of Chicago Press, 1946.

Morris, Eric. *Blockade.* London: Hamish Hamilton, 1973.

Moscos, Charles C., Jr., ed. *Public Opinion and the Military Establishment.* Beverly Hills: Sage, 1971.

Mosley, Leonard. *Power Politics: Oil in the Middle East.* New York: Random House, 1973.

Murphy, Robert D. *Diplomat Among Warriors.* New York: Doubleday, 1964.

North, Robert C.; Holsti, Ole R.; Zaninovich, M. G.; and Zinnes, Dina A. *Content Analysis: A Handbook and Applications for the Study of International Crises.* Evanston, Ill.: Northwestern University Press, 1963.

Oglesby, Carl, and Shaull, Richard. *Containment and Change.* New York: Macmillan, 1967.

Organski, A. F. K. *Population and World Power.* New York: Knopf, 1961.

Parry, J. H. *Trade and Dominion.* London: Weidenfeld and Nicolson, 1971.

Petrov, U. "Formation of Soviet Foreign Policy." *Orbis,* 17 (1973):819–50.

Riker, William. *The Theory of Political Coalitions.* New Haven: Yale University Press, 1962.

Rohri-Wedge, U. J., and Wedge, B. "The Role of Perception in International Politics." *International Studies Newsletter,* Fall 1973.

Rokeach, Milton. *Beliefs, Attitudes and Values: A Theory of Organization and Change.* San Francisco: Jossey Bass, 1968.

————. *Nature of Human Values.* New York: Free Press, 1973.

Rosenau, James. *Public Opinion and Foreign Policy.* New York: Random House, 1961.

Rostow, Walt W. *The Stages of Economic Growth.* Cambridge: Harvard University Press, 1960.

Rummell, R. "Some Empirical Findings on Nations and Their Behavior." *World Politics,* 21 (1969):226–41.

Rush, Myron. *The International Situation and Soviet Foreign Policy.* Columbus, Ohio: Merrill, 1970.

Sarkesian, Sam S. *The Military Industrial Complex: A Reassessment.* Beverly Hills: Sage, 1972.

Schelling, Thomas C. *Arms and Influence.* New Haven: Yale University Press, 1966.

———. *The Strategy of Conflict.* Cambridge: Harvard University Press, 1960.

Schumpeter, Joseph. *Imperialism and Social Classes.* Cleveland: Meridian, 1955.

Schwartz, Morton. *The Motive Force of Soviet Foreign Policy.* Denver: University of Denver Press, 1971.

Seabury, Paul. *Power, Freedom and Diplomacy.* New York: Random House, 1963.

Seale, Patrick. *The Struggle for Syria.* New York: Oxford University Press, 1965.

Singer, David, ed. *Quantitative International Politics.* New York: Free Press, 1968.

Siverson, R. M. "The Evaluation of Self, Allies and Enemies in the 1956 Suez Crisis." *Journal of Conflict Resolution,* 16 (1972):203–10.

———. "Role and Perception in International Crisis: The Cases of Israeli and Egyptian Decision Makers in National Capitals and the United Nations." *International Organization,* 27 (1973):329–45.

Snyder, Richard C.; Bruck, H. W.; and Sapin, B., eds. *Foreign Policy Decision Making.* New York: Free Press, 1962.

Stassen, G. H. "Individual Preferences Versus Role-Constraint in Policy Making: Senatorial Response to Secretaries Acheson and Dulles." *World Politics,* 25 (1972):96–119.

Stoessinger, J. G. *Nations in Darkness: China, Russia and America.* New York: Random House, 1965.

Strachey, John. *The End of Empire.* London: Gollancz, 1959.

Stupak, R. J. "Dean Rusk on International Relations: An Analysis of His Philosophical Perceptions." *Australian Outlook,* 25 (1971):13–28.

Thayer, Charles Wheeler. *Diplomat.* New York: Harper, 1960.

Thornton, Archibald P. *The Imperial Idea and Its Enemies.* New York: St. Martins Press, 1959.

Tucker, Robert W. *The Radical Left and American Foreign Policy.* Baltimore: The Johns Hopkins University Press, 1971.

Ulam, Adam. *Expansion and Coexistence.* New York: Praeger, 1968.

Waltz, Kenneth N. *Man, The State and War.* New York: Columbia University Press, 1959.

Weinstein, F. B. "The Indonesian Elite's View of the World and the Foreign Policy of Development." *Indonesia,* 12 (1971):97–131.

Westerfield, Bradford. *The Instruments of American Foreign Policy.* New York: Cromwell, 1963.

White, Ralph. "Misperception and the Vietnam War." *Journal of Social Issues,* 21 (1966):103–22.

Williams, Glyndwr. *The Expansion of Europe in the Eighteenth Century.* New York: Walker, 1966.

Winslow, Earle M. *The Patterns of Imperialism.* New York: Columbia University Press, 1948.

Wolfers, Arnold. *Discord and Collaboration.* Baltimore: The Johns Hopkins Press, 1967.

Zimmerman, William. *Soviet Perspectives on International Relations.* Princeton: Princeton University Press, 1969.

Part II

Ahmed, Jamal M. *The Intellectual Origins of Egyptian Nationalism.* New York: Oxford University Press, 1960.

Assad, Thomas. *Three Victorian Travellers.* London: Routledge and Kegan Paul, 1964.

Berger, Murroe. *Bureaucracy and Society in Modern Egypt.* Princeton: Princeton University Press, 1957.

Blake, Robert. *Disraeli*. New York: St. Martins Press, 1967.

Blunt, Wilfrid Scawen. *My Diaries*. London: Martin Secker, 1932.

————. *Secret History of the English Occupation of Egypt*. New York: H. Fertig, 1932.

Bowman, Humphry. *Middle East Window*. London: Longmans, Green and Co., 1942.

Brondley, Alexander M. *How We Defended Arabi and His Friends*. London, 1884.

Calvocoressi, Peter. *Suez: Ten Years After*. New York: Pantheon, 1967.

Cecil, Gwendolyn. *The Life of Robert Marquis of Salisbury*. London, 1921.

Chamberlain, Joseph. *A Political Memoir 1880–92*. Edited by C. H. D. Howard. London: Batchworth Press, 1953.

Chirol, Valentine. *Fifty Years in a Changing World*. London, 1927.

Colvin, Auckland. *The Making of Modern Egypt*. London: Seely and Co., 1906.

Crankshaw, Edward. *The Forsaken Idea: A Study of Viscount Milner*. New York: Longmans, Green, 1952.

Crewe, Robert Offley Ashburton Crewe-Milner, First Marquis of. *Lord Rosebery*. London: Harper and Brothers, 1931.

Cromer, Evelyn Baring, 1st Earl of. *Abbas II*. London: Macmillan, 1915.

————. *Modern Egypt*. 2 vols. London: Macmillan, 1908.

————. *Political and Literary Essays*. 3 vols. London: Macmillan, 1908–1916.

Dayan, Moshe. *Diary of the Sinai Campaign*. New York: Harper and Row, 1966.

Dicey, Edward. *England and Egypt*. London, 1881.

Dodwell, Henry Herbert. *The Founder of Modern Egypt*. Cambridge: The University Press, 1931.

Eden, Sir Anthony. *Full Circle*. Boston: Houghton, Mifflin, 1960.

Eisenhower, Dwight. *Waging Peace, 1956–61*. Vol. 2. New York: Doubleday, 1965.

Epstein, Leon. *British Politics in the Suez Crisis*. Urbana: University of Illinois Press, 1964.

Finch, Edith. *Wilfrid Scawen Blunt, 1840–1922*. London: Jonathan Cape, 1938.

Finer, Herman. *Dulles Over Suez*. Chicago: Quadrangle, 1964.

Hourani, Albert. *Arabic Thought in the Liberal Age*. London: Oxford University Press, 1962.

Issawi, Charles. *Egypt at Mid-Century*. New York: Oxford University Press, 1954.

James, Robert R. *Rosebery*. New York: Macmillan, 1963.

Jarvis, H. Wood. *Pharaoh to Farouk*. London: J. Murray, 1953.

Kedourie, Elie. *The Chatham House Version*. New York: Praeger, 1970.

————. *England and the Middle East: The Destruction of the Ottoman Empire, 1914–21*. London: Bowes and Bowes, 1956.

Knaplund, P. *Gladstone's Foreign Policy*. New York: Harper and Brothers, 1935.

Lacouture, Jean and Simone. *Egypt in Transition*. London: Methuen and Co., 1959.

Landau, Jacob M. *Parliaments and Parties in Egypt*. New York: Praeger, 1954.

Landes, David. *Bankers and Pashas*. Cambridge: Harvard University Press, 1958.

Langer, William L. *The Diplomacy of Imperialism*. New York: Knopf, 1951.

Leslie, Shane. *Men Were Different: Five Studies in Late Victorian Biography*. Freeport, N.Y.: Library Press, 1967.

Little, Tom. *Egypt*. New York: Praeger, 1958.

Lloyd, George. *Egypt Since Cromer*. 2 vols. London, 1933–34.

Love, Kennett. *Suez, the Twice-Fought War*. New York: McGraw Hill, 1969.

Magnus, Philip, *Gladstone, A Biography*. London: J. Murray, 1954.

————. *Kitchener, Portrait of an Imperialist*. New York: E. P. Dutton, 1959.

Mansfield, Peter. *The British in Egypt*. New York: Holt, Rinehart, and Winston, 1971.

Marlowe, John. *Cromer in Egypt*. New York: Praeger, 1970.

————. *A History of Modern Egypt and Anglo-Egyptian Relations, 1800–1953*. New York: Praeger, 1954.

Mathews, Joseph J. *Egypt and the Formation of the Anglo-French Entente of 1904*. Philadelphia: University of Pennsylvania Press, 1939.

Medlicott, William Norton. *Bismarck, Gladstone and the Concert of Europe*. London: Athlone Press, 1956.

Milner, Alfred. *England in Egypt*. London: E. Arnold, 1892.

Monroe, Elizabeth. *Britain's Moment in the Middle East, 1914–56*. Baltimore: The Johns Hopkins Press, 1963.

Moreley, John. *Life of William Ewart Gladstone*. London: Macmillan, 1903.

Pudney, John. *Suez: De Lesseps' Canal*. New York: Praeger, 1969.

Ramm, Agatha, ed. *The Political Correspondnece of Mr. Gladstone and Lord Granville, 1876–1886*. 2 Vols. Oxford: Clarendon Press, 1962.

Robinson, Ronald; Gallagher, John; and Denny A. *Africa and the Victorians*. New York: St. Martins Press, 1961.

Rothstein, Theodore. *Egypt's Ruin: A Financial and Administrative Record*. London, 1910.

Royal Institute of International Affairs. *Great Britain and Egypt, 1914–1951*. London, 1952.

Safran, Nadav. *Egypt in Search of Political Community*. Cambridge: Harvard University Press, 1961.

———. *From War to War*. New York: Pegasus, 1969.

al-Sayyid, Afaf Lutfi. *Egypt and Cromer*. New York: Praeger, 1968.

Storrs, Ronald. *The Memoirs of Sir Ronald Storrs*. New York: G. P. Putnam Sons, 1937.

Symons, M. Travers. *Britain and Egypt: The Rise of Egyptian Nationalism*. London: C. Palmer, 1925.

Taylor, A. J. P. *The Struggle for Mastery in Europe, 1848–1918*. Oxford: Clarendon Press, 1954.

Thomas, Hugh. *Suez*. New York: Harper and Row, 1966.

Tignor, Robert L. *Modernization and British Colonial Rule in Egypt, 1882–1914*. Princeton: Princeton University Press, 1966.

Vatikiotis, P. J. *The Modern History of Egypt*. New York: Praeger, 1969.

Wallace, Donald Mackenzie. *Egypt and the Egyptian Question*. London, 1883.

Ward, A. W., and Gooch, G. *The Cambridge History of British Foreign Policy, 1783–1919*. Cambridge: The University Press, 1923.

Wingate, Ronald. *Wingate of the Sudan*. London: Murray, 1955.

Zayid, Mahmud Yusuf. *Egypt's Struggle for Independence*. Beirut: Khayats, 1965.

Index

Abbas II, Khedive, 234–35, 239, 241, 242, 243, 245, 247, 254, 270
Abdou, Mohammed, 176, 198, 233–34, 242, 253
Abdullah, King of Jordan, 298–300
Abdullah Pasha, 187
Academics, American: debate on Vietnam policy of, 3–8, 138, 141–42; role in foreign policy process of; 6–12, 49–50, 93, 137, 332–33
Acheson, Dean, 321
Acton, E. H., 171
Adly Pasha, 275
Affectivity, as determinant of variance in perception, 324–25
Afghanistan, in British world view, 190, 219, 236–37, 251–52
Aflaq, Michael, 108
Africa: cultural messianism in, 39, 57; in British world view, 163, 191, 217, 260
Africa and the Victorians, 21, 162, 163, 205–06
Ala, Husain, 294
Alexandria: commercial role of, 158–59, 180; riots and bombardment of, 188, 195–96, 201, 206–07
Algeria, 58, 289
Ali Fehmi Pasha, 187
Allenby, Edmund, Field Marshal, 259, 267–68, 272–73, 274, 275, 277
Alliance for Progress, 47
Allied ideal type perceptual syndrome: defined and described, 63–64, 66, 73–78, 80–83, 85–87, 94, 102, 315–16; in British situational view of Egypt, 170, 177; in British general view, 218, 231, 249, 260, 291
Allison, Graham, 10, 24, 25
American foreign policy. *See* United States
American Legion, 57
Americans for Democratic Action, 57, 125
Amery, Julian, 302
Anglo-Egyptian Agreement of 1954, 284–85

Anglo-Egyptian Treaty of 1936, 281, 284
Anglo-French Declaration, 239
Anglo-Iranian Oil Company, 57, 293–94
Appeasement, Morgenthau on, 54
Arab-Americans, 125, 129
Arabi, Ahmed: emerges as nationalist leader, 152, 176; as central figure in 1882 crisis, 182–88, 194–95, 197–98, 200–01, 203–07; mentioned, 211, 217, 225, 232, 235, 298
Arab-Israeli conflict: as influence on British policy in Egypt, 286–88; in American world view, 326–30
Arab nationalism, in Egypt, 279–80, 298
Arabs: and frontier dynamics, 28, 58; and cultural messianism, 39; view of Israel, 50–51, 85–86; in Iranian world view, 96; in American world view, 111–12, 326–30; U.S. policy toward, 123–28; as imperialists in Egypt, 151–52; British policy toward, 251, 285–86; in British world view, 298, 300–02, 306; world view of, 298. *See also* Arab world view under France; Great Britain; Israel; United States
Aramco, 56
Arbenz, Jacobo, 4
Armenian population in Egypt, 236, 241
Asia, in British world view, 260
Aswan Dam, 288–89
Attlee, Clement, 283
Austria-Hungary: in British world view, 216, 231, 249; British policy toward, 220, 229, 263
Austrian population in Egypt, 169
Al Azhar, 158, 199

Baath party, 37, 108, 300
Baghdad Pact (CENTO), 124, 127
Balfour, Arthur, 241, 266
Bandung Conference, 298
Bangladesh, U.S. policy toward, 9
Bao Dai, 300
Bay of Pigs, 4

365

Belgian Congo, in American world view, 89

Ben Gurion, David, 77, 287

Benson, Ezra Taft, 90

Berlin blockade, in American world view, 148

Bevan, Aneurin, 289–90

Birch, David, 32

Bismarck, Otto von: policy of, toward the Ottoman Empire, 160, 162, 216; mentioned, 84

Blacks, American, in Arab-Israeli conflict, 129

Blunt, Wilfrid Scawen: view of Egypt, 152–53; involvement with Egyptian nationalism, 196–201, 206; mentioned, 241, 252, 254, 257, 258, 272, 297

Boer War, 37

Bonaparte, Napoleon. *See* Napoleon Bonaparte

Boyle, Harry, 240–41

Brezhnev, Leonid, 42, 48

Bright, John, 203

British Commonwealth, British policy toward, 296

British population in Egypt, 169

Bryce, James, 224

Buckley, William, 148, 321

Bulgaria, 219, 224

Bundy, McGeorge, 4

Bureaucratic determinism, 23

Bureaucratic vested interests: defined and described, 10, 40–41, 55–56, 113, 140, 145, 147; as British situational motive in Egypt, 169, 174, 200, 206–07, 212, 227–28, 240, 255–56, 273–74, 305; as British general motive, 191–93, 219, 250, 262, 264–65; summary estimate of, in Egypt, 309–10

Cambodia: in American world view, 112; U.S. policy toward, 118, 134

Campbell, Sir George, 167–68, 201–02, 223

Capability, as indicator in ideal type perceptual syndromes, 64–66, 69–72, 96

Capability distance, 63–68, 70, 75, 103–04, 315–17

Capability self-image, 103–04

Carr, Edward, 15

Castro, Fidel, 73–74

Cave mission, 168, 170–71, 178

Central Asia, in British world view, 189–90, 219

Central Intelligence Agency (CIA): role in 1953 Iranian coup, 57, 80; role in 1957 Syrian coup attempt, 109, 126; mentioned, 56

Chamber of Notables (Egypt), 178, 184–86, 200, 206

Chamberlain, Joseph, 37, 84

Change in foreign policy: discussed, 105–08; at situational level, 108–10; at general level,

110–12; at general strategy level, 112–15; at systems aims level, 115–16

Cheetham, Milne, 267, 270

Chiang Kai-shek, 69–70

China: in American world view, 6, 21, 69–70, 75–76, 91, 112–15, 135, 138–39, 143–44, 146; as nation-state, 36; in Japanese world view, 68, 317; in Iranian world view, 94, 96, 102; as example of divided state, 134; in British world view, 290; world views of, 316

Christian revolt in the Balkans, 151, 161–62, 165–66

Church, Frank, 321, 326–29

Churchill, Winston, 260–61, 265, 283, 321

Clayton, Sir Gilbert, 268

Clemenceau, Georges, 205

Clifford, Clark, 11, 115, 144

Closed mind–open mind, as determinant of variance in perception, 84, 91, 325

Coexistence, as Soviet umbrella strategy term, 138–39

Colombia, in American world view, 88

Colonial ideal type perceptual syndrome: defined and described, 63–64, 70–78, 80–83, 85, 94–95, 316; in Arab world view, 298

Colons, in Algeria, 58

Colvin, Sir Auckland, 184, 197, 198, 199, 206, 216, 235

Communist party (China), 37

Communist party (Soviet Union), 37

Complex ideal type perceptual syndrome: defined and described, 62, 64–66, 73–77, 81–83, 87–88, 94–96, 102, 111–13, 118, 315; in British situational view of Egypt, 178–79, 201, 204, 224–25, 240, 252–54, 272–73, 301, 303–04; in British general view, 217, 231, 240, 290; in American general view, 328

Concert of Europe, 189–90, 192–94, 207, 217, 220–21

Congress, U.S., 145

Congress of Berlin, 189–90, 192–93

Congress party (India), 278

Containment, as umbrella term for U.S. general strategy, 10, 52–53, 115, 118–19, 123–24, 127, 138, 318

Control systems, international, 29, 30, 181. *See also* Egypt—control system

Controllers general, in Egypt, 173, 182

Cookson, Charles, 173, 183

Copeland, Miles, 124, 284

Copts, Egyptian, 86, 158, 180–81, 199, 243–44, 246

Cosmopolitan-parochial, as determinant of variance in perception, 84, 91, 325

Cromer, Evelyn Baring, First Earl of: world

view of, 152–53, 311, 324; view of 1882 period, 184–85, 197–201; policies of 1887 period, 212–14, 216; view of 1887 period, 227, 258; policies of, after 1887, 232, 235–36, 242–44, 253; view of, after 1887, 233–36, 241–45, 266, 270
Cuba: Bay of Pigs crisis in, 4, 74; missile crisis in, 9; world view in, 73–75; in American world view, 90, 148. *See also* Cuban world view, under Union of Soviet Socialist Republics; United States
Cultural distance, as perception determinant, 63–68, 70, 74, 103–04, 315–17
Cultural messianism, as foreign policy motive: defined and described, 39, 57, 154, 314; as British situational motive in Egypt, 154, 174, 208, 227–28, 256, 274, 278, 304–05; as British general motive, 164, 191, 194, 219, 251; summary estimate of, in Egypt, 310
Czechoslovakia, policy of, toward Egypt, 288

D'Aunoy, Count, 226
Dayan, Moshe, 302
Decazes, Elie, 168, 173
Decisional style, 64–66, 69–72, 97
Decision-making: in foreign policy process, 7–12, 14, 62, 106–07, 318–20; American academic role in, 7–12; central role players in, 54–55, 320–21; American, in Vietnam crisis, 135–38, 145
Decision-making, locus of, 64–66, 69–72, 97
Defense, as foreign policy motive: defined and described, 42–43, 68, 74, 82, 95, 97, 118, 145, 314–15; as British general motive, 164, 191–92, 218, 219, 249–50, 262, 294–95; as British situational motive in Egypt, 167–68, 173–74, 200, 206, 210, 214, 227–29, 240, 255–56, 273–74, 278, 281, 305; summary estimate of, in Egypt, 309–10
De Gaulle, Charles: external personal power drive of, 20, 42–43; Middle East policy of, 128; world view of, 139
Delcassé, Théophile, 238–39
De Lesseps, Ferdinand, 159, 197
De Lisle, Lord, 223–24
Derby, Edward Stanley, 14th Earl of, 160–61, 167, 173
Detachment quotient, as determinant of variance in perception, 324, 329–30
Détente, as umbrella strategy term, 119
Deterrence theory, 20, 120, 136
Dhofar, in Iranian world view, 94, 96, 102
Dinshawi affair, 243–44, 246
Diplomatic probes, 12, 93, 330–32
Directional thrust of foreign policy, 99–100, 103, 106, 112

Disraeli, Benjamin: as imperialist proponent, 84; in Suez Canal purchase, 160; policy of, toward Ottoman Empire, 160, 164, 166, 268
Domestic forces interaction, 64–66, 69, 71–73
Dominican Republic: and ideological messianism, 40; under Trujillo, 57, 90; in Cuban general view, 73–75
Domino theory, as perceptual metaphor, 314
Dufferin, Frederick Blackwood, First Marquis of, 209, 211
Dulles, John Foster: decisional role of, 9; Suez policy of, 9, 123, 288–89, 307; idiosyncrasies of, 90, 322; and rollback, 118

Eastern Europe, Soviet expansion in, 49
Economic vested interests
—domestic investments, as foreign policy motive; defined and described, 35, 56, 96–97, 140; as British general motive, 293, 295–96
—investments abroad, as foreign policy motive: defined and described, 37, 79, 125–26, 129–30, 140; as French situational motive in Egypt, 159–60; as British situational motive in Egypt, 162, 167–68, 170, 172–74, 177, 201, 205–07, 225–26, 273–74, 305; summary estimate of, in Egypt, 308, 310
—trade, as foreign policy motive: defined and described, 34, 68; as British general motive, 164, 190–93, 219, 250, 262, 293, 295–97; as British situational motive in Egypt, 225–26, 229, 256, 274, 278, 305; summary estimate of, in Egypt, 308, 310
Economist, 172
Edelman, Maurice, 301
Edelman, Murray, 8–9
Eden, Anthony: as example of personal determinism, 24–25; policy of , in Suez crisis, 277, 284–85, 289, 290–92, 299, 303–06
Efficacy, as determinant of variance in perception, 325–26
Egypt: Dulles's policy toward, 9; in Eden's world view, 24–25; in British world view, 68; in Israeli world view, 77–78, 83; in formation of United Arab Republic, 109; in American world view, 110, 327; U.S. policy toward, 123–24; decisional process in, 158, 181, 186, 205, 275; debt of, 159, 168; army in, 182–84, 186–88, 196; coup of 1952 in, 284–86
—control system: before British invasion, 181–82, 184, 186, 208; under British, preprotectorate, 211–14, 234, 236, 239, 240, 242, 243, 245–46, 247; after World War I, 257, 268–69, 271–72, 274–75, 277–79, 282, 284

—nationalism in: before British invasion, 180–83, 187, 189, 194, 199, 203, 207; before World War I, 225, 230, 232, 241, 243–46, 254–55; in early Wafd period, 266–68, 270–71, 273; Arab-Egyptian mix of, 279–80, 283–85, 298

Eisenhower, Dwight, 123, 126, 288–89, 291, 307

Eisenhower doctrine, 288

Ellsberg, Daniel, 7

Empathetic ability, as determinant of variance in perception, 84, 91, 325

Enemy ideal type perceptual syndrome: defined and described, 62, 64–65, 73–78, 81–82, 85–87, 89, 91, 94–96, 102, 107, 109, 118, 136–37, 148, 315; in British situational view of Egypt, 169–70, 174, 179, 204, 224–25, 303–04; in British general view, 191, 217–18, 220, 231, 235, 247–49, 260, 290

Ethiopia, in British world view, 237–38

Ethnic interest groups, 58, 125–26, 128–30

Evans, Lincoln, 291

Expectations: and perceptual change, 106–16, 131–32, 143–47, 319–20; of British in Egypt, 174–79, 208–10, 228–30, 231, 257, 267, 274–77, 298, 306–08; and diplomatic probing, 231

Fahmy, Mustafa, 243, 266

Far East: in British world view, 237, 240, 249; British policy toward, 263

Farid, Mohammed, 246–47

Farouk, King, 158, 278, 282–84, 298

Fashoda, 238–39, 255

Federation of Arab Emirates, in Iranian world view, 94, 96, 102

Fells, Anthony, 302–03

Ferguson, Sir James, 226–27

Fortress America, as umbrella strategy term, 118

Fourteen points, 15

France: foreign policy motivations of, 20; as nation-state, 36; and cultural messianism, 39; view of Germans of, 61, 160–61, 189, 205; in Arab world view, 85; U.S. policy toward, 123; imperial policy of, in Egypt, 157–60; in British world view, 163, 170, 172, 174, 190, 192, 216–17, 220–22, 224, 226, 230, 231–32, 234–35, 237–40, 242, 249–50, 259, 292; British policy toward, 165–66, 217, 220–21, 223, 229, 231–32, 236–40, 251–52; policy of, in Egypt, prior to 1882, 183, 185–89, 203–05, 208–09; policy of, in Egypt, after 1882, 212, 215; world view in, 238–39; role of, in Suez crisis, 289, 294, 300, 306; in German (Nazi) world view, 316

Franco, Francisco, 57, 89, 323

Franco-Prussian War, 160

French population in Egypt, 169

Freycinet, Charles Louis de, 186, 188–89, 205

Frontier dynamics, as foreign policy motive, 38, 57–58

Fuad, Sultan, 259, 266–68, 272, 278, 280

Fulbright, J. William, 48–49, 66–67, 91, 136, 146–47, 320, 326–29

Gaitskell, Hugh, 299, 301

Gambetta, Leon, 185, 189, 195, 197, 198, 200, 201, 206

Gamson, William, 14, 131

Gaza Strip raid, 77, 286–87

General Assembly (Egypt), 246–47, 253

Geneva Agreements, 134

German population in Egypt, 169

Germany: as example of divided state, 134; in British world view, 163, 170, 172, 191, 216–17, 231, 236–37, 247–48, 253–54, 259–60, 262, 264, 280, 282; British policy toward, 165–66, 232, 237, 250–52, 263, 296; in French world view, 189, 205. *See also* German world view under France; Poland

—Federal Republic of Germany: view of France, 61; view of USSR, 139

—Nazi Germany: foreign policy motivations of, 11, 46, 83; impact on liberalism of, 15; and Hitler's 1940 speech, 36; view of Poland, 68; in Israel's world view, 83; perceptual tendencies in, 316

Ghuli, Butros Pasha, 243–46

Gladstone, William Ewart: Midlothian speeches of, 151, 153, 161, 166, 180, 219; view of Egypt, in 1876 period, 167, 175; world view of, in 1882 period, 183, 189–90, 193, 217, 231, 261, 320; view of Egypt, in 1882 period, 183, 203, 205–08, 225, 272; general world view of, 320–21

Goldwater, Barry, 29–30, 42–43, 48, 148

Gordon, Charles, 162, 213–14

Gorst, Sir J. Eldon, 245–46, 252

Goschen, George Joachim, 171, 173, 202

Graduated compellence, 137–38, 143

Grandeur, as foreign policy motive, 38, 57–58. *See also* National grandeur

Granville, G. G. Leveson Gower, Second Earl of, 185–88, 227

Great Britain: religious messianism of, 39; cultural messianism of, 39, 57; defense in, 43; frontier dynamics and, 58; world view of, general, 68; in Iranian world view, 80; in Arab world view, 85; in American world view, 102; U.S. policy toward, 123; view of

USSR, 139; general motivation of, in Egypt, 153–55, 157–60; Liberal radical view in, 180, 182–83, 185, 190, 202–03, 207, 218, 222, 224, 272
—general foreign policy motivations: in 1876, 161, 163–64; in 1882, 190–92; in 1887, 218–19; in 1914, 249–50; in 1921, 260–62; in 1956, 292–94
—general system of aims: in 1876, 164–66; in 1882, 192–94; in 1887, 219–21; in 1914, 250–52; in 1921, 262–65; in 1956, 291–97
—prevailing situational view: in 1876, 166–72; in 1882, 194–203; in 1887, 221–24; in 1914, 252–54; in 1921, 265–72; in 1956, 297–304
—prevailing world view: in 1876, 160–63; in 1882, 188–91; in 1887, 216–18; in 1914, 247–49; in 1921, 259–60; in 1956, 289–92
—situational motivational system: in 1876, 172–74; in 1882, 203–08, in 1887, 224–28; in 1914, 255–56; in 1921, 272–74; in 1956, 304–05
—*See also* British policy under Arab-Israeli conflict; Asia; British Commonwealth; Far East; Germany; India; Ireland; Ottoman Empire; Pakistan; Palestine; Rumania; Russia; Sudan; Union of Soviet Socialist Republics; United States. *See also* British world view under Afghanistan; Africa; Arab-Israeli conflict; Asia; Central Asia; China; Egypt; Ethiopia; Far East; France; Germany; Hungary; India; Ireland; Italy; Ottoman Empire; Russia; South Africa; Sudan; Union of Soviet Socialist Republics; United States
Greece: and cultural messianism, 39; and ideological messianism, 40, 57; imperialism of, in Egypt, 151–52; British policy toward, 251, 292
Greek population in Egypt, 169
Guatemala: 1954 coup in, 4; in American world view, 102

Hanbury, R. W., 224
Hansen, Clifford P., 326–29
Hartington, Spencer Cavendish, Marquis of, 190, 202–03, 207
Hatfield, Mark, 328
al Hawrani, Akram, 108
Hicks, William, 212
Hidden hand, in colonial image, 70–72
Hinchingbrook, Viscount, Earl of Sandwich, 291
Historical experience, as perceptual determinant, 60
Hitler, Adolf: world view of, 11, 68; and liberalism, 15; 1940 speech of, 36; external personal power drive of, 41–42; and anti-Semitism, 61; as imperialist example, 84
Hobson, John A., 21–22, 25, 35, 37, 70
Hobson-Lenin imperialist motivational attribution, 23, 35, 70–72, 81, 135, 143
Hoffmann, Stanley, 3, 155
Hoopes, Townsend, 11, 19, 133
Hostile ideal type. *See* Enemy ideal type perceptual syndrome
Humphrey, Hubert, 146–47, 328
Hungary, in British world view, 297, 306
Husain, Kamil Pasha, 247, 257

Ibrahim Dervish Pasha, 188, 195
Idealists, in international relations theory, 15, 31
Ideal types, defined and described, 63–64
Ideological messianism, as foreign policy motive: defined and described, 40, 57, 74, 79; as British general motive, 164, 191–94, 265; as British situational motive in Egypt, 207, 278
Ideological projection theory, 107, 141, 323–24
Idiosyncratic perceptual determinants, 60, 90–91
Imperial ideal type perceptual syndrome: defined and described, 63–64, 67–68, 73–77, 94, 96, 102, 106, 109, 111, 316; in British situational view of Egypt, 170–72, 174, 176–77, 179, 190, 193, 199, 201, 204, 207, 221–22, 224–25, 240–41, 245, 249, 252–58, 267–73, 277, 285, 297–98, 302–04; in British general view, 218, 232–36, 240, 249, 259–61; as seen in American view of Arabs, 327
Imperialism: Hobson's analysis of, 21–23; defined and described, 26–30, 33–34, 55, 155, 157; in Egypt, 151, 157
India: as multinational state, 36; in British world view, 162, 190, 219–20, 236–37, 250; British policy toward, 293, 296
Indonesia, in American world view, 112
International relations theory and foreign policy, 8, 11–12, 14, 49–50, 52–53
Iran: American role in 1953 coup in, 56–57, 108, 154, 308; world view in, 80–84; foreign policy system values of, 99–101; foreign policy directional thrust of, 100; foreign policy system of aims of, 101, 103–04; general foreign policy strategy of, 104–05; parametric value of, 163; in British world view, 250–51, 293–94, 302. *See also* Iran world view under Arabs; China; Dhofar; Federation of Arab Emirates; Great Britain; Iraq; Union of Soviet Socialist Republics; United States
Iraq: Baath party of, 37; in Iranian world view,

94–96, 102, 104; in American world view,
109; U.S. policy toward, 124; rivalry with
Egypt, 280; 1956 crisis in, 302, 308
Ireland: British policy toward, 37; as determinant of British world view, 160–62, 180, 207
Islam, and Egyptian nationalism, 158, 181, 280
Ismail, Khedive: role in 1876 British policy,
168, 171, 175–78; mentioned, 159, 162,
181–82, 203, 212, 235, 254
Israel: and frontier dynamics, 38, 58; and defense, 43; foreign policy motivations of, 46,
50–51; world view in, 77–78, 83; in Arab
world view, 85–86, 124–25, 299; U.S. policy toward, 123–28; role of, in Suez crisis,
286–89, 294, 300, 306; in British world
view, 300–02. *See also* Israeli world view
under Arabs; Egypt; Germany—Nazi Germany; Syria; Union of Soviet Socialist Republics; United States
Italian population in Egypt, 169
Italy: in British world view, 216, 231, 237,
259, 280; British policy toward, 220, 229,
232, 237, 251

Jackson, Henry, 66–67, 91, 148, 320–21,
326–29
Jameson Raid, 236
Japan: view of China, 68, 317; in American
world view, 69–70; in British world view,
237, 252, 280; military dictatorship in, 316
Jews, in France, 86–87
Johnson, Lyndon: decision of, to bomb North
Vietnam, 3; and imperialism, 37; world view
of, 105–06, 139, 272; Southeast Asian pol-
icy of, 118; decision of March 31, 1968,
127, 133–34, 145–47
Johnson doctrine, 115, 145
Joint Note (1881), 185–86, 194, 196, 199, 200
Jordan: viewed as imperial puppet, 85; in
American world view, 88, 109; U.S. policy
toward, 123, 154; in 1956 crisis, 302
Josephson, Matthews, 17–18
Joubert, M., 171, 173

Kaplan, Morton, 98, 155
Karami, Rashid, 110–11
Kayhan, 94, 96
Kedouri, Elie, 267
Kemal, Mustafa, 152, 242–46, 265, 298
Kennan, George, 20, 83, 115–16, 118, 139
Kennedy, John F.: and ideological messianism,
40; world view of, 105–06; Vietnam role of,
113, 137; as nascent dove, 135
Kennedy, Robert, 133, 146–47
Khrushchev, Nikita, 9, 42

King, James E., Jr., 17
Kissinger, Henry: foreign policy decisions of,
9; as realist theorist, 17–20, 49, 65, 67, 91,
148
Kitchener, Horatio Herbert Kitchener, Earl of,
238, 246–47, 252–53, 255, 258, 266
Korea, 4, 134
Kosygin, Aleksei, 42, 48
Kruger, Stephanus Johannes Paulus, 236–37
al Kuwatli, Shukri, 4, 123, 126

Labour party, 285, 290, 293–95, 297–306
Lampson, Miles (later Lord Kilearn), 282–87
Lascelles, Sir Frank, 177
League of Nations: and liberal doctrine, 15;
British policy toward, 263
League of Three Emperors, 164, 197
Lebanon: U.S. intervention in, 1958, 4,
110–12, 126; identity range in, 86
Legislative Council (Egypt), 234, 247
Levantines, in Egyptian commerce, 158, 180,
182
Lenin, Nikolai, 22, 23, 35, 70–72, 81, 135,
143
Lever, Harold, 301
Liberal Constitutional party (Egypt), 274
Liberalism, expressed as national self-
determination, 15
Liska, George, 115, 145
al Liwa, 242
London Times: correspondent of, in Cairo,
169–71, 182–83, 185, 194–96, 207, 221–22,
225–26, 253, 259–60; view of Egypt, 172,
201, 222–23, 248–49, 252, 254, 255, 256,
260–61, 272
Loot, as foreign policy motive, 34
Lowe, Robert, 178
Lumumba, Patrice, 89
Lyons, Richard Pemell, First Earl of, 168, 173

McCarthy, Eugene, 133, 147
McCarthy, Joseph, 91, 290
McGovern, George, 146–47, 321
McNamara, Robert, 11, 137, 144
McNamara doctrine, 4, 8, 136
Mahdi, Mohammed Ahmed, 212–13
Malet, Sir Edward, 183, 185, 187–88, 196,
198, 206
Mamelukes, 157–58
Manchester Guardian, 241, 255, 298
Marchand expedition, 238–39
Marlowe, John, 182, 187, 196, 277
Maronite church, 86
Marshall Plan, as cultural messianism, 47
Martin, John Bartlow, 24
Maslow, Abraham, 32

Mediterranean agreement, 217
Mesopotamia, British policy toward, 251
Messianism, 38
Mexico, U.S. policy toward, 57
Middle East, U.S. policy toward. *See* Arab-Israeli conflict
Middle East Defense Organization, 285
Midlothian campaign, 151, 153
Militarism, 22, 41
Military-industrial complex, 35, 47, 56, 140
Military vested interests, as foreign policy motive: defined and described, 41, 96–97, 140; as British situational motive in Egypt, 208, 228–29, 240, 256, 273–74, 305; as British general motive, 250, 261–62, 264–65, 294; summary estimate of, in Egypt, 310
Milner, Alfred, 152–53, 198, 216, 233, 235, 241, 266–72, 274–75
Modigliani, Andre, 14, 131
Mohammed Ali, Khedive, 158, 212
Mohammed Riza Pahlavi. *See* Shah of Iran
Mondale, Walter, 147
Moon, Parker Thomas, 22
Moore, Sir Thomas, 302
Morgenthau, Hans, 14–17, 20–21, 25, 31, 54, 66, 87, 136
Morocco, 85, 289
Morrison, Herbert, 291, 293–94
Moslem. *See* Islam
Moslem Brotherhood, 281–84
Mossadegh, Mohammed: as CIA victim, 4, 56–57, 80, 154; in American world view, 88, 289, 308; in British world view, 293–94
Motivation, foreign policy: defined, 31; as aspect of ideal type perceptual syndromes, 64–66, 68–72, 97
Motivational systems, 313
Mt. Lebanon, 86
al-Muayyad, 242
Munro-Ferguson, R. C., 223–24
Muskie, Edmund, 147
Mussolini, Benito: as imperialist, 37, 84; external personal power drive of, 42; world view of, 68

Nabulsi, Suleiman, 88, 123, 159
el-Nahas, Mustafa, 278–79, 218–84, 302
Napoleon Bonaparte: external personal power drive of, 41–42; world view of, 68; as imperialist, 84
Nasser, Gamal Abdel: in Anthony Eden's world view, 24–25; in Israeli world view, 83; U.S. policy toward, 123, 126, 288; as Arab leader, 286; in British world view, 290–92, 298–303, 305–06; mentioned, 152, 244, 281, 285, 286, 288–89, 298

National Front (Iran), 278
National grandeur, as foreign policy motive: defined and described, 36–37, 97, 142, 145, 314; as British general motive, 164, 191–92, 215, 250, 261–62, 265, 294–95; as British situational motive in Egypt, 194, 206, 228, 256, 274, 278, 284–85, 304–05; summary estimate of, in Egypt, 308–10
Nationalism: defined and described, 36–37, 60, 69, 84–85, 87, 145–46; and New Left, 47. *See also* Egypt, nationalism in
National Liberation Front (Vietcong), in American world view, 141
National party (Egypt), 186–87, 196, 198, 201, 206
Nehru, Jawaharlal, 298
Neutrals, in ideal type representation, 65
New Left, 23, 47–48, 49, 322
New Statesman and Nation, 259, 260, 261, 269, 273, 297, 298
New York Times, 88
Ngo Dinh Diem, 113
Nixon, Richard: world view of, 146, 320–21; mentioned, 9, 128, 134
Nixon doctrine, 115, 145
Normative theory, 332–33
North Atlantic Treaty Organization, 67, 293
Northbrook, Thomas George Baring, First Earl of, 207
Northcote, Sir Stafford, 167
North Vietnam: Johnson's decision to bomb, 3–4; American policy toward debated, 6, 133–34, 141, 146; in American world view, 68, 76, 112–15, 141, 143–44, 146
Nubar Pasha, 175–77, 181, 210, 212, 215, 222, 235

October War, 326–31, 333
O'Donnell, F., 202
Oglesby, Carl, 21, 23, 25, 29, 30, 56
Oil, as economic interest group, 56, 125–26, 128–30
Oman, Iranian interest in, 94, 100
Open mind–closed mind, as determinant of variance in perception, 84, 91, 325
Ottoman Empire: suzerainty of, over Egypt, 158–59, 257; in British world view, 163, 217, 220–21, 222, 230, 232, 235, 237, 248–49, 253–54; British policy toward, 165–66, 183, 185–88, 200, 208–09, 217, 219, 221, 223, 226–27, 229, 232, 247, 250–52, 257, 263; and the Arab world, 216
Outrey mission, 170

Paget, R. T., 290
Pahlavi, Mohammed Riza. *See* Shah of Iran

Pakistan, British policy toward, 293, 296
Palestine, 86, 280, 286; British policy toward, 292, 296
Palmerston, Henry John Temple, Third Viscount, 158
Pan Islam, 232, 248
Parametric value: defined and described, 101–04, 317; in British foreign policy aims systems, 164–65, 190, 192, 218, 220, 230, 231, 234, 237, 249–50, 261–62, 272, 280–81, 309
Parochial-cosmopolitan, as determinant of variance in perception, 84, 91, 325
Participant excitement, as foreign policy motive: defined and described, 37–38, 56; as British situational motive in Egypt, 208, 305; summary estimate of, in Egypt, 310
Party of the Institutionalized Revolution (PRI, Mexico), 278
Peace movement, in United States, 143–44, 146
Peace theory, 11, 12, 49–50, 52–53, 93, 313, 326–32
Pentagon Papers, 7
Perceptual balance, 25. *See also* Psychological balance
Perceptual rhythm, 313–15
Persian Gulf, Iran's interest in, 82, 96, 100, 114
Personal determinism, and foreign policy, 24–25
Personal power drive, domestic, as foreign policy motive: defined and described, 41–42, 55, 68, 82, 96–97; as British situational motive, 208, 228, 305; summary estimate of, in Egypt, 310
Personal power drive, external, as foreign policy motive; 42, 55, 68, 82, 96–97
Philosophy of a Revolution, 298–99
Pilisuk, Marc, 4–5, 7
Point Four, 47
Poland, in German world view, 68
Population, as foreign policy motive, 34
Power in international relations, 15–21, 23, 25–26
Prevailing situational view: defined, 59; for British in Egypt, 166–72, 178, 182
Prevailing world view: defined and described, 10, 33, 45, 58–59, 78–79, 97, 102, 111, 318; rhythmic change in, 11, 313–15; for Great Britain, 160–63, 179, 188–90
Psychological balance: Anthony Eden and, 25; theory of, 39, 61, 79, 106
Public, role of: in foreign policy decisional process, 106–07, 140–48, 317–18; in U.S. policy in Vietnam, 317–18

Rapoport, Anatol, 4–6
Realists, in international relations theory, 15–21, 23, 25–26, 31, 60, 79, 87
Religious community identity, 89
Religious messianism, as foreign policy motive: defined and described, 38–39, 57; as British general motive, 164, 191, 193
Revisionist historians, 21–22, 25–26, 31, 100–01, 117, 140, 147–48
Rhodesia, and frontier dynamics, 58
Riaz Pasha, 177, 209, 233
Riforma, 216
Riker, William, 15, 16, 20, 25, 32, 79, 277
Ring, Baron de, 206
Robens, Alfred, 300
Rogers Plan, 128, 130, 328
Rojas Pinilla, Gustavo, 88
Role, as perceptual determinant, 60–61, 67, 79, 83, 90, 99, 107, 124–25, 320–22
Rollback, as umbrella term for strategy, 53, 118, 318
Rome: and imperialism, 37; world view of, 316
Roosevelt, Theodore: on imperialism, 37, 84; external personal power drive of, 42
Rosebery, Archibald Philip Primrose, Fifth Earl of, 219, 235
Rothschild, House of, 160, 197
Rumania, British policy toward, 251
Rushdi, Hossein, 266, 268
Rusk, Dean, 19, 139
Russia: and frontier dynamics, 38; in British world view, 158, 163, 170, 172, 190, 192, 216, 217, 220, 224, 231, 235, 237, 249, 250, 259–60, 262, 264; view of Germany, 161; British policy toward, 165–66, 220, 229. *See also* Union of Soviet Socialist Republics
Russian population in Egypt, 169

Saddiq, Ismail, 171–72, 175, 177, 181
Said, Khedive, 159
as-Said, Nuri, 298, 300, 308
Saleh, Allahyar, 88
Salisbury, Lord, 258
Salisbury, Robert Gascoyne-Cecil, Third Marquis of: policy toward the Ottoman Empire, 161, 178, 231, 232, 236, 238; world view of, 217, 219, 320–21, 324
Sami, Mohammed, 198
Saturday Review, 172
Saudi Arabia: oil interests of, 56; viewed as imperial puppet, 85; British policy toward, 251
al-Sayyad, Ahmed Lutfi, 242
Schelling, Thomas: and doctrine of graduated

compellence, 4, 8, 137, 144; on mixed motives, 20, 137
Schumpeter, Joseph, 22, 25
Self-confidence, as determinant of variance in perception, 326
Seymour, Frederick, 188–89, 195, 198, 203, 207
Shah of Iran, Mohammed Riza Pahlavi: in Iranian perceptions, 80–82; in American world view, 88; world view of, 94–96
Sharett, Moshe, 77, 287
Shawish, Abd al-Aziz, 247, 259–60
Sherif Pasha, 176, 178, 182, 184, 187, 209, 210
Sidky, Bakir, 280–81, 283
Sidky-Bevin Agreement, 283
Slavery, opposition to, as foreign policy motivational factor, 39, 57, 162–63, 165–66, 190, 213, 219
Snyder, Richard, 24, 31, 55, 320
South Africa, in British world view, 236–37, 240
South Vietnam, in American world view, 68, 76–77, 112–15, 144
Spain: and religious messianism, 39, 57; under Franco, 57, 89
Spectator, 172
Stalin, Joseph, 42, 48
Strategic lines, general, 101–04
Strategic planning, 331–32
Sudan: U.S. support of coups in, 108; British policy toward, 212–13, 219, 252, 283–85; in British world view, 232
Suez Canal, 159–60, 164, 168
Suez Canal Company, 159–60, 289, 303
Suez crisis, U.S. role in, 123
Sukarno: in British world view, 298; mentioned, 112
Sunni Islam, 86
Syria: U.S. support of coup attempt in, 4, 108–10, 123, 126; Baath party of, 37; view of Israel, 50–51, 85; in Israeli world view, 317; in American world view, 327
Syrian population in Egypt, 236, 291
System aims, foreign policy, 100–01, 103
System values, foreign policy, defined and described, 98–101, 103

Taiwan, in American world view, 69–70, 74–75
Taylor, A. J. P., 160, 189, 196
Teach-ins, 4–8
Tewfik, Khedive, 178, 181, 194, 212, 225, 230, 233–34, 239
Thailand, in American world view, 112
Third World states, British policy toward, 296

Tignor, Robert L., 196
Time, 88
Tito, in American world view, 87
Tonkin Gulf decision, 136
Triple Alliance, 193, 217, 236, 237
Trotsky, Leon, 57
Tshombe, Moise, 89
Tucker, Robert W., 23, 26
Tunisia, 85, 289
Turkey: policy toward Syria, 108–09; British policy toward, 285; in Greek world view, 316–17. *See also* Ottoman Empire

Umma party (Egypt), 242–47, 253, 255
Union of Soviet Socialist Republics: in American world view, 6, 11, 21, 23, 44, 67, 75–76, 83, 91, 102, 109, 110–11, 112–15, 117–18, 123, 126–31, 134–35, 141, 143–44, 146–47, 290, 326–31; foreign policy decisional process in, 9; and Cuban missile decision, 9; as multinational state, 36; ideological messianism in, 40, 57; foreign policy motivational system of, 46, 48–49, 53; in Cuban world view, 73, 75; in Israeli world view, 81–82, 94–96, 102; in Arab world view, 85–86; policy of, toward Syria, 109; in containment theory, 115–16; in British world view, 283, 290–92, 297, 305–07; policy of, toward Egypt, 288, 307; British policy toward, 295–96. *See also* Russia; United States, in Soviet world view
United Fruit Company, 27, 322
United Nations, British policy toward, 296, 306–07
United States: policy toward Vietnam, criticism of, 3–7, 35–36, 133–34; foreign policy motivations of, 21, 46–48, 154; as nation-state, 36; and cultural messianism, 39–40; and ideological messianism, 40; and military vested interests, 41; in Cuban world view, 73–75; in Israeli world view, 77–78; in Iranian world view, 80–84, 94, 96; in Arab world view, 85–86, 124; foreign policy directional thrust of, 100; foreign policy system of aims of, 105, 107–32; policy of, in Syria, 108–10; policy of, in Lebanon, 110; policy of, toward Arab-Israeli conflict, 123–32; in British world view, 284–86, 291–93, 306–07; British policy toward, 293, 295–96; policy of, in Suez crisis, 307; in Soviet world view, 331–32. *See also* U.S. policy under Bangladesh; Bay of Pigs; Cambodia; Great Britain; Iraq; Israel; Jordan; Mexico; North Vietnam; Sudan. *See also* American world view under Arab-Israeli conflict; Arabs; Belgian Congo; Berlin block-

ade; China; Colombia; Cuba; Egypt; Great Britain; Guatemala; Indonesia; Iraq; Japan; Jordan; North Vietnam; South Vietnam; Syria; Taiwan; Thailand; Union of Soviet Socialist Republics
U Nu, 298
U Thant, 133, 146

Values: political, as perceptual determinant, 7, 60, 61, 67, 83–84, 87, 91, 93, 98–99, 187, 313–14, 322–25; and ideology, 40, 88–90, 91, 107, 141–42, 147; intensity of, 323–25
Veroff, Joseph, 32
Versailles Conference, 266–67
Vested interests. *See* Bureaucratic vested interests; Economic vested interests; Military vested interests
Vietcong, in American world view, 141
Vietnam: in American world view, 75–76, 118; as example of American general policy change, 112–15, 133–48
Vietnam, Democratic Republic of. *See* North Vietnam
Vivian, Henry Hussey, 162–63, 173, 175–77

Wafd party, 242, 266, 274, 277–84, 298, 302
Wall, Major Patrick, 303
Walrond, Osmond, 266
Watani party, 242, 246–47, 248, 253–54, 260, 266, 274
Wedgwood Benn, Anthony, 291, 300, 301

Wegg, George, 301
Westernized Oriental Gentleman (WOG), 68–71, 73, 77, 109, 110, 113, 144, 172, 175–77, 179, 181, 194, 225, 230, 233, 234, 243, 266, 269, 316
Wilson, Sir Rivers, 168, 176
Wilson, Woodrow: Fourteen Points and, 15, 270; and ideological messianism, 40, 57
Wingate, Sir Francis Reginald, 258, 266–67
Winslow, E. M., 22, 25, 41
WOG. *See* Westernized Oriental Gentleman
Wolff, Henry Drummond, 216, 221–23, 226, 228, 229–30
World view: defined and described, 10, 11, 33, 60–61, 97, 107; importance of, for peace theory, 11, 12, 78; tendencies in, 91–92

Yom Kippur War. *See* October War
Young Egypt, 281–82, 284
Younger, Kenneth, 290

Zaghlul, Fathi Bey, 243–44
Zaghlul, Saad, 152, 242–43, 245, 247, 253, 255, 265–67, 274–75, 277–78, 281, 298
Zaire. *See* Belgian Congo
Zilliacus, K., 300, 306–07
Zionism, 280, 299–300
Zionists: as ethnic pressure group, 125–26, 128–30; British policy toward, 251
Zobeir Pasha, 213